Philosophy in Schools

All of us ponder the big and enduring human questions—Who am I? Am I free? What should I do? What is good? Is there justice? Is life meaningful?—but this kind of philosophical interrogation is rarely carefully explored or even taken seriously in most primary and secondary school settings. However, introducing philosophy to young people well before they get to college can help to develop and deepen critical and creative thinking, foster social and behavioral skills, and increase philosophical awareness.

Philosophy in Schools: An Introduction for Philosophers and Teachers is an invaluable resource for students and practitioners who wish to learn about the Philosophy for Children movement and how to work its principles into their own classroom activities. The volume provides a wealth of practical information, including how to train educators to incorporate philosophy into their daily lessons, best practices, and activity ideas for every grade level, as well as assessment strategies. With contributions from some of the best practitioners of Philosophy for Children, *Philosophy in Schools* is a must-have resource for students of philosophy and education alike.

Sara Goering is Associate Professor of Philosophy at the University of Washington, Seattle, Washington, USA. She is Program Director at the Northwest Center for Philosophy for Children (http://depts.washington.edu/nwcenter/) and has previously developed philosophy outreach programs in Boulder, Colorado, and Long Beach, California.

Nicholas J. Shudak is Assistant Professor and Division Chair of Teacher Education at Mount Marty College, USA. He is also the Director of the Master of Education program at Mount Marty College through which he works with in-service teachers, helping bring philosophy into their classrooms.

Thomas E. Wartenberg is Professor of Philosophy at Mt. Holyoke College, USA. He is author of *Big Ideas for Little Kids: Teaching Philosophy through Children's Literature*. His website—http://www.teachingchildrenphilosophy.org—was awarded the 2011 Prize for Excellence and Innovation in Philosophy Programs from the American Philosophical Association and the Philosophy Distribution Center.

Routledge Studies in Contemporary Philosophy

For a full list of titles in this series, please visit www.routledge.com

Philosophy in Schools

An Introduction for Philosophers
and Teachers

**Edited by Sara Goering,
Nicholas J. Shudak, and
Thomas E. Wartenberg**

Routledge
Taylor & Francis Group

NEW YORK AND LONDON

First published 2013
by Routledge
711 Third Avenue, New York, NY 10017

Simultaneously published in the UK
by Routledge
2 Park Square, Milton Park, Abingdon, Oxon OX14 4RN

*Routledge is an imprint of the Taylor & Francis Group,
an informa business*

Library of Congress Cataloging-in-Publication Data

Philosophy in schools : an introduction for philosophers and teachers / edited by
  Sara Goering, Nicholas J. Shudak, and Thomas E. Wartenberg.
    p. cm. — (Routledge studies in contemporary philosophy ; 47)
    Includes bibliographical references and index.
  1. Philosophy—Study and teaching. I. Goering, Sara. II. Shudak,
Nicholas J., 1975– III. Wartenberg, Thomas E.
    B52.P515   2012
    107.1—dc23
    2012034697

ISBN: 978-0-415-64063-3 (hbk)
ISBN: 978-0-203-08265-2 (ebk)

Typeset in Sabon
by Apex CoVantage, LLC

Printed and bound in the United States of America by Publishers Graphics,
LLC on sustainably sourced paper.

Contents

PART II
Ideas for Bringing Philosophy into the K–8 Classroom

PART III
Ideas for Philosophy at the High School Level

Preface
"Do Not Delay"

Roberta Israeloff

It's 4:45 p.m., and the suburban high school classroom is brimming with students. They've pushed the desks into a crude circle, folding back on itself in several places to accommodate the crush, and still there aren't enough seats: many sit on the floor, on the window ledge. At the biweekly meeting of the Philosophy Club, as usual, it's standing room only.

I'm visiting because, as director of the Squire Family Foundation, which advocates for more precollege philosophy in our schools, I've heard about the philosophy program in this district, pioneered and sustained by a philosophy-loving history teacher. Accompanying me is a reporter from a local newspaper who is writing an article about the club. She has a list of questions she wants to ask and has been waiting for two hours for a break, but the discussion shows no signs of waning. Not only are the students eager to share ideas—the topic at hand is, "Can a 'bad' action yield good consequences, and vice versa?"—but they're also directing the discussion, taking turns, drawing out reticent talkers, and shushing those who can't stop. It strikes me that a casual observer couldn't be faulted for thinking that the club was leaderless. Only those who know teaching from the inside out could appreciate how much work the teacher had already expended: so thoroughly had her students internalized the essence of Socratic dialogue and civil discourse that she could take a seat and become another participant.

Finally, at about 5:00 p.m., apologizing for the interruption, the reporter explains that she needs some quotes from the students for the story she's writing. Would they break for a moment to talk about why they enjoy coming to this club?

Several people speak, one more enthusiastic than the next, but two responses stand out in my mind to this day. A girl who's been very vocal all afternoon says, "This is the only period of the day when anyone asks us what we think. Every other period, we're just spitting back what they tell us we have to know, our parents, our teachers. Here, we get to think and figure things out for ourselves."

And then a boy who hasn't spoken up very much says, "When I first joined this club, I was a very prejudiced person. I hated blacks, I hated Muslims, I hated gays. . . . But I've learned to understand things through other people's eyes. Being in this club, hearing people speak about their own experience, I realize that mine isn't the only perspective, that everyone has a story, a point of view. It's made me a more accepting person. I'm not filled with hate."

These students aren't "privileged"—this isn't a gold-coast suburb but a solidly middle-class community. There's no way to know whether a student is on the dean's list or academic probation—the club is open to all. And just about all of them gave eloquent voice to why philosophy matters and how it can transform classrooms across the country. What more can we ask of students than that they learn to think for themselves, while also learning that their own thoughts aren't the only thoughts that need attention. Philosophy simultaneously opens up the world within and without: by studying it, which really means joining the ongoing, millennia-old conversation, we begin to plumb and reformulate our deepest-held beliefs, and to do so in dialogue with others.

As such, philosophy seems a natural and uncontroversial addition to the curriculum of American elementary and secondary schools. Yet we've all heard at least four arguments countering this claim.

The preeminent objection is logistical. Some argue there isn't enough time in the school day to add a new course—even one which is at the foundation of every other discipline. In truth, we can't really read a novel, discuss the causes of a war, or dissect a frog without stumbling over philosophical issues. We may choose to ignore them, or label them differently, but they're there.

Others claim there's no incentive to add a course that won't boost test scores. Yet because philosophy undergirds all subject matters, it's a pretty safe assumption that the critical thinking skills students learn in philosophy will show up in other classes, and will help improve writing and clear thinking no matter what subject is under discussion.

To rebut the charge that philosophy is too difficult for young students, just talk to a two-year-old who can't stop asking "Why?" or a teenager who can't stop arguing. Children are natural philosophers. Most jump at the opportunity to explore the "big" questions.

Perhaps the most rigorous charge comes from those who worry that philosophy belongs to academic philosophers and then worry that a little philosophy, especially if not "properly" taught, will be worse than no philosophy at all.

But think for a moment of basketball, as an Australian philosopher recently proposed to me. An NBA all star and a kid shooting hoops in the schoolyard are playing at different levels and with different rules, but they're both playing basketball. Essentially, it's the same game. Now think of science. We don't delay science instruction until college because younger students can't grasp the concept of natural selection or the theory of relativity. Rather, we devise ways to bring students and science together in age-appropriate ways.

The initiative to bring philosophy into precollege classrooms, which began slowly, with a few pioneers—most prominently Matthew Lipman and Gareth Matthews—has been gathering momentum over the past 40 years, thanks to the dogged efforts of a few pioneering philosophers. It is fast gaining critical mass: witness the over 60 philosophy professors, teachers, and graduate students who attended a mini-conference on Philosophy for Children as part of the American Philosophical Association's Pacific Division meeting in San Diego, in April 2011. Long overdue, the conference from which this volume derived drew a wide range of precollege philosophy fans who share a goal but differ, as is to be expected, in terms of how to best accomplish it.

Many essential issues remain on the table. We need to determine how to best train teachers to do philosophy with young children, to persuade those making educational policy decisions that investing in philosophy will be a sound investment, to counter those who worry that philosophical discussions will degenerate into unproductive discussion groups, to rebut the mistaken notions that either there are no right answers or that every answer is equally valid, to evaluate the programs that already exist and export those that are successful. The essays in this volume consider many of these issues. Difficulties and real differences of opinion exist, but the problems are not insurmountable, especially if the philosophical and educational communities join forces to find consensus.

As the particulars are hammered out, I'm remaining steadfast in my claim that philosophy and younger students belong together. In truth, the precollege philosophy initiative isn't just about calling attention to a woefully neglected discipline; it's the vanguard of an educational reform movement whose goal is to reclaim and redirect education. The new vision includes but doesn't dwell on accountability, observed results, scripts, and scores; rather, it seeks to ensure that education always begins in wonder. We've become so obsessed with answering questions that we've forgotten the importance of questioning answers. We've become so mesmerized by testing that we've neglected the value of class discussions that end leaving students with the slightly uncomfortable feeling that they know a little less than they did before. We need more classes that challenge students' core beliefs, classes in which we have sufficient time, room, and safety to uncover the unexamined assumptions we all hold dear and hold them up to the light of reason, so that we can restructure them to be more sound, more valid, more respectful, more insightful, and reflective. Philosophy provides us with the unique opportunity to become more responsible both in our personal relationships and as citizens in a democracy, and we should seize it.

We also have to keep repeating—because this point really goes against today's educational current—that education is not a business, and students aren't consumers. Education has a business aspect: money is needed, exchanged, spent, raised, accounted for. But just because an enterprise partakes of business doesn't define education as a business, certainly not in the way selling plumbing supplies is a business. Knowledge isn't a commodity or an accessory—it's not for sale, and the teacher-student relationship isn't one between a seller and a buyer. Teachers and students aren't equals—which isn't to say that it's not a transformative relationship. Each learns from the other all the time, but the contract between them is different than the one with the person who sells you soap or sneakers.

In our rush for accountability, we can't discount the fact that the fruits of educational labors sometimes don't appear for years. How many of us have recalled, years and sometimes decades later, a teacher's comments about a novel; a discussion that raised more issues than it laid to rest; a question that still pends, unanswered. What we learn in dialogue-driven classrooms can't be confined. Learning, set in motion, keeps happening; it blossoms at unpredictable moments. Just because we haven't figured out how to accurately measure the potential for learning, which the study of philosophy holds out as its greatest contribution, doesn't mean it's not worth learning.

Think of those students in the philosophy club. They came after school and stayed until dinner time because it provided them with opportunities they couldn't find elsewhere in the school day. No one twisted their arms to come. And by the way, when I left at 5:45 p.m., the discussion was still going strong.

"Be philosophical about it," we say to one another. In doing so, we all understand that we're not exhorting each other to expound on Kant or Mill, but rather to adopt a perspective from which we can view things in a more productive and accurate context; to view our situation through a lens through which every issue being considered is given its due, its time, its importance, and respect.

Epicurus says, "Let no one delay the study of philosophy while young nor weary of it when old." If only educators in the United States had heeded this advice. Perhaps it's not too late.

Introduction

*Sara Goering, Nicholas J. Shudak,
and Thomas E. Wartenberg*

Reading, writing, and arithmetic are often considered the foundational subjects in education. Science, history, and art follow quickly, with the aim of helping students appreciate the lessons of the past, figure out how to understand the world around them, and perhaps make their mark in it. Philosophy, sometimes regarded as the mother of all disciplines, rarely makes an appearance in K–12 curricula. To many people—professional philosophers, educators, and lay people alike—this fact is none too surprising. Philosophy has a reputation for being esoteric, abstract, dense, and difficult. Yet the questions of philosophy—about ethics, justice, identity, knowledge, and the nature of reality—have puzzled nearly all of us at some point. Rather than accepting that philosophical thinking is too difficult, the authors in this volume believe that philosophizing is not only suitable for, but readily done by young people, and that schools will benefit from its inclusion in K–12 education.

Philosophy for Children came into existence as an educational reform movement in the early 1970s, with the writing of *Harry Stottlemeier's Discovery*. This little book by Matthew Lipman, an academic philosopher concerned with the nature of his children's education, depicts fifth graders raising and exploring challenging philosophical questions in their everyday lives: questions about logic, reasoning, the nature of the mind, the way people ought to treat each other, and what we can and cannot know. Lipman's idea was to offer children an entry into philosophical thinking that—unlike the more difficult and dense prose of academic philosophy—would resonate with their own concerns and struggles. Others shared this belief in children's capacity to think philosophically and helped to develop a movement designed to give uptake to their philosophical questions, and guidance in grappling with them.

After 40 years, it seemed appropriate to bring together practitioners of Philosophy for Children to discuss the movement, its opportunities to enhance K–12 education, and the creative methods practitioners had developed to unite children and philosophy. So, in the spring of 2011, a mini-conference took place prior to the annual meeting of the Pacific Division of the American Philosophical Association organized by Thomas Wartenberg,

Sara Goering, and the late Gareth Matthews.[1] Although most of the participants had been involved in teaching philosophy at the precollege level for many years, the sheer number and diversity of the different types of philosophical interventions that were described during the two days of the conference made a huge impact on all of the participants, including the three coeditors of this volume. Many of the participants had been working in semi-isolation, more or less unaware of the wonderful efforts of their coworkers in this growing field of philosophical endeavor.

It was from a desire to communicate to others interested in precollege philosophy the sense of community and excitement that was evident during the mini-conference that the present volume was conceived. It is not, however, a mere collection of papers presented at the conference, though some of the papers had their origins there. Rather, we conceive of this volume as taking inspiration from that event, but as incorporating other contributions that help broaden its reach, both in terms of the types of contributions included and the geographical scope of the contributors.

The Philosophy for Children movement is truly international in its scope and diverse in its programs. Indeed, even the name "Philosophy for Children" is too limited in that some of the programs represented in this volume target the elderly as well as the young, and many of the young people who participate in the programs would bristle at being called children. Nonetheless, we have retained this nomenclature in honor of the heritage of the attempt to bring philosophy to young people earlier than their first year in university.

There is a long tradition, traceable back to *The Republic* of Plato, of seeing philosophy as the province of the elderly. For many, the image of the toga-clad old men in Raphael's painting *The School of Athens* captures the proper participants in a philosophical dialogue: elderly men with the leisure to discuss topics of no direct relevance to people's lives. But, as the contributions to this volume so eloquently demonstrate, nearly everything about that image is mistaken: women as well as men can engage in the practice of philosophy; the young are perhaps even more apt for philosophizing than the elderly; much of philosophy is very relevant to people's lives; and philosophy can be done even in the midst of a fully engaged life.

So, in some sense, the contributors to this volume are united in their desire to overturn the traditional picture of philosophy and to demonstrate its importance in the daily lives of human beings at every stage of their lives. Although the focus of the volume is on teaching philosophy to precollege students, its scope is broader than that, for its ultimate aim is a rethinking of the assumptions that guide the current practice of this ancient subject.

WHY PHILOSOPHY FOR CHILDREN?

Although many of the contributions to this volume make a case for teaching philosophy to students prior to their attending college or university, the importance of this question requires that we briefly address it here. Our brief discussion is not meant to be definitive, but to indicate some of the reasons why we believe that introducing philosophy to precollege students is valuable and perhaps even crucial.

1. A first reason to teach philosophy to precollege students is that they have a real interest in philosophical questions and deserve the opportunity to discuss them in a classroom setting. Anyone who has spent time with young children knows that they are constantly asking "why?" and trying to figure out the world. Like philosophers, they are puzzled by why things are the way that they are. In giving children an opportunity to discuss philosophy in a school setting (or some other location), one is only responding to their own desires and demonstrating an interest in their concerns.

2. A second reason to teach philosophy to precollege students is that doing so will teach them a wide range of intellectual skills necessary for academic success. In order to be able to take part in a philosophical discussion, a child has to master a range of skills from careful listening and assessing the validity of what she has heard to developing an argument in support of a position she holds. These skills lie at the heart of not only academic success, but leading a thoughtful life. By introducing young people to philosophy, one gives them an opportunity to develop these crucial skills.

3. A final reason for bringing philosophy into precollege classrooms is that a democratic society needs citizens who can take part in the democratic process in a meaningful way. This requires that they be able to critically assess arguments made in the political arena, take part in rational discussions about political goals and policies, and be able to communicate their views carefully and coherently. When children participate in philosophical discussions, they learn to listen carefully and respectfully to their peers, to disagree politely (even if passionately), and to be open to revising their views in the face of good reasons. As such, they are acquiring the very skills that they will need to be effective citizens in a democratic society.

THE STRUCTURE OF THE BOOK

The book is divided into four parts. The first—models for getting philosophy to young people—introduces a variety of different ways in which professional philosophers have introduced philosophy to precollege students. Some of them may seem obvious to you. If you want philosophy in a classroom, for instance, you probably should teach teachers how to teach it. But other ideas are less evident. Can college students or even parents be effective teachers of philosophy? Does it make any sense for a school to have a "philosopher in residence"? And would anyone go to a philosophy summer camp? These are some of the questions for which you will find answers in the chapters that make up this section of the book. The wide scope of programs through which philosophy has been introduced into classrooms shows the creativity and inventiveness of proponents of this educational reform movement.

Many people assume that philosophy is not a suitable subject to teach children who are younger than high school age. If you share some of that skepticism, you'll be surprised by the chapters in the second section of this book, for they focus on different ways of introducing philosophy into the K–8 classroom. If you thought philosophy was dull and abstract, you will be surprised by how inventive practitioners have been in devising ways to tap into the philosophical thinking of younger students and help hone their thinking skills. They have used children's literature, games, and other methods to excite the minds of even—as in the case of the preschool programs developed by the Gauts—very young philosophers.

Philosophy at the high school level is a more expected topic. Many European countries, for example, have mandatory philosophy courses for secondary school students. But how would such courses fare in the United States? The chapters in the third part of this anthology each present a different attempt to engage high school students in doing philosophy. They range from the introduction of more standard sorts of philosophy courses to ways to find philosophy in more standard curricular materials. Other authors show how contests, websites, and after-school clubs can engage high school students in philosophy. Each chapter highlights topics and/or styles of philosophical engagement that speak to students in their adolescence, including those who excel in school generally as well as those who have been turned off by standard classroom dynamics and expectations. All hope to show that philosophy raises issues that most students in this age group want to discuss and care deeply about.

Probably the skeptic in all of us wonders how well philosophy fares prior to college. Do students really get something out of their engagement with philosophy? Is it just a pleasurable pastime, or are they genuinely learning something? These questions fall under the rubric of "assessment," the subject of the final section of the book. There are a variety of strategies for assessing the efficacy of precollege philosophy programs, from participant observations to careful statistical studies that meet standards for empirical research. Both of these strategies are represented here, as you will hear from a teacher passionately committed to teaching her students philosophy to psychological researchers interested in assessing the cognitive development of young philosophy students. Reading this section, you can't help but be impressed by the positive results that precollege philosophy has had and that are testified to in a variety of different ways.

This anthology is not a compendium of scientific research on teaching philosophy to precollege students. Its emphasis is practical. It is a handbook, something we hope that the eager practitioner can use to develop a philosophy program of her own. By seeing the wide range of techniques that people have used to introduce young students to philosophy and the impressive results such attempts have had, the interested practitioner can find both encouragement and practical suggestions for teaching philosophy at the pre-college level. All of the contributors to this book have found their efforts immensely rewarding. Our hope is that this volume will inspire many others to follow in our footsteps.

NOTE

1. The mini-conference was sponsored by the Pacific Division of the American Philosophical Association, the Committee on Pre-College Instruction in Philosophy of the American Philosophical Association, the Squire Family Foundation, the Northwest Center for Philosophy for Children, and Mount Holyoke College.

Part I

Models for Getting Philosophy to Young People

1   Teachers Bringing Philosophy into the Classroom

Wendy Turgeon

With a growing interest in introducing philosophy to children, it is imperative that we engage in an open and functional dialogue on how best to achieve this goal. A wide range of models exist: undergraduates visiting classrooms, teaching degree programs for doing philosophy with children and young people, and individuals who craft their own methods of bringing philosophical inquiry to precollege students. The Institute for the Advancement of Philosophy for Children (IAPC) model based at Montclair State University) represents a formal program that focuses upon preparing practicing teachers to integrate philosophy into their classrooms. It also trains professional philosophers, graduate students in philosophy and education, and many professionals in the education field to help implement philosophy in classrooms. Many practitioners of philosophy with young people have been inspired by the writings of Matthew Lipman, Ann Margaret Sharp, Maughn Gregory, and all of the IAPC, as well as the creative practices demonstrated by many of the authors included in this volume. This chapter will offer advice for interested *practicing teachers* on how they can best prepare to introduce philosophical inquiry into their classrooms—from preschool through high school—with success and enjoyment. This essay will also address some potential challenges to this endeavor.

GETTING STARTED: "PHILOSOPHY WITH CHILDREN?—I AM INTRIGUED"

Many teachers who encounter the idea of philosophy for and with children are engaged by the concepts of community, dialogue, contentious questions, and lived learning. In many cases they discover the idea of "doing philosophy for children" from a book, website, newspaper article, or workshop. These educators are well skilled in teaching and working with children. They understand the perspectives and needs of children and young adults; they are versed in cooperative learning and integrative teaching that stress the importance of involving students in reflective inquiry. Teachers perceive themselves to be good listeners and facilitators of children's learning, and philosophy seems like a natural extension of this relational model of education.

In many of these ideas they are correct. These important skills and attitudes serve teachers well in leading their students in philosophical discussions.[1] However, what many teachers *do* lack is sustained training in and appreciation for *philosophic* inquiry, and this often derails their good intentions. Philosophy is not a required subject in many U.S. colleges. Those in teacher training programs often find their schedules so tightly packed that the luxury of exploring disciplines that do not directly connect to teacher certification is unavailable to them. For those who do take philosophy courses, they are usually peripheral to their focused education studies and are often part of a general education core taken early on in their undergraduate career. Even teachers abroad who have studied philosophy as part of their high school or teacher training program consider it to be a matter of recognizing the great philosophers and mastering their theories. Teaching philosophy means instructing students in the history of ideas. While this approach may find a place as an elective course in high school, it certainly appears irrelevant for younger students.

In some cases, interested teachers can participate in a workshop, such as those sponsored by the IAPC and by other centers around the country; these can help them become more familiar with this way of parsing human experience. Teachers who have participated in such workshops often return to their schools as experts in philosophy for children (p4c) and are given the task of training other teachers in philosophic inquiry. With just a workshop acquaintance, they either present a version of p4c that heavily resembles whole language or literary analysis, or they simply equate it with cooperative and discussion-based learning. Since many teachers consider themselves already well versed in such methodologies, they easily dismiss the need to see the program as requiring careful and sustained apprenticeship in philosophical theory and methodology. In our society, there is a general belief that philosophy simply means having opinions and beliefs, and everyone has plenty of those. Philosophy is believed to be an activity that we all can do naturally.

But what do we mean by "philosophy for children"? How can we explain the notion to interested teachers? Characterizing the enterprise as philosophy, we must be vigilant in keeping front and center the nature of our inquiry as *philosophical*. In doing this, we can still acknowledge the nature of philosophy as pluralistic but also maintain that it is distinctive from other forms of intellectual inquiry. What must we collectively do so as to mark both the unique distinctiveness of philosophy for children and also accommodate a range of models? What family resemblances might we seek? Or, to take a Socratic turn, what does *not* count as philosophy? While I might be favoring a model that looks suspiciously or fortuitously (depending on your perspective) like the IAPC model, I am consciously inviting us to be open to other models that offer what I will be labeling "genuine philosophical inquiry with children."[2]

BUILDING DEFINITIONS—WHAT IS *"PHILOSOPHY* FOR *CHILDREN?"*

How we define *philosophy* may play a crucial role in shaping the nature of our model of philosophy for children. One way to approach the project of constructing a definition is to recognize what philosophical inquiry is not:

1. The simple asking of questions.
2. The answering of questions where there is "no right or wrong answer."
3. The sharing of different viewpoints without some sustained examination of each.
4. Word play: games without a reflective piece.

While these sorts of actions may be described as a form of "pre-philosophy," we run the risk of misrepresenting philosophy and shortchanging the participants if we allow any form of questioning to be considered philosophy. However one conceives of the activity of philosophy, one must reflect upon how this is indeed *philosophy* and not some other act of inquiry. Philosophy does not simply mean an expression of opinions, beliefs, or feelings about events and ideas. At the same time, we want to be cautious about defining the arena of philosophical discourse too narrowly or as limited to one vision of what philosophy ought to be. Philosophy is more than logical argument. We want to strive to negotiate an authentic meaning open to plural interpretations but maintain integrity to the discipline. As our working definition, let us propose the following:

> "philosophy"—inquiry, the exploration of the great ideas, the asking of open-ended and foundational questions, participation in engaging activities which generate a better understanding of a concept at a general level.

Some concepts that can generate a philosophical turn include friendship, truth, love, honesty, tolerance, self, identity, courage, hope—among many others.

When we speak of "Philosophy with/for *children*," what do we mean by that latter term?

> "children"—how young/how old? We want to be mindful of the age range which might generate different *pedagogies* and perhaps use different definitions/versions of philosophy.

For example, if we are working with very young children in a preschool or kindergarten setting, we want to encourage them to explore and develop the art of words. Very young children are just beginning to become wordsmiths, and they love playing with language as much as with dolls and trucks. As they grow into the elementary school years, they begin to master the art of the question and work on their listening skills. How does language "mean" the world around them? How can they put ideas together to make meaning? Who are they? What is the world? This process continues on through the later years at the elementary school level as children continue to hone their skills of questioning, listening, responding, and building on the ideas of their community.

As children move into the middle school years, their self-awareness intensifies as they become acutely aware of themselves amid their peers and the adults in their lives. The topics of their personal conversations relate to different avenues for inquiry, highlighting the sameness and difference in their worlds. We find high school students deeply committed to sustained inquiry informed by attentive logical reflection, creative applications of the Great Conversation, and interacting with the larger society.

All children and young people wish to be taken seriously—as indeed do adults. Philosophical inquiry can connect the child to the adult in ways that reveal and make manifest their common challenge of being human. Although we suggest a form of building from skills to broad conceptual structures, philosophy in the classroom does not represent a geometric curriculum model of linear development. Perhaps a more apt metaphor would be that of a spiral: ideas are continually revisited and reworked in light of new experiences, new insights, and a changing community environment.

Where can this sort of inquiry take place? Well, naturally we might first think of the classroom, but it pays to be open to a multiplicity of venues: the general classroom, an afterschool club, a dedicated philosophy class, a library program, even casual settings with parents and friends. And we find successful philosophical engagement in formal competitions such as ethics bowls or international competitions.[3] Teachers can find exiting venues in which to make room for philosophical inquiry, even if their formal class time is limited for this.

Perhaps more important than thinking of a place is to consider developing a *space* in which participants can engage in philosophy through talking/dialogue, writing (communal or individual), debate, collaborative construction, games, artistic creations, individual and shared projects. Teachers can be creative in how they engage their students collectively and individually in philosophical inquiry. But teachers need to be clear about what they are doing with their students, where this can take place (physically but also conceptually), and what precisely their role may be.

So, armed with a general working definition of the ideas behind "philosophy for children" and beginning to think of modalities through which philosophy can be included in the lives of their students, how can teachers begin to prepare to work with their students?

TEACHER PREPARATION: BUILDING KNOWLEDGE, SKILLS, AND DISPOSITIONS FOR PHILOSOPHICAL INQUIRY

Traditionally, professional philosophers have been trained extensively with a careful reading and analysis of the history of philosophy through primary documents and commentaries. They tackle the problems in the recognized areas of philosophy such as epistemology, metaphysics, logic, politics, aesthetics, ethics, etc. And often they apprentice within a particular philosophic tradition that uses its favored methodology to view and critique other approaches and ideas. Professional philosophers have often majored in philosophy in their undergraduate studies and gone on to complete extensive graduate work at the masters or doctorate level as well as ongoing self-education during and afterward.

With much of the literature that discusses philosophy with children and youth, there is minimal discussion of a sustained study of philosophic issues. Philosophy is deemed a natural human activity, indeed as virtually instinctive. This unfortunately is often the view proposed by well-meaning proponents of philosophy for children.

In properly preparing the classroom teacher to engage students in philosophic reflection, it is a disservice to overemphasize the naturalness of the philosophic perspective. The writings of Gareth Matthews (Matthews 1982, 1992, and 1996) may be easily misinterpreted to suggest that children are naturally philosophic to the point that we need do nothing to encourage, promote, or develop such inclinations. In such a reading, our job is to get out of the way of innate curiosity and philosophic proficiency. By extension, it might be assumed that the adult need only rediscover one's "inner child" to find a full-blown philosopher waiting to spring out and function in a thoughtful and critical manner. Of course, Gareth Matthews is not arguing this point, and indeed it is most unhelpful and confusing to both teacher and students to operate under these assumptions. The prevalence of fallacious reasoning in every corner of the world bears out a genuine need for training in thinking skills. But initial enthusiasm can lead us in this direction, and we must be cautious about overestimating the presence of philosophical inquiry in children and ourselves. "My philosophy of—whatever" is a common enough phrase that we tend to see philosophy as nothing but an open and enthusiastic expression of beliefs. "What I like about philosophy is that there are no right or wrong answers," is a common comment among novice practitioners.

The failure to prepare teachers to some level of basic competence in philosophy as a technical craft thereby runs the risk of losing the philosophic perspective and can ultimately result in the teacher's loss of interest and focus in "doing philosophy" with students. For example, when teachers abandon the Lipman novels in favor of using trade literature, it can be a reflection of an inability to recognize and sustain philosophic dialogue as much as it might be a dissatisfaction with the literary qualities of these novel-texts. The teacher thus reverts to familiar material, literature, or topical issues from the news, and the discussions evolve into lively literary analyses or freewheeling opinion sharing. Captivating and vital though they may be, such debates can be impoverished of *philosophic* astuteness. (Please note the qualifiers here: "often," "can"—there are, of course, exceptions and literature can function quite well as a catalyst for philosophic discussion.[4])

However, it would be impractical to insist that the teacher return to college to earn an undergraduate major or complete a graduate level program in philosophical history or problems before they are prepared to work in teaching philosophy in the precollege classroom. Such expectations would be quite discouraging to the typical classroom teacher and would clearly lessen the appeal and practicality of any philosophy for children program.

Teachers and administrators are loath to commit to any program that requires an extended preparation since it is assumed that one's teacher training equips the teacher to work with any and all curricula and students. Teachers quickly realize that the teacher certification process touches but the tip of the educational iceberg and are usually strong advocates of on-the-job learning. So both teachers and administrators are reluctant to embark on a formal program that might require that they learn an entire new discipline or way of teaching. This presents something of a quandary for the dedicated p4c educator. Specifically: to what extent ought an educator be familiar with the philosophical tradition so as to initiate and support an authentic philosophic inquiry in the classroom? How much background knowledge, practice, and ongoing mentoring is necessary and practical? The good news is that interested and motivated teachers can become quite well prepared without embarking on a new degree.

A solid knowledge base and an active and self-aware use of philosophical tools are necessary for teachers to be successful in implementing genuine philosophical inquiry. Let us begin by proposing the following knowledge and skills base for teachers who wish to engage their children/young people in philosophical inquiry:

1. The ability to recognize philosophic issues and problems and distinguish them from other types of inquiry and to use materials such as stories, the news, anecdotes, dilemmas, philosophical writings meaningfully in the promotion of *philosophical* inquiry; here some familiarity with the philosophical tradition and an active engagement with texts, primary and secondary, would be enormously helpful.

2. The dispositions, skills, and techniques needed to assist children in acquiring and developing their critical thinking skills, specifically the developing ability to note logical structures in living dialogue and the skill to assist the children in honing their own thinking techniques. Examples might include distinguishing forms of arguments/disagreements and comprehending the epistemology of philosophical inquiry: facts, opinions, theories, ideas.

3. An attunement for the questions of philosophy and a practiced ability to recognize their presence in the world as they emerge from discussion and daily living.

The first requires a cache of ideas and problems that can be recognized as philosophical in the comments and questions of the children. A quick list might include some of the following: What is truth? Where do our ideas come from? What makes something real? What is the self? What makes an action right or wrong? Can we understand the world around us? What is beauty?

This ties into knowledge of the history of ideas and sensitivity to topical categories but it also references point 3, the skill of seeing philosophical issues and questions within the concrete comments and examples of the children and any materials that are being used. The second speaks to the need of methodological techniques to facilitate the sharpening of children's tools of inquiry.

If we assume that some training is needed and profitable for the teachers, what sources might we recommend? There are numerous introductions to philosophy written for undergraduate courses and for general reading. Such introductions should be well written, not assume a vast store of knowledge of ideas but also offer rich and meaningful support for adults—the teachers. Two short but quite excellent texts are Thomas Nagel's *What Does It All Mean?* (Nagel 1987) and Roger Scruton's *An Intelligent Person's Guide to Philosophy* (Scruton 1999). While academic texts abound that function as primary source readers or secondary accounts of historical philosophy, one source is Jostein Gaarder's novel *Sophie's World* (Gaarder 2007). Gaarder's account of the history of philosophy may be deemed sketchy and slanted to some degree, but it is accessible and absorbing for someone new to philosophical ideas. It serves as an excellent and quite engaging introductory platform upon which to build a more sustained and nuanced appreciation of some of the ways in which philosophers parse the world.

Reading the primary sources is always to be desired; finding beginning to intermediate reading lists of philosophical classics is a fairly easy enterprise. One can also use topical collections of questions both to promote philosophic dialogue with students and to assist the teacher in developing their "philosophic ear." Finally, news stories, literature, and curricula materials can also be plumbed for philosophic dilemmas but may need modeling in order to distill the philosophical potential. In England, Roger Sutcliff has developed some excellent resources.[5]

Another approach is for teachers to take advantage of local colleges' course offerings in philosophy. For example, a course dedicated to a survey of Western philosophy could provide teachers with a sustained and guided reading of the classic works within a community of fellow participants. This might be a fruitful enterprise for colleges to consider—offering courses that teachers can take as nonmatriculated students (not formally enrolled in a degree program) or perhaps developing certificate programs in the discipline of philosophy. This could offer an opportunity to expand a philosophy department's perspectives beyond the general education course offerings and/ or the traditional graduate school preparation models. St. Joseph's College in New York is approved by the New York State Education Department (NYSED) to offer a concentration in philosophy for child study majors.[6] This would prepare elementary teachers directly to work within the discipline of philosophy as part of their educative mission. Graduate degrees that are attractive to practicing teachers can include opportunities for sustained study of philosophy itself and philosophy in the classroom.

In addition to gaining knowledge about the history of philosophy, teachers may want to explore the range of methodologies advocated by proponents of philosophy for children and young people. These range from positions that advocate for the children to control the entire trajectory of the conversation to those which establish a far more active role for the facilitator in shaping and nurturing the topics chosen and the course of the dialogue. Teachers would do well to read the theory behind the concept—from the pedagogical materials created by the IAPC to the many practitioners from around the world who have developed their own approaches or adapted Lipman's model in creative ways.

Once the teacher has had an opportunity to encounter philosophic ideas and issues, they then begin to practice philosophical inquiry within their classes. Whether they use formal curricula (Lipman's specially written stories or those by Phil Cam, Karin Murris, and others) or self-developed curriculum materials as a springboard, they must begin to lead their students in the development of critical and creative thinking, reflecting on the issues of importance as chosen by the children. Together the class forges a community of philosophical inquiry. But what happens then? What kinds of challenges and problems might they encounter in their classrooms?

SOME COMMON PROBLEMS FACED BY NOVICE PHILOSOPHY TEACHERS

What are some of the typical problems encountered by teachers in implementing philosophy for children and young people? In noting these, we hope to provide clues for teachers to self-correct and address these problems as they arise in their own classrooms.

Many teachers experience great difficulty distinguishing philosophy from science, religion, garden-variety opinion, psychology, and other areas where human knowledge cannot claim factual certainty. For example, novices are often quite confused about what makes a topic a philosophic one instead of, for example, scientific. Exposure to and practice with philosophic questions will help them develop their philosophic ear, but it is also helpful to directly address these distinctions. While it might seem easy to depict science as dealing with observable facts and philosophy as with unobservable concepts, it is not quite so simple. At the cutting age of science, theories struggle with other theories, and philosophical thinking and science intertwine. Which questions can, in principle, be settled by scientific method, and which ones cannot? This might serve as a foundational lightning rod for distinctions. Ethical discussions often become an exchange of legal fact checks or sociological descriptions of beliefs and practices. Learning to distinguish descriptive from prescriptive claims and the various types of prescription (legal, prudential, ethical) moves one toward ethical thinking rather than sociological or legal thinking.

When it comes to religion, teachers are even more concerned and reluctant to engage their (public school) students in such discussions. This is a difficult area: philosophical considerations of God and religion are not simply historical reviews, nor are they theological claims based on faith. But such subtleties can be difficult for the neophyte philosopher. Until children have acquired some experience in critical thinking and philosophical distinction making, they might be ill-prepared to approach the topics of God and religion. That is not to discourage or forbid such discussion but rather to recognize that it is fraught with potential misunderstanding and misinterpretation. Once children have achieved such tools of inquiry (into their secondary educational level[7]), then it would be appropriate to engage them in such reflections. At the same time, it must be remembered that not all religions or sects see a role for rational analysis in comprehending religious experience. That itself can be open for discussion. At the very least, our educational system should be doing more to educate our children on the meaning of religion in its doctrinal senses and its impact on our global community.

Then there is the issue of critical thinking skills. We would like to assume that all of us adults have already achieved a high degree of proficiency in thinking skills such as constructing sound and strong arguments, recognizing and avoiding fallacious reasoning, using logical patterns of reasoning in ethically astute ways, etc. However, we recognize that this is not always the case. Familiarity with Bloom's taxonomy, De Bono's thinking skills or Piagetian stage theory does not constitute a rigorous and sustained ability to think clearly, compassionately, and creatively within a philosophical context. But how might we best introduce or nurture our teachers in the conscious awareness of and focused development of these aspects of thinking? Perhaps some version of Lipman's *Harry Stottlemeier's Discovery*[8] may be helpful in revisiting informal logical thinking for the teacher as well as for the student. Another text that might be worth perusing is Anthony Weston's *A Rulebook for Arguments* (Weston 1992). Catherin McCall argues persuasively for the importance of some formal training and practice in logic in her recent text *Transforming Thinking* (McCall 2009). In this work, she offers numerous examples of conversations with children and young adults and carefully analyzes the quality of the dialogue as philosophical or not, indicating ways in which teachers might assist their students to develop reasoning skills. The construction of a genuinely philosophical dialogue requires some sense of concept development or articulation, and ultimately the conversation must move forward, even if only to reveal further complications and complexities. This is far more difficult to achieve than one can easily imagine. A lively interchange of ideas is not philosophy *as such*, nor is a rigorous debate. Peter Worley, also of the United Kingdom, argues for logical rigor in any philosophical dialogue and offers models for teachers to practice and implement in their own classrooms (Worley 2011). Accomplished teachers are good thinkers, but they will also want to become acutely aware of their own thinking processes so that they can better guide their students in meta-reflection on their own thinking.

In *Philosophy in the Classroom* (Lipman, Sharp, and Oscanyan 1980) and in Sharp and Splitter's *Teaching for Better Thinking* (1995), there is an excellent discussion on guiding teachers into a better appreciation of the differences among types of inquiry. For example, one of the most difficult challenges for a teacher is using anecdotal examples productively. The tendency is to affirm these personal accounts as illustrating a concept and perhaps lose the concept in the process. Adults are just as guilty as children here—witness discussion in the political arena. The teacher must make a concerted and conscious effort to monitor discussions for such digressions. This is critical since a successful philosophic discussion must move forward to some degree. That is, a better understanding (albeit, even if "better" here means only more complicated) of the topic must be sought. A self-conscious focus on the nature and role of examples facilitates the development of a conversation into a philosophic inquiry.

Finally, there is the tendency among teachers, and many who introduce discussions about ethics into children's lives, to teach the "truth" about the ideas under examination. There are many works of children's literature that are designed to teach a particular moral lesson. In cases like this, the teacher may be anxious that the students "get it right" and teach the ideas that they want the children and young people to have. There is a place for didactic instruction, but philosophy ought to allow for more ownership of the ideas by the participant themselves. At the very least, this approach should be entered into consciously and with some problematizing: self-discovery and generation of ideas are key in many approaches to philosophy. However, if the teacher is instructing students about a particular philosopher's ideas, then a more didactic approach makes sense. But is this "doing philosophy"?

Simply by considering these typical challenges and potential detours, teachers can do much to avoid them. So, let us consider the teachers who have prepared themselves to introduce philosophy and are finding positive reactions from their students. What we can suggest to continue their own personal growth in philosophical acumen?

MOVING FORWARD: ONGOING PROFESSIONAL DEVELOPMENT IDEAS

To answer this question, it can be instructive to examine further the patterns of success and failure in the implementation of philosophy and children. We can also compare the development of a p4c practitioner with the development of practitioners in other fields. Professionals in fields such as medicine, engineering, and psychology recognize the need for ongoing professional development to stay current in their respective fields. What resources should be available and encouraged for the new elementary/secondary school teacher of philosophy? Some possible activities/programs could include the following:

- School or district-wide philosophical workshops and discussion groups of teachers
- On-site "philosophers" or visiting philosophers who can participate in and comment upon the course of classroom discussion in a helpful, constructive, and supportive manner
- School-based communities of teachers and local university faculty who collaborate on models of philosophical inquiry
- Online communities of teachers/faculty who can support one another as well as engage in dialogue on questions of substance
- A journal or newsletter of philosophic material designed for *teachers*
- Organizations such as PLATO, a recently founded organization in the United States to promote the teaching of philosophy, and SAPERE in the United Kingdom, which invite precollege teachers to become involved in the broader philosophical community as well as to participate in learning opportunities in their respective communities

I would suggest that successful precollege philosophy teachers can find creative and fulfilling ways for themselves to engage students in productive philosophical dialogue. Just as teachers fully expect to continue "life-long learning" to sharpen and grow their pedagogical tools, we might encourage likewise a continuing engagement with philosophy as a form of human reflective experience. The educational world is accustomed to the idea of renewing certification or updating skills as a necessary part of teacher maturation and development. Such programs do not imply a lack in the teacher's training but rather echo the need for personal and professional growth in every field. Teachers embrace the excitement and value of ongoing learning as they witness it every day in their own classrooms. Philosophy can offer them opportunities to connect their passion for learning, their dedication to their students, and their own curiosity about the human experience.

NOTES

1. In fact, these skills are often available to practicing teachers while others struggle to achieve them.
2. In addition to the Lipman school of "p4c," we find more recent philosophers advocating for a more exploratory, poetic, therapeutic model of philosophy as a life form. These proponents tend to deemphasize the analytic approaches of the critical thinking forms of p4c in favor of both a more holistic notion of inquiry and an insistence on the primacy of children's autonomy in charting their dialogues. Writers such as Walter Kohan, David Kennedy, Barbara Weber—to name but a few—advocate for the radical open-endedness and creative journeyings of philosophy.
3. See the International Philosophy Olympiad: http://www.philosophy-olympiad.org/
4. A number of essays in this volume will make a strong case for the use of stories for philosophical inquiry. My point here is that in the hands of a trained philosopher, these sources are productive and engaging. For literature to function as a philosophical prompt, it requires the skills and abilities of a trained philosophical facilitator. Otherwise, the nature of the ensuing conversation, delightful though it may be, may not explore philosophical ideas.
5. See *Dialogueworks* in the UK—http://www.dialogueworks.co.uk/index.php/home
6. This concentration in philosophy for future elementary educators requires 30 credits in philosophy (the history of Western philosophy and a range of topics courses), including 9 credits focusing on philosophy in the classroom.
7. This is the view of the author and it is only fair to note that other theorists and practitioners may argue for early engagement with philosophy of religion.
8. This is Lipman's novel for fifth/sixth graders that introduces formal and informal reasoning.

REFERENCES

Gaarder, J. (2007) *Sophie's World* New York: Farrar Strauss and Giroux.

Lipman, M., Sharp, A. and Oscanyan, F. (1980) *Philosophy in the Classroom* Philadelphia: Temple University Press.

Matthews, G. (1996) *The Philosophy of Childhood* Harvard: Harvard University Press.

———. (1992) *Dialogues with Children* Harvard: Harvard University Press.

———. (1982) *Philosophy and the Young Child* Harvard: Harvard University Press.

McCall, C. (2009) *Transforming Thinking* New York: Routledge.

Nagel, T. (1987) *What Does It All Mean?* New York: Oxford University Press.

Scruton, R. (1999) *An Intelligent Person's Guide to Philosophy* New York: Penguin Books.

Sharp, A. and Splitter, L. (1995) *Teaching for Better Thinking* Melbourne, Victoria: Australian Council for Educational Research.

Weston, A. (1992) *A Rulebook for Arguments* Indianapolis: Hackett Publishing Co.

Worley, P. (2011) *The If Machine* New York: Continuum.

2 The Need for Philosophical Frameworks in Teacher Education

Nicholas J. Shudak

INTRODUCTION

Teaching has long been a highly thought-of profession. It is often referred to as one of the noblest professions, if not the noblest. Plato's Athenian Stranger suggests that teaching and being taught are the "first among the noblest things" (Pangle 1980, 24 [644b]). Aristotle is said to have also valued teaching, and is attributed with saying that "Those who educate children well are more to be honored than they who produce them; for these only give them life, those the art of living well" (Ryan and Cooper 2013, 17). And similarly, Cicero's oft-quoted question—"What noble employment is more valuable to the state than that of the man who instructs the rising generation?" (Sadker and Zittleman 2009, 8)—suggests as much, too. And though the "flowery tributes to teaching" (ibid. 9) are nice, teacher-educator Amee Adkins reminds us that teaching resides in the moral and sacred domains of life, and because so, it is nothing to be taken lightly (Adkins 2006).

The teacher education discourse is seemingly in agreement on these points. Teaching is definitely worthy of the accolades found in complimentary statements. And especially for those who enter the profession, teaching, and one's motivations for doing so, are worthy of serious thought. Foundations-based textbooks written for preservice teachers are replete with chapters dedicated to helping students think more fully about teaching and becoming clearer as to why they would even want to teach.

In alignment with such discursive impulses, this chapter develops a model to help preservice teachers think about teaching more philosophically. As used in a foundations-based course, this model challenges students to consider teaching as a textured or layered concept comprised of three "conceptual personae" (Deleuze and Guattari 1994). According to this model, teaching is viewed in terms of its *relational*, *liberal*, and *practical* personae—RLP—which, when taken together, provide a fuller and more philosophical understanding of this thing called teaching. My hope is that in using this model to think more deeply and philosophically about teaching, students are actually in the process of developing a broader, more informed, and robust philosophy of education. What this chapter endeavors to do, then, is to develop the conceptual basis of this model for use in teacher education classrooms.

Before doing so, however, it is necessary to dig into a unique and powerful movement in teacher education that might render philosophical inquiry obsolete: a movement that makes philosophical frameworks similar to those put forth in this chapter and in this volume all the more necessary. The movement I'm referring to is the teacher effectiveness movement.

A DOUBLE-EDGED SWORD

Our recent era has seen an increase in the development of high stakes measures of accountability for teacher education and the profession of teaching. Ostensibly this push is a focused attempt toward "ensuring that every student has an effective teacher in every classroom every year" (MET Project 2010, 1), toward closing achievement gaps of all kinds, toward increasing levels of educational attainment by students in the United States, and toward increasing our educational competitiveness on a global scale. It is also a push predicated on the profound belief that the teacher matters.

In the United States, this push has turned into a significant movement regarding teacher effectiveness or quality. In his remarks to the Hispanic Chamber of Commerce on March 10, 2009, President Barak Obama famously commented that "From the moment students enter a school, the most important factor in their success is not the color of their skin or the income of their parents, it's the person standing at the front of the classroom . . . America's future depends on its teachers" (U.S. Department of Education September 2011, 1). President Obama's comments are echoed by many other educational authorities.

The Measuring Effective Teaching (MET) Project commissioned through the Bill & Melinda Gates Foundation is also forthright on this point. This project's main goal is "to develop and test multiple measures of teacher effectiveness . . . [and] to improve the quality of information about teaching effectiveness available to education professionals" (MET Project 2010, ibid.). On the point of whether the teacher matters, MET candidly states that a teacher "has more impact on student learning than any other factor controlled by school systems including class-size, school size, and the quality of after-school programs—or even which school a student is attending" (ibid.). For MET, large school reform depends on the quality of teachers in classrooms.

Such sentiments are reinforced by veteran teacher and author Paul Chance. Through his research specifically directed toward effective teaching, Chance minces no words. On his terms, "there is nothing anyone can do to improve student achievement that is as important as providing highly skilled teachers. Nothing" (Chance 2008, 1). For Chance, the elephant in the room is always teacher quality, such that the "quality of teaching is not only the most important factor in student learning, it's so far out in front that it doesn't even matter what comes in second" (2). This isn't to say that other variables do not matter. It is to say, however, that the many historical variables used to explain achievement levels are still not as powerful as good teaching. And arguably, this is how Chance wants it: for teachers to think and feel that regardless of the difficulties they and their students face, that learning and achievement is going to happen because of quality teaching.

One of the outcomes of this movement and the research undergirding it is a keen focus from disparate corners on teacher preparation, and in particular, the clinical experiences within those programs. From one corner comes the U.S. Department of Education report titled "Our Future, Our Teachers." This report squarely places teacher quality in the hands of teacher preparation programs. If our country is going to transform public education, according to the Secretary, then "the first step is with how we handle teacher preparation—what happens before many teachers even step foot in the classroom (U.S. Department of Education September 2011, 1). Of the areas of concern mentioned in this report, making sure programs provide rigorous clinical experiences is one. Similarly, and from another corner comes a report from the National Council on Teacher Quality (NCTQ). The authors of this report advocate for a more robust student teaching experience as a way to improve teacher quality through teacher preparation (Greenberg, Pomerance, and Walsh 2011). In addition, from another corner comes the National Education Association's (NEA) three-point plan for improving teacher quality. In line with what has already been mentioned, this plan would increase a student's clinical and classroom experience by requiring a full year of student teaching residency (Van Roekel 2011).

As laudable as this focus on teacher quality through teacher preparation is, it is also a double-edged sword; there is liability to be had. The liability is seemingly significant for those interested in philosophy in schools. With such an emphasis on increasing the expectations of and hours in clinical experiences at the preservice level, which is also a focus on the methodological considerations for being in such experiences, multiple opportunities for students to take philosophically oriented coursework outside of the minimum requirements—even if there are any—is shrinking. Furthermore, and within preparation programs that might be part of the increasing trend toward alternative route certification, philosophically oriented courses are essentially nonexistent. They are being replaced by a focus on observable and replicable techniques, strategies, and skills. The Relay Graduate School of Education in New York City is an excellent example of this.

The Relay Graduate School of Education (Relay) is named after the research from Sanders and Rivers (1996) indicating that students most benefit from three good teachers in a row, from the *relay* of one good teacher to another. Relay is quite unique. It is a stand-alone accredited college of teacher preparation, something the United States hasn't seen since the "normal school" days of two-year teacher preparation that had gone extinct around the mid-20th century. What is also quite unique about Relay is that nearly all of the instruction is in module form around techniques, rather than through coursework and curriculum.

The goal of Relay is to upend teacher preparation as a way to improve public education. Norman Atkins, Relay's president, hopes to make this improvement by helping Relay's students focus on strategies, skills, and techniques that are proven to increase classroom performance and student achievement (Otterman 2011, 24). To do this, students learn through a module format focusing on roughly 60 teaching techniques. As Otterman reports, "There will be no campus, because it is old-think to believe that a building makes a school. Instead, the graduate students will be mentored primarily at the schools where they teach. And there will be no lectures" (ibid.).

If any theory is to be taught, Atkins insists that it will be solely for the purpose of expanding on a core practice. This is a distinct break from the three-credit hour courses many traditional programs offer in the realms of learning theory and philosophy of education. Otterman also reports that at Relay, there is no mention of the canonical heavyweights such as Dewey, Gardner, Freire, or Vygotsky that are oftentimes found in traditional programs. On the importance of theory and philosophy in relation to practice, she quotes Brent Maddin, Relay's provost, as saying, "To make a crude analogy, if I am learning to become a blacksmith, I also don't learn how to be a pipefitter . . . I also don't read a ton of books about how to shoe a horse. What I do is show up and shoe horses" (ibid.). Here we see the double-edged sword in action. If Relay is any indication of where this laudable movement toward teacher effectiveness might take teacher preparation, then left to the wayside in favor of focusing on replicable strategies are the philosophies of education that provide preservice teachers with an intellectual backdrop to help deepen, enlighten, and enliven the hearts and minds of their future students.

For teachers interested in philosophy and philosophers who are interested in teaching, this is definitely disturbing. In such a human-to-human profession where vulnerability is in play at almost every moment and in almost every interaction, philosophy is needed. The import of and connection to philosophy, then, in this most human of professions is quite simple.

As a subject, philosophy helps us come to know the great ideas and purposes of human life and the multitude of considerations involved in living that life. Moreover, though, as a type of study and a way of being, philosophy is a form of nourishment; it keeps us focused on the crucial questions of human life, on the very things that make us human. Borrowing from Jacob Needleman, there is a yearning in the human heart that only philosophy can satisfy, a yearning to remember the purposes of humanity. Without that remembering, without the nourishment philosophy provides, the human being essentially becomes thingified and dies (Needleman 1982, 3).

Admittedly an essential part of teaching is procuring student learning that results from using proven strategies and techniques. Relay and similar programs should be applauded for their intractable stance on this. However, teaching cannot be separated from the philosophy that questions the purposes, the kinds, the degrees of student learning and the effect that learning has on our humanity. Similarly to teaching and learning, teaching and philosophy are inextricably in relationship.

Acknowledging the importance of this relationship, RLP brings to a confluence both teaching and philosophy. As was mentioned at the outset of this chapter, RLP is designed to help preservice teachers think about *teaching*; to help students in preparatory programs develop a more sophisticated position regarding the whys and wherefores of teaching and its relationship with learning. It is important to note that my hope for this model is that it is but one of many models students in teacher preparation programs countenance during their journey toward becoming a teacher.

INTRODUCING THE RLP MODEL

RLP is indebted to the philosophical and educational movement called Philosophy for Children. In particular, RLP finds its springboard in an article written by Matthew Lipman, progenitor and early advocate of the movement. In his article, Lipman discusses the possibility of redesigning philosophy with accessibility to elementary school children and focuses on the importance of the education of elementary school teachers.

On Lipman's terms, philosophy should undergo redesign especially if the consequence is also a redesign and betterment of the educational process starting at the elementary level. However, such redesign is entirely "contingent upon the preparation of teachers who have a love of ideas and a concern to establish a community of inquiry in the classroom" (Lipman 2000, 212). Lipman's concern is that philosophy is unlikely to reach the elementary classroom if it does not have a place in the classrooms in which teachers are prepared. Though he provides several insights into how this might happen, his comments regarding thinking are particularly instructive.

A common charge of philosophy is that it is interested in clarity of thought. With that said, it makes sense that Lipman is concerned with the role of thinking in the educational process, especially at the elementary level. Of special concern is what Lipman refers to as the "absence of conceptual components" within approaches to the teaching of thinking. What many of these approaches lack is "access to the philosophical repertoire of concepts" (208) that helps students move their thinking beyond mere steps in the troubleshooting or problem-solving process and explore issues regarding value and purpose. In this sense, the conceptual persona that comprise RLP help preservice teachers think of teaching as more than following steps in a process or replicating techniques. The hope is that it helps students move their thinking about teaching into the conceptual realms involving purposes and value. Again, my reservations about the Relay model is that, because of philosophy's absence, its students do not experience thinking about teaching in conceptual senses but only in terms of troubleshooting and replicable practices.

What follows, then, is the philosophical and conceptual framework used in my work with preservice teachers. As teaching is essentially a human-to-human activity, I begin with the notion that teaching is relational and progresses through to the liberal and practical personages respectively.

TEACHING IS RELATIONAL

In his short story, "The Kid Nobody Could Handle," Kurt Vonnegut's teacher protagonist—George M. Helmholtz—exclaims that "Making sure everybody has a corner [of the universe] is about the biggest job we teachers have" (Vonnegut 1968, 275). For Helmholtz, one's corner of the universe is that place where everything makes sense, where hope is fulfilled, and passion is requited. Subject matter is often that place for teachers, and it is their job, according to Helmholtz, to help students find their own corner through subject matter.

Vonnegut's Helmholtz exemplifies the relational persona of teaching. In his axiomatic phrase, Helmholtz implicates teachers, students, and subject matter, and binds them all together. On this point, and borrowing from philosopher John Passmore, whatever teaching is, "[t]here is a familiar logical point to be made about [it]: it is a triadic relation" (Passmore 1980/2012, 364). Though the points on this triad are oftentimes labeled teachers, students, and others (Power 1982); or teachers, pupils, and subjects (Passmore), I prefer Parker Palmer's view of the triad as consisting of students, subjects, and self (Palmer 1998).

In Palmer's terms, this relational triad represents the life and work of a teacher, such that one cannot fully grasp what teaching is without coming to terms with each point in the triad. He refers to these points as the tangles of a teacher's life that oftentimes get us into trouble. For Palmer, though, "When you love your work that much—and many teachers do—the only way to get out of trouble is to go deeper in. We must enter, not evade, the tangles of teaching so we can understand them better and negotiate them with more grace, not only to guard our own spirits but also to serve our students well" (Palmer 1998, 2).

The first two entanglements representing points of the triad are quite commonplace: subject matter and students. For Palmer, subjects and students are both quite large and complex, and therefore our knowledge of each is generally "flawed and partial." With that said, however, our job as teachers is to go deeper into each one of them and to do so for a purpose. As Palmer sees it, our purpose is to help "guide our students on an inner journey toward more truthful ways of seeing and being in the world" (6), and the way to do this is through subject matter. Recalling Helmholtz's comments that the job of the teacher is to help students find a corner of the universe, Palmer would agree, and he would have teachers help by using subject matter as a means toward seeing and being in the world in more truthful ways, as a means toward finding their corner. In my view, this position routinely gets left out of teacher preparation: that the subjects we study are in the curriculum because they help us see the world. How revolutionary, especially at the elementary level. To connect—relate—students with subject matter in such a way, though, largely depends on the ability of the teacher to do this for him- or herself. Thus, we are brought to Palmer's third point in the relational triad of teaching: the self.

Though the first two points are common, the third—the self—"is rarely given its due" (2). For Palmer, "Teaching, like any truly human activity, emerges from one's inwardness, for better or worse" (ibid.). As teachers, our ability to help our students weave webs of connectivity to subject matter and with the world is a direct reflection of whether we can do it for ourselves. In other words, and again borrowing from Helmholtz, the question the teacher must ask and answer is whether he or she has a corner of the universe located through subject matter. The question of teaching, then, becomes a question of selfhood.

As intimated above, focusing on the self is also a focus on the purpose of education and its value, and is a focus that many preservice teachers find uncomfortable. Asking a group of preservice teachers, regardless of intended level of teaching, about how subject matter has helped them make sense of the world, usually quiets the room quickly. This isn't necessarily a bad thing. I choose to look at it as being a moment in their lives when they've been asked to think about something they've never before thought about. This is exciting and maddening all in one. Exciting because as a class we can embark together on something unique; maddening because they've spent roughly 12 years of their lives in classrooms and with curriculum and are scarcely prepared to countenance a question whose answer should come screaming from their lips. That students generally cannot answer this is an indication that both the purpose and value of systematic education in many of their lives—and in society—is not to make meaning, and, is an indication of the importance of helping students think about teaching in the relational sense.

TEACHING IS LIBERAL

When discussing a liberal personage of teaching, I make sure to stress that we are talking about liberal in the classic and small "l" sense of the word. Liberal as we discuss it pertains to human freedom and borrows from the same root from which the term *liberty* is derived. I also discuss with them the notion that this form of liberal is related to studying the "liberal" arts, the *septem artes liberales*, or the seven disciplines deemed necessary in antiquity for a free citizen to be able to know, understand, and make decisions in a society. Looking at teaching in accordance with this conceptual persona is to view teaching as freeing: teaching should enlighten, enliven, and enrich students' lives so that they can do more because of and after one's teaching than before, hearkening to Adkins's point about the moral and sacred domains of teaching. There are a few key authors I use to help students think *about* teaching in this liberal sense.

Of the volumes written by John Dewey, one of his most influential pieces for a teacher education audience is an article written for *The New Republic* in 1922. In this public intellectual piece, Dewey makes a very clear case for why education is important to society, and especially to one where the proliferation of information is inexpensive and always ready. Dewey states simply that "the profit of education is the ability it gives to discriminate, to make distinctions that penetrate below the surface" (Dewey 1922/1940, 157). He would have us think of education, and by extension teaching, as something that protects individuals from becoming a being for another's purposes: to protect individuals from becoming "dupes." Thinking about what we do as teachers as something leading to "a trained habit of discriminating inquiry and discriminating belief, [as helping students] look beneath a floating surface to detect the conditions that fix the contour of the surface" (ibid., 160) is to look at teaching as freeing students from the debilitating "gulping habit of mind" that causes one to become a "dupe," or another's duplicate. Teaching, then, on Dewey's terms is liberal in that the teacher has the students' individual freedom to think and act in mind.

Poet, author, and social critic James Baldwin agrees. According to Baldwin, adults "are easily fooled because we are anxious to be fooled. But children are very different. Children, not yet aware that it is dangerous to look too deeply at anything, look at everything, look at each other, and draw their own conclusions" (Baldwin 1963/1986, 326–327). In his "Talk to Teachers," Baldwin is imploring teachers not to destroy this impulse in children; that the impulse to question deeply is what essentially makes us human; and in a society, this is what keeps us free. Baldwin is clear on this point, a point echoing Dewey's. Baldwin forthrightly states that "The purpose of education, finally, is to create in a person the ability to look at the world for himself . . . To ask questions of the universe, and then to learn to live with those questions [as] the way he achieves his own identity" (326). Should a society fail in this, should a society fail to bring up such individuals through systematic schooling, then that society will perish. At the least, our teaching should focus on an examination of self and society so as to make it better for both, and that's freeing.

During the semester I turn from the likes of Dewey and Baldwin—who focus more so on the normative level of education, purposes, and value—and direct students' attention to Jean Anyon's classic study that illustrates the liberal potential of teaching. In her enduring research connecting social class and school curriculum, Anyon makes a case that the educational experiences and opportunities students have in classrooms and over time is connected to future occupational experiences and opportunities later in life

(Anyon 1983). To do this, she analyzes five fifth grade classrooms in terms of the curriculum and pedagogy that students experience. Based on her methodology and theoretical lens focusing on social class, Anyon concludes that the "types" of classrooms students are in has a profound effect on individual creativity, expressiveness, ability to plan, skillfulness in terms of relating to others and authority versus resisting, and one's astuteness when it comes to manipulating tools and symbols of power within societies.

Directly relating this to the liberal persona of teaching, using Anyon helps students analyze their own educational backgrounds and autobiographies for the differences in the cognitive and behavioral skills that were developed over time that might have helped or hindered their pursuit for a professional career. Anyon also helps students understand more concretely what Dewey, Baldwin, and others are saying about purposes and values, about individual freedom, and about how teaching should help others do more. The liberal classroom in this sense helps instantiate Horace Mann's exclamation that schools are the "great equalizer" of society.

TEACHING IS PRACTICAL

This last persona is the one that students most easily come to see and understand. And though much of the semester is spent trying to get students to look at teaching differently through the relational and liberal aspects of teaching, it seems necessary to also focus on the very real, applicable, and practical parts of teaching that are part of the teacher effectiveness movement. To do this, I rely heavily on teacher and author Paul Chance.

As stated at the outset of this chapter, Chance and the research he relies on suggests that there is no other variable more important to student achievement than the teacher in front of the classroom. In *The Teacher's Craft*, Chance breaks down and discusses 10 essential skills a teacher must possess in order to improve student achievement. Of the 10, I specifically focus on 5 of them: climate, objectives, feedback, assessment, and motivation. Rather than simply summarizing what Chance says, I rather discuss my rationale for including these five. My rationale, however, is rooted in how Chance would have us think about teaching.

Chance's definition of teaching, a definition upon which the skills he discusses are built, is simple and memorable. On his terms, "Teaching means doing things that improve the rate, durability, and transfer of learning" (Chance 2008, 3). In other words, teaching means doing those things in classrooms and with students that increases how quickly students learn concepts, how long that learning lasts, and the degree to which that learning affects the other domains of students' lives. His book provides the skills to do this.

As my course is connected with observational experiences in the schools, I focus on five skills that are largely observable. The first concerns the importance of setting up a *classroom environment* conducive for learning. Using Chance's terms, good teachers "do" things to/in their classrooms for the sake of learning. This ranges from making the room an attractive place to be, to preventing group chasms from taking over, as well as to communicating with students in positive and affirming ways. A quick survey of students indicates that they've had teachers whose classrooms were good places to be for a variety of reasons, and other teachers whose classrooms resembled cold, gray, rainy days. Having students focus on the importance of the classroom environment is also a focus on the very practical things a teacher can do to affect student learning.

Second, I focus on the importance of having teaching *objectives*. As teaching is something that should be purposeful and directional, objectives help keep teachers and students on the path toward learning. According to Chance, an objective is nothing more than a clear idea as to what you're doing in the classroom, how you're going to do it, and why. There are four characteristics of good objectives. First, objectives should simply specify what it is students should observably be able to do after successfully completing the lesson. This helps the teacher focus on the fact that students should be able to do more after the lesson and because of teaching than before. Second, an objective should provide the students with some achievable challenge. Here, Chance echoes Vygotsky's "zone of proximal development" wherein the lesson is challenging enough to keep interest and be a bit of a struggle, but not too difficult where confusion and frustration set in. Thinking of lessons as an exciting challenge is, unfortunately, an unfamiliar thought to many preservice teachers. Third, good teaching objectives are always shared with the students at the outset of the lesson and are regularly revisited during the lesson. By sharing objectives, this helps both the teacher and students track progress. Fourth, and perhaps most important, objectives should be written down. Having written objectives for each lesson isn't a draconian measure by administrators to limit the creativity of the teacher. No. Having written objectives provides focus and structure to a lesson, which is essential. Regarding objectives, Chance is very clear on his position. He states that "the teacher who sees his day as a series of specific challenges, with each challenge spelled out clearly as a performance objective, will get better results than the teacher, however well-intentioned, who hasn't a clue what he wants his students to be able to do at the end of the day" (31). Writing good objectives is a very practical way to be a good teacher.

Third, I focus on the importance of *feedback*. In borrowing from the field of engineering, Chance defines feedback as input to a student based on output from that same student. As the goal of teaching and education is to improve student performance, feedback is essential. It lets the students know how they are doing in terms of their performance but also lets the teacher know how she is doing. Good feedback, according to Chance, is brief, unambiguous, specific, corrective, honest, immediate, and frequent. In class we discuss these seven hallmarks of effective feedback and reflect on our own schooling experiences to remember those teachers who were exemplars at providing feedback. Feedback is something that can be observed when visiting classrooms, too. Focusing on feedback also helps bring the practical into the realm of the relational.

Assessment has become a dirty word in education lately as it is deemed as the tail wagging the educational dog. However, the fact of the matter is that assessment is essential to being a good teacher. Simply put, "assessment means *gathering information from students to guide instruction*" (91). As assessment is an ongoing process occurring throughout every lesson, it is intimately entwined with teaching. Thinking of teaching in this most practical of senses simply means to constantly monitor student progress. And monitoring student progress toward achievement is also a way to monitor how well the teacher is teaching. During the semester, we focus on different ways to assess progress.

Last, I focus on the importance of *motivation*. We've all been in those classrooms that have breathed life into us, as well as in those classrooms wherein the students looked like debilitated patients in an asylum. According to Chance, providing students with experiences in which to succeed is the key to motivation, such that nothing succeeds like success. Discussing motivation in education is quite tricky. The conversation seems to be dominated by two powerful yet opposing camps. On one side are those who believe in rewards as a way to help students succeed, and on the other side are those who believe that rewards are demotivating and actually punish students. Chance believes that rewards do not undermine motivation, but also believes that the success of rewards largely depends on how they are used. With that said, Chance provides us with eight guidelines for using rewards as a way to motivate and help students succeed. As many students have innumerable and variable experiences with rewards and success, they actually like talking about this. Motivating students is also one of a preservice teacher's biggest fears. Of all the things discussed when talking about the practical persona of teaching, motivation seems to be the most popular.

CONCLUSION

My hope for this chapter was to show that there is a need in teacher education for helping students think more philosophically about what it is they want to do and why when it comes to teaching. Should philosophy make a larger impact in K–12 settings, it also needs to have an impact in teacher education, and as laudable as the effectiveness movement is, philosophy cannot be pushed aside. I also set out to provide the readers with a type of framework—RLP—for helping think about teaching conceptually and philosophically, as being one concept comprised of three personas. The framework above is but one way to help bring philosophical thinking into preservice programming.

Through student evaluations and comments, many seem to like RLP as a framework for thinking differently about teaching. Generally, and at first, many are suspicious of thinking about teaching as a triadic relationship involving students, subject, and self all geared toward making meaning of the world. The biggest obstacle is for them to reframe their minds to think that schooling is actually a place where meaning is made. There are two reasons for this. First, many students make meaning through culture, family, and friends rather than through curriculum. Second, and borrowing from Lipman, I'm not sure many teacher education programs are intent at helping preservice teachers use subject matter as a conceptual tool to make meaning. By the end, though, this seems to make great sense to them, and some have even commented that they have become better students in their content courses because of this.

Regarding the liberal persona, I have found that most students struggle with this for similar reasons as stated above: they are simply not used to thinking that curriculum and pedagogy are enablers of the human mind and spirit. Unfortunately many are set on the belief that third grade is to prepare you for fourth grade, or that Algebra I is to prepare you for Algebra II, so on and so forth. They are hesitant to fully embrace that teaching is something freeing.

Of the personae, the practical seems to be the one most students gravitate toward. Admittedly this is what the teacher effectiveness movement is predicated on—observable behaviors of teachers that lead toward student achievement—and is generally what people think about when they think of teaching. With that said, I think any framework for thinking about teaching also needs to embrace what it is that teachers "do" in classrooms, to borrow once again from Chance.

In concluding this chapter, I'd like to comment that I think the teacher effectiveness movement is very important as it has its focus on both the importance of teachers in terms of procuring student achievement, but also a focus on the experiences students have while in those classrooms—of course, all revolving around achievement. Though many are not fans of the accountability movement attached with teacher effectiveness, it puts a lot of responsibility on the shoulders of the teacher, and isn't that how we should want it? If teaching is really worthy of the tributes that started this chapter, it's only because the job is actually that important.

REFERENCES

Adkins, A. (2006) "Not to Be Taken Lightly: Education in Moral and Sacred Terms" *Journal of Thought*, 41(3): 23–27.
Anyon, J. (1983) "Social Class and the Hidden Curriculum of Work" In *Hidden Curriculum and Moral Education: Deception or Discovery* (ed. H. A. Girioux) 143–167. Berkeley, CA: McCutchan.
Baldwin, J. (1963/1986) "A Talk to Teachers" in the Price of the Ticket: Collected Nonfiction 1948–1985 New York: St. Martin's/Marek.

Chance, P. (2008) *The Teacher's Craft: The 10 Essential Skills of Effective Teaching* Long Grove, IL: Waveland Press.

Deleuze, G. and Guattari, F. (1994) *What Is Philosophy?* New York: Columbia University Press.

Dewey, J. (1922/1940) *Education as Politics* New York: G. P. Putnam's Sons.

Greenberg, J., Pomerance, L., and Walsh, K. (2011) *Student Teaching in the United States* Washington, DC: National Council on Teacher Quality.

Lipman, M. (2000) "Do Elementary School Children Need Philosophy?" In *Philosophical Documents in Education* (eds. R. F. Reed and T. W. Johnson) 207–212. New York: Longman.

MET Project (2010) *Working with Teachers to Develop Fair and Reliable Measures of Effective Teaching* Seattle: Bill and Melinda Gates Foundation.

Needleman, J. (1982) *The Heart of Philosophy* New York: Jeremy P. Tarcher/Penguin.

Otterman, S. (2011) "Ed School's Pedagogical Puzzle" *New York Times*, July 21, 1–10.

Palmer, P. (1998) *The Courage to Teach: Exploring the Inner Landscape of a Teacher's Life* San Francisco: Jossey-Bass Inc.

Pangle, T. L. (ed.) (1980) *The Laws of Plato* Chicago: University of Chicago Press.

Passmore, J. (1980/2012) "The Concept of Teaching" In *Classic and Contemporary Readings in the Philosophy of Education*, 2nd ed. (ed. S. M. Cahn) 362–370. New York: Oxford University.

Power, E. J. (1982) *Philosophy of Education: Studies in Philosophies, Schooling, and Educational Policies* Englewood Cliffs, NJ: Prentice-Hall.

Ryan, K. and J. M. Cooper (2013) *Those Who Can, Teach* Belmont, CA: Wadsworth.

Sadker, D. M. and Zittleman, K. R. (2009) *Teachers, Schools, and Society* New York: McGraw-Hill.

Sanders, W. L. and Rivers, J. C.(1996) *Cumulative and Residual Effects of Teachers on Future Student Achievement* Knoxville: University of Tennessee Value Added Assessment System.

U.S. Department of Education (2011) "Our Future, Our Teachers: The Obama Administration's Plan for Teacher Education Reform and Improvement" Washington, DC.

Van Roekel, D. (2011) *Leading the Profession: NEA's Three-Point Plan for Reform* Washington, DC: National Education Association.

Vonnegut, K. (1968) *Welcome to the Monkey House* New York: Dial Press.

3　Elementary School Philosophy

Thomas E. Wartenberg

INTRODUCTION

It is with great excitement that I have witnessed the growth of the philosophy for children movement over the past 5 years. When I became interested in teaching philosophy to precollege students some 13 or so years ago, I felt that I was working more or less in a vacuum. I think that my experience was shared by many who attempted in one form or another to engage the minds of young and curious children with philosophical ideas and puzzles.

Nowadays, such isolation seems to me to be unthinkable. One factor in this is the World Wide Web, which has made websites such as the one I developed—http://www.teachingchildrenphilosophy.org[1]—accessible from anywhere on the globe with Internet access. Another is the work in the United States of the Squire Family Foundation, which has not only supported the efforts of philosophers like myself, but has also helped to create a network of like-minded individuals.[2] These efforts have reached fruition in the creation of the Philosophy Learning and Teaching Organization (PLATO) network for precollege philosopher teachers and their supporters.[3]

But one feature of this heartening trend concerns me: its emphasis on teaching philosophy to high school students. Don't get me wrong. I have no objection to bringing philosophy into the curricula of secondary schools and, in fact, think it would be a very positive development in the American educational system to have philosophy as a part of the high school curriculum. So, my only reservation about this is that insufficient effort has been directed to the teaching of philosophy to much younger children: elementary school-children whose ages range from 6 to 11. And it is this that I think is a problematic feature of the current state of the philosophy for children movement.

One reason why philosophers may be wary of attempting to teach philosophy in grade school is that it requires a very different approach than that which many professors routinely employ in their college courses. While one can pretty easily conceive of how to adapt a college course to juniors and seniors in high school, many philosophers may simply throw up their hands in frustration at the suggestion that they attempt to teach philosophy to six-year-olds. "What do you do?" they might wonder. "Teach comic book versions of the Platonic dialogues? Does doing this even make sense?"

In this chapter, I'm going to show you that elementary school philosophy does make sense. Not only that, it is an exciting endeavor that yields amazing results. But it is true that teaching philosophy to children at such a young age requires rethinking the nature of the discipline and, in particular, how we initiate students into its wonders. Specifically, it requires us to differentiate teaching students about the range of answers that have been given by philosophers to central questions in the discipline from fostering student engagement in the actual doing of philosophy.

To have a grasp of what philosophy is, one has not only to master a range of different intellectual skills; one also has to have an understanding of what counts as a philosophical issue and how philosophers have attempted to resolve them. In teaching philosophy at the college or university level, one can emphasize either of these different aspects. So courses in the history of philosophy, for example, will tend to stress the acquisition of knowledge about what constitutes a philosophical issue and how the significant philosophers in the tradition have attempted to solve such issues. Introductory courses can also have this emphasis, although I think it is more common at this level to foster students' ability to think philosophically, say, by presenting them with a range of traditional philosophical puzzles, such as how one can know that one is not a "brain in a vat."

Our goal in teaching philosophy to young children is to get them to engage in the activity of actually doing philosophy rather than to teach them what philosophical positions there are, for example, on the reality of numbers or the morality of telling a lie. While children may not have the patience to listen to someone telling them about Kant's rigorism in regard to lying, they become really engaged in discussing why *they think* lying is wrong. And what I have found is that children are perceptive philosophers at a very young age. So let me explain how I get them to engage in philosophical discussions.

PICTURE BOOK PHILOSOPHY

The approach that I have developed for teaching philosophy to elementary school children relies on children's picture books to initiate a discussion among the children themselves. I adopted this approach when I first started teaching philosophy in elementary schools because I wanted to make it as easy as possible for the teachers to begin teaching philosophy. Since they already were required to teach picture books as well as to develop their students' oral language skills, I thought that using picture books to teach philosophy would allow the teachers to begin teaching philosophy without actually adding a new subject into their already full schedules. Instead, they could just teach the books they normally would, but do so using a different methodology.

What is that methodology? First, it involves asking the children a series of open-ended questions designed to elicit their reactions to philosophical puzzles and issues that are presented in the book they have just heard read to them. Our facilitators have "question sets" that are designed with that purpose in mind. Unlike many traditional teaching methods, however, our goal is not to tell the student that his or her answer is either right or wrong. Instead, we turn to the other students in the class and ask them whether they agree or disagree with what has been said, and to back up their responses with reasons.

This is the core of our method of "teaching" philosophy to elementary school children. Rather than attempting to transmit knowledge from one who possesses it to one who does not—one standard way of thinking about the process of education—we focus on getting our young students to participate in a discussion with one another that is both rational and respectful. It is rational because the children are asked to state their positions, back those positions up with reasons, critically consider the opinions of the classmates, and to explain why they disagree with what their classmates have said when they do or why they agree. It is respectful because we suggest that everyone has something to contribute to our discussions, so that each participant in the discussion must be treated with respect.

Central to this method is reducing the focus on the teacher. Traditional classroom setups are ones in which the students are all focused on the teacher, and the teacher is the center of attention, even as the children vie for her attention. Using a horseshoe, our sessions allow the children to see one another—as well as the board on which we record their answers as well as charts about the book—so that they come to see each other as partners in a group discussion.

The books that we discuss with the children are chosen for their philosophical richness. Although some people assume that we would choose books that have definite morals—such as that lying is wrong—that we can teach the children, that is actually the opposite of what we are looking for. We are looking for books that take an important concept that is of philosophical interest—it could be stealing, but also bravery, reality, truth, or even art—and make certain features of that concept appear confusing or problematic. This is because we want the children to become puzzled about the concept and therefore be interested in discussing it with one another.

THE FACILITATOR OF PHILOSOPHICAL DISCUSSION

Each discussion is initiated by a question posed by the discussion leader, often the classroom teacher but really any adult interested in fostering philosophical discussions among young people. Although I have developed lists of such questions both on my website and in *Big Ideas for Little Kids* (Wartenberg, 2009), I urge the discussion leaders to adapt them to their own situation. Nonetheless, I think it is useful to provide the discussion leaders with questions that have been selected for their philosophical relevance. This allows adults without specialized knowledge of philosophy to lead such discussions.

Although I have generally argued that teachers or other adults leading philosophical discussions among children do not have to have an expertise in philosophy in order to get their students/children to participate in philosophical discussions, some understanding of philosophy or, at least, specific philosophical issues is quite helpful. One reason for this is that, in her role as the facilitator of the discussion, the facilitator has to notice when something of philosophical significance has been said so that she can redirect the discussion. In order to do this, the discussion leader has to recognize philosophically significant contributions that children make.

In a discussion I recently witnessed among second grade students in San Jose, California, the facilitators were parents, and they had neither specialized philosophical training nor a great deal of experience in leading philosophical discussions. (It was their third "test flight.") They were discussing one of the books that I regularly use in elementary schools, Margaret Wise Brown's *The Important Book*.

That book has a simple structure. For a number of different objects—the ones that were chosen as ones to discuss with the children were an apple, a spoon, and you—the book proceeds in a formulaic manner. First, it presents one feature of the object as "the important thing" about that object. So, for example, it says that the important thing about an apple is that it is round. Then, the book lists a number of other properties that the object has. In the case of an apple, it says that it also is shiny; squirts when you bite it; and is juicy, among other things. Finally, the book reports its claim about the important thing about the object: that it is round in the case of the apple.

The discussion leader in this case read the children one page of the book and then paused to have them discuss what they thought the important— and other—things about the various objects were. After discussing the nature of apples, the kids got the hang of it, and they really got into discussing the nature of spoons, the second object chosen by the discussion leader from the book.

In order to focus the discussion on spoons' essential properties, they were asked to say things that they thought all spoons had in common. (This way of understanding "the important thing" about a spoon was one that the adults leading the discussions chose.) The list the children came up with was quite impressive. Among the things included were that they have bowls, you eat with them, some spoons are used for measuring, spoons can be used for stirring, spoons have handles, etc. When they were then asked by the facilitator to look over the list of things they had said—their comments were recorded on a large tablet by another parent—and say what they thought the important thing about a spoon was, two characteristics were chosen by the students: spoons are bowls with sticks on them, and spoons are for eating. The second facilitator put stars next to each answer. At this point, the facilitator moved along to the next topic of conversation: What is the important thing about *you*?

Although the facilitator did an excellent job of getting the children to say what they thought and whether they agreed or disagreed with their classmates, he let an amazing opportunity slip past. In saying what they thought the important thing about a spoon was, the children had presented two very different views that could have become the topic of a more abstract, higher level discussion. While I, as a professional philosopher, could see that the children had put forward two different fundamental conceptions of "thinghood" or objectivity, that is, what makes things in general the types of things that they are, the parent understandably did not recognize this.

To see precisely what opportunity was missed, let's consider the children's different responses more carefully. One of them said that a spoon was something you eat with. This conception of "spoonhood" focuses upon the basic function that spoons have in human life. At least arguably, spoons have the unique function of making it possible for us to consume liquids that cannot be eaten with our hands because they are, for example, hot or "gooey." If you accept this claim, then you would implicitly be assuming that, at least for things like spoons (i.e., artifacts), their nature is determined functionally.

It's interesting to note that the children did not all accept this particular functional account of the nature of spoons. Some of them pointed out that spoons also had the function of stirring. Perhaps these children came from homes in which people baked and cooked frequently, so they thought of spoons primarily in this context. Other children, perhaps on the basis of similar experiences, asserted that spoons were used for measuring. Clearly, when thought of functionally, spoons have multiple "important things" about them.

This multiplicity of functional characterizations of spoons may have given rise to a child's attempt to characterize the nature of a spoon in a nonfunctional manner. As I noted, she claimed that a spoon was simply a bowl with a stick attached to it. In so doing, she was implicitly privileging the *physical structure* that an object has to have to be a spoon, at least in her view of the matter. And a physical, structural understanding of the nature of objects stands as a good alternative to a functional one.

Let me just add that I actually learned an important philosophical lesson from this discussion. In thinking about children's discussions of *The Important Book* (Brown 1990), I had previously noticed that the children had more or less replicated a distinction that Heidegger draws in *Being and Time* (2010) between two ontological characteristics of objects: their "ready-to-hand-ness" and their "present-at-hand-ness"; or, as I just put it, a functional and a structural characterization of objecthood. This distinction is also one developed by the pragmatists. And both Heidegger and the pragmatists argue that a functional characterization of entities' nature is more basic than a structural characterization.

Although I was not satisfied with this claim, I hadn't seen a way to argue for the alternative view. But that is just what the children did. First, they put forward a number of different functional characterizations of the nature of a spoon, none of which really seemed more basic than the other. Then, they suggested that it was possible to give a structural characterization of spoons that all spoons would fit despite differences in the material out of which they were composed and the specific shapes that they have: they are bowls-on-a-stick (or with a handle). What this suggested to me was that because spoons have this particular physical structure, they are able to fulfill a number of different functional roles, none of which could be identified as *the* specific role that spoons fulfilled. The children had given me a lesson in metaphysics, the area of philosophy concerned with the basic structure of things.

Before moving on, let me also point out that what I was discovering about metaphysics I learned from a conversation that the children had and not from the contributions of any single child. This is an important feature of such discussions, namely, that the viewpoint(s) that emerge(s) are the result of a group process to which each of the individuals contribute but that cannot be reduced to the sum of their individual contributions, for each participant learns from what the other participants say.

With this philosophical background, we can see that there was an opportunity for a philosophically literate facilitator to move the children's discussion from one about the features that spoons have in common to a discussion of how one decides what the most important feature of spoons is. Without the ability to recognize the significance of the different characterizations of the most important thing about a spoon, the parent facilitator thus missed out on an opportunity to turn an interesting discussion among second graders into a genuinely philosophical one. The transformation of a discussion from one about empirical objects to one about the nature of objects and their essential properties is exactly what is needed in order to have children develop their philosophical skills—to allow them to approach abstract issues through specific examples.

I have discussed this example in detail because it illustrates why having some background in philosophy is important for those interested in helping children discuss philosophy with one another. Although children can learn from having a philosophical discussion, having a philosophically knowledgeable discussion leader can significantly enhance the learning that takes place . . . but only, of course, if the leader is able to see the philosophical opportunities that are available on the spot.

WHAT IS GAINED THROUGH PHILOSOPHICAL DISCUSSION?

I now want to emphasize how the discussion that these children had about spoons and their properties highlights the fact that there are two different learning processes that take place during elementary school philosophy discussions. The first is the more obvious: children learn something about the philosophical issues that they discuss amongst themselves under the watchful eye of a caring adult. As the facilitator of the discussion told me later that day, his daughter was so excited by the philosophy discussion she took part in that, when he picked her up from school, she began wondering what the important thing was about many of the objects they passed on their way home: a car and a building being the two he mentioned. This shows that participating in this type of philosophical discussion can really stimulate the thinking of elementary school children. Having thought about what the important thing about a spoon is, this young child began to think about objects in a different way, as she wondered whether everything had an important property, just like spoons.

Clearly, when the discussion children have is philosophically sophisticated, they will have a better chance for thinking more deeply about the philosophical issues involved. But even when a discussion fails to achieve all that it might—and I believe that all discussions at any level have this characteristic for there are always untapped possibilities that we can see as we consider the course that a discussion took—children can be stimulated to think in a more nuanced and critical manner.

But there is another, perhaps even more important aspect to the learning that takes place through philosophy sessions for elementary school children. By taking part in a discussion that is facilitated in the manner I have described, children learn to have a genuine discussion with one another whose goal is the acquisition of knowledge. People who have not focused upon schools may not realize that children are not generally taught to interact with each other in a way that fosters their respect for the opinion of their classmates. Too often, the teacher remains the focus of the students' attention, leaving other students in the role of competitors for that limited commodity. To change this, students need to be taught to listen to one another, to take others' views seriously, and to back up their ideas with reasons. None of these skills—and they are skills that children can learn—are ones that the traditional dissemination of knowledge model of education emphasizes. But they are crucial skills to have as a human being functioning in a confusing and contentious world. And they are the skills that lie at the heart of our method of conducting a philosophical discussion.

In some of my previous writing on philosophy for children, mostly notably in my book, *Big Ideas for Little Kids: Teaching Philosophy through Children's Literature* (Wartenberg, 2009), I have emphasized that *anyone* can facilitate a philosophical discussion among young children. So it might seem as if the present chapter involves a change of my views. I would characterize it as involving a shift in emphasis. I have here emphasized how a facilitator's knowledge of philosophy as a discipline can *enrich* children's philosophy discussions. But, as I have just pointed out, even when a children's philosophy discussion does not attain the level of abstraction that one might desire for a richer philosophical discussion, there are many ways in which the children can benefit from taking part in it. The two I have pointed out are that (1) they can learn to apply philosophically significant ideas to their experience, as that young girl did when she wondered if everything she saw had an important feature or essence as did the objects discussed in *The Important Book*; and (2) they can learn to be part of a supportive intellectual community with their peers through which they learn to think for themselves. So even if we admit that having a philosophically savvy facilitator can open up new channels for elementary school philosophy discussions, children will gain a great deal from such discussions even if opportunities for fuller, more philosophical discussions are not always taken.

In addition, it is important to realize that facilitation is a skill that a person will inevitably learn from the doing of it. It is important not to discourage people with little or no background in philosophy from attempting to facilitate philosophical discussions among young children. Once they become engaged in this endeavor, they will find themselves learning both how to facilitate and what counts as a philosophical question. So, even in light of my previous discussion, let me affirm that anyone can facilitate philosophical discussions—and will learn how to do so by their very attempt at doing so. All of us learn from our mistakes as facilitators, so that no one need think that they lack the requisite skills for making the attempt, so long as they are willing to think and learn.

CONCLUSION

I began this chapter with a worry: that the philosophy for children movement was too focused on teaching philosophy in high school. What I hope the reader will take away from my discussion is how fertile the ground for philosophy is in elementary schools. Although one has to be inventive in thinking about how to "teach" philosophy to young children, they really are primed for philosophy by the fact that the world they inhabit presents them with puzzling features that they are trying to make sense of. We owe it to them to help them find ways to resolves their quandaries, rather than to simply ignore them and hope they "mature." Philosophy for children is one avenue for channeling children's natural inquisitiveness into productive and socially useful channels that also benefit the children themselves.

NOTES

1. At last count, there were approximately 20,000 page views per month to the website. It also has some pages in Spanish.
2. See http://www.squirefoundation.org.
3. See http://plato-apa.org.

REFERENCES

Brown, M. W. (1990) *The Important Book* New York: HarperCollins.
Heidegger, M. (2010) *Being and Time* J. Stambaugh and D. J. Schmidt, trans. Albany, NY: SUNY Press.
Wartenberg, T. (2009) *Big Ideas for Little Kids: Teaching Philosophy through Children's Literature* Lanham, MD: Rowman & Littlefield.

4 A p4c Experiment
The High School
Philosopher in Residence

Benjamin Lukey

A P4C HAWAI'I CLASSROOM

The question selected by the discussion for inquiry was, "What are the reasons, when we are in a life or death situation, we lose sight of reality?" It had narrowly been chosen over other top contenders, such as "Is it better to face a harsh reality or develop a fake one to stay sane?," "What are the reasons people sacrifice their morals for their own survival/benefit?," and "Can I assume someone's personality and priorities would change in a survival situation?"

The students in this 10th grade English class had just read the first two chapters of *Lord of the Flies* and were interested in how one's survival instinct might trump one's moral beliefs. Over the course of the next hour, the students probed philosophical issues familiar to many in academic philosophy. Many thought that one's moral beliefs are part of one's identity and to go against those beliefs is to go against oneself. Others pointed out that our moral beliefs may sometimes come into conflict with each other and provided examples from their daily lives. This, in turn, led to the question of where these beliefs come from that make up our identity and whether they are genuinely "our" beliefs. They wondered when we are allowed to change our moral principles/beliefs and whether changing your behavior in certain groups or situations is being "fake." The students began to focus on the issue of lying and whether it was ever justified. One student surprised the class by saying he thought that lying and cheating were justified to get ahead in life. His rejection of the social norm (a norm at least in this class) led students to wonder whether their beliefs about lying were just a product of their upbringing and society and hence not "really true." The class ended as the students were discussing whether the reality of the "jungle" is more "real" than the reality constructed in society (while at the same time attempting to define "real").

While the breadth and depth of the philosophical inquiry was exhilarating, for myself, the teacher, and the students, what was even more impressive were the dynamics of the classroom community. Seated at tables arranged in a circle, the students were actively concerned with making sure that everyone in the circle was heard from. Using the yarn "community ball," a ubiquitous element of p4c Hawai'i,[1] there were many instances when the more active students would often immediately pass the ball to someone who hadn't spoken yet or spoken in a long time, deferring their own contributions so that they could hear from others. When the one student said he had no problem lying and cheating to get ahead in life, others were respectful. Rather than putting him on the defensive, they tried to genuinely understand his reasoning, and eventually many incorporated it into their developing views on morality, identity, and society. There was another visitor with me that day, a researcher from Japan, and she was amazed at how focused the students were throughout the entire 60-minute inquiry; a group of 25 normally rambunctious teenagers made the class feel like a (good) university seminar.

The teacher for the class described above was a relative newcomer to philosophy for children and p4c Hawai'i. She had only begun teaching at Kailua High School at the beginning of the 2010 school year, when she was confronted with an entire department committed to p4c. In one of her reflections she wrote:

> My first encounter with the Kailua High School English Department left me feeling a bit confused and overwhelmed. "We do P4C, Philosophy for Children," one teacher said, "You use this yarn ball and everyone sits in a circle. It's something we all do in the English department." [. . .] I hadn't even had time to figure out where the bathroom was and I was already sinking into a deep confusion. Every first day at a new school comes with some feelings of disorientation and uncertainty, which is expected; but it was the word "philosophy" that scared me. At my previous schools I had quickly jumped on the opportunity of creating shared school-wide strategies, reading curriculum, and writing programs, but I have never shared a *philosophy* before. Instead of using a shared strategy or common assessment, we were sharing a common foundation for which we would build our understanding of how teaching and learning occurs in our classroom communities.

Starting from confusion, she had, in less than two years, transformed her classroom into a place that in many ways represents the aims of p4c Hawai'i—to create intellectually responsible communities of philosophical inquiry. This had been my first visit to this particular class, and I found it immensely gratifying to see so many elements of p4c Hawai'i pedagogy come to fruition such that I was fortunate to merely be one of the participants in the discussion, patiently waiting my turn to share my own thoughts. The circumstances and efforts that made such an experience in this 10th grade classroom possible, however, are the result of meaningful collaboration among skilled teachers and myself over the past five years, as part of p4c Hawai'i's Philosopher in Residence initiative. The purpose of this chapter is to provide readers with a greater understanding of p4c Hawai'i and this unique and extraordinary role of high school Philosopher in Residence.

P4C HAWAI'I AND THE PHILOSOPHER IN RESIDENCE

When people hear that I work as a high school Philosopher in Residence (PIR, which I prefer to pronounce "peer"), they often assume that I teach introductory philosophy courses for high school students ("What else would a philosopher do?"). Sometimes, those more familiar with the worldwide P4C[2] movement often assume that I conduct Lipman-esque inquiries with high school students. Neither of these assumptions is true. Yet, to explain what being a p4c Hawai'i Philosopher in Residence does entail requires a bit of context.

Ever since Thomas Jackson introduced p4c to Hawai'i in the mid-1980s, one of the defining characteristics of p4c Hawai'i has been its commitment to working with classroom teachers in Hawai'i's public schools. It has been part of our mission to find every way possible to support these teachers, both in their classrooms and as faculty in a school setting. This has aided the teachers to develop their own intellectually safe communities of philosophical inquiry and to grow as colleagues engaged in philosophically fruitful reflections on issues that matter to them. All this has helped to create a deep-seated commitment among the teachers to p4c as a basic approach to teaching, not just another passing programmatic fad. Until recently, much of the focus had been on working with teachers in elementary school classrooms, where they had the freedom to set aside time for p4c each week.

My own experience with p4c Hawai'i began as a graduate assistant, where I trained under Dr. Jackson and veteran p4c teachers in the Department of Education (DOE) before facilitating philosophical inquiries (often using the Lipman novels and teacher manuals) on my own in elementary schools. I was fortunate to work in this capacity for three years, working with many excellent elementary school teachers and developing my own approach to doing p4c with young children. After my tenure as a graduate assistant, I continued to volunteer in some classrooms, but other duties and obligations quickly filled my time.

At the same time I was drifting away from p4c Hawai'i, the center of gravity for p4c Hawai'i pedagogy was shifting. Philosophy graduate students were no longer funded in supporting p4c. However, while the involvement of philosophy graduate students in p4c was waning, there were still several DOE teachers creating innovative p4c-inspired curricula and pedagogy. Most teachers practicing p4c in their classrooms had taken an introductory course in philosophy for children from Dr. Jackson at University of Hawai'i at Manoa. Several of these teachers continued to work with Dr. Jackson as they pursued advanced degrees in education at the university. At Kailua High School (KHS),[3] two such teachers—Amber Makaiau and Chad Miller—were pursuing their master's degrees (and eventually their doctorates) while incorporating p4c into their curricula (in social studies and English, respectively). Their continuing academic collaboration with Dr. Jackson encouraged their classroom innovation, and they were achieving impressive results in their respective classrooms. Their students were performing well in their classes and on the high stakes tests: Hawai'i State Assessments and Advanced Placement exams. More importantly, their students were engaged and speaking positively about their English and social studies classes with other students and teachers.

Since they were teaching at the same school, Miller and Makaiau were able to support each other in the face of pedagogical challenges and skepticism from those in the school administration. Wishing to expand this support network and responding to the requests of several teachers who had become interested in p4c because of the noticeable gains in student performance, Makaiau and Miller taught a University of Hawai'i course. Although the course was successful in introducing the theory behind philosophy for children and many aspects of the p4c pedagogy developed by Jackson, Makaiau, and Miller, it became clear that ongoing support for a network of several teachers was not feasible for Makaiau and Miller by themselves. If more teachers were going to actually implement p4c in their classrooms, they needed supplementary support.

Thus, the p4c Hawai'i team decided that, with the support of the Uehiro Foundation[4] and private donors, we would pilot a high school Philosopher in Residence. The position would begin as part time, under the supervision of Dr. Jackson.[5] I agreed to attempt to translate my experience and competence with p4c in an elementary school context into the high school context. I would begin working with teachers who were already interested in bringing p4c Hawai'i into their classrooms (initially, these were teachers from the English or Social Studies Departments, those who'd worked most closely with Miller or Makaiau), and then extend into the classrooms of other teachers. There were two immediate challenges. First, my role was very different from that of a p4c facilitator in an elementary school classroom: I was not at the high school to teach or do p4c with the students, but rather to support the teachers in incorporating p4c Hawai'i pedagogy into their curricula so that *they* were comfortable and competent as p4c teachers. A second challenge was that I was unfamiliar with the KHS curricula and socio-academic context; I had limited knowledge of Hawai'i's high school standards and of the common problems faced by KHS students and teachers. What I discovered, however, was that many of the aspects that characterize p4c Hawai'i were essential in overcoming these challenges.

BEGINNING THE EXPERIMENT

As mentioned above, the idea of intellectually responsible communities of philosophical inquiry lies at the heart of p4c Hawai'i. Though experiencing it for oneself is perhaps the best path to understanding this concept, I will try to explain four key aspects that have guided my activity as a Philosopher in Residence and helped me overcome the two challenges described above.

Not in a Rush

The predominant feeling in a typical U.S. high school is of being in a rush. Whether it is bells marking the beginning and end of class periods; or the relentless pressure to learn X, Y, and Z by the appointed date; or the stress of teachers knowing that taking an extra week reviewing fractions means the class will never get to triangles; the onrush of time is unyielding. The typical school day and the typical faculty meeting are often efficient, but they tend to prioritize the urgent over the important. The rush was somewhat familiar from elementary school but was so much more intense as I began working at the high school. Some of us are fortunate to be able to do our best thinking under pressure, but philosophy is typically not a timed activity. Recognizing that the purpose of philosophical inquiry is not necessarily a definite answer but rather an expanded awareness of the complexities of our concepts and beliefs, we are more rewarded by slowing down and digging into questions than by rushing to the next "destination." As a high school PIR, I have been sensitive to concerns about *wasting* time, but I have been a consistent advocate for *taking* time. And because I know from experience that not being in a rush does, in fact, lead to greater progress in one's thinking and the inquiry, I am able to reassure teachers that not being in a rush is different from wasting time. Once the teachers experience the change in student engagement, thinking, and learning that comes as a result of taking time, they are better able to make time for philosophical inquiry. Thus, a role that emerged for me as a high school PIR was to help teachers and students take and make time for philosophical activity and pedagogy.

The importance of this role became clear soon after I started working at KHS. In a meeting with the KHS English teachers during my first year as PIR, the detailed agenda indicated that the meeting would focus on "vertical teaming," the alignment of curriculum such that students would continue to develop their skills as they matriculated through high school. However, as is often the case, many other activities and responsibilities kept the meeting from getting started and its members from focusing on the agenda. Anxiety rose as people realized they were behind schedule. Then, Dr. Jackson, who was also at the meeting, asked them to make a distinction between what is urgent and what is important. This prompt helped teachers defer anxieties about scheduling and administrative expectations so that they could think about what is important about school, English, reading, writing, etc. The ensuing discussion was unhurried, focused, illuminating—and, in the end, accomplished nearly everything that was on the original agenda. The experience illustrated for the teachers that what is important and what is urgent are not always incompatible, or that deciding to focus on one or the other necessarily creates tension. Indeed, we can discuss things that are important without having to sacrifice our urgent responsibilities. The idea that "we're not in a rush" is perhaps the most basic understanding of p4c in Hawai'i, but the complete thought, as articulated by Dr. Jackson, is that "although we aren't in a rush to get anywhere, we *do* have an expectation that we will get *somewhere*."

Intellectual Safety

Part of creating an environment in which wonderment and questioning are encouraged and rewarded involves fostering intellectual safety. In his article, "The Art and Craft of 'Gently Socratic' Inquiry," Thomas Jackson describes this attitude:

> Certainly, classrooms must be physically safe places. For dialogue and inquiry to occur they must be emotionally and intellectually safe as well. In an intellectually safe place there are no putdowns and no comments intended to belittle, undermine, negate, devalue, or ridicule. Within this place, the group accepts virtually any question or comment, so long as it is respectful of the other members of the circle. What develops is a growing trust among the participants and with it the courage to present one's own thoughts, however tentative initially, on complex and difficult issues. (Jackson 2001, 5)[6]

If the class or the faculty community of inquiry is intellectually safe, then people can voice beliefs that are tentative and uncertain without fear, and wonderment and questioning can take root.

Although intellectual safety may become a predominant part of an elementary school culture, as it has at Waikiki Elementary School (one of p4c Hawai'i's "model" schools), high schools are not usually associated with intellectual safety. Teachers, like all thinkers, are also susceptible to the negative effects of a lack of intellectual safety.

Often the biggest threat to intellectual safety comes not from students but from outsiders observing the classroom. Whether it is other teachers, administrators, or consultants, their purpose in observing a class is usually to evaluate the classroom teacher. Often the observation is conducted for only a fraction of the class period and without much information about the context of the lesson. These factors put the classroom teacher on the defensive, inhibiting open inquiry into the class content or pedagogy. Hence, my goal as a beginning PIR was to establish myself as a member of the classroom community. I participated in classes, even when there was no philosophical inquiry, sometimes even taking quizzes and tests with the students. In conversations with teachers after class, I strove to listen, understand, and appreciate their grasp of the class material and their approach to teaching. I purposely did not participate with a philosophical or pedagogical "agenda"; my contributions to faculty inquiry were genuine questions of curiosity or puzzlement. As a result, I found that teachers felt more intellectually safe to examine difficult questions (either about their content area or about their philosophy of teaching) and collaborate with me and others in addressing those questions. The following reflection from one of the English teachers describes this role of the PIR as an intellectually safe member of the teacher community:

> At first, I would clearly explain the role of the PIR. Oftentimes, people are threatened by visitors of a classroom, especially repeat visitors. I would assure them the role of the PIR is not necessarily punitive, but it is a tool to help push the communities, push the thinking, and a tool to push the reflection of practices. One of the most valuable aspects of a PIR is that the PIR is another set of eyes that can understand what is happening within the community, thinking, classroom, and with the teacher. More importantly, this PIR has visited many other classrooms so he or she may have a wider view of what is happening beyond the classroom. Lastly, since the PIR has the ability to visit other classrooms, the PIR can suggest practices he or she has seen in other classes that work. (Tolentino 2009)[7]

The prompt for the above reflection was "If you were to suggest to another teacher that they work with the PIR, what would you tell them to expect and why, if at all, would you recommend such collaboration?" The fact that Mr. Tolentino's initial thought concerned the "threat" of classroom visitors reveals both the general lack of intellectual safety when it comes to visitors as well as work that I had done to overcome that perceived threat. I had purposely avoided being seen as a consultant, armed in advance with all the answers and ready to provide solutions to whatever ails the classroom teacher, and instead became a co-inquirer. The goal of an inquiry is deeper understanding, and this remains the case when discussing lesson plans and teaching practices. My ability as PIR to see a variety of lessons, class dynamics, and teaching styles enabled me to provide valuable examples and evidence in such inquiry.[8]

Wonder

Socrates is widely credited with saying that philosophy begins in wonder, and it remains true today. Yet wonderment is not typically rewarded in a variety of school contexts. By the time most students reach high school, the sense of wonder they experienced, both academically and socially, has been replaced with cynicism: they feel that it is no longer "cool" to be in awe of, or confused by the complexity of their outer and inner worlds. Jackson identifies this loss as the situation to which education, specifically p4c, must respond:

Frequently, by the time children reach 3rd grade, the sense of wonder with which they entered kindergarten—wonder out of which authentic thinking and thus thinking for oneself develops—has begun to diminish. By 6th grade it has practically disappeared. Children's thinking focuses instead on what the teacher expects. A major contributing factor to this loss of wonder is the failure to properly nurture the true voices of children. Due to a variety of pressures, both internal and external, the typical classroom teacher does not appear to have time for children's genuine wondering and questioning, from which structured inquiries can grow. (Jackson 2001, p. 4)

With one small change, Jackson's words above could equally apply to teachers and administrators as they do to students: "Due to a variety of pressures, both internal and external, the typical classroom teacher does not appear to have time for [his or her own] genuine wondering and questioning."

There is a narrow bandwidth of tolerance for wonder in high school. Engaged and focused curiosity is highly valued (and rare). More often, wonderment seems terribly inefficient for classroom learning; there are limitless things to wonder about, but in any particular hour a teacher needs to keep students focused on learning a particular skill or chunk of knowledge. An abundance of curiosity, persistently asking "why," is seen as both juvenile (think of a typical four-year old) and disruptive. Moreover, even if a student's question is complex and relevant, the teacher may not feel comfortable answering it due to uncertainty or time constraints. Accordingly, my role as PIR was to not only bring wonder back into the student and teacher communities of inquiry, but also to remind that wonder can be rewarding and productive.

It was very easy to model wonder: I was being reintroduced to subjects that I had either found fascinating in high school or had since gained an appreciation of. I was in a new cultural environment working with highly motivated and talented teachers, from whom there was much to learn. However, during in-class and after-class discussions with students and teachers, my background in philosophy and p4c helped me articulate how my wonder and curiosity was driving/helping me to make meaning of all this new information and experiences. It was this process of making meaning and hence of making learning meaningful that teachers recognized as what they valued in their students.

During one of the English Department faculty meetings, a teacher finally felt intellectually safe enough to ask a colleague a question she had wondered about for years. The question was not academic (and also somewhat personal, which is why I will not share it here), but it led to a highly engaging inquiry that energized the rest of the meeting, which is still remembered by the teachers as one of the most productive faculty meetings they'd ever had. Wonder had become an accepted and appreciated aspect of their professional community, and they experienced firsthand how this wonder drives our search to create meaning of the world and make education meaningful.

Digging beneath the Surface

When a classroom and a faculty have questions and wonder about the topic at hand, have the time to explore those questions, and have a community intellectually safe enough to genuinely explore those questions and the connections to other experiences and thoughts, people should rightfully expect some kind of progress to be made as a result of such inquiry. p4c Hawai'i generally refers to that progress as "digging beneath the surface." One of the reasons that "digging beneath the surface" is a helpful phrase to use here is because different people make different kinds of progress; furthermore, there are many different ways to make progress in one's own thinking. In a community we may each recognize that our inquiry helped us make progress in our thinking—we can agree that we dug beneath the surface—but each of us may have experienced that progress in a different way. Because each of us thinks differently and makes progress in various ways, we cannot expect a uniform answer to our inquiry (though it may be nice when genuine uniform agreement happens). However, we can hope that we make connections between our ideas and beliefs or think about these ideas or beliefs in novel ways. Through this novelty and connection making, we may experience the confusion that both results from complexity and also drives us toward deeper complexity in our thinking.

In p4c Hawai'i, we use the "Good Thinker's Tool Kit" (GTTK) to measure and foster progress in an inquiry. Developed by Dr. Jackson (Jackson 2001, p. 11), the seven "letters" of the Toolkit help us articulate the kind of thinking that we already tend to do in inquiry, whether scientific or philosophical. By becoming more aware of the kind of thinking we're engaging in, we are able to consciously push the inquiry to deeper levels. In addition to confusion and complexity, the variety and frequency of Toolkit letters used can help us understand how we dug beneath the surface.

It is in "digging beneath the surface" that I contribute in ways that are most recognizable to other academic philosophers. Both Amber Makaiau and Chad Miller have made the GTTK part of their curricula (e.g., Makaiau uses it in her Ethnic Studies course to help students form thought-provoking questions for their self-concept research). As other teachers want to adopt and adapt the GTTK, I can offer needed clarification of the thinking concepts involved or suggestions of how they might be adapted for certain subjects.[9] However, I most often help teachers and students dig beneath the surface by highlighting the many opportunities for philosophical depth.

In the classroom, I have often found that students are interested in a very complex philosophical question, the depth of which may not be immediately appreciated. In one of the freshman Ethnic Studies classes, the students were reading and discussing the novel *The Tattoo*, by Chris McKinney. In the novel, an "auntie" is described who is fiercely protective and affectionate, but who swears at the kids continuously and eloquently and is said to do so lovingly. The students all wrote their questions from the chapter up on the board and voted on the question they would most like to talk about (a process referred to in p4c Hawai'i as "Plain Vanilla"): "Can you really use the phrase fu**** little sh** as a term of endearment?" The teacher suspected that the question had received the most voted because it was about cursing and was amusing to the students (she was likely correct about several of the votes), but as the inquiry started, the complexities of the question emerged.[10]

My interest in the inquiry was purposefully visible, I wanted to communicate to the students and teacher that they were really digging beneath the surface. I repeatedly expressed appreciation for the student's examples and questions and occasionally provided examples or thought experiments that helped bring into focus the issues that we were struggling with. The teacher and I continued the inquiry after the class for another hour (thankfully, it had been the last class of the day), both of us grateful that the "amusing" question had gotten the most votes. On the surface, a teacher without the support of the PIR may have brushed this question off as a joke or had trouble helping the students examine their interests with intellectual rigor.

Cultivating philosophical sensitivity and appreciation is also very important in teacher meetings, where it can often enrich teachers' commitment to the concrete duties at hand. Recently, a high school educational consultant organized an all-day meeting of the KHS English Department to come up with a list of goals to pursue throughout the year. The overarching goal was to create a culture of writing at the school. The teachers successfully created a list of goals and were energized by the meeting. Because I was fortunate enough to participate in that meeting, I was able to identify a philosophical question that was lurking beneath the surface of the discussion. Two days later, during an after-school departmental meeting, I raised this question: "Why *should* there be a culture of writing?"[11] This prompted a rich philosophical discussion on the putative intrinsic worth of writing. Eventually, we were able to articulate a shared belief that writing has value because the individual's beliefs and ideas carry value; and that individuals who are not competent in writing may not be able to attain their full potential in terms of contributing to society and public discourse, at least in contemporary American society. However, that the teachers reached a conclusion is less important than the fact that they engaged in a process of grounding their commitment to a plan of action in their deeply held beliefs about individuals and education. Philosophical progress in the inquiry directly contributed to their pedagogical theory and practice.

It is important to emphasize this teacher-oriented role of the PIR. Just as it is important to help students become more philosophical in their thinking, the PIR must help teachers step back from the daily grind of teaching to view and reflect on the theories and foundations of their practice. Rather than simply worrying about "how to," teachers must regularly revisit and consider their teaching philosophy so that they can create objectives, lessons, and activities to bring this philosophy to the classroom.

THE EXPERIMENT CONTINUES

I am currently in my fifth year as KHS's Philosopher in Residence, and while certain aspects of this experiment have come into focus, new challenges are continuously emerging, making the role just as stimulating as it was when I first began. One of the aspects that has come into focus is that the high school PIR works just as much (if not more) with teachers as with students. This has required both a shift on my part toward education and philosophy of education, and a recognition of teachers as philosophers. In speaking of p4c, Maughn Gregory, the current head of the Institute for the Advancement of Philosophy for Children (IAPC), has made it clear that the goal is not to simply stick academic philosophers into K–12 classrooms; rather, *philosophers* must have a philosophy of education before they can begin to work effectively with students and teachers. While working in elementary schools, my primary aim was to do philosophy with children. Now, my primary aim is to collaboratively improve education, most concretely at KHS, by sharing my strengths in philosophy and p4c with high school students and teachers. I recognize that my philosophy of education differs from many whom I encounter in the schools, but having a grounded philosophy of education places me in the discourse with students, teachers, administrators, and education advocates.

In my years at KHS, I have come to recognize that the ability and motivation to pursue philosophical inquiry is just as keen among high school teachers as it is among students. Teachers want to think, and they want to engage their students; however, they feel a professional obligation to rush through content and projects so that students are prepared for tests and have assessable products each unit. They *are* philosophers but do not have time to recognize their abilities or develop confidence in them.[12] The challenges that teachers face in becoming active philosophers are very similar to those faced by students. Students are besieged by tests and often must deal with a lack of resources and unsafe environments; these same problems create obstacles for teachers as well. However, teachers often face an additional obstacle in that they are often not viewed as philosophers.[13] Instead, teachers are often disparaged as an obstacle in the interaction of the two groups of philosophers, that is, the professional philosophers conducting P4C lessons and inquiries and the students participating in these lessons and inquiries. It is important to recognize teachers as philosophical peers. Though our training may be very different, together we are engaged not only in the philosophical discourse on education, but also in the various philosophical discourses connected to our different content areas and intellectual interests.

Our aim at KHS has been to broaden the community of inquiry to include more co-inquirers, from all areas of the high school faculty. Part of the motivation for this is educational—we want to improve education at KHS. Another part of it, however, is personal—teachers find their jobs more fulfilling when they are an active member of the p4c community of inquiry. What we see in p4c classrooms from kindergarten through 12th grade is a deeper engagement (or a reengagement) with schooling fueled by reinvigorated intellectual energy. This happens with teachers and administrators as well. Rather than thinking of meetings as mandatory drudgery, teachers see them as opportunities for reconnecting to what is important in education and as a means of tangibly improving their own practices. Just as p4c students may view themselves as intellectual contributors, a community of p4c teachers' inquiry is more collaborative and philosophical.

It has been essential that the energy behind expanding the p4c community has come from the teachers. Recently, KHS decided that it wanted to devote a significant portion of one of its professional development days to p4c. Rather than have myself or Dr. Jackson facilitate a workshop, veteran p4c practitioners who had been working with the PIR were the ones who facilitated small-group inquiries with their colleagues. The intellectual invigoration and enthusiasm for discussion and learning from and with one's peers was nearly palpable and continues to fuel the growing number of teachers who are becoming involved with p4c and working with the PIR.

One of the most effective ways to broaden the community has been to offer, through the University of Hawai'i, a p4c course for which teachers can earn professional development credits. Though I serve as the nominal instructor, the course is co-facilitated by all the participants. This not only serves as a more representative experience of p4c in the classroom, but also helps establish a structure wherein teachers look to their fellow co-inquirers for insight and wisdom. I have ideas, but I do not know how p4c will be incorporated into a teacher's particular (e.g., math, science, foreign language, etc.) classroom. Those particular practices will be developed in collaboration with many in the community of inquiry. One of the first to take the course was a teacher of Japanese language. Through inquiries and conversations with English and social studies teachers, school counselors, and me, the Japanese teacher developed philosophical lessons that contributed to the aims of the class. Furthermore, she developed confidence in being able to facilitate those philosophical lessons. This same process is being repeated by teachers from every department within the school.

The long-term goal is to make p4c and a PIR part of the culture of KHS. We are identifying teachers who might also excel in the role of Philosopher in Residence, so that the position is one that is funded directly by the school. p4c Hawai'i recently hired a KHS teacher as an additional PIR to meet the demand at the school. While the position is still funded from outside the school, the benefits of having school faculty serve as a PIR are considerable. Involvement in school planning and school-wide professional development is far more extensive, and the trust-building phase of being in another teacher's classroom is far shorter.

Though the progress has been gradual, classes such as the 10th grade English class described at the beginning are now more common. Philosophy has become part of the school's self-identification and is embedded in the school's new vision statement: "Kailua High School students are mindful, *philosophical thinkers* prepared to pursue their goals and create positive change in the world."

NOTES

1. The rationale behind the community ball, and instructions for making one, can be found under the "Getting Started" resources at www.p4chawaii.org.
2. "P4C" capitalized refers to the worldwide movement begun by Matthew Lipman and Ann Sharp. "p4c Hawai'i" is left in lowercase letters for two reasons: first, "philosophy" is intentionally lower case to distinguish it from the academic activities carried out in university departments; second, "children" is intentionally lower case to differentiate it from the category of Children—p4c in Hawai'i is philosophy for all in the community, not just those who are younger than 18. Thus, the lowercase "p4c Hawai'i" indicates the movement in Hawai'i away from the academic discipline found in Departments of Philosophy and toward a broader conception of "children" as anyone who remains full of wonder and open to examination of his/her beliefs and experiences.
3. Kailua High School is a small public high school (2011 total enrollment = 852) located on the windward side of Oahu. Ethnically, the school is multicultural, with Native Hawaiians making up the largest portion of the student body (54%). Students at Kailua High School are faced with many of the same social (domestic violence, discrimination, substance abuse), economic (approximately half of the students receive free and reduced lunch), and political issues that face other students in the state of Hawai'i.
4. From their website (www.rinri.or.jp): "The main goal of the Uehiro Foundation on Ethics and Education (UFEE) is to encourage research and public discussion about ethics and education and the inter-relationship between them." The UFEE has generously provided p4c Hawai'i with seed money to develop a model of improving schools through philosophy for children.
5. The position began working with approximately 8 teachers, visiting the classroom of each at least once per week. Serving as PIR is now only one role of a full-time position. Now that there are more than 20 teachers working with the PIR, p4c Hawai'i provides two PIRs for Kailua High School, each of whom works with approximately 10–12 teachers. Eventually, we hope that the school takes ownership of the position, and the PIR will be solely dedicated to working with students and teachers at the school. We estimate that a full-time PIR, without any other teaching or administrative duties, could work responsibly with about 25–30 teachers.
6. Citation page numbers are from pdf copy of article available from the p4c Hawai'i website: http://www.p4chawaii.org/wp-content/uploads/2011/05/Gently-Socratic-Inquiry.pdf.
7. Taken from end-of-year evaluation of PIR initiative conducted by p4c Hawai'i.
8. The large number of variables within any community of inquiry—the particular strengths and personality of the classroom teacher is one of the most determinative—make it challenging for anyone to understand a particular community of inquiry; yet without this understanding, improvement is likely to be superficial at best.

9. For example, the health occupations teacher was interested in applying some of the practices of "Problem Based Learning," used at the John A. Burns School of Medicine (the local medical school that her students take field trips to), in her classroom case studies. I helped construct a similar process making use of the Toolkit letters A (assumptions), I (inferences), and E (evidence), which were familiar to the students, so that students would see that the type of thinking they were practicing in other subjects, such as English) was practically useful in the medical profession.

10. Though the students were not aware of the philosophical labels of their efforts, they struggled with issues in philosophy of language, such as whether the meaning of the word is objective or dependent upon the intention of the speaker and/or the perception of the interlocutor. The sociopolitical dimensions of language were also explored as students tried to get a clearer understanding of whether a word could be oppressive merely because of its social history, even in cases where the intentions of the speaker were benevolent.

11. This is a question that I think Socrates himself would have taken great interest in.

12. Furthermore, they have not been trained to bring philosophy into their content area; there is not yet a teacher training program in Hawai'i that develops teachers to do this.

13. This does not apply to the relatively small number of those fortunate to teach the discipline of philosophy in K–12 classrooms (many of whom have received advanced degrees in philosophy), but rather the majority of K–12 teachers who have received specialized training in other areas and often had minimal positive experiences with philosophy.

REFERENCE

Jackson, T. (2001) "The Art and Craft of 'Gently Socratic' Inquiry" In *Developing Minds: A Resource Book for Teaching Thinking*, 3rd ed. (ed. A. Costa) Alexandria, VA: Association for Supervision and Curriculum Development.

5 Creating Engaging Philosophy Summer Camps

John Simpson

Taking philosophy out of the classroom and offering it through a summer camp experience presents an interesting set of challenges. These challenges are not unique to the summer camp experience and exist to one degree or another in any attempt to introduce philosophy outside of traditional classroom settings and expectations. Summer camps will encounter and compound most, if not all, such issues beyond alternatives due to both the length of camp programs and the specific expectations around them. The aim of this chapter is to share a set of conceptual and concrete programming tools that have demonstrated success. These tools are based on what has been learned through the development of EUREKAMP, the philosophy summer camp program at the University of Alberta.[1] The approaches shared here, particularly the section on micro-philosophy discussions that stands as a challenge to traditional thinking about what counts as philosophy, will likely also serve as helpful additions to a toolkit for in-school approaches to philosophy as well.

Before going further, it is important that the reader understand what this chapter is *not* about: it is not about the general necessities to be taken into account when running a camp program. Things like what to charge for camp fees, whether you should use waivers or hold-harmless agreements, what to do with medications, how to pay your staff, where to source craft supplies, and what works best for sign-in and sign-out policies are not the sort of thing that will be touched on here at all, unless they are particularly relevant to developing a *philosophy* summer camp program. Make no mistake, these sorts of issues are important, and any program that you run will struggle to be successful if you neglect them, but they are not what this chapter is about. The best way to address them is to find someone with experience running the closest thing to the program you envisage running, and put them in charge of the logistics of your camp, leaving you free to look after the programming. Failing this, find the most successful nearby program like the one you want to build and model the minutiae of your program after theirs. If they provide snacks, then you provide snacks. If they provide t-shirts, then you provide t-shirts. If they use a waiver, then you use a waiver. Do not worry about needing to differentiate yourself on these logistical items; they are the cost of admission to meet the expectations of parents and children in your area around what it means to attend the type of program you are offering. You have enough to worry about when it comes to putting *philosophy* into your program, so do not re-create parts of the model that are already working.[2]

The caveat of the previous paragraph aside, there are two pieces of general camp management that you must know upfront. Consider them the golden rules for success when providing programming to children—*any programming whatsoever*. They go double for philosophy programs given the misunderstandings that are possible with them. They are simply this: (1) give children responsibility in accord with your expectations of them in every way that you are able to, and (2) ensure that you are communicating regularly and openly with parents and any other adults involved. Setting all the philosophy components aside, these are the reasons that parents and campers continually say that EUREKAMP is the best camp program in which they have participated.

The first rule matters because, on the whole, children know when they are being pandered to, offered platitudes instead of substance, and what it means to be given plastic scissors instead of "real" scissors; and they don't appreciate such things. It is doubly counterproductive to do these sorts of things in a program meant to work with philosophical ideas and issues because some of the most serious and dangerous things in our lives are the ideas we encounter. If a child believes you do not trust them at the craft table, then as a matter of reciprocity of trust they are less likely to trust your claims that a discussion is truly open and that they really can say what they think or feel.

The second matters because it is the parent or adult administrator that you never talk to that will cause you the most problems, not your campers. Speaking regularly to parents helps ensure that they have the requisite knowledge to navigate what they are told or not told by their child. This is paramount in terms of having parental buy-in to such a high degree that they talk positively about your program to others and thereby become informal ambassadors. It is also essential in preventing concerns or accusations from arising around your program and your delivery in the first place. Talk to each parent every day, and you will be rewarded. Fail to do so, and you will suffer the consequences.

AVOIDING THE EIGHT-HOUR DISCUSSION CIRCLE

The Institute for the Advancement of Philosophy for Children (IAPC) has a five-stage model for conducting philosophical inquiry with children.[3] These five stages are (1) the use of a stimulus material to prompt thinking on a certain topic or direction, (2) the creation of a set of questions to guide a discussion-based inquiry session, (3) the discussion-based inquiry, (4) a review of the process by the participants of the inquiry, and (5) an activity intended to conclude the topic and/or provide some practice for a particular skill or disposition. This model was built with classrooms in mind, and it leverages their characteristics, occurring during a scheduled time and looking a lot like a discussion circle to anyone unfamiliar with the subtle differences. Applying this standard model outside the classroom becomes increasingly difficult as the similarity to the classroom diminishes. Table 5.1 shares some important contrasts between a stereotypical classroom and a summer camp program.

Reflection on these differences should make it clear that the standard model will be a challenge to implement in the camp environment. As a consequence, some changes are required: some to avoid difficulties and some to leverage opportunities. The most significant change will be giving up the standard conception of what it looks like to do philosophy with children (and possibly the assumption of what it looks like to do philosophy at all). Why? One reason: the standard model is simply not sustainable beyond about 90 minutes, and so continually returning to it to fill an eight-hour day is going to be both unappealing to your target audience and frustrating to implement for your camp team. Put another way, if your camp looks like "sit in a circle and talk for eight hours camp," then no one, not even professional philosophers, are going to register their children to attend it.[4]

A philosophy summer camp must be approached as a summer camp first and a philosophy program second. In short, it must both be and appear to be physically active and fun. While philosophy can be done in such a way that it meets such expectations, no one is going to believe that it does as long as an infinite chain of discussion circles is what comes to mind when thinking about your program. Even more importantly, you will struggle to provide a program that is anything other than either an infinite chain of

Table 5.1 Comparing classroom-based philosophy programs to summer camp-based philosophy programs

Classroom	Summer Camp
Philosophy is a special period once a week	Philosophy is constantly present and possible
Time is limited by other curriculum goals	Time is limited by abilities of campers and staff
Almost anyone at all could be in the classroom	Campers self-select to be part of this program
Students know each other in advance	Campers rarely know each other in advance
Facilitator is often a professional educator	Facilitator is often not a professional educator
Formal programming and expectations	Informal programming and expectations.

discussion circles or a regular summer camp with some philosophy programming grafted onto the side of it if your camp is based solely on the standard model. To be successful in providing a *philosophy* summer camp, you will need to embrace at least one new model for doing philosophy with children. Three that have proven to work within the camp environment are shared here: activity-based stimulus, activity-discussion fusion, and micro-philosophy.

Activity-Based Stimulus

The easiest way to begin moving beyond programming that looks and feels like it was meant for a classroom is to manipulate the IAPC model so that all the components remain but in a way that complements a summer camp program. There are many ways that this could be done, but the one that has proven itself at EUREKAMP has been combining the first and last stages of the model (the initial stimulus and the closing development activity) into a longer series of stimulus-development activities that happen before attempting the middle three stages (question development, discussion, and reflection on the process). Typically this produces a program that on any given day looks like two half days of directed programming that each conclude with a facilitated discussion among the program participants around questions that result as they respond to the programming just experienced. This approach has been so generally successful that it forms the backbone of the EUREKAMP experience for both our participants and our program designers.

Note that while a planned program results from this approach, efforts are also made to ensure that both the plan and the delivery are flexible. In any week of scheduled discussions, only about half to two thirds of them actually take place. The rest are vetoed by camp staff based on their assessment of the inability of the camp to hold a profitable discussion at the time. The holes these make are filled with other activities planned as hole fillers or swapped for sessions planned to happen later in the week. Just as often, discussions become possible in unexpected places, and adjustments are made to accommodate these as well. Some of the best philosophy just happens, and your program should be designed to capitalize on this as soon as it does.

Core to the success of activity-based stimulus is the necessity that it is the activity *itself* that prompts camper questions rather than some imposed metaphor or other lens through which the activity is to be viewed. Metaphors are better when developed than given, because this is the only way to be confident that they are understood. Further, because the hoped-for discussion topics are meant to be central to the campers and arise directly out of their experience, the activity had better make these issues central.

As an example, suppose that you wanted to prompt a discussion around fairness with this approach. To do this you would find an activity that forces one set of campers to exclaim, "That's not fair!," while another group proclaims just as adamantly, "Yes it is!" Such fairness disputes often arise naturally, but they do not arise regularly enough to be counted on for camp programming. If a discussion around fairness is your goal, then you must create situations that lead to these disputes. You must also be prepared for when the discussion topic you thought you were raising is not the one that actually gets raised. With this in mind it is better to consider what you are doing as setting the conditions for the possibility of the existence of a discussion around a certain topic rather than making any such discussion certain. For the most part, raising disputes around social-political or ethical issues like fairness are easy, but issues in metaphysics, epistemology, and the like can be prompted with clever design as well.

As evidence that it is possible to prompt clear philosophical discussion around philosophical issues that it might not be expected that children would be able to notice, let alone discuss, and as an illustration of what is meant by making sure that the inherent nature of the activity must prompt the questions raised, the following example is offered. The very first year that EUREKAMP ran, a day directed entirely toward philosophy of science was planned. In addition to all the science camp-like things that it enabled, the hope was that it would allow the campers to talk and think about science. There was no certainty about what sorts of discussions might be possible, and the plan was to simply try and prompt as many philosophy-of-science issues as possible and see what caught.

One activity was intended to put the scientific method front and center. This activity split campers into teams, each of which was given the same set of eight different chemicals, in all enough to make three things: a rubber ball, oobleck, and some really nice store-bought quality slime.[5] The campers were split into groups and told that they had to see what interesting things they could make by combining the chemicals and by following a three step process: record what they mixed, record the result, and then share the recipe and results with the other groups.[6]

When the activity was over, we all sat down in a very large circle in the hope of having a discussion around how the method used was important to actually making discoveries. The first question asked by the facilitator wasn't even one of the prepared questions. It was just a summarizing question of habit, "So, what did we just do?" The response was silence, the kind that typically accompanies questions with obvious answers asked to large groups. Eventually a camper said, "Science" like it was meant to be the end of the discussion, because what else could we be doing? Of course, from the perspective of a facilitator, this wasn't all that helpful so they held out for a better answer: a longer one with reasons and descriptions. They didn't get it. What the facilitator got when choosing the next—and only—hand in the air was, "No, we weren't doing science." Echoing what they must have thought was the absurdity felt by everyone else in the circle at this remark, the camper who said they just did science shot back "Of course we were!" and followed it with a list of all the things that made it science (the test tubes, the chemicals, the mixing, etc.). Unfazed, the challenger simply replied that while all those things were true, that didn't make it science. Science was something that was done in school and was about getting right answers, about making experiments work. What had just happened wasn't about that sort of thing at all: it was more exploratory, and so while it looked like science, it wasn't *really* science. Conversational pandemonium broke out, everyone had something to say about this, and they were all saying it at once. Eventually some order was restored, and the group engaged in a wonderful discussion about what science is, what it should be, and how it should be taught. Quite an achievement for a wide assortment of 8- to 12-year-olds.

While this activity has never produced exactly the same discussion—and sometimes no discussion at all—packing it alongside other science-related activities has ensured that the whole unit regularly succeeds in prompting strong discussions about science and technology. Prompting discussions in campers around philosophical issues that even professional philosophers have difficulty tackling is a matter of experience design and a little patience.

Activity-Discussion Fusion

Certain activities allow for discussions around philosophical issues to take place within the activities themselves. Such activities typically contain a combination of philosophically interesting material or stimulating tasks that naturally produce philosophical conundrums, while at the same time integrating the spaces necessary for such discussion. Through this fusion, they act as fully packaged philosophical activities to the point that following the activity up with a discussion, or what is often referred to as a debrief, would be forced and met with an air of dismissal from the campers. Two examples of this sort of activity are the games Mafia and BaFa' BaFa'.

Mafia is a murder mystery game that assigns secret roles to a few of the participants, thereby setting up a tension between the participants designated as mafia members (who are trying to remove non-mafia players from the game) and all the non-mafia designated players (who are trying to remove all the mafia players from the game).[7] Between the short periods of the game where the participants with particular roles make their moves in secret, there are longer periods where all the participants discuss their reasons for thinking who should be removed from the circle on the grounds that they are part of the mafia. Once two or three games have been played, such that the participants understand the roles through practice and observation, the discussion period comes to act as a laboratory for the formation of many modes of reasoning. It also becomes a place to explore the ethics of fairness and game playing. Whether through articulating who could or could not be mafia based on the available information or a discussion of the consequences of cheating, Mafia opens up a space for a wide variety of philosophically related skills and discussions around logic and fairness.[8]

BaFa' BaFa' is a simulation game that aims to improve the cultural competence of participants by placing them in a situation that inevitably leads to deep misunderstandings between two fictional cultures even though there is no necessary conflict between the practices of each of them.[9] As designed, the emphasis of the program is for most of the discussion to take place during the debriefing that follows the activity generating the cultural conflict. At EUREKAMP, we created a variation, because in our experience, discussion at the end of the activity is inherently lackluster, seemingly because it is now "out of game" and so of substantially less immediate value to campers. Making space for discussions within the game itself, particularly following each cross-cultural visit, results in discussions that are much more philosophically interesting and valuable. Once the observers have made their report on the other culture and a short discussion about how to approach future visits has taken place, short discussions around the nature of language and the ethics of culture are regularly had during the game itself.

In the case of both these games, the discussions are typically shorter than those produced in traditional communities of inquiry, and, they lack the formality that normally accompanies a community of inquiry within standard models of philosophical discussion. In exchange for this lack of formality, the experience frequently provides topics that are much more central, controversial, and contestable than the formal discussions that they replace would have been. The immediacy of being *in* the game produces a strong desire to push forward, and fusing the activity and the discussion into a single entity is the way to capitalize on this. This approach is most easily employed when ethical, social-political, and raw critical thinking challenges are what is to be included in the program. But, as with activity-based stimulus, an openness toward exploiting the philosophical moment as it arises is important to successfully incorporating philosophy into a camp in a way that feels natural. With this in mind, be prepared to scratch plans for follow-up discussions with various activities and instead move the discussions inside activities as warranted. Just make sure that the activity as a whole does not slow down too much, or the camper experience may suffer as a result.

Micro-Philosophy

As philosophy for children is usually conceived, indeed as Western philosophy as a whole is usually conceived, acts of philosophy require that a great deal is either written or said. This is understandable because the only way we have of knowing just what someone is thinking is to observe the products of their thinking. Because most ideas judged to be philosophically interesting are full of complications, many words are needed to share the nuances of the idea with each other. This makes our predisposition to count only large volumes of language as acts of philosophy a function of our need to be certain in our judgments, but massive speech acts are not necessary to doing philosophy per se. Even people who say very little to nothing at all may be thinking very philosophical thoughts.

Within the camp environment, micro-philosophy typically happens when a counselor salvages a statement by a camper that might otherwise have been ignored. This is an attempt to realize the potential of the statement to raise an interesting discussion. This move by the counselor is typically a challenge to the original speaker to justify the statement made or to redirect a question to other campers. Either a challenge or an answer could be given by the counselors themselves, but it is more effective to draw in another camper to this cause and thereby create a conversation that is removed from the usual counselor-camper power relation. The exchange between the campers need not be long—it is neither necessary nor desirable to draw these conversations out—since what matters is the inherent acknowledgment of the original statement and the possibility that an otherwise unknown alternative position is shared.

Consider the following example. While building a bat house during a camp, one little boy says, "Why are we doing this? Bats are stupid!," at which point a nearby counselor does a curious thing (at least from the perspective of the little boy) and says to a little girl nearby who is suspected of having a different perspective, "Why do you think we are doing this? Will you tell <little boy's name> if you agree that bats are stupid and why?" Assuming the little girl responds, then the micro-philosophy discussion has been started. From this point forward, it's entirely up to the facilitator and the two participants to decide where it goes and how far. It may last about three to five more sentences depending on whether the little girl agrees/disagrees with the little boy, and if so, how much. Depending on the plan for the activity, this sort of intervention may help prime campers for a larger discussion on some related topic, or a least illuminate viable issues for future discussion.

The value of micro-philosophy goes beyond priming larger discussions. In particular micro-philosophy interventions stand to do three additional things. First, they can be used to stand against a kind of subtle intellectual bullying by creating spaces where alternative ideas from the speaker's peer group are given room to exist. In such cases, were it not for the explicit creation of a conversation by a counselor, campers holding alternative views would likely just have sat in silence, possibly filled with the apprehension that everyone else was also silent because they agreed with the speaker. In this way, an attempt at micro-philosophy challenges children to pay attention to what they say while also acknowledging the speaker and validating them as a member of the community, yet without necessarily extending this validation to what they are saying.

Second, ensuring that the campers respond to one another is crucial in terms of building the community of inquiry by assisting campers in making connections. This is important early in the progression of any camp and especially so in the case of a philosophy-based camp because community building is of vital importance to the realization of the goals of the program.

Last, the micro-philosophy that happens in such discussions often really *is philosophy*. Where is the philosophy? It is in the content of the conversations themselves, even if short and incomplete, and in the thinking that inevitably follows the mildly antagonistic acts that often initiate these discussions.

Successfully inserting micro-philosophy into a summer camp program will likely be less easy than the simplicity of the idea may suggest. It requires a different approach to preparing for philosophical discussion and the striking of a balance between over-stalking these statements and letting them pass. Campers quickly learn who the over-stalkers are and adjust their behavior to accommodate their presence by not talking at all. It is also extremely tiring for the counselors to continually track these statements, rapidly assess their potential merit, and then to attempt to initiate a connection with another camper alongside all their other responsibilities.

Two pieces of advice should assist any attempt to implement micro-philosophy discussions into your program. First, initiating these sorts of conversational connections on the fly is a skill that can be learned through practice. Start with tasking your program team to start one such conversation a day, and then move to two conversations and so on. By the end of a few weeks of camp, it will come more naturally. Second, don't worry about making perfect connections. What matters is that the speakers are confronted with both an opportunity to explain themselves and to be faced with an alternative perspective from their peer group. If the camper that you draw in doesn't allow for either of these possibilities to be realized, then you can always offer a third camper the opportunity to participate in the discussion.

A SAMPLE DAY OF PROGRAMMING

One of our core programming days comes from a program called *Ideas Safari* that features the question "Who am I?" as the grounding idea around the first day at camp. It is a fun theme that combines inward reflections with outward declarations in a way that really helps build a community of inquiry from a collection of mostly strangers and generate some interesting philosophical discussions.

The first activity of the day asks campers to create silhouettes of themselves on giant sheets of paper and to place inside the silhouettes pictures or words that capture who they are.[10] Of course, it is a challenge to trace oneself, so this creates a natural need to partner up, and so right away the new camp community is being built.[11] This community is further reinforced when the campers are asked to introduce—not themselves—but their partner to the rest of camp. An alert and knowledgeable team of staff and volunteers will be watching the things that the campers have written on these silhouettes and will already be planning on how to incorporate these into the upcoming week of programming.

In addition to all of them building the group, this activity also sets up campers to think about essential properties of the self. To follow up on this, campers are asked to use sticky notes to cover up those things that are not essential to who they are or anything "You don't need to be you." Experience with this activity has shown that campers differ wildly in their views, with some of them saying that nothing can be taken and others defining themselves by narrow criteria such as "I play baseball." Creating an atmosphere where these choices can be discussed in small groups as they are made has proven to be particularly effective, especially where the counselor with each group is able to note the contrasts and agreements within the group and initiate discussion of these features, treating this activity as a hybrid between an in-game discussion and an opportunity to create micro-philosophy discussions. Depending on the sorts of issues raised, this activity may provide for a short community of inquiry directed toward the issues being noticed by the campers.

After framing the first activity as an exploration of who the campers are, the next activity becomes an exploration of who they would like to be. This is done explicitly by asking them to create a mask that represents who they want to be. This exercise serves as another opportunity for micro-philosophy that can prompt thinking on a topic and solicit possible discussion topics for later. The masks are important because they allow the campers to playfully explore the issue of what makes them who they are. They are also important because they set the stage for the culminating activity for the day: the design and performance of a play that features all of the campers within each team and the alternate personas that they have created.

While every discussion is different, we have found many profitable discussions raised around topics like, "When you wear a mask, are you a different person?," "Why do people wear masks?," "Is there one most important thing about each person?," "Can you or anyone else know who you *really* are?," and "Can anyone be completely evil or completely good?"[12]

The next activity is a challenge to the campers. They are asked to create small plays in teams that feature both who they are and the individual represented by the mask they just made. Later these plays are performed for the other campers, recorded, and watched again. The plays developed are always zany, poignant, and rich with philosophical material to prompt discussion. All three of the models discussed above are put to work during this phase of the day's programming in various ways depending on the issues raised. This is a period of time that is particularly ripe for the prompting of micro-philosophy discussions because of the dynamic nature of this creative process and the inevitable jockeying for key roles in story design. In summary, it is a significant act of imaginative play that is rich with philosophical possibility. It is also a favorite to share with parents because it showcases the creativity of their children and allows them to see a glimpse of the source of the ideas that their camper is bringing home.

Of course, throughout the day there is space for "regular" games, lunch, afternoon snack, and location changes. Attempting to implement a similar program that ignores these components will inevitably suffer push back from many fronts.

ONGOING DEVELOPMENT

In the span of four years, EUREKAMP has grown from a one-week proof of concept with 24 campers to six separate camp programs covering a wide range of topics including food, game theory, and the fine arts. The success of these programs is due in large part to the careful attention of the program development and delivery teams. The focus of this attention is always first and foremost on the challenge that generated the approaches shared here: how to do engaging philosophy outside of the classroom? By keeping attention on this initial question rather than the answers it has produced, we have been able to arrive at some interesting innovations and a marked degree of success. It also ensures that we are not (often) caught expecting children fit our camps when it should be our camps that are made to fit the children.

This is not said to take away from the generalized approaches that have been shared here since they have proven to work well at engaging campers with interesting ideas. Rather, this constant engagement with the core challenge needs to be recognized because the approaches shared are merely workable answers in response to the challenges and not *the* only answers. We are constantly on the lookout for new ways to provide adventures in ideas for curious children. Hopefully, having read some of our successes, you'll be in a better position to begin your own expeditions into wilds of philosophy beyond the classroom.

NOTES

1. EUREKAMP was started in 2009 by Philosophy for Children Alberta, an affiliate of the Institute for the Advancement of Philosophy for Children and housed inside the Philosophy Department at the University of Alberta. The first year featured one camp that served as a proof of concept. In 2010 the program was expanded to four different theme camps across four separate weeks. In 2011 the number of camps was doubled with two camps running in each of four weeks. The 2012 summer camp season brought a further expansion, adding two new programs for children aged five to seven years and three programs offered per week over each of four weeks.
2. An excellent source for materials to assist you sorting out the logistical aspects of your program is the American Camping Association (http://www.acacamps.org/). In particular, they have a publication called *Basic Camp Management*, which can be quite helpful in navigating these issues.
3. For details about this five-stage model beyond what is provided here, acquire a copy of the *Practitioner's Handbook* from the IAPC (http://cehs.montclair.edu/academic/iapc/).

4. As proof of this, I offer the very first attempt made by well-meaning students within the philosophy department at the University of Alberta to offer a summer camp program. The description and images used made it look exactly like a "sit in a circle and talk about ideas for eight hours camp." No one signed up. When faculty members who knew about the program were asked why they had not signed their children up, the response given was simple: "It looked boring."

5. The chemicals were all standard things that might be found around the home with the exception of liquid latex, which we screened all the participants for allergies to prior to the activity. Recipes for these items can be found through a simple search. You might find oobleck by another name though. It is a mixture of cornstarch and water and a clear example of a non-Newtonian fluid because it does not respond in expected proportion to the force applied; it is hard when you put pressure on it and runny when left alone. The name comes from a Dr. Seuss story titled "Bartholomew and the Oobleck." Ketchup is another example of a non-Newtonian fluid.

6. It is perhaps important to note that we shared the plans for this activity in advance with about five different teachers. Each teacher asked said that the activity was a bad idea because it did not have a clear goal, and with all the different combinations (40,320 possible combinations with 8 chemicals), the campers were going to simply end up frustrated. Of course this didn't happen, and the campers had made everything we intended in about 40 minutes. In addition to making all the things we had prepared for them to make, they also made a whole lot of variations on slime, all of which they found much more fascinating to modify the recipe for than any of the things we had hoped for them to make. We learned another important lesson here about not treating camp like a classroom and trusting children to play and explore on their own terms.

7. Mafia also goes by the name of Assassin or Witch Hunt, and many rule variations can be found on the Internet with a simple search. There is also a commercial version of the game available under the name *Werewolf*. Resist the temptation to introduce too many of the possible variations too fast. The simplest versions will be challenging enough, and keeping things simple up front will allow for a greater depth of exploration around the simple game dynamics. Also note that *the* key to successful experience is the ability of the narrator to weave the actions of the players into an interesting story that the players are constructing rather than simply acting as a referee who ensures that the right moves are being carried out at the right times by the right people. If you want participants to talk about the game during the game, then they need to care about the game, and the narrator is crucial for this.

8. One of the favorite exchanges between two campers led to a discussion about just what is necessary to play a game at all. The campers realized the complications that arise when enforcing the rules necessitates following them as well:

Camper A: I accuse Camper B of being Mafia.
Camper B: You saw me get picked when we had our eyes closed!
Camper A: Did not!
Camper B: Did too. I saw you peeking!
[Insert heavy silence full of multiple realizations.]
Camper C: Wait a minute . . .

9. Created by Dr. Garry Shirts and published and marketed by Simulation Training Systems of San Francisco, CA.

10. This is a great gathering activity since it is really easy to accommodate all the inevitable late arrivals on the first day.
11. There is lots of potential for micro-philosophy here, and starting to use them now both further accelerates the building of community and sets the expectations for later.
12. The last question arises more often than might be expected given how regularly campers make masks of both superheroes and villains.

6 Precollege Philosophy Education
What Can It Be? The IAPC Model

Maughn Gregory

"Philosophy for Children" (P4C) is the phrase Matthew Lipman used to refer to an idea that, he says, "just exploded in my head one day"[1] in the late 1960s: that children should have the opportunity to practice philosophy. Lipman was then a professor at Columbia University, distraught at the inability of students and administrators to resolve deep political conflicts without resorting to hostility and even violence. In 1969, Lipman introduced a new literary genre with the publication of his first philosophical children's novel, *Harry Stottlemeier's Discovery*. A few years later he moved to Montclair State College (now University) where, in 1974, he founded the Institute for the Advancement of Philosophy for Children (IAPC) with his colleague Ann Margaret Sharp. Over the next 40-plus years, Lipman and Sharp developed Philosophy for Children into a K–12 curriculum, a dialogical pedagogy, a professional development model for philosophy in schools, and a philosophy of education.[2] Their work attracted the interest of philosophers and educators around the world—hundreds of whom studied, trained, and conducted research at the IAPC and established affiliate centers in the United States and some 50 other countries. In 1985 the International Council for Philosophical Inquiry with Children (ICPIC) was chartered in Denmark, and it has called world conferences every other year since then.

Over the past four decades, a body of curriculum materials, empirical research, and philosophical writing on philosophy for, of, and with children and adolescents has built up, amounting to thousands of academic books, articles, and doctoral dissertations, from scores of countries. Precollege philosophy education is the topic of dozens of academic conferences or special conference sessions every year, in every part of the world, and has been the primary thematic focus of six academic journals,[3] as well as an occasional theme of numerous other journals in philosophy and education.[4] Much of this work has little or no relationship to the Lipman/Sharp program; indeed, the diversity of curriculum materials, pedagogical approaches, and theoretical frameworks developed for precollege philosophy education represents not merely different approaches to that work, but different conceptions of what it means to teach philosophy to children or to engage children in philosophical practice. Practitioners around the world today use phrases like "Philosophy with Children," ". . . with Children and Adolescents," "Philosophy in Schools," and "Philosophy for Young People," to refer to their own work, and in the research literature these phrases are used interchangeably to refer to any program that engages children in philosophical dialogue—as opposed, especially, to high school philosophy courses patterned on introductory college courses.

In this chapter, I describe the ideal we have evolved for this work at the IAPC, challenges we have faced, innovations we have attempted, questions we've developed that we can't answer yet, and how all of this has altered our conception of what it means to do philosophy with children.[5] That Philosophy for Children is now in its fifth decade means that it has already outlived many other educational programs and movements. In another sense, however, it is still a newcomer, both in education and in philosophy. Indeed, the idea of introducing children and philosophy to each other still strikes many educators and philosophers as odd and in need of special justification. So I will preface my description of how we do this with a few words about why we do it, which derives from conceptions of philosophy, children, and education.

PHILOSOPHY, CHILDREN, AND EDUCATION

We construe philosophy very broadly as a yearning or wondering toward meaningfulness, of which truth or reasonable belief is a necessary aspect. Philosophy for Children directs this wondering into collaborative inquiry into questions about ethical, aesthetic, epistemological, political, and other philosophical aspects of experience. We rely on the Deweyan notion that these traditional branches of academic philosophy signify aspects of most people's ordinary experience rather than remotely intellectual or esoteric subjects, and on the growing awareness advanced by Lipman (Lipman, Sharp and Oscanyan 1980), Matthews (1980, 1996), and others: that children's experience is just as replete with these philosophical dimensions as is the experience of adults.[6] Philosophical wonder is but one element of the freshness of fascination young children might bring to any experience. Their inquiries are as playful as they are serious, and the philosopher's primary task is help them deepen and extend their inquiries by learning to be more deliberate (e.g., to listen better to each other), to make their reasons more apparent, and to begin to think about their own thinking.[7]

In contrast, by the time children reach adolescence, they have typically lost their ability to become easily fascinated and have begun to be troubled by existential questions such as, What does it all mean?, and What is it all for? Another way to say this is that part of the meaning of adolescent self-absorption is philosophical.[8] The philosopher Jacob Needleman, who created a high school philosophy course in the 1980s (Needleman 1982a, 1982b), wrote of that experience:

I know now one undoubted fact about adolescence. It is a time when the Question of myself is a natural companion, a light that soon flickers and goes out. Often, it is simply degraded under the term "self-consciousness," in its negative sense. (1982a, 94)

I see the power of great ideas to start and support this special sort of questioning in young people. I see how easily and naturally it comes to them. Yet, without the help of such ideas presented to them in a definite way, this questioning may never get started or never move them very far. Yet, at least before they are "fully grown adults" with a "secure identity role" in society, this questioning is there all the time. . . . But who sees it? Who honors this questioning? Who supports it in our world? (Ibid., 112)

This kind of existential questioning, or questing to know oneself, addresses both "the meaning of it all" and how one's own life can be lived meaningfully—the cosmic and the personal aspects of wisdom, which was philosophy's original focus in the ancient Eastern and Western schools. In this regard, it is significant that Yale psychologist Robert J. Sternberg has cited Philosophy for Children as one of only three educational programs he found that "seem particularly related to the goals of . . . teaching for wisdom" (2003, 163). The idea that formal education should include "teaching for wisdom"—should aim broadly at individual and collective well-being, in aesthetic, political, and moral terms, as well as in narrower, economic terms—is at least as old as Socrates and has been a perennial theme in philosophy that continues to the present day (Needleman 1982a; Noddings 2005; Nussbaum 2010; Palmer 1993; Rose 2009; Sternberg 1999, 2001, 2003).

Lipman and Sharp's Philosophy for Children instantiates Dewey's fundamental insight that education means learning to interact more intelligently and purposefully with the problems and opportunities that confront us here and now (Lipman 2004a). For Dewey, the school curricula represent various kinds of (culturally valued) meaning—mathematical, historical, scientific, sociological, literary, musical, etc.—that are already latent in children's experience. The purpose of schooling is to help children to recognize these kinds of meaning—that they already have mathematical, scientific, and aesthetic experience—and to learn ways of thinking and acting that enhance the meaning (i.e., the value of those experiences). If philosophy has a place in schools, it is likewise to help children enhance possibilities for meaning in their experiences, but encompassing ethical, aesthetic, political, logical, and metaphysical meaning.

Although the IAPC has promoted Philosophy for Children as an effective means of reaching educational objectives such as improved reasoning, creativity, and social skills, for most of us involved in this work these benefits are auxiliary to the benefit of children having the chance to do their own philosophical inquiry: to become aware of the aesthetic or the ethical in their own experience; to share their puzzlement and excitement; to inquire into the problematic; and to formulate their own judgments about what is what, how things relate, and how their corner of the world could be more just or more beautiful. Rather than see this kind of inquiry as something instrumental to other kinds of learning, many philosophers of education have argued the reverse: that much of the rest of one's education should be considered instrumental to this kind of existential inquiry.

P4C AS A PROCESS APPROACH TO PHILOSOPHY EDUCATION

As Judith Suissa has argued (2008), the ways that philosophical content and method are sometimes taught in precollege programs make these programs as liable as any other school subject to become dryly academic in ways that obstruct the meaning philosophy might have for young people. Programs that focus on argumentation and the critical function of philosophy—which I will call the "process approach"—tend to prioritize questions of truth or even of logical validity over questions of meaning. Programs that focus on traditional content areas of academic philosophy (whether organized historically or thematically)—which I will call the "content approach"—tend to treat philosophy as a predetermined body of knowledge to be mastered for its own sake: topics of professional interest mostly abstracted away from a student's own experience. I will describe the process and the content features of Philosophy for Children and explain how each resists these perils of emptiness.

The method developed in the early 1970s by Lipman and Sharp for engaging children in philosophical inquiry, though often embellished and varied in practice, has endured mostly intact since then. Lipman rearticulated the method in 2003 in terms of five stages:

1. The offering of the text [Students read or enact a philosophical story together].
2. The construction of the agenda [Students raise questions for discussion and organize them into an agenda].
3. Solidifying the community [Students dialogue about the questions as a community of inquiry facilitated by an adult with philosophical training; discussion continues over subsequent philosophy sessions until the inquiry agenda is finished, or until the students agree to move on to another reading/topic].
4. Using exercises and discussion plans [The facilitator introduces relevant philosophical activities to deepen and expand the students' inquiry or to help them practice particular skills].
5. Encouraging further responses [These include, e.g., self-assessment of philosophy practice, art projects, action projects, and personal philosophical reflection].

The central practice of Philosophy for Children is the community of inquiry: a practice of collaborative dialogue that engages young people in cognitive moves such as creating hypotheses, clarifying terms, giving and evaluating reasons, offering examples and counterexamples, questioning assumptions, and drawing inferences—as well as social moves like sharing perspectives, listening attentively, helping others make their point, and challenging and building on other people's ideas (Fisher 2008; Gregory 2008a; Kennedy 2004a). The facilitator of these dialogues neither leads the students to a predetermined answer nor attempts to validate every opinion as equally sound. Instead, she models and prompts the kinds of behaviors just mentioned, helps students to see the argument structure that emerges in each dialogue, and encourages them to follow the inquiry where it leads, that is, in the direction of the strongest arguments and evidence (including the evidence of feelings). The goal of these inquiries is for the students to arrive at one or more reasonable philosophical judgments regarding their own questions (Gregory 2008a), with the expectation that doing so will require each person to reconstruct or "self-correct" the understandings, opinions, feelings, and/or values she began with, at least partially.

Lipman's design of P4C as education for improved thinking (Lipman 2003, 2008) falls squarely within the norms of Socratic pedagogy, which, as Nussbaum explains it, combines a focus on "the child's ability to understand the logical structure of an argument, to detect bad reasoning, [and] to challenge ambiguity," with a focus on "Socratic values," such as being "active, critical, curious, [and] capable of resisting authority and peer pressure" (2010, 72). Lipman used the phrase "multidimensional thinking" to refer to his tripartite of critical, creative, and caring thinking as irreducible facets of normative inquiry (see Lipman 2003, chs. 11–13). In fact, Lipman's work provides a theoretical grounding for Suissa's concern that exclusive focus on philosophy's critical function ignores the importance of imaginative reflection and of philosophy's relationship to the social and natural world. Lipman also drew on the work of Peirce scholar and Dewey colleague Justus Buchler to posit as the aim of philosophical inquiry, not rational belief, but "ethical, social, political, and aesthetic judgments . . . applied directly to life situations" (2003, 279).

But perhaps Lipman and Sharp's most important contribution to critical thinking and precollege philosophy education was the way they conceived and then operationalized the social dimension of thinking, which has both epistemological and pedagogical import. First, thinking that is rational (i.e., reliant on sound arguments and good evidence) may not be reasonable, for which it must also be informed by diverse perspectives and subjected to the critique of one's (disciplinary) peers. We acquire the ability to reason as we participate in linguistic (i.e., cognitive communities), and that ability is heightened when we make our thinking accountable to others, especially others whose facility in one or more kinds of thinking is more practiced than our own. When I externalize my thinking in dialogue with others, I make it accountable to theirs. As they ask me for clarification, point out mistakes in my reasoning, develop my ideas in new directions, tell stories that expand my perspective, etc., I have the opportunity, not only to strengthen my understanding of the particular topic, but also to interact with, mimic, and internalize some of the kinds of skillful thinking the others demonstrate.

The most important factor in this model is the skilled philosophical facilitator (Kennedy 2004b): a person who respects children as persons and listens to them with a sensitive philosophical ear; who is procedurally rigorous but is comfortable with ambiguity; who approaches philosophical inquiry with both playfulness and reverence; who is comfortable making transparent her own wondering, reasoning, and self-correction. Most of the people who have prepared for and practiced this kind of facilitation under the auspices of the IAPC fall into three categories, each with typical strengths and weaknesses: university faculty of philosophy, graduate students in philosophy or education, and schoolteachers.

Some of the university faculty who have taken an interest in Philosophy for Children have become our most important resources, not only for promoting this work and providing professional development to teachers, but also for developing the program's theory, methods, and materials. All of this, however, depends on the professors becoming excellent P4C practitioners themselves. Philosophy professors who facilitate children's dialogue are uniquely prepared to appreciate the philosophical implications of what the children say and do, to model and prompt good reasoning moves, and to help the children keep track of the structures and the intricacies of the extended arguments that emerge in their dialogues. They also have experience in teaching and classroom management, much of which transfers to the context of secondary and even primary schools. However, university faculty who are prepared, willing, and supported by their institutions to work with children on a regular basis are extremely scarce. Some who experiment with the program have found either that the work did not suit them (perhaps because they were uncomfortable not being the arbiter of knowledge in a dialogue), or that working with children and schoolteachers would not be deemed sufficiently scholarly by their universities and professional organizations to count toward their professional advancement. This last point—the reluctance of academic philosophers to take professional interest in children's philosophical practice—is a damaging bias that the growing vitality of the fields of practical and precollege philosophy are beginning to undermine.

I began practicing Philosophy for Children as a graduate student at the University of Hawaii, which, under the direction of Dr. Thomas E. Jackson, has had the most extensive and longest-running Philosophy in Schools project in the United States.[9] Both there and in New Jersey I have seen graduate students in philosophy and education develop into highly skilled facilitators with children and devote some or all of their graduate studies to this work. Some of the advantages of having graduate students work with schools are that children often see them as hip and so respond to them more enthusiastically; teachers are often less intimidated by them than by university faculty; and to be frank, their labor is cheaper. Some of the disadvantages are that their star quality can be a detriment if the children associate doing philosophy too closely with the personality of the graduate student; that many graduate students have little or no experience in teaching or working with children and so struggle with issues of classroom discipline; that some graduate students are prone to the same problems of ego and professional planning that beset some university faculty; that it can be very difficult to secure regular funding for graduate student assistantships to do work that is not directly related to university teaching or research; and that graduate students are only with us a few years at a time.

Teachers bring a number of advantages to the role of facilitator of children's philosophical dialogue. They are skilled in classroom management and have established habits of discipline with their students. They know their students well and interpret their words and actions better than visitors can. Their expertise in one or many areas of curricula makes it easy for them to help the children make connections between philosophy and the other disciplines. And many of them are experienced in conducting group conversation (Haroutunian-Gordon 2009). Helping teachers learn to facilitate philosophical dialogue has become the focus of our Philosophy in Schools project at the IAPC because in spite of the challenges, we believe this is the surest way to realize the ideal described above, of giving children the opportunity to practice philosophy with integrity and regularity.

One of the challenges of this approach is that teachers with minimal preparation in critical thinking sometimes struggle to learn principles and strategies of argumentation. Another is that the kind of classroom discussion many teachers are used to is strongly didactic: neither open ended (the teacher's role is to guide students to discover for themselves a predetermined answer), nor truly collaborative (the discourse pattern is strongly teacher centered) (Nystrand, Wu, Gamoran, Zeiser, and Long 2003). The only alternative to didactic discussion many teachers can imagine, initially, is a "circle time" or "town meeting" discussion, in which participants are encouraged to express their opinions on an equal footing, without being criticized or judged for what they say. It takes some time for some teachers to understand philosophical dialogue—a collaborative inquiry aimed at sound judgment requiring the reconstruction of beliefs and values—as a distinctive practice.

To meet these challenges the IAPC has developed a rigorous program of professional development for teachers (certified by the State of New Jersey), usually conducted as a series of full-day workshops with a cohort of teachers at a school. In these workshops we move back and forth between theory—the study of program objectives and methodology from academic sources—and practice: we conduct several sessions of our own philosophical inquiry, using the IAPC curriculum but not pretending to be children. In these inquiry sessions, teachers learn to recognize philosophical questions and ideas, to follow the unfolding of a complex philosophical argument, and to notice how the moves of the facilitator reinforce the quality of the discourse and help it advance in the direction to which it tends. We draw attention to distinguishing features of this kind of "inquiry dialogue," such as maintaining a slow pace, tracking the arguments that unfold, waiting to speak until we can help move the inquiry forward, paying attention to others in the group, keeping our remarks brief, and directing our comments to the entire group.

In helping teachers to articulate their own philosophical questioning and thinking, and to recognize the rich philosophical meaning latent in their curriculum and in their students' questions and ideas, we (and they) can't avoid thinking philosophically about education. Making philosophical inquiry a regular part of the classroom experience both necessitates and induces broader educational reforms (e.g., toward student empowerment, reasoning across the disciplines, inquiry-based pedagogy, community decision making, and the abandonment of curriculum that does not enrich the student's experience). Indeed, the implication of children's philosophical practice for educational reform is one of the most important and most-often addressed topics in the academic literature around the P4C movement (Golding 2011; Gregory and Laverty 2009; Lipman 1985; Lipman and Sharp 1978; Lushyn 2003; Lyle 2008).

P4C AS A CONTENT APPROACH TO PHILOSOPHY EDUCATION

As a process approach to philosophy education, Philosophy for Children teaches a multidimensional and collaborative inquiry process that children and adults can use to think through and with the subject matter of philosophy. In that regard, P4C is also a content approach, though it eschews the traditional content approach to teaching philosophy that emphasizes canonical philosophical problems, concepts, arguments, and key figures within established subdisciplines. Instead, P4C draws students' attention to philosophical concepts like justice, person, mind, beauty, cause, time, number, truth, citizen, good, and right. These concepts are not only foundational to the arts and sciences but are already implicated in children's experience, and are necessary for understanding and improving that experience. Splitter and Sharp (1995, 130) characterize such concepts in terms of "3 Cs"—that they are central to human experience (rather than trivial); common to most people's experience (rather than esoteric)—yet contestable—or essentially problematic. P4C attempts to help students learn to discern such philosophical concepts wherever they arise, to develop their own "philosophical ear" (Gregory 2008a, 1).

Teachers new to philosophy may also take some time to develop a "philosophical ear," during which time they may miss the philosophical meaning of their students' talk. This is the reason we begin teacher preparation and their initial philosophy practice with the IAPC curriculum: Lipman's philosophical children's novels and the activity books he and Sharp developed around them. Although any stimulus material can be used to prompt a philosophical inquiry, the IAPC curriculum has the following unique benefits, especially for teachers and students new to philosophy:

- Lipman's novels model children having their own philosophical dialogue, with and without adults, thus dramatizing and illustrating inquiry strategies.
- Philosophical concepts and issues are easily identified in the novels and further explained in the manuals, helping students and teachers recognize philosophical dimensions of their experience.
- Exercises and Discussion Plans in the manuals help students practice thinking moves and concept development skills.
- Characters in the IAPC novels raise philosophical questions and ideas from the philosophical tradition so that children may consider these in their deliberations (Gregory 2008a, 13).

THE IAPC CURRICULUM

Excerpt from *Elfie* (Lipman 2004b, 4–5)

Today Seth said, "Elfie hardly ever talks. Maybe she's not for real!"

That just shows how wrong he can be! Maybe I don't talk much, but I think all the time. I even think when I sleep. I don't have fancy dreams. I just think, when I'm asleep, about the same things I think about when I'm awake.

Last night I woke up in the middle of the night and I said to myself, "Elfie, are you asleep?" I touched my eyes, and they were open, so I said, "No, I'm not asleep." But that could be wrong. Maybe a person could sleep with her eyes open.

Then I said to myself, "At this moment, am I thinking? I really wonder."

And I answered myself, "Dummy! If you can wonder, you must be thinking! And if you're thinking then, no matter what Seth says, you're for real."

Discussion Plan: On being beautiful, from *Wondering at the World* (Lipman and Sharp 1986, 97)

- What is the difference between an ordinary house and a beautiful house?
- What is the difference between an ordinary tree and a beautiful tree?
- What is the difference between an ordinary song and a beautiful song?
- What is the difference between an ordinary day and a beautiful day?
- Could you have very ordinary features, and still be beautiful?
- Could you have very unusual features, and still be beautiful?
- Could you be beautiful, even though lots of people think you aren't?
- Are there people you know who are beautiful in some ways but not in others?
- Is it possible that every person is beautiful in some ways?
- Is it possible that no person is beautiful in every way?
- Can a person do beautiful things? If so, can you give an example?
- Is a person who does beautiful things a beautiful person?
- Could you be a beautiful person if you did lots of things that weren't nice?

> **Exercise: Same and different, from *Looking for Meaning* (Lipman and Sharp 1982, 287)**
>
> Say whether you think these sentences have the same or different meanings.
>
> 1. None but girls are in this class. This class contains only girls.
> 2. Only men and women are in this class. No boys or girls are in this class.
> 3. Some members of this class are boys. Some boys are members of this class.
> 4. Everyone in this class is a girl. Each person in this class is a girl.
> 5. If it's a member of this class, it's a boy. If it's a boy, it's a member of this class.

In our professional development workshops, we also spend time reflecting on the nature of philosophical questions and how they differ from, but often hide behind psychological, historical, scientific, theological, and other kinds of questions. We ask teachers to talk about philosophical questions they have wondered about throughout their lives. We also practice taking questions that may not be recognizably philosophical and reconstructing them into questions ripe for philosophical exploration. We encourage teachers to see themselves as embarking on a long-term personal inquiry into the nature of philosophy and the theory and practice of engaging children in philosophical inquiry.

Following the introductory workshops, each teacher in the cohort is assigned a Philosophy Coach from the IAPC: a faculty member or graduate student who attends the weekly philosophy sessions. The coach typically facilitates the first several sessions while the teacher observes, then takes turns with the teacher facilitating and observing and helping the teacher reflect on the sessions, and eventually provides support while the teacher facilitates most sessions. Teachers in schools distant from Montclair are also assigned Philosophy Coaches, with whom they communicate in an online dialogue forum. They use a Reflection on Philosophy Session form (Gregory 2008a) to help them evaluate their sessions and ask for specific kinds of advice from their coaches. They also submit video segments of their sessions to their coaches.

While philosophy sessions are happening in the schools, the IAPC coordinates a number of kinds of supervision and support. Philosophy Coaches participate in a "P4C Coaching Group" at the IAPC, in which faculty and graduate students exchange ideas and concerns, take turns showing video segments of philosophy sessions (led by us and by the teachers we work with) for group critique, and discuss shared standards of practice. The Institute conducts monthly Philosophy for Teachers (P4T) sessions in which the teachers and we exchange ideas and concerns, observe and discuss video segments, or read and discuss relevant research articles. Teachers are also regularly invited to events sponsored by the Institute, including colloquia, follow-up workshops, study groups, and Summer Seminars. The IAPC records the teachers' professional development credit for these events. All of this represents a tremendous investment of personnel hours, which is by far the most precious of the Institute's resources, and for this reason we are limited to working with no more than a few schools at a time.

Two kinds of assessment are important to the practice of Philosophy for Children: self-assessment conducted by communities of children and adolescents doing philosophy; and external assessment of those communities, conducted by teachers and by the Institute. In addition to the Reflection on Philosophy Session forms described above, the IAPC has designed a number of Observation Guides (Gregory 2008a) for teachers to use to assess video recordings of their philosophy sessions. Student self-assessment is part of the practice of the community of inquiry, as the ideal of self-correction requires that participants become aware of, and improve their own inquiry skills and outcomes. The IAPC has designed instruments for students of different ages to conduct collective self-assessments. The Institute also conducts annual evaluation surveys of students and teachers to learn about how they are experiencing the program.

STANDARDS, CHALLENGES, AND QUESTIONS

Several Philosophy for Children centers and federations around the world have designed credentialing programs. Teachers and graduate students who work with the IAPC may be endorsed as "Philosophy for Children Practitioners" by completing 25 hours of workshops, seminars, or other coursework in Philosophy for Children; 25 hours of supervised practice of philosophy facilitation; and a formal self-assessment of a video-recorded philosophy session, and after a formal assessment of the same recording is made by IAPC faculty. Teachers with Institutional endorsement assume primary responsibility for conducting their philosophy sessions, with only periodic visits from IAPC coaches. They become mentors to new graduate students and to other teachers doing their initial P4C practice, and they are invited to collaborate with IAPC faculty in conducting research, developing and testing new curriculum, and making academic presentations. As long as philosophy is practiced in a school, the Institute continues to conduct P4T sessions, professional development, and program evaluation, while phasing out of intense individual coaching frees Institute personnel to begin new relationships with other schools.

The practice of engaging children in rigorous but open-ended philosophical dialogue facilitated by philosophers with training in pedagogy and educational theory or by teachers with training in philosophy, has generated a tremendous amount of scholarship in the last 40-something years, including epistemological (Bleazby 2011; Siegel 2008), political (Burgh, Field, and Freakley 2006; Weber 2008), ethical (Cam 1994; Splitter 2011), and even aesthetic (Moore 1994; Sharp 1997) theory justifying and critiquing the ideal and empirical studies that identify factors and conditions that account for its success (Murphy et al. 2009; Trickey and Topping 2004). The participation of IAPC faculty in ongoing philosophical and empirical research in these areas is a necessary component of our work in curriculum development, in refining program methods, and in our personal growth as classroom practitioners. For this reason, Lipman and Sharp made the IAPC a center of scholarship, where the journal *Thinking* is edited and published, visiting scholars are invited from around the globe, academic colloquia are hosted, faculty and students are sponsored to participate in conferences and research projects, and partnerships are forged with like-minded philosophical and educational centers and organizations.

Three kinds of problems continually threaten to undermine our work. One is a change in school administration (i.e., the replacement of the school principal or district superintendent who approved the funding and provided the leadership for introducing philosophy into the school system). Because philosophy is not mandated in the curriculum, it is vulnerable to this kind of disruption. Another challenge is the implementation of federal, state, or district educational standards or testing systems that consume so much time and energy that schools and teachers find it difficult to make time for anything not mandated. In these cases our strategy is to point to research that shows that philosophy is likely to help children meet the new program objectives or standards. A third challenge is cutbacks in university support to the Institute. One important reason we have been able to work so closely with schools in the past was that the cost of doing so was not born entirely by the schools but was subsidized by the university, in the form of faculty assignments and student assistantships. The loss of that support in recent years has diverted much of our time and attention toward pursuing grant funding.

Our experience implementing and reconstructing this model of Philosophy in Schools over the last several years has left us with a number of questions that can only be answered in the years ahead. The most pressing question for us is this: given the standard we have evolved for basic practitioner endorsement, how much time and resources should we realistically expect to invest in order to bring a cohort of teachers to meet that standard? Are there more cost-efficient ways to help teachers reach the standard, perhaps over longer periods of time? Beyond the basic standard, what kinds of philosophical expertise can teachers develop by working with us, apart from taking formal degree programs in philosophy? In what ways and to what extent can philosophical inquiry become part of other school subjects like mathematics, history, and character education? And what kinds of opportunities can we offer to experienced P4C teachers to encourage them to continue their study and practice of philosophy? What are the best ways to persuade philosophers to be concerned about pedagogy and to reflect on their own?

Our experience has also helped us to rethink what it means to do philosophy with children in some details. It has reconfirmed our conviction that reasoning is an indispensable part of, but not the whole of vibrant philosophical dialogue. It has given us the opportunity to continue to find philosophical meaning in the experiences and the thinking of children and teachers in school settings. It has caused us to be clearer and more insistent about the nature of inquiry that should structure philosophical dialogue so that it does not dissipate into an endless and incoherent exploration of associated ideas. It has caused us to reconstruct our recommendations for using the Instruction Manuals that accompany the philosophical novels in the IAPC curriculum.

Most important, our experience has reconfirmed the fundamental premise of Philosophy for Children: that children and adults without academic philosophical training are capable of discerning ethical, aesthetic, political, and other philosophical dimensions of their own experience; of recognizing problematic aspects of that experience; and through a process of rigorous and conscientious dialogue, of inquiring toward judgment and action capable of resolving what was problematic. That is our ideal, the experience we aim for when we sit on the rug with a group of children to do philosophy for an hour or so. As with all educational practice, the real is sometimes far from the ideal; but the real can also surpass the ideal and give us new ideas about what is possible.

NOTES

1. Lipman makes this remark in the BBC documentary *Socrates for Six-Year-Olds* (1990). Tony W. Johnson gives a more detailed account of the intellectual and social genealogy of Lipman's idea in a section on "The Origins of Philosophy for Children," in Johnson 1995, 123–127.
2. See "IAPC Timeline" at http://cehs.montclair.edu/academic/iapc/timeline.shtml, accessed 10/22/08.
3. *Thinking: The Journal of Philosophy for Children* (Montclair, NJ: IAPC, 1979 to present); *Analytic Teaching and Philosophical Praxis* (La Crosse, WI: Viterbo University, 1981 to present, online at http://www.viterbo.edu/atpp); *Critical and Creative Thinking: The Australasian Journal of Philosophy in Education* (Federation of Australasian Philosophy in Schools Associations, 1993 to 2009); *Childhood & Philosophy: A Journal of the International Council of Philosophical Inquiry with Children* (2005 to present, online at http://www.periodicos.proped.pro.br/index.php?journal=childhood); *Diotime: Revue Internationale de Didactique de la Philosophie* (*Diotima: International Journal of Teaching Philosophy*) online at www.crdp-montpellier.fr/ressources/agora/D034017A.htm; and *Tafakor va koodak* (*Thinking and Children*, published by Iranian Institute for Humanities and Cultural Studies).

4. These include *Journal of Philosophy of Education* 45(2) (2011); *Educational Philosophy and Theory* 43(5) (2011); *Gifted Education International* 22(2/3) (2007); *Metaphilosophy* 35(5) (2004); *Inquiry: Critical Thinking Across the Disciplines* 14(2) (2000), 16(4) (1997), and 17(1) (1997); and *Early Child Development and Care* 107(1) (1995); as well as journals in Colombia, Germany, and Iran.
5. Some parts of this chapter are adapted from parts of three earlier papers: Gregory 2002, 2008b, and 2009.
6. "It was my hunch that children were primarily intent on obtaining meaning—this is why they so often condemned school as meaningless—and wanted meanings they could verbalize. . . . Philosophy might be indispensable for the redesign of education, but to make this happen it would itself have to be redesigned" (Lipman 1996, xv).
7. For more on doing philosophy with young children, see Cam et al. 2007; Daniel 2005; Fields 1995; Kennedy 1991, 1996; Lipman 1991; Matthews 1980; McCall 1989; Murris 1999; Sharp 2000; and Shea 2004.
8. For more on doing philosophy with adolescents, see Hannam and Echeverria 2010, Lipman 1986, McCall 2006, Rondhuis 2005, and Weinstein 1982.
9. See http://www.p4chawaii.org, accessed 5/23/12.

REFERENCES

Bleazby, J. (2011) "Overcoming Relativism and Absolutism: Dewey's Ideals of Truth and Meaning in Philosophy for Children" *Educational Philosophy and Theory* 43(5): 453–466.
Burgh, G., Field, T. and Freakley, M. (2006) *Ethics and the Community of Inquiry: Education for Deliberative Democracy*, 2nd ed. Melbourne: Thomson Social Science Press.
Cam, P. (1994) "A Philosophical Approach to Moral Education" *Critical and Creative Thinking* 2(2): 19–26.
Cam, P., Fynes-Clinton, L., Harrison, K., Hinton, L., Scholl, R. and Vaseo, S. (2007) *Philosophy for Young Children: A Classroom Handbook* Deakin West, Australian Capital Territory: Australian Curriculum Studies Association.
Daniel, M-F. (2005) "Learning to Dialogue in Kindergarten: A Case Study" *Analytic Teaching* 25(3): 23–52.
Fields, J. I. (1995) "Young Children as Emergent Philosophers" *Early Child Development and Care* 107(1): 57–59.
Fisher, R. (2008) *Teaching Thinking: Philosophical Enquiry in the Classroom*, 3rd ed. New York: Continuum.
Golding, C. (2011) "Educating Philosophically: The Educational Theory of Philosophy for Children" *Educational Philosophy and Theory* 43(5): 413–414.
Gregory, M. (2009) "Philosophy for Children as a Process and a Content Approach to Philosophy Education: A Response to Judith Suissa" Paper presented at the Annual Conference of the Philosophy of Education Society of Great Britain, New College, Oxford University.
———. (2008a) *Philosophy for Children Practitioner Handbook* Montclair, NJ: Institute for the Advancement of Philosophy for Children.
———. (2008b) "Philosophy in Schools: Ideals, Challenges and Opportunities" *Critical and Creative Thinking* 16(1): 5–22.
———. (2002) "Are Philosophy and Children Good for Each Other?" *Thinking: The Journal of Philosophy for Children* 16(2): 9–12.

Gregory, M. and Laverty, M. (2009) "Philosophy and Education for Wisdom" In *Teaching Philosophy* (ed. A. Kenkmann), 155–173, London: Continuum International.

Hannam, P. and Echeverria, E. (2010) *Philosophy with Teenagers: Nurturing a Moral Imagination for the 21st Century* London: Network Continuum Education.

Haroutunian-Gordon, S. (2009) *Learning to Teach Through Discussion: The Art of Turning the Soul* New Haven, CT: Yale University Press.

Johnson, T. W. (1995) *Discipleship or Pilgrimage? The Educator's Quest for Philosophy* Albany: State University of New York Press.

Kennedy, D. (2004a) "Communal Philosophical Dialogue and the Intersubject" *International Journal for Philosophical Practice* 18(2): 201–216.

———. (2004b) "The Role of a Facilitator in a Community of Philosophical Inquiry" *Metaphilosophy* 35(5): 744–765.

———. (1996) "Young Children's Moves" *Critical and Creative Thinking* 4(2): 28–41.

———. (1991) "Young Children and Ultimate Questions: Romancing at Day Care" *Analytic Teaching* 12(1): 59–64.

Lipman, M. (2008) *A Life Teaching Thinking* Montclair, NJ: Institute for the Advancement of Philosophy for Children.

———. (2004a) "Philosophy for Children's Debt to Dewey" *Critical and Creative Thinking* 12: 1–8.

———. (2004b) *Elfie*, 2nd ed. Montclair, NJ: Institute for the Advancement of Philosophy for Children.

———. (2003) *Thinking in Education*, 2nd ed. Cambridge: Cambridge University Press.

———. (1996) *Natasha: Vygotskian Dialogues* New York: Teachers College Press.

———. (1991) "Philosophy Is Also for the Young, at Least Possibly" *Thinking* 9(3): 27.

———. (1986) "Can Education for Thinking Take Place in High Schools Too?" *Administrators Journal* 3(2): 14–19.

———. (1985) "Philosophical Practice and Educational Reform" *Journal of Thought* 20(4): 20–36 (response by Kurt Baier: 37–44).

Lipman, M. and Sharp, A. M. (1986) *Wondering at the World* Montclair, NJ: Institute for the Advancement of Philosophy for Children.

———. (1982) *Looking for Meaning* Montclair, NJ: Institute for the Advancement of Philosophy for Children.

———. (1978) "Some Educational Presuppositions of Philosophy for Children" *Oxford Review of Education* 4(1): 85–90.

Lipman, M., Sharp, A. M. and Oscanyan, F. (1980) *Philosophy in the Classroom.* Philadelphia: Temple University Press.

Lushyn, P. (2003) "Some Reflections on the Ecology of Pedagogical Space" *Thinking* 16(3): 4–11.

Lyle, S. (2008) "Dialogic Teaching: Discussing Theoretical Contexts and Reviewing Evidence from Classroom Practice" *Language and Education* 22(3): 222–240.

Matthews, G. (1996) *Philosophy of Childhood* Cambridge, MA: Harvard University Press.

———. (1980) *Philosophy and the Young Child* Cambridge, MA: Harvard University Press.

McCall, C. (2006) *Thinking Adventures: A Book for High School Pupils and a Teacher's Guide to Thinking Adventures* Edinburgh: Scottish Executive Education Department.

———. (1989) "Young Children Generate Philosophical Ideas" *Thinking* 8(2): 22–41.

Moore, R. (1994) "Aesthetics for Young People: Problems and Prospects" *Journal of Aesthetic Education* 28(3): 5–18.

Murphy, P. K., Wilkinson, I.A.G., Soter, A. O., Hennessey, M. N. and Alexander, J. F. (2009) "Examining the Effects of Classroom Discussion on Students' Comprehension of Text: A Meta-Analysis" *Journal of Educational Psychology* 101(3): 740–764.

Murris, K. (1999) "Philosophy with Preliterate Children" *Thinking* 14(4): 23–33.

Needleman, J. (1982a) *The Heart of Philosophy* New York: Alfred A. Knopf.

———. (1982b) "Teaching Philosophy to Adolescents" *Thinking: The Journal of Philosophy for Children* 3(3/4): 26–30.

Noddings, N. (2005) *Happiness and Education* Cambridge: Cambridge University Press.

Nussbaum, M. (2010) *Not for Profit: Why Democracy Needs the Humanities* Princeton, NJ: Princeton University Press.

Nystrand, M., Wu, L. A., Gamoran, A., Zeiser, S. and Long, D. A. (2003) "Questions in Time: Investigating the Structure and Dynamics of Unfolding Classroom Discourse" *Discourse Processes* 35(2): 135–200.

Palmer, P. J. (1993) *To Know as We Are Known: A Spirituality of Education* New York: HarperCollins.

Reed, R. F. (1994) "Radical Empiricism" *Analytic Teaching* 14(2): 33–41.

Rondhuis, T. (2005) *Philosophical Talent: Empirical Investigations into Philosophical Features of Adolescents' Discourse* (PhD Diss., Dept. of Developmental Psychology, Utrecht University, The Netherlands). Accessed May 15, 2012: url: http://igitur-archive.library.uu.nl/dissertations/2005–1004-200025/UUindex.html.

Rose, M. (2009) *Why School? Reclaiming Education for All of Us* New York: The New Press.

Sharp, A.M. (2000) *The Doll Hospital and Making Sense of My World: Instructional Manual* Camberwell, Victoria, Australia: The Australian Council for Educational Research, Ltd.

———. (1997) "The Aesthetic Dimension of the Community of Inquiry" *Inquiry: Critical Thinking Across the Disciplines* 17(1): 67–77.

Shea, P. (2004) "Offering a Frame to Put Experience in: Margaret Wise Brown Presents Ideas as Opportunities to Very Young Children" *Thinking* 17(3): 30–37.

Siegel, H. (2008) "Why Teach Epistemology in Schools?" In *Philosophy in Schools* (eds. M. Hand and C. Winstanley) 78–84. New York: Continuum International.

Socrates for Six-Year-Olds, produced by the British Broadcasting Company. 1990. Oxford, UK: SAPERE, DVD.

Splitter, L. J. (2011) "Agency, Thought, and Language: Analytic Philosophy Goes to School" *Studies in Philosophy and Education* 30: 343–362.

Splitter, L. J. and Sharp, A. M. (1995) *Teaching for Better Thinking* Melbourne: Australian Council of Educational Research.

Sternberg, R. J. (2003) *Wisdom, Intelligence, and Creativity Synthesized* Cambridge: Cambridge University Press.

———. (2001) "Why Schools Should Teach for Wisdom: The Balance Theory of Wisdom in Educational Settings" *Educational Psychologist* 36(4): 227–245.

———. (1999) "Schools Should Nurture Wisdom" In *Teaching for Intelligence* (ed. B. Z. Presseisen) 55–82, Arlington Heights, IL: Skylight Training and Publishing.

Suissa, J. (2008) "Philosophy in the Secondary School—a Deweyan Perspective" In *Philosophy in Schools* (eds. M. Hand and C. Winstanley) 132–144, London: Continuum.

Trickey, S. and Topping, K. J. (2004) " 'Philosophy for Children': A Systematic Review" *Research Papers in Education* 19(3): 363–378.

Weber, B. (2008) "Hope Instead of Cognition? The Community of Inquiry as a Culture for Human Rights Based on Richard Rorty's Understanding of Philosophy" *Thinking* 18(4): 23–31.

Weinstein, M. (1982) "Teaching Ethics in Secondary School" *Analytic Teaching* 4(2): 15–18.

7 Does Philosophy Fit in Caxias? A Latin American Project

Walter Omar Kohan

This chapter introduces an educational and philosophical project that is still very much alive and in process. The project—Does Philosophy Fit in Caxias? Public School Bets on Thinking—is housed in two public schools in the city of Duque de Caxias, a suburb of Rio de Janeiro, Brazil, that may be characterized as an urban poverty zone. The project involves philosophizing with students *and* the creation of a teacher education agenda in which teachers study and practice the art of facilitating philosophical experiences with their students. Created in 2007, it is sponsored by the Center for Philosophical Studies of Childhood (NEFI) at the University of the State of Rio de Janeiro (UERJ), and includes roughly 20 teachers and 400 students from ages 6 to 70—with the latter as part of an adult literacy class.

The teacher education plan includes several workshops ranging between 20 and 40 hours each. The workshops occur within the schools and in residence on the campus of UERJ on the island of Ilha Grande. These workshops are mainly experimental, and sessions have basically two forms: "experiences of thinking" and "thinking the experience." The former are initially conducted by the coordination team and progressively by all participants, with their support throughout the planning of the session. They consist in philosophizing as a process of "problematizing," "dialoguing," and "conceptualizing." Each session is free to choose its strategies, texts, etc., as soon as they unfold the aforementioned triad. Along with the workshops, the program includes regular meetings at the designated schools and at the university. Students of UERJ who are studying in pedagogy and philosophy also take part in these activities. The participating students also attend workshops at the university, and they and their teachers have participated in two international conferences organized in Rio. Since the beginning of the project, one teacher has completed a master's thesis that takes the project as an object of research, and two others are in the process of doing so.

Though still relatively new, this project has received significant attention. TV Escola—a national educational network—has produced a one hour program on the project, and a book on it has recently been published (Kohan and Olarieta 2012). There is also an Internet site dedicated to the project and its work (www.filoeduc.org/caxias). The project demonstrates that extra-campus extension activities are as essential to the university's mandate as are teaching and research. Rather than the transmission of knowledge from university to community, extension is here understood as a form of research in which "insiders" and "outsiders" together think through the problems and opportunities with which the experience of philosophy presents them.

PATHS TO EXPERIENCE PHILOSOPHIZING

Given the centrality of collaborative philosophizing in our project, our goal has been to organize an experience without predetermined methods or curriculum materials, and to approach pedagogical practice like the artist, who needs skill and practiced sensibility, but also a radical openness to the world. Materials and techniques are at service of the pedagogical setting just as they are for a musician or a painter. We offer principles, texts, and philosophical questions to teachers as materials that each one works with in her own way. None of them are inflexible, nothing has always to be included or avoided—they represent elements for thinking about the "what" and the "how" of philosophical practice. We list some of our shared action principles or "gestures" in an appendix at the end of the chapter.[1] What follow are some theoretical principles that sustain our project.

The Importance of Being Aware of Ignorance

The understanding of philosophy that we affirm was born with Socrates to the extent that his practice was a public exercise of the word, through questioning and problematizing. Dissatisfied with the dominant ways of life in the *pólis*, Socrates called them into question and pushed his fellow citizens to confront their problematic assumptions.

Importantly, Socrates was understood to be wise because of his relationship with ignorance;[2] he was aware of his ignorance, and this made him the wisest person in Athens. Even knowing that he would never reach a consolidated form of knowledge, he doggedly sought it. He lived to search and searched to live a life worth living. Importantly, Socrates never claimed to be Master of anyone. He did not transmit any knowledge, but generates learning. In this way he suggests a stance for the philosophy teacher: one who causes learning without claiming the status of a teacher; not being a master, his followers emerge.[3] The Socratic position is inspiring in the way it opens a space for the practice of educational philosophy as a living exercise of thinking, instead of as a transmission of knowledge. This means that the teacher does not plan philosophical experiences aiming to transmit knowledge (or "values" or "competences" or whatever) to her students but because of the meaning and sense of thinking experiences themselves and the learning they eventually might generate.

Another inspiring figure for our philosophy teacher education perspective is Simón Rodríguez, a Venezuelan of the 19th century, named by his disciple, Simon Bolivar, "The Socrates of Caracas."[4] Like Socrates, he was a relentless critic of his society, calling its foundations into question, walking around the city confronting the dominant ways of life. He also dedicated his life to "educating" people—interrogating them, challenging them to seek out other possible worlds. Like Socrates, he criticized the masters as transmitters of knowledge who equated education with a technique for the dissemination of knowledge. He also was a disturber of the social status quo, with a pedagogical, philosophical, and political project of transformation. Both the Athenian and the Caraqueño spoke a language other than their contemporaries; both were considered exotic, extravagant, strangers in their own city, and ultimately dangerous to the established order.

The Caraqueño said, "We invent or we err."[5] The claim is philosophical, pedagogical, political, and existential. To truly educate all the people, in knowing and doing, for a common life to come which is as yet unknown, we cannot rely on any dominant models of education. We must invent it. Any imitation will reproduce the logic of submission and extermination that has reigned in Latin America for centuries. Monarchical schools teach sophisticated skills of reasoning such as the Aristotelian syllogism to justify the subjugation of the Indians. Instead, we must educate the real owners of the land, those dispossessed by the colonial power. We must think feelingly, painting a reality of freedom for all the inhabitants of our own terrain. The truth is not out there waiting to be discovered; rather it is part of an ethics and a politics that can make this part of the world a place of true freedom for all who inhabit it, a place like no other on earth.[6] Following Rodríguez, our program seeks to rethink the notion of education from the ground up, to work with individual and groups who have been marginalized or subjugated—and through shared philosophizing—to envision a future reality for all of us (Rodríguez 2001b). Particularly with adult students we emphasize the philosophical disposition of making our experience of the world strange; of seeing the ordinary as extraordinary; of finding no naturality or normality in culture, concerns that would be unlikely to be raised in the given process of schooling.

Intellectual Equality between Teacher and Student

Everyone has an equal capacity to learn, everyone is able to do what any human being is able to do, affirmed J. Jacotot a couple of centuries ago.[7] The same intelligence operates in creating a piece of art as in cleaning the street. This principle—simple, difficult but also clear—disrupts the normalization process characteristic of the school. The teacher is not supposed to explain what she knows and have students accept it: each one must seek and find for themselves, in the company of others, their own way. This is what a true teacher cannot fail to know or practice—that she needs to learn and teach so as to generate learning that the other wants to provide herself. It is necessary that the other learn, first of all, that she is able to learn and think like everyone else. The teacher needs to know that in terms of capability, her intelligence is no more and no less than any other intelligence, whatever difference in experience and any other respects they have. As such, the teacher's entire task reconfigures itself. It is no longer supported by the knowledge that has to be transmitted, or the skills that the other must achieve, but in caring for the way the other wants to learn. What matters is that the other wants to learn, to seek and never stop seeking. It also doesn't matter *what* the student learns—what matters is that she learn and keep learning forever, with full attention. There is nothing we should expect the student to learn except to continue learning; and there is no method to this other than the student's. As such, the philosophical experiences aim to provoke the seeking of experience and thinking itself. They do not aim to "teach to think" but the will, desire or inspiration to "learn to think" and keep learning to think endlessly.

Emphasis on Experience

Inspiration for our project also came from French thinkers such as Foucault, Deleuze, and Derrida. From Foucault comes a tentative relationship to claims of truth, and a wariness about the modern disciplinary structures of schools and how they affect individuals within them (Foucault 1997). From his thinking, we suggest that the teacher's task is not only to transmit truths, but to question, by experience, her relationship to truth. The idea of experience inhabits the practice of philosophy considered as an exercise or experience of thinking, in which form and content are always mutually imbricated, continuously trying to think in another way without consecrating or legitimizing what is already thought and known, but always searching to think and learn in other ways. In doing philosophy together, we learn not only about ourselves, but we also better understand the relationships of power from which we emerge, relationships that we may be able to refuse or transform in order eventually to be different. Foucault calls this a "critical ontology of ourselves" (Foucault 1994a). Foucault, like Deleuze, taught us the indignity of speaking for others.[8]

In this way, we stop thinking of education as a training device to promote certain forms of subjectivity by means of a normative discourse on what ought to be, and began to think it as a friendly, introductory practice of opening spaces that disrupt the dominant dynamic in schools. Teachers and students can take part in new forms of being and, in Deleuzian terminology, new becomings. We also learn to differentiate between childhood and children, and to mistrust the form of temporalization that divides life into chronological stages. "Becoming-child" or "child block" is a way of being in the world that is associated with the quality of experience, rather than one's age.[9] Within "majoritarian" education (curricula, laws, parameters, institutions) lives "minoritarian" education, and Deleuze helps us to think the latter within the interstices of the former. It also affirms the importance of conceptual creation, which is a dimension of philosophy crucial to our work (Deleuze and Guattari 2005). Learning presupposes attention to signs: to learn means to decipher the signs of the world, of people, of life (Deleuze 2004). There is no univocal correspondence between teaching and learning—someone can teach and nobody learn, and someone can learn without anyone teaching. Finally, we learn that the teacher who pretends to be a model teaches nothing: we only learn with those who propose gestures that are sensitive to difference.[10]

Derrida also teaches us to see the paradoxical relationship between teacher and method (Derrida 1986). A path is needed, as well as planning, resources, texts, sensitivation strategies, evaluations. But philosophy escapes from any method. The best method used in the most accurate way may not provoke a philosophical experience, which can occur *against* a method, or with an anti-method.

Taking Philosophy Outside the University

From Giuseppe Ferraro—a Neapolitano and a friend—we learn the necessity of taking philosophy outside the walls of the university and into the city, and even into the outskirts, at the extremes, where it seems to have always been absent, and yet which is its more proper and vital space. We learn that philosophy can only be practiced among friends, because rather than simply being a quest for knowledge (as the word is commonly translated), philosophy is a knowledge of desire, of searching, and of friendship. Philosophers do not philosophize together because they are friends, but they become friends when they philosophize together (Ferraro 2010a, 5).

Ferraro teaches that philosophical knowledge is not about things, but about the taste[11] that these things have, how and why we feel them in one way and not in another—the way they are, what they are and nothing else. Philosophy helps us to think if someone or something is being what she or it truly is, if she or it lives a life with the strength and joy that could be living. Philosophy is a way of looking at what we are, and thinking whether we are what we truly are. It is a sort of interior gaze, provoked by the encounter with other perspectives, which moves us to understand and transform what we are. It is a form of affection—both to affect and to be affected—of bodies thinking together (Ferraro 2010b, 18). Ferraro also teaches us that philosophy can be a way to find, together, in concert, the voice of words. It is at the edges of the city that the excluded voice finds its words in experiences of philosophy. It is only at the outskirts, where it doesn't seems to be able to be what it is, that philosophy finds out what it truly is. For philosophy, to leave the walls of academia is not a promenade; it is the possibility of being truly itself (Ferraro 2010a, 8–9).

Philosophy for Children

Matthew Lipman created the contemporary form of *philosophy for children*, and with it a very large philosophical movement emerged. Ann Sharp worked tirelessly to disseminate the project. The very idea of our project is inspired by Lipman and Sharp, if only by the original formulation of the possibility and the crucial importance of putting philosophy and children together in educational institutions. Although we do not adopt their program, and even affirm significant differences in our way of conceiving philosophy, childhood, and the sense of how they meet, we have learned much from Lipman and Sharp.

Among other things, we have learned from them to place the utmost importance on the coherence between what we think and what we do, and on the form of our practice in educational institutions. This is a crucial issue in teacher education, which is no longer thought of as the transmission of theoretical and methodological supports, but as a site where we practice ourselves what we expect to practice with students. The practice of philosophy turns on the experience of *questioning*, and immersion in philosophical practice assumes an implicit trust in its transformational power. As such, philosophical practice represents a major challenge to the traditional educational position of the teacher that mainstream institutions insist on spreading (Lipman 1988, 11 ff.). Lipman and Sharp have led us into a process of learning to unlearn how to be a teacher, all the while remaining open to the emergence of new, affirmative ways that are revealed by the experience of philosophy in action.

The idea of community of philosophical inquiry is essential to this process. Philosophy is not an individual's lonely, introspective, reclusive task. It may be so in another space. But in the common meeting, it is quintessential dialogical practice, where what matters is not to have the truth or to quote the masters, but the voicing of the collective inquiry, which tends always to show the complexity of the problems under discussion, and different ways of approaching a question, or of attempting to think it through. Above all, in community of inquiry, philosophizing becomes an opportunity to meet with each other—with other thoughts and with the thoughts of others (Lipman 2003, 81 ff.).

Philosophy as Rebellion: "It's Enough!"

Subcommandant Marcos is the intellectual leader of the Zapatista movement, which erupted in the Lacandon Jungle in the Mexican state of Chiapas in 1994. Marcos is a university graduate in philosophy who at some point of his life travelled from Mexico City to Chiapas to live the reality of oppression and exclusion of the indigenous Chiapanecos, and in this experience to build a singular political movement of resistance to that reality. From the Zapatistas we have learned, above all, a way of thinking state politics.

The meaning of Zapatista politics is inscribed in the epigraph, "Today we say 'it's enough!'" presented in the First Lacandona Jungle Declaration, on January, 2, 1994 (EZLN 1996, 33).

"Today we say 'it's enough!'" indicates a period of time—500 years—during which ancient Mexican indigenous people have fought against the invaders who stole their land, their food, their wealth, their lives. It also indicates an action in the first person plural: *"we say."* A collective voice, one people, a common force that expresses resistance: words as a form of rebellion. Finally, it indicates a loud voice, an exclamation, a cry that breaks the apparent calm, the silence. It is the sign of a limit, a point that cannot be passed beyond; a marking to this ancestral time that justifies and gives a meaning to it. The Zapatistas announce a new policy: no excluded ones, no hierarchies, no false representations. In this policy, there are no longer those who command and those others who obey, those who know and those who are ignorant, those who legislate and those who abide by the laws. Zapatism is an equality politics asserted by the fact of difference. Our philosophy project adopts this general stance and infuses the work of Marcos in our philosophy discussions. Marcos wrote many stories—for example, "The Story of the Search," "The Story of the Looks," "The Story of the Mirrors"—which bring together elements of pre-European American mythologies and contemporary European thinkers, and which are inspiring texts for philosophizing with children.[12] They show a complex, open, incomplete world, in which human life requires thinking for oneself and with others. The Zapatista movement also makes us see policy in more colors, because Zapatistas write not only stories and letters, but embody the life they are becoming through music, painting, costume, street theater and media spectacle. The strength and pain of "it's enough!" affirms a colorful expression of life.

Philosophy as a Creative Sensibility

The last of our inspirations is a Brazilian poet—Manoel de Barros—an artist and creator from the epic tropical wetlands of the Pantanal. In fact, the sense and feeling of the philosophical experience that moves us comes very close to that of the artistic experience: the tone of creative sensibility. In addition, Barros is an inventor of infancies, of a special relationship with childhood, both in his writing and thinking. His presence is very strong in our practice. He inspires us with the beauty of the writing and the creative exercise of his thought—aesthetics and invention bound in each other's service. The epigraph that heads his volume of poetry—*Infancy: Invented Memories*—serves as a manifesto: "All that I do not invent is false" (Barros 2010, 3). For Barros, as for Simon Rodriguez, invention is a criterion for truth. It may be that not all inventions are true, but if all we do not invent is not true, then we also know that something that we do not invent cannot be true. Creation is the gateway to the world of truth.

The poet of the Pantanal has taught us to unlearn a diminutive and schematic view of childhood, opening doors for a more powerful, rich, and complex one. The child's world in his writing is one of intimacy with things and the world, in a "child block" of vital force and creative energy. His poetry shows the strength of a childlike form of being and seeing the world. He teaches us the ugliness and poverty of the diminishing gaze so often applied to childhood, and finds a special strength in the thinking associated with attending to what normally is regarded as small or useless. Read with equal pleasure by students and teachers, his writing breaks down disciplinary boundaries and methodological strictures. His texts lead us into a rich, powerful, and beautiful exercise of thinking. Let's consider, for example, his poem "A didacts of invention," where he offers a number of examples of how to touch the intimacy of the world. In the last sentence, he affirms: "To dislearn eight hours a day teaches the principles," (Barros 1993) and this is, in fact, a principle of our work. Because of his irreverent relationship with syntax and grammar, which demands that we unlearn a standard form of writing, he also inspires us to think beyond standard forms, and thereby beyond the world in which they constrict us, to other possible worlds.

Appendix

Here are some of our shared action principles or "gestures" available to teachers (NEFI 2011). Their inspiration is multiple, and they are constantly changing from the outcomes of our practice.

GESTURES OF AFFIRMATION

What, in Our Perspective, Is It Important That the Teacher Do in Her Practice?

1. Encourage the participants to listen and to dialogue with each other. Highlight the similarities and the differences between the perspectives presented. Ask for clarification when what was said seems confused. Seek to deepen each perspective, and encourage participants to do the same.
2. Ask "why," and persist in asking. Insist on consistency. Problematize the sense of what is happening.
3. Help participants to explore each question in depth. Do not bombard them with questions, but explore each of them.
4. Don't be bothered by silence. Try to observe different forms of attention. Participation is not always in spoken form.
5. Discourage long monologues so that voice is shared within the group; orchestrate scattered ideas, stitching them together as a collective dialogue.
6. Do not impose anything that the group does not need. For example, if the group requires rules, they must produce them themselves.

GESTURES TO AVOID

What Practices Inhibit, in Our Consideration, the Potential of Philosophical Thinking?

1. Lecturing.
2. Attempting to control, discipline, or evaluate what a student knows.
3. Answering a question in a way that ignores or occludes doubt.
4. Voicing moral judgments about students' thoughts and affirmations.
5. Talking too much. Open questions, briefly put, are preferable. Contributing an anecdotal or opinionated conversation in like manner.
6. Seeking to solve personal problems, although the conversation often helps to think through those problems.

WAYS OF THINKING TOGETHER ABOUT OUR WORK

What Dispositions Contribute to the Work We Are Fostering to Unfold?

A. Dispositions Concerning the Questions and Topics Investigated

1. Is our thinking stimulated by our inquiry?
2. Do we wonder, express curiosity, and become deeply involved in the discussion?
3. Do we think the same way as we did before the inquiry, or have we changed our position?
4. Do fresh questions arise? Are some of our questions transformed by the inquiry?

B. Dispositions Regarding the Participants

1. Do we help to build an atmosphere of trust, in which everyone felt that their thinking would be heard carefully?
2. Do we encourage the participants to express their views when they seem doubtful about joining in?
3. Do we try to involve as many participants, in as many different ways, as possible?
4. Do we promote dialogue between participants, rather than between participants and teacher?
6. Do we foster cooperation in the inquiry?
7. Do we take the views of the participants into consideration, giving each the opportunity to be heard, understood, and responded to?
8. Are we sensitive to the length of each intervention?

9. Do we avoid manipulating the inquiry to impose a point of view?
10. Do we help students to relate their ideas with their experience and with other knowledge?

C. Dispositions Regarding the Inquiry

1. Do we seek to bring the dialogue to a deeper conceptual level through problematizing assumptions or implicit values?
2. Do we try to focus the discussion when it becomes too abstract or unclear?
3. Do we take care to explore the inquiry's direction, implications, and assumptions in a search for underlying reasons and not an exchange of opinions?
4. Do we help to avoid the idea that philosophical investigations serve only to confirm predetermined answers?
5. Do we trust and help others to trust that there may be growth in philosophical inquires?
6. Do we help participants to clarify and develop what they say?
7. Do we help to connect and relate the ideas of the participants through suggesting, for example, lines of convergence or divergence?
8. Do we encourage participants to explore positions that they do not agree with?
9. Do we point out possible contradictions, and in other cases, consistencies?
10. Do we indicate possible ways of continuing of the inquiry?

NOTES

1. These examples have been taken and rewritten from NEFI 2011, 58 ff.
2. This presentation of Socrates comes from Plato's *Apology of Socrates* in Plato 1997, 20d ff.
3. "Socrates" presents this argument against the accusation of corrupting the youth in Plato, *Apology of Socrates* in Plato 1997, 33a–b.
4. See letter from Bolívar to Santander, from Pallasca, December 8, 1823. In Rodríguez 2001c, 117.
5. This phrase appears many times in his writings. Cf., for example, Rodríguez 2001c, 185.
6. This idea is developed in *Sociedades Americanas*. In Rodríguez 2001a, 193 ff.
7. The principles of Jacotot are presented in the first chapter "Une aventure intellectuelle," in Rancière's book *The Ignorant Schoolmaster* 1987.
8. This is what Deleuze said in an interview with Foucault, «Les intellectuels et le pouvoir». In Foucault 1994b, 309.
9. Cf. Plateau «10. 1730—devenir-intense, devenir-animal, devenir-imperceptible » (Deleuze and Guattari 2001, 284 ff.).
10. Cf. the Introduction of *Différence et Répétition* (Deleuze 2003).
11. Etymologically, to taste (sabor) and to know (saber) share the same root in Italian.
12. These stories can be found at http://enlacezapatista.ezln.org.mx/.

REFERENCES

Barros, M. (2010) *Memórias inventadas. As infâncias de Manoel de Barros* São Paulo: Planeta.

———. (1993) "Uma didática da invenção" In *O Livro das Ignorãças* (ed. Barros, M.) Rio de Janeiro: Civilização Brasileira.

Deleuze, G. (2004) *Proust et les signes* Presses universitaires de France.

———. (2003) *Différence et Répétition* Presses universitaires de France.

Deleuze, G. and Guattari, F. (2005) *Qu'est-ce que la philosophie?* Paris: Éditions de Minuit.

———. (2001) *Mille Plateaux* Paris: Éditions de Minuit.

Derrida, J. (1986) "Les antinomies de la discipline philosophique" In *La grève des philosophes, Ecole et philosophie* (eds. Derrida et al.), Paris: Osiris.

EZLN. (1996) *Documentos y comunicados* México: ERA.

Ferraro, G. (2010a) *Filosofia fueri le mura* Napoli: Filema.

———. (2010b) *La scuola dei sentimenti* Napoli: Filema.

Foucault, M. (1997) *Surveiller et punir* Naissance de la prison: Gallimard.

Foucault, M. (1994a) *Dits et Écrits 1954–1988.* Vol. IV (1980–1988) Paris: Gallimard.

Foucault, M. (1994b) *Dits et Écrits. 1954–1988.* Vol. II (1970–1975) Paris: Gallimard.

Kohan, W. O. and Olarieta, F. (eds.) (2012) *A escola pública aposta no pensamento* Belo Horizonte: Autêntica.

Lipman, M. (1988) *Philosophy Goes to School*, 2nd ed. Philadelphia: Temple University Press.

———. (2003) *Thinking in Education* Cambridge: Cambridge University Press.

NEFI (2011) *Caderno de materiais* Rio de Janeiro: UERJ.

Plato. (1997) *Plato: Complete works* (ed. Cooper, J. M., with Hutchinson, D. S.). Indianapolis, IN: Hackett Publishing.

Rancière, J. (1987) *Le maître ignorant* Paris: Fayard.

Rodríguez, S. (2001a) *Obra Completa* Tomo I. Caracas: Presidencia de la República.

Rodríguez, S. (2001b) *Obra Completa* Tomo II. Caracas: Presidencia de la República.

Rodríguez, S. (2001c) *Cartas* Caracas: Ediciones del Rectorado de la UNISER.

Part II

Ideas for Bringing Philosophy into the K–8 Classroom

8 Philosophical Rules of Engagement

Thomas Jackson

To the reader of this chapter: I love the work I do, learning and doing philosophy for children (p4c). I began and have continued to learn to do p4c in Hawaii since 1984. I love what p4c has made possible for me and the teachers, students, and educators with whom I have met in Hawaii, the mainland United States, China, Japan, Brazil, Korea, Austria, and Switzerland. I love how teachers and students come to love p4c; what it does for them in school and out, changing and enriching their lives; and, for the teachers, how it empowers their professional practice as they internalize what we in Hawaii now call "the philosopher's pedagogy." I love the excitement in the K–12 classrooms I get to spend time with on a regular weekly basis when the teacher and students realize that it's "p4c time," a special time where we will inquire together, in the intellectually safe community we have developed, into topics and questions *they* have chosen, questions that have arisen out of their interests, be it in English, Social Studies, Math, or questions that arise out of their own wonderings about the world in which they find themselves. The questions range across the landscape from "Could Santa die?" (K) and "Who made numbers . . . because they never end!" (1st grade) to "Why do kids have to judge each other by the way they look, act, etc.?" (8th grade).

For most of the teachers and students with whom I work, there is no longer a question of the value of what we are doing together. Indeed, together we are working to expand the impact of p4c throughout our schools and communities. In addition, the "hard data" that this approach works and has impact beyond standardized test scores continues to grow as well.

What follows is an effort to share with you the framework we have developed and some of the concrete strategies for implementing this framework that is producing the exciting results indicated above. I will assume that many of you reading this are encountering p4c for the first time and so, hopefully, begin at the beginning.

PILLARS OF P4C

At p4c Hawaii we have found that the adventure of doing philosophy with children (K–8) is supported and enhanced when the adventure is conceptualized in pillar form. As this chapter will show, the pillars we use are *Community*, *Inquiry*, *Reflection*, and *Philosophy*. In the space that follows, each of these pillars are explained in terms of both why and how they are part of doing philosophy for children.

It is not an accident that Community comes first in this list. As indicated above, the intention of doing philosophy in a classroom setting is to inquire together into topics that arise from the interests of the community (students and their teacher) in philosophically responsible ways. For this to happen, it is *essential* to begin by building and sustaining an intellectually safe community conducive to philosophical inquiry.

Pillar 1: Community

At the outset, it is useful to think of your community as something that will grow and develop through stages of beginning, emerging, and mature communities. This is important because, as this development occurs, the role of the teacher will shift from teacher/facilitator/participant to participant/teacher/facilitator. In other words, as the community matures, the student members will internalize the roles, vocabulary, and protocols (social and cognitive) that are the hallmarks of an intellectually safe philosophical inquiry community. Students will become co-facilitators as well as participants, allowing the teacher to become a participant among participants. Indeed, in a mature community, apart from the teacher's physical size, identifying the teacher would not be an easy task. In a beginning community, the teacher's role will be strong and direct as students gradually learn the "rules" of the community.

At the outset it is also important to be mindful of the nature of your community. Two important factors are age and backgrounds of your students. We have found that beginning to do p4c at the pre-K, K–1 levels is importantly different from later grade levels. We have developed a "Start-Up Kit" for pre-K and K–1 levels precisely because of the wide range of developmental experiences young students bring to the classroom. For example, it may or may not be their first experience in a group setting. They may or may not have attended preschool. They may or may not have experienced sitting in a circle, taking turns, and so on. They also will have come from a wide variety of family and cultural backgrounds. All of this just adds to the adventure!

At the upper end of the age level, in middle school, a different set of challenges presents itself. Depending on the school experiences to that point, students may resist the idea of sitting in a circle, taking turns, speaking out in front of their peers, or responding to questions to which they may not know the answers. The very idea of an inquiry where no one knows in advance where the discourse may go can be confusing, frustrating, even threatening for some students. Don't be discouraged! There is plenty of evidence of success once students come to see that this "game" is very different. The initial resistance melts as they come to see that p4c time is *their* time, where *their* thoughts and ideas are central. It is not about what the teacher thinks, or about a predetermined answer the teacher is looking for but what the community (teacher and students) can develop together out of their thoughts about what matters to them. Some examples will follow later!

The beginning of the p4c Hawaii classroom experience is seating everyone in a circle. For this first and most, if not every subsequent session for p4c time, the class, including teacher, sit in a circle. For many this may be their first experience in such a configuration. The importance of the circle cannot be overemphasized! In a circle, each participate is able to see each other, to make eye contact with each other, to see directly the impact on each other of what is being said or done. The circle creates the possibilities for more intimate engagement and commitment, vulnerability and trust. Participants are better able to hear what others are saying and also to see how they are saying it; in other words, the facial expressions and mannerisms of those who are speaking. The circle also facilitates seeing the impact on each other of the interaction. What is the impact of acceptance or rejection? Of careful listening as opposed to indifference?

Your first activity together, an experience central to every beginning p4c community in Hawaii (K–University) is the making of a Community Ball (CB). The CB will become a moving source of focus and energy that facilitates weaving together the voices that will contribute to each inquiry that unfolds in all the sessions to follow. Here are the materials you'll need to make your first CB: (1) an empty cardboard paper towel core, (2), a skein of multicolored yarn, (3) one zip-tie, (4) scissors.

Here is the procedure:

(1) Place the zip-tie through the center of the paper towel core. The teacher begins wrapping the yarn around the paper towel core while the student next to him/her feeds the yarn from the skein. As the teacher is wrapping, he/she is responding to the questions she has prepared for this first session. These questions can be anything the teacher thinks will draw out the children, such as, "What is your favorite food (or music)?" or "What do you like best about school?" The objective is to select questions that will be easy, yet engaging, drawing out each student in some degree. When the teacher finishes speaking, he/she passes the cardboard to the student beside her, who begins to wrap and respond to the questions as the teacher takes over feeding the yarn. This process—one person wrapping and speaking, and his neighbor feeding the yarn—continues until all have had the opportunity to speak to the question. This activity creates a sense of mystery and excitement and often the beginnings of intimacy as students share some surprising responses to the questions.

(2) When finished wrapping, hold onto the zip-tie while pulling the yarn off the core.

(3) Zip-tie must remain in the center of the yarn coil.

(4) Loop and fasten the zip-tie, pulling it as tight as possible, forming a bagel shape from the yarn.

(5) Cut through the yarn at the outer edge, creating your own pom-pom CB!

There is often delight when the CB emerges as the end result of these efforts.

Once the group has made the ball, the teacher presents two rules: (1) the person with the ball is the speaker of the moment. That person, when finished, may pass the ball to whomever he or she wishes. (2) If one receives the ball, one *always* has the right to pass. In a beginning community, the teacher, of course, has the right and responsibility to intervene, even without the CB, if circumstance requires.

This activity anticipates many of the features that will be central to the community. First, everyone is seated in a circle. (We've done this with up to 40 high school students in the circle.) Second, each person has the opportunity to speak, allowing everyone in the circle to hear every other voice in the circle responding to questions that invite an easily accessible response from each participant, including the teacher. Third, upon completion, the CB becomes a symbol of a powerful symbolic shift in the circle regarding the authorization of the right to speak.

This activity has proven effective with groups from kindergarten through university, and in places as diverse as China, Japan, Brazil, Austria, and Kenya.

Having completed the making of a CB, which can take more than one period, an early, vital concept to introduce and explore together with the community is that of "Intellectual Safety": *All participants in the community are free to ask virtually any question or state any view so long as respect for all is honored.* It is important to share this statement with the community in age appropriate ways and to discuss together behaviors that contribute to and detract from intellectual safety in the community. The presence or lack of safety is one criterion of a "successful" session that is discussed later in this chapter.

Creating and maintaining intellectual safety allows for thoughts to be expressed that might not be expressed otherwise. "Raw thoughts"; tentative, not yet formed thoughts; "spontaneous eloquence" all become possible in an intellectually safe community. Intellectual safety does NOT mean participants are simply being "nice" and "polite" with each other. Intellectual safety makes possible intellectual courage (to speak one's authentic thoughts). Speaking one's authentic thoughts then brings with it the intellectual responsibility to clarify, to ask for and give reasons for what one says. (See "Good Thinker's Toolkit section below.)

The intention in creating and maintaining this intellectually safe community is to provide a foundational context for inquiring into and achieving a deeper understanding of questions and topics that arise out of and are sensitive to the interests of the community: that is, to say, to conduct a p4c Inquiry.

Pillar 2: p4c Inquiry

The idea of Inquiry covers a large territory. There are different discipline-specific forms of inquiry such as mathematical, scientific, historical, psychological, and philosophical, each with its own criteria. A p4c Hawai'i philosophical inquiry has the following five characteristics:

(1) **The source of the inquiry**—Whenever possible, the inquiry arises out of the questions and interests of the community, begins where the community is in its understanding, and moves in directions that the community indicates. A salient feature of p4c inquiry is its sensitivity to the interests and questions of the community, their thoughts, and where they take the topic. In an intellectually safe community, even very young children generate sophisticated lines of inquiry from deceptively simple beginnings. One kindergartner, in response to the question, "What do you wonder about?" answered: "The other night, while I was gazing at the stars, I wondered whether anything came before space." In the discussion that ensued, the children's exploration ranged from dinosaurs to God. Other inquiries have explored such topics as "Could there be a greatest number?" (3rd grade); "What constitutes a right?" and "What is the purpose of rights?" (5th grade); and "What is more important—friends, fame, or fortune?" (6th grade). Once children realize that the topics can indeed come from them and be pursued along lines they are interested in, the quality, creativity, and insight in their thinking is truly astounding.

There are a wide variety of possible sources, occasions, and topics for inquiry. Plain Vanilla is one strategy or "how to" for finding a topic and then giving shape to an inquiry. The name "Plain Vanilla" was inspired by the idea that just as there are a variety of possible triggers for inquiry, so too are there a variety of ice creams, vanilla being only one. "Variety," as they say, "is the spice of life!" There are lots of ways to begin an inquiry! A Plain Vanilla sequence proceeds as follows:

> Read—The community reads a paragraph or two, an episode, a chapter, or a whole story. Alternatively, the community could look at a painting, watch a video, read a poem, listen to a piece of music, or select a topic from a "wonder box" into which questions have been placed.
>
> Question—Each member of the community is asked to pose a question or comment based on the reading or other option mentioned above. These questions are then posted for all to see. (Optional: each person also writes his or her name next to his or her question or comment.)
>
> Vote—The community votes for the question or comment they would like to inquire into first.
>
> Inquire—The community inquires into the question selected, using WRAITEC (from the Toolkit).

(2) **Co-inquiry**—In p4c inquiry, no one, not even the teacher, knows either "the" answer to the question (if the inquiry begins with a question) or where the inquiry will lead. Any effort to guide an inquiry to a predetermined answer or outcome will compromise the process from the start. A p4c inquiry develops its own integrity, its own movement, going where "it" wants or needs to go. At various points it may bog down and need an occasional nudge, but in the main, the inquiry emerges from the context.

p4c inquiry is co-inquiry in the best sense. The teacher is an important, but not a privileged knower. In such inquiries, the children are not infrequently ahead of the thinking in the community, opening the inquiry down unexpected paths. What someone already "knows" too confidently in advance can interfere with participation in the unfolding inquiry.

(3) **The self-corrective nature of the inquiry**—Matthew Lipman, following in the pragmatist tradition of the American philosopher Charles Sanders Peirce, emphasized the centrality of self-corrective inquiry. In classrooms where inquiry has become an essential and ongoing activity, community members will change and develop their thought about a particular topic. "Before I thought . . ., but now I realize that. . . ." becomes an increasingly common comment in a maturing inquiry community in the course of a school year.

(4) **Inquiry tools (WRAITEC)**—p4c inquiry is more than a conversation or sharing of ideas within a group. It is characterized by an intellectual rigor that certain cognitive tools help facilitate. These seven tools comprise the "Good Thinker's Toolkit." They are an important means for giving shape and direction to the notion that, although we aren't in a rush to get anywhere, we *do* have an expectation that we will get *somewhere*.

The Good Thinker's Tool kit (WRAITEC)©

[W] = *What* do you/we mean by . . .?

[R] = Are Reasons being offered to support claims?

[A] = Are we aware of and identifying key *Assumptions* being made?

[I] = Are we aware of *Inferences* being made and possible *Implications* of what is being said?

[T] = Is what is being said *True*? How could we find out?

[E] = Are *Examples* being given, or is *Evidence* being offered to support or illustrate claims?

[C] = Are there any *Counterexamples* to the claim being made?

As soon as possible, it is important to introduce members of the community to the individual letters of the Toolkit, the important skills they represent, and their interconnections. Sessions should be devoted to each tool and their interplay. Many teachers have each student make his own Toolkit for use during sessions. Here are a couple of examples of practice lessons that are lots of fun to do!

To practice [R] Reasons, to the students, say, "Imagine you are the teacher. A student turns in a homework assignment late. What would you consider a good reason and why?"

To practice [A] Assume & [I] If . . . then . . . and [T] True, to the students say, "*Assume* children were in charge of the world. *If* this were [T] *true*, what might happen?

To practice [E] Example & [C] Counterexample, pose the question: "Are all drugs dangerous? Can you give an example of a dangerous drug? Can you give a counterexample?"

As familiarity and facility with the various toolkit letters grows, so too does the depth of questions and the inquiries, both during the p4c sessions and in other content areas *and life beyond the classroom*!

(5) **Reflect**—Using the criteria below, the community evaluates how the session went, both in terms of community (intellectual safety, etc.) and inquiry. The following criteria are suggested. The teacher can present these to the group prior to beginning the inquiry cycle and again at the end of each session. The criteria fall into two categories, those dealing with how we did as a community and those dealing with the inquiry itself.

How did we do as a community?

- **Listening**—Was I listening to others? Were others listening to me?
- **Participation**—Did most people participate rather than just a few who dominated?
- **Safety**—Was it a safe environment?

How was our inquiry?

- **Focus**—Did we maintain a focus?
- **Depth**—Did our discussions scratch beneath the surface or open up the topic?
- **Understanding**—Did I increase my understanding of the topic?
- **Thinking**—Did I challenge my own thinking or work hard at it?
- **Interest**—Was it interesting?

At the end of the session, members of the community can be asked to indicate by a "thumb-up, thumb-middle, or thumb-down," their response to each of the above criteria.

In addition to the above criteria, with a maturing community it is highly recommended to ask each student to write a written reflection on whether or not he experienced any *progress* in his own thinking as a result of the Inquiry. There are at least three possible, different, sometimes overlapping kinds of progress: (1) complexity/confusion: any encounter with a complex topic, especially in the beginning, can lead to confusion. To recognize confusion in oneself and celebrate one's courage to be with this confusion is an important form of progress, especially in a school testing culture that is overwhelmingly about single correct answers; (2) connection of ideas: often in an inquiry, one will hear perspectives not thought of before, leading to new connections for oneself; (3) emergence of an answer: at any point *an* answer, however tentative, can emerge.

At the end of any given session, individual participants may experience any or some combination of these forms of progress, depending on the inquiry. It is important to stress that individuals can experience very different forms of progress in any inquiry depending on their starting point with the topic or question.

Pillar 3: Reflection

Reflection as a pillar of p4c Hawai'i refers not only to the reflection that occurs at the end of each inquiry, as indicated above, but also to reflection on the entire process of p4c, the pillars themselves, and the fidelity of the participants to the values that the pillars represent. One such reflection concerns the role of the teacher/facilitator.

The teacher/facilitator is pivotal to the success of p4c inquiry. In the beginning it will be the teacher/facilitator who introduces the ideas behind such inquiry. He/she will be responsible for establishing, monitoring, and maintaining the safety within the group. This will include monitoring the proper use of the CB and calling on each other and seeing that members have ample opportunity to speak as well as permission to remain silent. With younger grades, for example, one problem that often appears initially is that boys only call on boys, girls call on girls, or close friends call on each other.

In a beginning community, the teacher/facilitator conducts the lessons that involve making the Toolkit and follow-up lessons that focus on a particular tool. For most students and many teachers, "inference" and "assumption" are little more than vocabulary words. The group needs to spend time on developing deeper understanding of what these terms mean. Similarly, what makes a reason a good reason, how counterexamples function, and how one might go about finding out whether a given claim or statement is true may be areas where understanding is currently quite shallow. In early sessions the teacher should call attention to uses of the various tools and encourage their use.

It is the teacher/facilitator, especially in the beginning, who sets the pace for the group. "Not being in a rush" depends on a teacher being sufficiently comfortable with silence and "wait time" beyond what is typical in most classrooms. It requires a teacher/facilitator whose own sense of wonder is still alive and who is keenly interested in what the authentic thoughts of the community are on a given topic; one who is comfortable with uncertainty, not eager to push for closure but willing to allow an inquiry to move where "it" and the community seem to want to take it. He/she must be willing to risk not knowing the answer, to indeed be a co-inquirer in the quest for an answer.

Initially the teacher/facilitator needs to make the crucial judgments about using Good Thinker's Tools. The teacher/facilitator is the one who asks for reasons, examples, and clarification; at the same time displaying letters that represent the particular tool requested; at once modeling and highlighting their use.

The teacher/facilitator assists in weaving threads of conversation into dialogue, asking who agrees or disagrees or has other thoughts about the topic at hand, offering a counterexample, asking "If what Tanya said is true, would it follow that . . .?" or making some other comment to nudge the dialogue along. This is especially delicate and challenging because a major objective is for the children to internalize and thus take over these skills and behaviors. They need as much opportunity as possible to try them out, and providing these opportunities is the teacher's responsibility.

It is the teacher/facilitator who brings a given session to a close and sees to it that the group conducts an evaluation. How long are inquiry sessions? With kindergarten children they last from 10 minutes to more than an hour. Sessions with older children tend to be more predictable in terms of length, but also more subject to the time demands of the school day and curriculum.

In this kind of inquiry, the teacher/facilitator's role is to be pedagogically strong but philosophically self-effacing. The teacher/facilitator should be firmly in control of the procedures but allow the content of the inquiry to unfold, as it needs to, rather than following his/her own desires. As indicated above, this role of pedagogical strength can be especially challenging since it is asking for the students to ultimately assume greater responsibility for the success of the sessions. Indeed, it cannot occur without their active, willing acceptance of this responsibility.

A strategy that we have found effective in creating this more active participation is the use of what we call "Magic Words." These words are playful "shorthand" for situations that can slow or disrupt the flow of a session. Here are a few examples: "POPAAT—Please One Person at a Time." In a lively session there is a strong temptation to speak out of turn, even with the presence of the CB. POPAAT indicates that this function of the CB has been forgotten by the community. When POPAAT is uttered, the protocol is for everyone to stop talking and to begin again only when respect for the designated speaker has been restored. It is the role of the teacher/facilitator to vigilantly enforce this rule. Note that not observing this rule infringes on the Intellectual Safety of the session. Another example is "GOS—Going Off Subject!" GOS indicates that the person who uttered it senses that inquiry has moved away from the chosen focus. The community votes at this point to see if it agrees and if it wishes to continue with the GOS or return to the initial question. A final example is "LMO—Let's Move On!" LMO indicates that the person who uttered it senses that we're bogged down in our session and it's time to move forward. Again, the community votes to see if they agree. If the majority agrees, it moves on, perhaps to a new topic or question. Note that one need not be in possession of the CB to say a magic word.

As the community grows and matures it will move from beginning to emerging, where the other members of the community internalize the protocols, call on each other, and spontaneously begin to use the Toolkit letters and so on. Finally, in a mature community, the teacher/facilitator will be a coequal facilitator/participant.

Pillar 4: Philosophy

In my experience, for a variety of complex reasons, many educators and parents I've met in my work around the world have a neutral to negative response to the word Philosophy, particularly when connected with children. They see philosophy as something rather esoteric, removed from everyday experience and concerns, difficult to understand, perhaps not even suitable for children. As a result, in working with teachers and parents in recent years I have found it useful to clarify philosophy and its connection with children in the following way: first, if it's a "live" audience, I like to ask if those present were at some point in their life a child. This is met with smiles of acknowledgment and raised hands. Next, I ask how many still think they have something of the child within them. The response is the same. I next ask them how many wonder about things. I then point out that a philosopher well known to some of them—Plato—pointed out long ago that philosophy, whatever else it is, begins in Wonder! To elaborate, I then playfully suggest that philosophy, whatever else it is, first, involves both Content and Activity; and second, that philosophy comes in two "varieties": Big P and little p, each of which has both Content and Activity. It is Big P Content and Activity that most people tend to associate with philosophy.

> Big P Content includes Philosophers like Socrates, Aristotle, Kant, Wittgenstein, Nagarjuna, Samkara, Confucius, Lao-tzu, Ibn Sina, etc.; Areas such as Metaphysics, Epistemology, Ethics; and Schools, Movements, and Worldviews such as Daoism, Empiricism, Feminism, Phenomenology, Hermeneutics, etc.
>
> Big P Activity refers primarily to professionals teaching, studying, reading, writing, publishing, and presenting their work at conferences based on the aforementioned content.
>
> Little p Content refers to the set of beliefs we begin to acquire at birth that continue to inform our experience, becoming the framework with which we make sense of our world. To the extent that we have beliefs, we *have* a philosophy. We are social beings from the beginning, and the family and culture which meets and greets us makes possible our growth into the human community. We are, however, not passive in this encounter, as anyone with young children knows. The younger we are, the more persistent are the "But why's?" that greet our adult responses to them in our efforts to answer their increasingly deep questions. A colleague pointed out to me recently in connection with her grandchild that "A young child can take you very deep, very quickly!"

> Little p Activity refers to the fact that we don't passively acquire this content but engage it almost from the beginning. Arising from our innate sense of wonder, with the acquisition of language questions soon arise naturally with the persistent "But why?"

We are thusly born philosophical, eager to wonder, engage, question, learn from and challenge the world around us. It is this child-like energy that p4c taps into and is the primary source of its joy for parents, teachers, and students. Perhaps one of the most important "lessons" of rediscovering one's own "little p" philosophical capacity is, in an encounter with one's own child or students, to resist the temptation to immediately answer their questions, but rather to see it as an invitation to an inquiry and respond by asking first "What do you think?" Children and students, sensing your genuine interest, soon jump at the occasion!

In the practice of p4c Hawai'i, the center of gravity is on little p philosophy. That is, the emphasis is on the beliefs, questions, and topics that arise from the students themselves (Inquiry, First Characteristic). Philosophical activity then grows from these initial beliefs and questions in the form of inquiry as has been outlined above. They are co-inquiries, self-corrective, informed by the active use of the Good Thinker's Toolkit. Teachers soon are applying the Plain Vanilla structure to a wide range of content and subject areas. This has been particularly important in teachers being able to practice philosophy in their middle and high school classrooms. Philosophy is no longer an "extra." It is now seen primarily as an activity, a particularly effective way of engaging any content that presents itself. Seen and practiced this way as little p, it does not require prior experience with Big P. (This, of course, is in no way to diminish the importance of Big P in its own right and as a resource to be drawn upon if desired.) Philosophy comes to be seen, when applied in a classroom context as I have endeavored to present in this chapter, as what we are now referring to as a "philosopher's pedagogy." Perhaps most satisfying of all is that when this pedagogy is applied to oneself, it leads to what Socrates called "the examined life."

I hope, as a result of reading this, you will be inspired to give p4c a try. The journey of p4c will have its ups and downs. It is most challenging if you are the only one at your school doing p4c. It is imperative that you have support all along the way if possible. The more teachers and grade levels that are involved, the better it is. In Hawai'i we have two model schools. Waikiki Elementary School, where we've been working for 12 years, has almost 100 percent participation. This means that after kindergarten, you have students who "know the routine." At Kailua High School, where we have been working for 8 years, whole departments are embracing the philosopher's pedagogy, buoyed up by students who also embrace the approach and actively participate in making it work. This book contains lots of suggestions from lots of good people who will no doubt be willing to help you if you ask!

9   Developing Philosophical Facilitation
A Toolbox of Philosophical "Moves"

David Kennedy

YOUNG CHILDREN AS CRITICAL REASONERS

Young children, who for purposes of this chapter I will ask the reader to visualize as five- to eight-year-olds, already have considerable experience in at least two dimensions of philosophical thinking. One dimension is wonder, which we might define as a deep curiosity that most often expresses itself in questions, some of which could be classified in thematic groups like "metaphysics," "aesthetics," "ethics," and so on. In the various philosophy for (or "with") children curricula that have emerged in the last half century, the preferred stimulus for encouraging this sense of wonder and eliciting these questions is the philosophical novel or story, and we can identify two types of such stimuli.

The first may actually be said to represent a new genre of children's literature—the philosophical novel for children. The novels of Matthew Lipman, founder of the Institute for the Advancement of Philosophy for Children (IAPC) provide an original model for this genre that has been widely imitated. Lipman's novels typically have these features: (1) No philosophical jargon of any kind is used, and no philosophers' names are mentioned; (2) The plots are prosaic—most take place in public schools—rather than fantasy or science fiction; (3) The novel itself portrays children engaged in philosophical dialogue with each other, with adults, or in combination, in completely ordinary language, for purposes of modeling communal dialogue; (4) The thematic structure of the novels is intuitively organized and nonsystematic. In the IAPC tradition, such novels are typically used, not to assign questions for group discussion, but to stimulate them. After a reading of an episode or short chapter, children generate their own questions, choose which one to start the conversation with, and proceed from there.

The second broad form of stimulus is the children's story with philosophical implications or overtones, of which there is a rich tradition in children's literature. These narratives do not model—directly anyway—philosophical dialogue, and often are plotted in fantasy, science fiction, or some alternate universe. As opposed to the Lipmanian novel, which covers many philosophical topics, children's books are often single themed. But they make up for their non-pedagogical emphasis and structure by their vividness and creative originality. At their best, they demonstrate the deep connection between literature and philosophy, whereas the deliberately philosophical novel tends to separate the two.

Beyond children's natural sense of philosophical wonder, a second dimension of philosophical experience young children already have is in the realm of language, which is the vehicle through which the questions that wonder gives rise to are expressed and answers given. I am thinking philosophically— or at least *pre*-philosophically—when I use language to reason—that is when I give definitions, classify someone or thing, point out contradictions in an argument, draw conclusions, entertain absent or nonexistent possibilities, talk about how things *ought* to be, and so on. And as a five- to eight-year-old, I do this all the time, whether I'm talking to or about my friends, or my school, or a story I read or saw, or whether I deserve the last cookie in the jar.

A community of philosophical inquiry is, we may say, a place where this way of talking is privileged—where teachers reward it with their careful attention and model it themselves. When that sort of a language space is set up, it is often surprising to see how quickly children learn to use it in a conscious and focused way. This is because they are learning it from each other as well as from the teacher, which makes of it a very powerful educational environment. But it does not happen automatically. It takes a thoughtful teacher to set up the environment, to identify, model and coach, not just its reasoning moves, but its group rules and practices, to help it stay on track and focused, and to work to provide just enough structure—not more and not less—for its own inherent structure to emerge.

This is both easier and harder than might appear at first sight. Harder because the teacher must be able to hear children reasoning when they do, and that takes overcoming the prejudice—widespread in adult culture— that they can't. It also involves going metacognitive—that is, thinking about thinking. If I said "It's a cat," for example, who would stop to note that I am making a classifying move, or that I am making distinctions and connections and thinking analogically when I say "It looks like a dog"? The teacher must learn—through paying careful and thorough attention to what children are saying—to recognize these reasoning moves in everyday language, and to feed that recognition back to her students.

The easy part is that these moves tend to happen spontaneously in a setting that involves group deliberation. If someone says "All cats are black" (an "all" statement), for example, the teacher won't have to call for a counterexample—it is virtually guaranteed that one will spring into someone's mind. More generally, the beauty and power of this kind of communal dialogue is its spontaneous, emergent quality—how we evoke each other's ideas as in a play whose lines we recite, however effortfully, without having had to learn them—a game that plays us rather than we it. Socrates called this "following the argument where it leads." But of course we can't follow it unless we recognize it. Through experience, we learn what to listen for.

What follows is a basic list of the sorts of critical reasoning moves that teachers can listen for when talking with children. Once she spots them, she can redistribute them among the group by pointing them out and naming them ("James just gave a counterexample"), introducing and modeling them herself ("I'm going to try and give a definition of 'freedom,' and you tell me if you agree or disagree, and why") or calling for a move ("Could someone restate Alicia's argument?"). The moves may be made more or less "visible" within a conversation. A teacher may, for example, emphasize one or more of them over the course of one or more sessions, as a kind of exercise within the larger discussion; or she may choose stories or episodes from novels that lend themselves better to practicing one or more of these moves. With that in mind, the dozen or so basic moves offered below are given in the order in which they might usefully be emphasized in a sequence of group conversations. For example, "Asking a question" is a cognitive move that comes naturally to young children, but which may not have been emphasized at home; or, even if it has, it may not have been consciously distinguished from a statement. Once young children can make such a move consciously, they are in a much better position to use it as a tool in a conversation. And since when we think together about the world we are most interested in questions rather than in already-formed propositions—for it is the question that leads to the emergence of new meanings—we place it first on the list.

THE TOOLBOX

Asking a question. The question is at the center of the thinking process. Besides soliciting questions about stories, you might devote whole sessions just to developing questions—and of course to writing them down, whether on the board or in students' philosophy journals And you might follow these sessions with discussions of how each question might be answered, and whether some of them have no answers at all, or would be answered differently by different people.

Agreeing or disagreeing. Young children sometimes acquire the misconception that disagreeing—and especially in public—is either disrespectful or dangerous, a hostile act. On the other hand, they might have the notion that to agree with someone's idea is to relinquish one's claims to at least partial ownership of it, and therefore needs to be resisted. But once they get the hang of how agreeing and disagreeing are used in a group dialogue, they quickly see that it can form the basis for moving the conversation forward. They discover that it can be just as powerful a move to build on other people's ideas as to discount them. Again, be sure to model the move yourself, to call for it (e.g., "James, do you agree or disagree with what Alicia just said?," or "Does anyone agree or disagree with what Alicia just said?"), or point it out whenever it happens ("So you are agreeing with Leroy, is that right?"), and indicate its significance through paralanguage.

Giving a reason. This move follows naturally from agreeing or disagreeing, and should always accompany it. The felt responsibility to give reasons may be the single most important disposition of reasonable discourse and reasonable people. So if James, for example, says he disagrees, immediately ask him, "Why? What is your reason for disagreeing?" And when you give a reason in the course of the discussion, be sure that you either announce that you are going to do so before you do it, or emphasize afterward that you have just done so.

Offering a proposition, hypothesis, or explanation. A proposition is an assertion that expresses a judgment or opinion—for example, "All dogs are brown," or "My mother is always right." If it's offered as a hypothesis, it doesn't make a truth claim or just makes a tentative one. Young children make propositions all the time, as does everyone else. The idea of doing philosophy is to learn to make propositions tentatively, and to develop the habit of examining them and determining if they need to be changed to better reflect the way the world is. As truth statements, propositions can be divided into three types—"All" statements ("All dogs are brown"), "Some" statements ("Some dogs are brown"), and "No" statements ("No dogs are brown"). One way to begin working on any given statement is to try to identify whether it is an "all," a "some," or a "no" statement. The realization that it takes only one counterexample to downgrade an "all" statement into a "some" statement—just one dog that is not brown—is often a powerful and intriguing idea for young children, and premonitory of the rigors of classical logic.

Offering an example or counterexample. Giving a counterexample is arguably one of the first critical moves that young children make, for they tend to come spontaneously to mind. As with all other moves, they should be identified as such by the teacher. Giving examples is the most immediate and concrete way to explore an argument. Like the majority of the moves in this list, you can orient whole sessions toward exemplification, as a kind of play exercise. Often you will find that young children think completely in examples—when you ask them a general question, they will respond with a story about something that happened to them or something they know. It is the facilitator's job to translate that example into a more general proposition and feed it back to the group for a response. For example, after James makes the assertion that mothers are always right, Jorge might tell a story about one time when his mother was wrong (counterexample), and Samantha may follow with a story about going to the mall with her mother, getting lost, asking directions, making several mistakes, etc. If you allow it, examples will continue without any move toward unpacking their implications—that is, what they are proving or disproving about the proposition that mothers are always right. So it is the facilitator's job to bring the group back to the more general question under discussion by helping children analyze the abundant examples they are offering and unpack their implications.

Classifying/Categorizing. Classifying and categorizing start from birth on the perceptual level, perhaps with the distinction between what is my mother and what is not. No one can make even the most basic sense of the world and how to survive in it without putting people, things, events, phenomena, qualities, etc. in classes and categories. Therefore, young children don't have to be taught how to classify, and in fact optimal human development could be said to reside in the progressive width, depth, clarity, flexibility, and complexity of our categories, or what Piaget called "schemes"—because the more adequate our schemes, the better we can handle what the world brings. Unless they are blocked by fear of some kind, young children work on this all the time. They are working, for example, on classifying teachers—good ones, poor ones, friendly ones, dangerous ones, helpful ones, genuine or hypocritical ones, etc., as well as on houses, neighborhoods, stores, television shows, parents, friends, siblings, dreams, foods, etc. Engaging in collaborative inquiry about key issues in one's life and in the world is one powerful way of pursuing this work, for the only way—apart from further experience—in which our ideas will grow and become more adequate is through examining them critically. Examining them in a group speeds up the process of self-correction and makes it more intense, as well as teaching us to do it by ourselves. There are many ways you can encourage this and make it visible in the group, but one of them is to begin to picture classes of things through Venn diagrams. If, for example, you made one circle that represented all the dogs in the world, and another circle that represented all the brown things in the world, what relationship would you put those circles in? And of course it can be continually reinforced verbally by using the words "all," "some," and "no" in your questions and clarifications.

Making a comparison. This move might be better put before classifying and categorizing, since it is the basis for grouping things into classes and operates through making *distinctions and connections* between things. I have to decide what something is *not* in order to determine what it is. If I decide that it is more like something else than not, I have to decide what criteria I'm going to use to group it with that other thing—its physical appearance, the way it acts, etc. If young children are classifying and categorizing as a matter of course, they are making distinctions and connections (i.e., they are comparing). If we engage them in conversation and really listen, we will see that a large part of their reasoning (like ours) is done through *analogy*—a bird is like an airplane or vice versa, a tree is like a human body in certain ways, a house can be like a person, etc. This kind of reasoning, which involves evaluating the similarities and differences or connections and distinctions between things on the basis of chosen criteria, can be directly practiced through playful exercises (e.g., "How is a _____ like a _____," or "What is the difference between _____ and _____"). It can also be practiced by pointing it out when it is done—when, for example, Samantha says "Dolls are not people"—or by calling for it, for example, asking an individual or the group as a whole, "How are dolls and people the same?" As with all of the moves on this list, it is best taught through learning to recognize it when it happens spontaneously in the course of the conversation, then taking advantage of that recognition by naming it and then repeating it consciously.

Offering a definition. Most thinking dialogues, whether among groups of young children or adults, quickly come to a point where a definition of terms is necessary for everyone to at least attempt to be on the same page.

In order to use any term, one has to be assuming *some* kind of definition of it, however implicit. Stating these definitions is not an easy thing, even among adults—what, for example, is the definition of "justice"?—and often a definition will change as the inquiry moves forward. You can be watching for those opportunities in young children's conversation to introduce the concept of "definition" and try it out—starting with simpler things, like "dog" or "doll" or "father," and moving gradually toward more complex concepts like "friend" or "fair."

Identifying an assumption. Every proposition or truth claim rests on a set of assumptions—things we consider to be the case either by definition—for example, "All dogs are four-legged creatures"—or by what we have noticed through experience—for example, "Some dogs are dangerous to humans." These beliefs about things and the world underlie the way we classify and categorize things, and therefore the judgments we make. It could be claimed that the most important and useful thing about thinking critically together is that it leads us to identify those underlying assumptions, many of which are either wrong or overgeneralized ("all" statements), and to correct them by thinking more carefully and responsibly about them. This is difficult work even for adults, for many of our most influential assumptions lie below the level of our awareness and are most often emotionally charged and invested. The best way for a facilitator (or anyone else) to learn to identify underlying assumptions is to work on identifying his or her own. Meanwhile, there are opportunities to introduce an awareness of underlying assumptions to young children through simple examples, which can be identified either in the course of conversations or through exercises, and their implications explored. If we assume, for example, that some dogs are dangerous to humans, how will that affect the way we approach a dog we don't know? If we assume that friends always share, what should we share with our friends? Our money? Our food? Other friends?

Making an inference. Assumptions lead us naturally into inferences, because inferring is the act of reasoning from something known or assumed to something that follows from it. For example, if I see dark clouds in the sky, I infer that it is likely to rain; or if I see a blush on someone's face, I infer that she is feeling embarrassed. If someone says to me, "Friends shouldn't act like that," I infer that he has certain assumptions about how friends should act. If we watch and listen carefully, we will see that young children are, like the rest of us, constantly making inferences. Although the value of teaching them the word "infer" or "inference" is doubtful, we can, when we notice an inference being made, either ask for or point out the basis on which it is made. If a child says to us, for example, "She's not my friend," we might respond with the question "What makes a person a friend?" and thereby encourage her to reflect on what is the basis of her inference.

Making a conditional statement ("if/then"). Conditional statements are inferences, as for example, "If it rains today, the streets will be wet," or "If you fight you might need to go to the hospital," in which the second statement follows logically from the first. Young children use these all the time.

You can follow up on these kinds of statements by exploring their logical implications. For example, you might answer "If you fight you might have to go to the hospital" with "Do people who fight *always* have to go to the hospital?" Or, "Is fighting the *only* reason that people go the hospital?" Young children often make conditional statements as normative judgments, meaning what one *should* do in any given situation—for example, "If you hurt your friends feelings you should say 'I'm sorry.'" This statement could be explored by asking if it's necessary—if you "have to" say you're sorry, and also by what else you could do if you hurt your friend's feelings, which puts us in the realm of exploring possibilities.

Reasoning syllogistically. A syllogism is a statement in which there are two premises that lead to a conclusion—for example, Premise 1: If you fight you will go to the hospital. Premise 2: You fought. Conclusion: You will go to the hospital. Again, young children reason this way all the time—it is embedded in the way we talk—but often it is hidden away or unstated. Consider a second grader's statement in a discussion about conflict. "Well yeah, but like, it's life. So I think you have to have it." If the statement is "unpacked" we see that it is syllogistic. Premise 1: Life always involves conflict. Premise 2: You are alive. Conclusion: You will be involved in conflict.

Self-correcting. Self-correction can happen both on the individual and on the group level. A group conversation that is developing is always self-correcting. This happens mainly through the use of examples. If someone makes the "all" statement "Friends never say mean things," and another person gives an example of a friend who said a mean thing to her, and yet she still considers her a friend, then the "all" statement must be corrected by reconstructing it as a "some" statement, that is, "Friends sometimes say mean things." Of course this will involve deciding together whether it is generally agreed upon by the group that being a friend absolutely excludes saying mean things to each other, which is a matter of definition. It is this kind of group reflection about the criteria we use to judge something to be this or that which is of tremendous value both to young children and adults. Facilitators should both model self-correction themselves—or offer stories about times they have self-corrected—and assure children that self-correction is a very positive thing.

Restating. This is a move that is based on what I consider the most important disposition to be cultivated through dialogical group thinking—listening. There are other moves that depend on active listening—clarification, summarization, connecting two or more points or arguments, or even a simple request for someone to repeat what they just said—that are as important, but this one is included because it shows the most direct evidence that children are in fact listening to each other, and because it is a skill that can easily be practiced. The teacher should model it continually, and also make a regular practice of asking children to restate what other people have said before they add another contribution to the discussion. It can also be practiced through exercises—for example, warm-up games in which one child makes a statement and the other restates it in different words, or some variation of that pattern.

Entertaining different perspectives. Entertaining different perspectives implies the ability to treat one's own perspective as one among many (or at least two). Piaget associates this capacity with the complete maturation of rationality in what he calls "formal operations," which assumes that we can entertain as many different perspectives as are mathematically (i.e., logically) possible in any given situation. It can also be associated with the democratic personality, if we understand the latter as a way of thinking that assumes a plurality of views, and understands its job as being to mediate them through the giving and the receiving of reasons. It is both a move and a tendency or disposition, and involves the ability to find similarities and differences; for in order to identify another perspective, we must have enough in common with it to recognize it as a perspective, and enough discrimination of differences to recognize how it is distinct from our own. It can be approached directly by the teacher by first modeling, then asking children to restate other people's ideas in their own words, and to offer summaries that identify multiple positions. There are also activities, designed for research like Piaget's "three mountain" experiment, in which a person stands in front of a model of a mountain and is asked to see what a doll set on the other side of the mountain "sees." An adaptation of this experiment could be made into a warm-up game for philosophical sessions.

PRACTICING THE MOVES

For those teachers who wish to concentrate on the moves to the point of removing them from the context of a conversation and practicing them directly, there is a powerful resource in the instructional manuals developed by Lipman and his colleagues to accompany each of his novels. The former include myriad exercises and discussion plans that probe both substantive themes and practice critical and creative thinking. For example, in *Getting Our Thoughts Together* (Lipman, 1998), which is the manual to accompany *Elfie* (a text appropriate for second graders), Leading Idea 3, "Distinctions" offers no less than six exercises on, in the words of the introductory paragraph, "being able to say how things are alike and how they are different." The exercise "On not being a tree" asks "How are these things not like a tree? A person, a cat, a flower, a shrub, another tree." And the exercise "Differences" asks "In what ways can these two things be different? Two thoughts, two thoughts about the same thing, the same thought about two different things, a thought and a memory, a thought and a dream" (p. 131).

Such exercises—of which there are thousands in the IAPC manuals, and which can easily be developed by the teacher herself—are certainly of great value, but nowhere near as effective as becoming aware of the moves and practicing them in the live, grounded context of a group discussion about some philosophical issue that is important to those participating, guided by a facilitator who can recognize them, highlight them, call for them, and model them herself. And the committed teacher has many options for training herself in this delicate, complicated, and intuitive practice, whose mastery is a life-long project.

The list expanded upon above, for example, can be used either as a worksheet or an evaluative checklist. As a worksheet, the teacher might ask older children to keep it in front of them during conversations and encourage them to identify what kind of move they are going to make before they make it. As a checklist, the teacher may videotape a conversation, then watch it with list in hand; more often than not one is surprised by how many moves one has missed or misinterpreted. And if facilitators have the good fortune to work in pairs, one member of the team can take notes as she adds ticks to the checklist, for later discussion with her partner. Given that the largest part of successful facilitation of philosophical dialogues—whether among children or adults—is in knowing what to listen for, the opportunity to analyze young children's reasoning after the fact represents a powerful learning tool for teacher-facilitators and would do well if it were made standard practice.

The List

Asking a question
Agreeing or disagreeing
Giving a reason
Offering a proposition, hypothesis, or explanation
Giving an example or counterexample
Classifying/Categorizing
Making a comparison
Making a distinction
Making a connection
Making an analogy
Offering a definition
Identifying an assumption
Making an inference
Making a conditional statement ("if/then")
Reasoning syllogistically
Self-correcting
Restating
Entertaining different perspectives

REFERENCE

Lipman, M. (1998) *Getting our thoughts together* Montclair, NJ: Institute for the Advancement of Philosophy for Children.

10 Philosophy in the Great Green Room
Early Children's Literature as Philosophy for Children

Rory E. Kraft, Jr.

Much of the philosophy for children movement focuses on working with middle and high school students. With rare exceptions, little attention is paid to work with elementary school students.[1] It is even harder to find a philosopher or educational theorist who takes seriously the possibility of doing philosophy by, for, or with pre-reading to early readers. This is despite philosophy and children being linked from the beginnings of Western philosophy. Plato, in the *Republic*, advocates starting society over with children; from these children the philosopher kings would come. Yet even for Plato it was important that the myths, poems, and stories told to the young already be set in place.[2] Plato's great myths were intended to lead to a better society, but they were not based in the mindset of the very young child. Traditionally, children's tales have been either directly moralistic, as in Aesop, or fairy tales. These tales stand in sharp contrast to most contemporary early children's literature, which to varying degrees has embraced Lucy Sprague Mitchell's Here and Now approach of telling stories connected with the actual lives of children.[3] But the change away from the fantastical also brought a move toward the acceptance of a philosophically informed understanding of epistemology and children's lives. This is perhaps best seen in the work of Margaret Wise Brown.

In this chapter, I examine how we can read Brown's work philosophically. I do this by focusing on the bunny trilogy of *Runaway Bunny*, *Goodnight Moon*, and *My World*, drawing out the philosophical connections to John Dewey through the influence of Mitchell, and then considering whether these works count as philosophy for the very young child. It is helpful to note at the outset that Brown was not aiming to foster knowledge of Plato, Aristotle, or even Dewey in these young children. Instead, Brown was using philosophically informed approaches and bringing young children to the very beginnings of doing philosophy. Children exposed to these works encounter challenges to their comfortable worldview, learn how to better understand their categories of knowledge, and find an appropriate outlet for the questioning central to a philosophical approach. I close with a consideration of how using these texts can be a form of doing philosophy itself, and as such I aim to broaden the understanding of the usefulness of early children's literature.

MARGARET WISE BROWN

Upon reading Brown's works, the first thing many notice is that the voice of the text is more authentically childlike than other children's books. Brown writes that "Children wrote these books and I was merely an ear and a pen. And also by some accident, one who shared their pleasure or inattention with them" (Brown 1949c, 13). Her familiarity with children's cadence and narratives comes directly from her days at the Bank Street School[4] observing children learn and play during the day and attending evening sessions learning the theories of Dewey, Edward Thorndike, and Sigmund Freud (Marcus 2001, 45). Brown wrote of the "feverish note-taking" from the time period that " '[o]ne had to be absolutely still and write very fast to catch' the stories and poems the students improvised" (quoted in Marcus 2001, 65) on the playground and in their classrooms.

Out of all of Brown's classic children's books, *Goodnight Moon* has captured popular attention and become the text most identified with Brown. On the surface it shows a small rabbit that is going to sleep in his nursery—a "great green room"—saying goodnight to the objects around him. The words are sparse, Clement Hurd's illustrations alternate between color and black and white, and there is a genuine soothing quality to the rhythm of the words. But for all of its apparent simplicity, *Goodnight Moon* contains sophisticated use of philosophy in its structure and content. As Leonard Marcus explains, "[i]n *Goodnight Moon* Brown was able to convey, as well as anyone has, a young child's liquid view of the world as a place both near at hand and vast beyond measure, toy bright yet shadow tinged, comfortingly familiar yet at times also fantastically strange" (Marcus 1997, 14).

The ordinariness of the great green room is belying. The structure is simple: the opening pages recount the items in a nursery, followed by a litany of goodnights to the objects of the room and the world beyond it. Marcus interprets the structure as a balance between the "voice of the provider, the good parent or guardian who can summon forth a secure, whole existence by naming its particulars" and "the voice of the child, who takes possession of that world by naming its particulars all over again, addressing them directly, one by one, as though each were alive, and bidding each goodnight" (Marcus 2001, 187). But what this interpretation misses is that it isn't only the objects of the room that are bid goodnight, but the objects of the world itself. Further, not every object of the room is spoken of in the second part; perhaps most notably the telephone is listed at the opening but not in the closing section. Further, we have goodnights to objects of objects (the bears and chairs of the second picture), imaginary objects ("nobody"), objects outside the room (the titular moon, stars), and things in general (air, noises everywhere). We see in this bedtime ritual an understanding of both the objects of the room, as well as the lack of distinction made between the room, the outside, and the nonsensical. When we couple the text with Hurd's illustrations, which Brown carefully controlled (Bliven 1946, 64),[5] we see that Brown has established a world with whimsy (a mouse that can be tracked from page to page), self-reference (the copy of *Goodnight Moon* on the nightstand), and homage to other children's books (the old lady from Wanda Ga'g's *Millions of Cats* becoming the quiet bunny lady). No detail of the book is accidental. It is this meticulousness of approach that shows that the philosophically informed aspects are intentionally placed and utilized as well. For example, Brown's structure closely follows Dewey's theory of perception. He notes that someone who has come to understand the distinction between the self and the world understands that "the train of ideas which seems to constitute the mind comes and goes, but this effects no change in the objects" (Dewey Early Works Vol. 2, 139). It is exactly this separation between the external world and the ideas of the mind that the bunny struggles to understand in *Goodnight Moon*.

Brown created worlds that are both familiar and challenging to children. The books drew on the experiences, language, and narratives of children, but pushed for the children to become more than themselves. The books were to be used not just as stories, but also as developmental tools. On the cover of an early work, Brown notes that "This book hopes to touch their imaginings and to suggest further imaginings in the realm of a child's reality" (Brown 1951, 79).[6] Brown's understanding of her stories as developmentally linked can be seen not only in her study of Dewey at Bank Street, but also in the manner in which she wrote them. A 1946 interview includes this observation about her language: "Brown also thinks that a book should include at least a couple of words too big and cumbersome for her youthful listeners, a theory which drives many child psychologists, teachers and librarians, professionally committed to safe and sane age-level words lists into shocking outrage" (Bliven 1946, 64). Brown's inclusion of "adult" words was not accidental; she believed that children "want words better arranged than their own, and a few gorgeous big grownup words for to bite on" (Bechtel 1958, 180). T.M. Rivinus and Lisa Audet find that Brown's "narratives begin with sentence structures typical of two- to five-year-old children. Later in the course of her stories, Brown helps pull the children up to a new level of linguistic knowledge by exposing them to words and structures slightly above their developmental level" (Rivinus and Audet 1992, 3).

Brown, however, was not just reproducing the ideas from Bank Street. Indeed her emphasis on and continued usage of animals as protagonists goes against the grain of Mitchell's approach. Rather than featuring real children in real child situations as would Mitchell, Brown simplifies the situations and, through use of animal stand-ins, makes the stories universal. The child need not worry if characters are redheaded, blond, or brunette or if that difference matters. Instead the rabbits, cats, and dogs of Brown's books could stand in for any and all children. Mitchell herself was not supportive of this nod toward fantasy, writing to Brown that she had "a resistance to the kind of illustrations . . . [because] animals have their own ways of loving & taking care of their children" (Mitchell 1951, 1–2).

THE INFLUENCES OF LUCY SPRAGUE MITCHELL
AND JOHN DEWEY

The genealogical beginning point for a philosophical analysis of Brown's books must be Bank Street and Mitchell. Upon arriving in New York in 1913, Mitchell visited with Dewey and psychologist Edward Thorndike to get advice about an educational career. She ended up attending "Dewey's lectures on the philosophy of education and Thorndike's lectures on educational psychology" (Antler 1987, 207). While attending Dewey's lectures she was exposed to the ideas that became *Democracy and Education*.

Under Mitchell's leadership, the Bank Street School served as a school, a teacher training center, and a writing laboratory. The schools that made up Bank Street were used as laboratories to "give the students the opportunity to explore first their own environment and gradually widen this environment for them along lines of their own inquiries" (Mitchell1921/1948, 15). The influence of the widening from the familiar to the less familiar at Bank Street can be seen in the gradual widening in Brown's use of the same technique in *Goodnight Moon*, from the familiar objects (the room), to the fanciful (nobody), to the unknowable (noises everywhere.)

Mitchell did not merely reiterate the theories of Dewey and others; she integrated them into her own theoretical understanding of intellectual development and its impact on the necessary structure for children's education and literature. Mitchell writes:

> We all know how long a child is in acquiring a correct use of the pronouns "me" and "you." And we know that long after he has this language distinction, he still calls everything he likes "mine." "This is my cow, this is my tree!" The only way to persuade him that it is not *his* is to call it some one [sic] else's. Possessed it must be. He knows the world only in personal terms. That is, his early sense of relationship is that of himself to his concrete environment. This later evolves into a sense of relationships between other people and their concrete environment. (Mitchell 1937, 17)

Mitchell explains here that children need to stake ownership of objects, to understand objects in relationship to ownership, to understand people and the environment in terms of ownership relations. This understanding of Mitchell's conforms to Dewey's statement that "Actual knowledge is concerned with relations. . . . These relations . . . are not mere objects or events. They are permanent connections which hold objects and events together, and make a unity of them" (Dewey Early Works Vol. 2, 76). While Dewey is speaking of knowledge being about relations, we can see similar approaches in Brown's *My World*. *My World* depicts a young rabbit making a series of connections between her own possessions and those of her parents. There are a number of links between this book and *Goodnight Moon*: the use of the rabbits, Clement Hurd's illustrations and the nursery appear to be the same ones from *Goodnight Moon* (though now no longer colored green.) Throughout, as with Dewey's approach, the rabbit's understandings and knowledge are generally relational. Thus we have the pairings of "Mother's chair. My chair" (4) or "My dog. Daddy's dog" (8). But these relational ownerships are not the totality of the rabbit's understanding. We also hear the rabbit's knowledge connected to these objects. Thus, we find out that "Daddy's dog once caught a frog" (8), and "When you catch a fish you make a wish" (21). It is intriguing also to consider the question that closes the book, "How many stripes on a bumble bee?" (33). This might be the first instance in which the rabbit begins to understand the world as apart from the ownership of its pieces.[7]

The additional influence by Mitchell on Brown is felt in the references—both visual and in text—to artists that had been impacted by Mitchell's Here and Now approach. Thus we find many of the images in Edward Steichen and Mary Steichen Martin's *First Picture Book* and *Second Picture Book* become the ordinary objects in *Goodnight Moon* and *My World*. For example, we see a clock, a comb and a brush, a pair of socks, a cake of soap, a toothbrush, a telephone, and a crib that resembles Hurd's crib illustrations in both *Runaway Bunny* and *My World*. In the *Second* book we see a boy playing with his bear, or "playing" at building with a hammer and nails, both of which are much as the child in *My World* does. Lest it be thought that these ordinary objects could be utilized by anyone and thus the commonality is accidental or coincidence, the introduction to the *First Picture Book* was written by Harriet Johnson, director of the nursery school program for Bank Street. These books were intended to help foster a child's understanding of the world through the perception of ordinary objects.

This focus on perception carries echoes of Dewey. In explaining the evidence for coming to understand our perceptions as linked (i.e., visual phenomenon is understandable only because of tactile perception), Dewey gives the example of "the child grasping for the moon, and crying because he cannot get it" (Dewey Early Works Vol. 2, 145). Without understanding spatial distance (which Dewey believes comes through the linking of the visual and the tactile), the child cannot understand why he cannot touch the moon that is after all *right there*. Not only does the example of the moon carry into *Goodnight Moon*, but the idea that the objects are all alike in their approachability to the child shows that the bunny has not yet wholly grasped distance and scale. Thus we say goodnight not only to the (very distant) moon, but also to the (very near) red balloon. Both objects are similar in their roundness and their *belonging* to the bunny as objects of perception. These objects are all important to the bunny; their importance is recognized in their belongingness and thus in their inclusion in the litany of goodnights.

The green room's objects are perceived by the bunny, but they are conceptually on the same basis as the objects outside. This corresponds with Dewey's beliefs about children's perception. While discussing how children come to possess the concepts of the world, Dewey considers children's drawings. In these pictures "[p]erspective does not exist, for the child's interest is not *pictorial representation*, but in the *things* represented; and while perspective is essential to the former, it is no part of the characteristic uses and values of the things themselves" (Dewey Middle Works Vol. 6, 277). The objects have importance as things themselves, not as the representations of them. This can perhaps be linked to both the flattened perspective of Hurd's illustrations as well as in the importance given to the objects themselves in the black and white illustrations in *Goodnight Moon* following the beginning of the goodnight litany. *Goodnight Moon* alternates between full color pages of the whole room and black and white pages that focus on the specific objects themselves. Often the objects in the black and white illustrations appear differently than in the color pages. For example, when the mittens are bid goodnight they are the lone objects on the drying rack, though they originally had been displayed with the socks next to them.

By focusing her books for very young children on their everyday experiences, Brown followed in the methods prescribed by Dewey. For Dewey the beginning point of instruction needs to be the "more or less superficial phenomena of child life" (Dewey Early Works Vol. 5, 174). Thus, the focus on the everyday, superficial objects of the child's nursery and household are an apt beginning point. These books ought to be understood as educational in Dewey's sense, though they don't provide new knowledge. This is because Dewey's understanding of the role of education was that it was to be "strictly interpretive or mediatory" enabling "the child to reconstruct his or her experience and grow" (Dewey Early Works Vol. 5, 174).

Dewey explains in *Democracy and Education* that, for children, an object gets its meaning from its use and the reactions that occur from interacting with it (29). This can be seen in the manner in which the young rabbit in *My World* interacts with the objects of the house. Will his soap make soapsuds as his father's did? Why is his (wooden toy) car different from his father's car? The progression from objects having meaning based upon use to the attempt to understand one's own place in the world through the use of the same or similar objects is alluded to when Dewey states that "A child sees persons with whom he lives using chairs, hats, tables, spades, saws, plows, horses, money in certain ways. If he has any share at all in what they are doing, he is led thereby to use things in the same way, or to use other things in a way which will fit in" (Dewey 1916, 32).

In a more subtle way, we can see the impact of Dewey in Brown's use of maps. Dewey believed that maps were an important way for children to come to understand their world. A map serves as a "summary, an arranged

and orderly view of previous experiences, serves as a guide to future experience; it gives direction; it facilitates control; it economizes effort, preventing
useless wandering, and pointing out the paths which lead most quickly and
most certainly to a desired result" (Dewey Middle Works Vol. 2, 284). But
children shouldn't be taught geography as we commonly understand it. The
use of maps was a method to understand the relationships between the world
and the objects of the world. It was a way to begin to understand one's placement within the world. This indirect influence of Dewey through Mitchell
can be seen in the early inclusion in the *Goodnight Moon* nursery of a map
on the wall of the nursery rather than the reproduced image from *Runaway
Bunny* of the mother rabbit fly-fishing for her child (Marcus 1997, 21, 23).[8]

It seems clear that Brown utilized much of Dewey's philosophical and
educational ideas in the formation of her own works. We see in the bunny
trilogy an attempt to encapsulate his epistemic theories of learning and engagement with the world in *Goodnight Moon* and *My World*.[9] In *My World*
we see relational reasoning. But Brown's use of philosophy does not end
with these texts. The Deweyian theme of engagement with the world runs
throughout many of her works. This engagement was purposeful and her
own choice—as shown by Mitchell's rebuke to Brown for the continued use
of fantasy. Brown had gone past Here and Now to create something new.

IS THIS PHILOSOPHY?

It seems clear that Brown was influenced by Dewey. Her works resonate
with Dewey's epistemic theories and carry out his vision of what it means
to meet children at their developmental level in education. What is less clear
is if these links are enough to say that these texts move beyond being philosophically informed to being philosophy proper.[10] What is at stake here
is to understand these works as not being merely work that can be used
philosophically—such as the use of L. Frank Baum's *Wizard of Oz* in Wartenberg's work (Wartenberg 2009, 89–94)—but to being actively and intentionally an engagement with philosophy. Are Brown's works philosophy for
the very youngest? It would be easy to dismiss this question as moot based
upon the belief that *any* learning is by its nature philosophy if it brings the
learner closer to wisdom. But that approach says too little of philosophy
and does not recognize contemporary understandings of academic disciplines. From my perspective, philosophy is more than just learning; it is a
method of questioning and approaching the world.

Brown conceived of her books as providing a space for children to think. She
believed that "[i]n quiet times and sleepy times a child can dwell in thoughts of
his own, and in songs and stories of his own" (Brown 1952, 166). This giving
of space for reflection and growth should be linked with her belief that the
"scientific books" are "in themselves only a limited study, and merely a tool
and a check to your own observations and to the delight and simplicity you
may by some happy accident still share with children" (Brown 1951a, 81).

In bringing together her direct observations of children and her theoretical knowledge of epistemology and child development, Brown was tapping into "a young child's most excessive awareness and needs" (Brown 1951a, 80).

All of this could be understood yet again as drawing on philosophy rather than being philosophy itself. Perhaps the best way to see that what these books were doing was philosophy is to understand that these children's books were steeped in Mitchell's Here and Now perspective and were intended not to be read *to* children, but rather to be read *with* children. Thus, we get the books speaking directly to children, drawing on children's humor, or encouraging children to grow beyond their current worldviews. It is all too easy to dismiss these moves as being simplistic, but we should remember Dewey's admonition that in determining the material and method of instruction, the beginning point needs to be the "more or less superficial phenomena of child life" (Dewey Early Works Vol. 5, 174).As we are concerned with perhaps the youngest age range with which we would consider doing philosophy, it may be enough to find that these works are philosophy because they start where the children are and pose admittedly gentle challenges to children, inviting them to rethink their ideas and understandings of the world. It is unclear to what extent the philosophical use of these works is contingent upon an adult reader guiding the child through the problems posed by the text, but then again, perhaps the same can be said of our undergraduate courses and any books used in philosophy for children.

DOING PHILOSOPHY IN THE NURSERY

This leaves unanswered the question about how to proceed from the knowledge that Brown was intentionally weaving philosophy into her texts to the actual doing of philosophy with the pre- and early readers for whom these texts are written. I have argued elsewhere that it is not enough to have a discussion about philosophy with children; the doing of philosophy requires a certain set of knowledge and skills to be done properly (Kraft 2012, 74). However, in the case of these quite young children—and specifically in the use of texts by Brown and others from the Bank Street Writers' Laboratory—it may be the case that the act of engaging with the text as something to be read *and responded to* is already to engage in the philosophical exercises for which the Dewey-influenced writers were calling.

When we move beyond the bunny trilogy to consider other works by Brown, we see her explicitly including calls for active engagement in her stories. In Brown's early work *Bumble Bugs and Elephants* (Brown 1938/2006)—which may be the first board book (Marcus 2001, 93)—we find her linking children's language and stories with a rich understanding of their worldview. In it we find not only word play ("Once upon a time, there was a great big bumble bug" (Brown 1938/2006, 1)), but also questions directed at the reader/child ("What do you know that is great big?" (17–18)). We see also for the first time the pairing of big and little objects for comparison, a recurring theme in Brown's works, and, through the illustrations, a constant reemphasis of what has come before. Thus the titular bumble bugs appear throughout the text, as do the big and little chickens, elephants, etc. Further, in a nod to the constant repetition of stories that children enjoy, the book ends at its very beginning, restating that "Once upon a time, there was a great big bumble bug" (21).[11] In reading *Bumble Bugs* these questions and word play, paired with Clement Hurd's bright illustrations, call for adults to get children to respond *and think* about the text. What does the child know that is tiny little? Can there be chickens larger than elephants? And best of all, it explicitly calls to be read and engaged with again and again.

One of the earliest, and ongoing examples, of being attuned to children comes in Brown's series of Noisy Books. These books follow the adventures of Muffin the dog as he tries to figure out what is going on around him by sound alone. In the first book Muffin has a bandage covering his eyes because of a cinder (Brown 1939); in subsequent books he is shut in a box (Brown 1940), needing to hop up to look out the window of a car (Brown 1951b), etc. The text of the books includes sound effects that lend themselves to children either reading the book themselves or having the book read to them, experiencing the world as Muffin does—through sound. For example,

> All about him he could hear the noises in the house. He could hear a broom sweeping / swish swish swish / Somebody taking the spoons off the table / clank clank clink clank / A telephone / ding a ling ring / A vacuum cleaner / mmmzzzmmmmmmmmm / And the cook in the kitchen beating eggs / bbbbbbbbbbbbbbbb / He could hear someone turning on the bath / swishshshhhsssss. (Brown 1942a)

Later in many of the texts, Brown turns explicitly to the children and asks them if they believe that Muffin could hear things such as a starfish "in a pool under a rock" (Brown 1941) or the stars coming out at night (Brown 1940). Alternately, the child is asked if it is possible that a particular sound is perhaps the sound of "a big balloon going up to the moon" (Brown 1947b), "an elephant tiptoeing down the stairs" (Brown 1950), or a "Big Brass Band crashing their instruments up on a cloud" (Brown 1951b). As Virginia Schonberg notes, "Coupled with the humor and participation in the Noisy Books is a poetry of observation, of awareness of the world about." (Schonberg 1963, 24). Eugene Scheel explains that in the writing of the Noisy Books, Brown checked in with children as to the proper sounds that objects make (thus correcting automobile horns to "AWRurrrrrrra," from "Honk Honk") (Scheel 1969, 73).[12] Further, he notes, the layout of the pages was done such that as Brown "zig-zags her questions across the page . . . the word pattern is being deciphered by the adult, the child has time to come up with the answer before the page turns" (74). In Scheel's opinion, it was this involvement with the child that caused the books to draw children into the books and demand repeated readings. They "remain classics because they bring the child directly into the work where he can participate in its action" (79). It seems clear, then, that the doing of philosophy with these books can be in many regards as simple as reading and participating in the books. What does Muffin hear? What do you (the child) hear? What can we know of the world through only our hearing?

Brown's ability to express the childlike fascination with, and apparent misunderstanding of adult categories, comes to full fruition with *The Important Book* (Brown 1949a).[13] In the text Brown lays out a series of the possible "most important thing" for objects with the categories being strangely off kilter from what might be expected. Thus we find that the important thing about grass is not that it "grows, and is tender, with a sweet grassy smell," but instead that it is green (10). Similarly, the important thing about an apple is that it is round, not that it is red, tastes like an apple, or is bitten into (14). As Schonborg notes "each page is like an opening on the world" because of the careful balance of Leonard Weisgard's illustrations with Brown's text (Schonborg 1963, 13). It is precisely the opening of the *child's* world that is at hand in the book. The categories are not adults', the schemas are not adults', and the humor is certainly not adults'. Despite the possibility that a child might become confused by these categories (though I think that they will sense both the properness of the categories and the humor implicit in them), "It is appropriate in that it has some facts about the sky and there is something comforting and thought provoking in the idea that 'the sky is always there.' One can hear a child saying, 'Yes it is, isn't it? When I go to bed and when I get up it's there'" (Schonberg 1963, 12–13). In Brown's *The Important Book* we see her grasping not just the joy of children's categories and language, but also a larger understanding of what this means for their worldview.

It is this engagement with a child's worldview that opens up the possibility for adults to do philosophy with the infants, toddlers, pre- and early readers. The Dewey-influenced authors who went through the Bank Street School's Writers' Laboratory, such as Brown, offer us the opportunity to not only to engage with and inculcate a love of reading in children. They have also provided us with rich texts that enable us to connect with these youngest of children at a level that is developmentally appropriate and to do what was intended by these texts—philosophy.

I realize that final claim is still a controversial one. But what Brown and others who went through Bank Street did in their works was to take the principles, theories, and understandings of Dewey and integrate them into the text, illustrations, and stories. The connections to Dewey's overall epistemology and his epistemic growth process are not accidental, nor are they an adjunct to the stories. These texts, by reaching out to children where they are, embracing their understanding of the world, and letting them play in the questions about the world that are natural for that developmental level, are the philosophy that can be done with the very youngest children. These works are not just children's literature; they are philosophy for children.

NOTES

I owe a large debt to three librarians for their roles in this paper. First, to my mother-in-law Christine Hall who brought Leonard Marcus's *The Making of Goodnight Moon* to my attention when I had, foolishly, forgotten our copy of *Goodnight Moon* when we visited her. Second, to Susan Uhler, the former interlibrary loan librarian at York College. Sue managed to find copies of almost every children's book I desired. I do not imagine that many academic librarians often get calls to find *It Looked Like Spilled Milk*, but when called upon she did a marvelous job. Finally, I would like to thank Beth Harris at Hollins University who was quite giving of her time and expertise when I was using the Margaret Wise Brown collections in their archives.

1. See Tom Wartenberg's *Big Ideas for Little Kids* for his own explanation of advice for doing philosophy with elementary school students.
2. Plato, *Republic* 377.
3. Mitchell's most articulate explanation of her approach (generally referred to as Here and Now) is in the *Here and Now Story Book*, 1921. Examples of stories that she believed were appropriate for children can be found both in that volume and the follow-up, 1937's *Another Here and Now Story Book*.
4. Mitchell founded the Bureau of Educational Experiments in New York in 1916. Since BEE's move to 69 Bank Street, it has generally been referred to as the "Bank Street School." This convention continues, though the BEE has since moved to West 112th Street.
5. He captures an exchange between Hurd and Brown discussing the illustrations: "I like the rabbit, he has a real sleepiness." "Yes, but I'm worried about the yarn; it loses personality and softness."
6. Quoting *The Fish with the Deep Sea Smile* jacket, which in turn is quoting a letter to the publisher of the book, E. P. Dutton.
7. Although it is possible to consider that the bee would "own" its stripes.
8. Mitchell's emphasis on geography is perhaps best seen in *Here and Now* at page 15.
9. I have largely omitted an analysis of *Runaway Bunny* here, though it can be read as an examination of the constancy of personal relationships. In this context of this chapter, the most important aspect of *Runaway Bunny* is its usage in *Goodnight Moon* both as an object in the green room and as an illustration on the wall.
10. Whenever I think of this question, I hear Wendy Turgeon asking "But is it philosophy?" My realization that this link needs to be more explicit is due to our conversations about philosophy with children more broadly.
11. This interest in repetition may in part stem from Brown's own interest in Gertrude Stein's writing. Brown later edited Stein's children's book *The World is Round*, which is written in a stream-of-consciousness narrative and includes a restatement of Stein's famous "A rose is a rose is a rose."
12. This exactness is seen in Brown's own notes. She notes at the beginning of the manuscript for "He Heard Seashells by the Seashore" (possibly the script for a record) that the sounds indicated in the text "should be the real sounds, not humans sounding like amateur self-conscious cats making second-rate meows."
13. Wartenberg provides an alternate reading of *The Important Book*, which focuses on her use of categories in order to understand metaphysics. While this is an apt reading of the text, what I offer here is one which I think comes to Brown's intent. This, I believe, is the central difference between doing philosophy with children's literature and my argument here that Brown is doing philosophy *in* children's literature.

REFERENCES

Antler, J. (1987) *Lucy Sprague Mitchell: The Making of a Modern Woman* New Haven, CT: Yale University Press.

Bechtel, L.S. (1958) "Margaret Wise Brown, 'Laureate of the Nursery'" *Horn Book Magazine* June 1958, 173–186.

Bliven, B., Jr. (1946) "Child's Best Seller" *Life* Dec. 2: 59–64, 66.

Brown, M. W. (1952) "Stories to Be Sung and Songs to Be Told" *Book of Knowledge Annual* 166–170.

———. (1951a) "Creative Writing for Very Young Children" *Book of Knowledge Annual* 77–81.

———. (1951b) *The Summer Noisy Book* Special Edition by E. M. Hale and Company, New York: Harper & Bros.

———. (1950) *The Quiet Noisy Book* New York: Harper & Row.

———. (1949a) *The Important Book* New York: HarperCollins.

———. (1949b) *My World* New York: Harper & Brothers.

———. (1949c) "Writing for Children" *Hollins Alumnae Magazine* Winter 22(2): 13–14.

———. (1947a) *Goodnight Moon* New York: Harper & Brothers.

———. (1947b) *The Winter Noisy Book* New York: HarperCollins.

———. (1942a) *The Indoor Noisy Book* New York: Harper & Row.

———. (1942b) *Runaway Bunny* New York: Harper & Brothers.

———. (1941) *The Seashore Noisy Book* New York: HarperCollins.

———. (1940) *The Country Noisy Book* New York: Harper & Row.

———. (1939) *The Noisy Book* New York: Harper & Row.

———. (1938) *The Fish with the Deep Sea Smile* New York: E. P. Dutton and Company.

———. (1938/2006) *Bumble Bugs and Elephants: A Big and Little Book.* New York: Harper Collins. (Reprint of W. R. Scott 1938 publication, with additional illustrations by Thatcher Hurd.)

———. (n.d.) "He Heard Seashells by the Seashore" Hollins University. Series 1: Manuscripts.

Dewey, J. (2008) *The Collected Works of John Dewey: 1882–1953.* Jo Ann Boydston, ed. Early Works, 1882—1898 (5 vols.), Middle Works, 1899–1924 (15 vols.), Later Works, 1925–1953 (17 vols.) Carbondale: Southern Illinois University Press.

———. (1916) *Democracy and Education* New York: Free Press.

Ga'g, W. (1928) *Millions of Cats* New York: Coward-McCann.

Hendley, B. (1986) *Dewey, Russell, Whitehead: Philosophers as Educators* Carbondale: Southern Illinois University Press.

Kraft, Jr., R. (2012) "More than Talking about Ideas: Expanding the Philosophical Use of Children's Literature" *Theory and Research in Education* 10(1): 71–75.

Marcus, L. (2001) *Margaret Wise Brown: Awakened by the Moon* New York: Perennial. (Reprint of 1992 Beacon Press publication.)

———. (1997) *The Making of Goodnight Moon* New York: HarperTrophy.

Martin, M. S. and Steichen, E. (1930) *First Picture Book* New York: Harcourt, Brace, and Company, 1930.

———. (1931) *Second Picture Book* New York: Harcourt, Brace, and Company.

Mitchell, L.S. (1951) March 29, 1951 letter to Margaret Wise Brown. Hollins University Archives (Series 4: Incoming Correspondence.)

———. (1937) *Another Here and Now Story Book* New York: E. P. Dutton & Co.

———. (1921/1948) *Here and Now Story Book: Two-Through Seven-Year Olds* New York: E. P. Dutton & Company.

Plato (1997) *Republic.* Trans. G.M.A. Grube, rev. C.D.C. Reeve. In *Plato: Complete Works* (ed. Cooper, J. M.) 971–1223, Indianapolis, IN: Hackett Publishing.

Rivinus, T. M. and Audet, L. (1992) "The Psychological Genius of Margaret Wise Brown" *Children's Literature in Education* 23(2): 1–14.

Scheel, E. M. (1969) *Margaret Wise Brown, The Foremost Innovator of Contemporary Literature for Children: Her Works and Life as Seen through Her Writings and Friends* Unpublished M.A. Thesis. Washington, DC: Georgetown University.

Schonborg, V. (1963) *An Examination of the Writings of Margaret Wise Brown with Special Reference to Uses of Fantasy and Reality* Unpublished B.A. Thesis. New York: Bank Street College.

Wartenberg, T. (2009) *Big Ideas for Little Kids* Lanham, MD: Rowman & Littlefield Education.

11 Teaching Philosophy to Young Children

Berys Gaut and Morag Gaut

This chapter explains how to teach philosophy to children as young as three years old. The method for doing so emerged from a collaboration between ourselves, who are, respectively, a professor of philosophy at the University of St Andrews, Scotland, and a teacher of three- to five-year-old children at Anstruther Primary School and St Andrews Nursery Centre in Fife, Scotland. The collaboration resulted in a book, *Philosophy for Young Children: A Practical Guide* (Gaut and Gaut 2011; hereafter cited as *PYC*), which consists of 36 detailed inquiry plans and an Introduction that explains how to use them. All the inquiries were tried out at Anstruther Primary School on children between the ages of 3 and 5, and many were also tried out on older children up to the age of 10. A statistical study showed some striking benefits: over the course of only 10 inquiries, there were marked increases in the number of relevant and unprompted reasons in response to philosophical questions produced by the two groups of three- and four-year-old children who participated in the study (Gaut 2010).

THE STRUCTURED METHOD

That one can teach philosophy to children as young as three will surprise many people. Indeed, there has been comparatively little work done by philosophy for children practitioners on this age group, the central focus being on children from the age of five or six upwards. But some writers have shown that three- or four-year-old children can participate in philosophical inquiries (e.g., Kennedy 1992; Murris and Haynes 2000). There are, admittedly, limits to the range of philosophical issues that young children can fruitfully discuss—they find some questions in epistemology difficult, for instance. Our inquiry "Dreaming of School" (*PYC*: chapter 7) asks the children to consider whether they are dreaming now, and many, though not all, three- and four-year-olds find it very hard to understand this as a possibility. But young children have no problems in understanding issues in many areas of philosophy. Indeed, in ethics and political philosophy, where concepts such as fairness play a central role, philosophical questions emerge naturally from the children's day-to-day discussions with friends about what it is fair to do and how they should share things. The inquiries in *PYC* cover political philosophy, environmental philosophy, social philosophy, ethics, esthetics, philosophy of mind, epistemology, and metaphysics; and with the exception of some topics in the latter two areas, even the youngest children, we found, can fully engage with the issues raised.

To teach philosophy to young children one has to tailor inquiries to the children's attention span. Inquiries at this age generally best last about 20–30 minutes, to reflect the length of time for which the children can easily concentrate. It is also important to be flexible about their length; if there are any signs of tiredness or restlessness, it is normally best to wrap up the inquiry swiftly.

The method we developed is prop based, since props, such as stories and pictures, help to stimulate and maintain the interest of young children. The stories need to be suitable for children of this age and should be clear, simple, engaging, and short, so that plenty of time for philosophical discussion is left. We wrote our own stories and commissioned pictures (all of which are included in the book). Writing the story allows us to address a single philosophical issue and to bring out the features that are relevant to it, whereas using commercially available picture books has the disadvantage that they are likely to raise several different kinds of philosophical issues, if they raise any at all, so that discussion may proceed in any number of directions and lose focus. Activities are also important, which can include pretending to be various things and sorting replies to questions into various categories. One particularly useful prop is a philosophy box, into which all the other props used in the inquiry are placed, and these are gradually brought out during the inquiry. This helps to create a sense of excitement and anticipation in the children, and even after several years many children fondly remember the philosophy box.

Interleaving the activity with philosophical questions also helps to focus children's attention and increase their concentration span. For instance, rather than reading a fairly long story and then at the end raising philosophical questions, it is better, where possible, to read a part of the story and then raise a philosophical question at that point, then resume the story after a short discussion. This breaks up the inquiry into smaller units and so stimulates interest by providing variety to the activities.

One must also discuss issues that children of this age can grasp. We noted that the youngest children may find some issues in epistemology and metaphysics hard to understand, and we do not recommend teaching formal logic to three-year-olds! The best way to teach the issues is by introducing concrete examples that the children can easily grasp and to which they can relate, as in the story of the Teddy Bears' Picnic, which we discuss below. Besides their role in enhancing interest, this is the second function of props, since, by exemplifying a principle or issue through a story, picture, or activity, young children can better understand what is at stake.

These, then, are the basic adaptations one must make for doing philosophy with young children. What is remarkable, however, is that so little has to be changed in the way that one would conduct inquiries with older children. Indeed, early on in our collaboration, we were struck by the fact that conducting an inquiry with three- and four-year-olds is not that different from running an undergraduate seminar at university level. Undergraduates often have to be steered to keep their comments relevant to the question posed, to respect each other's opinions, to listen carefully, to consider counterexamples and objections to their views, to grasp and develop distinctions, and so on, just as young children do. And undergraduates too benefit by considering abstract principles in relation to concrete examples (as indeed do all philosophers). The philosophical ability evinced is (usually) greater at undergraduate level, but the techniques for successfully running seminars are similar to those for conducting inquiries with young children.

The most distinctive feature of our method is not specific to running inquiries with young children but has general relevance. It lies in the way that the inquiry plans are structured. Each inquiry plan poses a clear question or set of questions, and for most of these questions, there is a pair of headings: "if the children answer yes" and "if the children answer no." Under each heading there is a further question, posed by the teacher, asking the children why they answered as they did, and then there is a list of some possible reasons for the children's answers. These provide examples of reasons that the children may come up with, and if they do not do so, the reasons can often usefully be introduced into the discussion. Many of the reasons also illustrate the use of counterexamples, principles, distinctions, and other philosophical techniques. Some of them are followed by possible objections to the reason, and in some cases follow-up questions that further explore the answer. The follow-up questions often generalize the answer or ask the children to consider possible objections to it. The structured method is in effect a kind of flowchart for taking different routes through an inquiry.

There are two advantages of the structured method of laying out inquiry plans. First, it gives the children philosophical questions to consider and helps to teach them key aspects of philosophical method. By giving possible reasons that illustrate philosophical techniques, such as making distinctions, generalizing examples to develop principles, looking for counterexamples, and so on, the children are taught philosophical heuristic skills (i.e., thinking skills for philosophical problem solving). Such heuristic skills also have wider applications in helping the children to acquire critical thinking skills, in general, and to come up with creative ideas (Gaut 2013). Second, the structured method helps teachers who have little or no background in philosophy (which will be true of the majority of teachers) to be confident that they are doing genuine philosophy, by providing them with philosophical questions and examples of philosophical techniques. By showing these teachers how to do philosophy, it also helps them to come up with their own responses to what the children say. It should be noted, though, that the possible reasons ought to be treated as mere suggestions, since the children are likely to come up with their own, different, and often interesting examples and points. The point is to use the reasons to help discussion when it is flagging and to sharpen the children's philosophical skills, not for the teacher to curtail or dominate the discussion.

The structured method is, so far as we are aware, unique to our approach. Most philosophy for children books provide a set of questions to be raised about the story or activity that is the basis for the inquiry, and some of the best of these books encourage the children to develop their philosophical abilities by showing them how to make distinctions, see the connections between different questions, and so on (e.g., Cam et al 2007; Wartenberg 2009). Our method builds on this kind of approach but does so more systematically, by laying out possible answers in greater detail and more explicitly and employing these answers more directly to illustrate philosophical techniques.

CONDUCTING AN INQUIRY

The best way to explain the method in more detail is to provide an example of its use: we'll discuss the first inquiry in our book, "The Teddy Bears' Picnic" (*PYC*: 12–13). Though we consider the first inquiry, it's worth noting that the inquiries can be conducted in any order.

When beginning inquiries with a group of children, it is important to explain some of the key terms and rules that govern their use. The first term to introduce is "philosophy," which in our experience children love to learn (it is, after all, a big word) and which is a bit of a tongue twister for some of them! The teacher should explain to the children the basic rules of an inquiry: They should think before they speak, listen to the other children, and respect others' opinions. In addition, only one child should speak at a time; each child should decide whether she agrees or disagrees with the others; and, most important, should give a reason for her answer. It's also important to tell the children that it is perfectly acceptable for them to change their minds, provided that they can give reasons for doing so. Paper cutout "Philosophy Helpers," each a character stating a rule, are very useful in reminding children of these rules. The rules need to be stated explicitly only during the first few inquiries, until the children are familiar with them, though having the Philosophy Helpers available in later inquiries is a good idea: to remind the children of the rules if need be. Sometimes, however, the children enjoy the recital of the rules so much that they insist on going through them, even when they are very familiar with them! One should also gradually teach children the basic concepts to use in philosophy, including those of an example, a counterexample, an objection, a principle, and a distinction.

Each inquiry plan starts with a statement of the philosophical topic and the aim of the inquiry. "The Teddy Bears' Picnic" is an inquiry in political philosophy, and its more specific aim is to get the children to discuss whether fairness is a matter of giving everyone equal shares or whether things should be distributed according to need—an issue that is still debated keenly by political philosophers. The statements of the topic and the aim are not meant to be conveyed to the children, but rather to help the teacher orient herself in the philosophical debate.

The props for the inquiry are listed next: in this case, two small teddies, a large teddy, a tablecloth, plates, and a cake. The next section of the plan introduces the story, which we wrote with a knowing nod to a traditional scenario. The two small teddies decide to have a picnic, lay out the tablecloth, put the plates and cake on it, and sit down. The teacher produces these props from the philosophy box and arranges them as in the story, invariably to the fascination of the children (the cake should, if possible, be a real one, which guarantees the children's keen interest). One teddy then asks the other how they should divide the cake, and they decide that it should be shared fairly.

The first, interleaved question is then posed to the children: how should the two teddies divide the cake if they are to do so fairly? Raising the question at this point gets the children to focus on the philosophical issue and to think about what they should say about it. Not surprisingly, almost all children say that the teddies should divide the cake equally between themselves. Toby (age four), for instance, suggested "cutting it two times and giving it to both of them."

The story then continues. The teddies decide that it is fair to divide the cake equally between them. At this point Big Teddy, who happens to be strolling along, sees the picnic and asks whether he can join in and have a piece of the cake. The teddies happily agree to this. But Big Teddy then says that he should have a bigger piece of cake than the smaller teddies, since he is much bigger and so needs more cake than they do.

The main question is then posed to the children: is it fair that Big Teddy has more cake? The question, given the context, is a concrete way of posing the issue of the relative merits of the conception of fairness as equal treatment, compared to the conception of fairness as requiring the satisfaction of needs.

The plan then addresses the two possible answers, affirmative and negative, to the question. The course of the inquiry will branch in one direction or the other, depending on the answers of the children, but in most inquiries (less so in this one) it is quite common at this point for the children not to agree with each other, so that both branches need to be explored.

The affirmative answer to the question is considered under the "If the children answer yes" heading. The teacher should ask the children why they think that it is fair for Big Teddy to have more cake. As always, they are encouraged to come up with reasons of their own in answer to the question. To help discussion, we list some possible reasons. These are useful for stimulating debate, bringing in relevant philosophical considerations, and illustrating philosophical method but are, recall, only suggestions.

Two possible reasons are given under the affirmative heading. The first is that Big Teddy will be unhappy if he doesn't receive more cake. Immediately after, we provide an objection that the two teddies will be unhappy if he does receive more cake. The children, should they take this line, are thus encouraged to think about the relative weights of the happiness of one person compared to the happiness of several (which is of course a nod in the direction of utilitarianism—the doctrine that we ought to maximize the general happiness).

The second possible reason is an endorsement of Big Teddy's view that since he is bigger, he needs more food, so it is fair that he has it. There is then a follow-up question, which asks the children to consider whether the general principle is true that we should always share things so that someone who needs more is given more. We also provide an example: if a child has a worse cold than another child, so he needs more tissues, should he be given more? The children are thus encouraged to move from a single, concrete instance, to consider the underlying principles of fair distribution.

These possible reasons are not the only ones that could be considered. A child might, for instance, say that since Big Teddy is much bigger, the two other teddies couldn't stop him from taking more cake. In that case, the teacher could ask the children to consider whether the fact that you can do something makes it fair—for instance, whether, if a bigger child took some cake from them, that would make it fair. There is, clearly, no way to anticipate all the possible reasons that could be given. However, we provide some of the philosophically more interesting ones, and, by giving many illustrations of how the discussion might go, a teacher who lacks a philosophical background can gradually acquire a sense of how to conduct a philosophical discussion.

The second possible answer to the question of whether it is fair for Big Teddy to have more cake is the negative one, discussed under the "If the children answer no" heading. Most children initially think that it is not fair for Big Teddy to have more cake. The teacher asks the children why they think this. We list four possible reasons.

First, the children might say that he is being greedy. The objection follows that he's not being greedy, since he needs more food. This is an example of getting the children to think about the meaning of terms: is it really greed if you take more of something because you need more?

The second reason is based on an analogy with the children's situation. They share things equally with other children, so in the same way Big Teddy ought to share things equally with the other teddies. The objection is then given that there is a difference in the situations: the children are not very different in size from others in their class, but Big Teddy is *much* bigger than the other two teddies. So the children are encouraged to think about the general principle at stake (that things ought to be shared equally), to look for support for that principle in their own experience (how they share with other children), and then to consider whether that support is really warranted—for there is a relevant difference between the two cases, since the children's needs, unlike the teddies', do not differ from each others' much. Thus the children are encouraged to consider making a distinction between the two cases.

The third possible reason is that if the cake is divided in favor of Big Teddy, he will be happy, but the two teddies will be unhappy, and that it is better if two teddies are happy than if only one is. This again is an invocation of utilitarian considerations about fair distribution. That the two teddies would be sad if they got less cake than Big Teddy is in fact one of the most common reasons that the children give.

The fourth possible reason is simply the statement that things ought always to be shared equally, which again encourages the children to think about the general principle. This reason is also a very common one for the children to give. For instance, David (age five) explained that each teddy should get the same sized piece of cake: "If that one gets one and that one gets one and that one gets one, that's fair enough."

In addition to support for, or objections to, the particular *reasons* the children might give, we also sometimes consider possible objections to the *answers* the children give, and we do so for this branch of the answer. The children are asked to consider a counterexample to their answer that it's not fair that Big Teddy should have more cake. We ask them whether their parents have more food on their plate than they do at mealtimes, and if so whether that is because their parents are bigger than they are, and so need more food. But if that's the case, surely it's fair that Big Teddy has more cake, since he is bigger than the other two teddies, just as their parents are bigger than they are? So do they now think that Big Teddy should have more cake? In our experience the majority of children now change their minds and agree that Big Teddy should have more cake. For instance, Elli (age five) said that the smaller teddies should have less cake "Cos they're only wee," and Katie (age three) thought that Big Teddy should have more "Cos that is the biggest."

So by considering a general principle (that things ought to be shared equally), and then a counterexample to it, most of the children will reject the principle and adopt a new one (that things ought to be shared according to need). In doing so, they have adjusted their principles in the light of their judgment about individual cases—an instance of what Rawls (1971: esp. 48–51) famously describes as *reflective equilibrium*: that is, the mutual adjustment of general principles and intuitions about particular cases to achieve overall consistency in one's set of beliefs. Not only have the children engaged in a genuine debate in political philosophy (about the correct principle of fairness in distribution), they have also done so using one of the most important methods of philosophical argument (reflective equilibrium).

The next section of the plan is the summary. The first part reminds the children what question has been discussed—in this case how to share things fairly. The second part summarizes what the children have said, and we list some of the possibilities. We often state these so as to bring out the general principles at stake to help the children to generalize their answers. In this case we list two possible principles: that things should always be shared equally, and that things should be shared according to need. Most children have changed their minds by the end of the inquiry, supporting the second principle rather than the first.

The inquiry plan then gives an optional follow-up activity. Here it is to divide the cake between the children and the teacher according to the principle of fairness accepted by the majority of children. If this is that the division should be according to need and the teacher cuts herself a larger slice of cake, there will likely be heated protests by most of the children! Cognitive dissonance is a wonderful thing.

Finally, for some inquiries we suggest an alternative version of the story for slightly older children. Children from the age of eight or so may feel that talking about teddies is beneath their dignity, so in the alternative story there are two twins, who take the place of the smaller teddies, and a taller friend, who takes the place of Big Teddy. All else remains the same, and this version of the inquiry runs just as successfully as the teddies version. As remarked, many of the inquiries in *PYC* have been successfully tried with the older children, and we think that, with alternative story versions in some cases, they are suitable for all age ranges in primary (i.e., elementary) school.

CONCLUSION: PHILOSOPHY FOR YOUNG AND OLDER CHILDREN

In teaching philosophy to young children, one has to adapt one's method to their motivations and abilities: one should keep sessions shorter, have lots of props to stimulate their interest, employ stories and examples that are comprehensible and meaningful to them, interleave activities with questions, and discuss issues that they can grasp. But what we have mainly stressed is that in teaching philosophy to young children, one should employ basically the same methods as one uses with older children or even undergraduates in a seminar context. One should try to get them to think about a philosophical question, to consider relevant principles, examine reasons in favor of and against those principles, make relevant distinctions, and so on. To do this we developed the structured method of laying out inquiry plans, which lists some of the possible answers and reasons that the children may give, and builds into those reasons examples of philosophical techniques, so that the heuristic skills of the children are advanced. Doing this also has the advantage that teachers who lack a philosophical background can proceed with confidence in teaching the inquiries, knowing that they are teaching genuine philosophy, and employing genuinely philosophical techniques. The common features of how to teach philosophy successfully far outweigh the specific differences between teaching philosophy to younger and to older children. In the end, teaching philosophy to young children is simply teaching philosophy.

REFERENCES

Cam, P., Fynes-Clinton, F., Harrison, K., Hinton, L., Scholl, R., and Vaseo, S. (2007) *Philosophy with Young Children—A Classroom Handbook* Deakin West: Australian Curriculum Studies Association.

Gaut, B. (2013) "Educating for Creativity" In *The Philosophy of Creativity* (eds. Paul, E. and Kaufman, S. B.) New York: Oxford University Press.

Gaut, B. and Gaut, M. (2011) *Philosophy for Young Children: A Practical Guide* London: Routledge.

Gaut, M. (2010) "Can Children Engage in Philosophical Enquiry?" In *Exploring Interdisciplinary Trends in Creativity and Engagement* (eds. McKenzie, B. and Fitzsimmons, P.) 195–203, Oxford: Inter-Disciplinary Press (e-Book).

Kennedy, D. (1992) "Using 'Peter Rabbit' as a Philosophical Text with Young Children" *Analytic Teaching* 13(1): 53–58.

Murris, K. and Haynes, J. (2000) *Storywise: Thinking through Stories* Newport, Pembrokeshire: DialogueWorks.

Rawls, J. (1971) *A Theory of Justice* Cambridge, MA: Harvard University Press.

Wartenberg, T.E. (2009) *Big Ideas for Little Kids: Teaching Philosophy through Children's Literature* Lanham, MD: Rowman & Littlefield.

12 Philosophical Children's Literature for Upper Elementary and Middle School

Claudia Mills

At one time in my life I took an introductory class in quilting. We spent some time studying the color wheel and exploring different color combinations arranged into patchwork patterns. By the end of the six class sessions, I found that my eyes had received an unexpected education. Now I saw quilt possibilities everywhere, in all directions, all day long. Wherever I looked I saw various color combinations and thought about each one, "*That* could make a great quilt!" The whole world became a quilt festival laid out before my newly appreciative eyes.

I want to suggest that the same is true with exposure to philosophy. As much as a set of specific skills or a defined body of literature, philosophy is a way of looking at the world. It invites us to see not colors, but questions. And once you start recognizing these questions, once you become alert to where they lurk, you come to see them everywhere. Some of these are conceptual questions that take the form "What is x?": "What is justice? What is freedom? What is reality? What is truth? What is goodness? What is beauty?" Some of these are normative questions that take the form, "What ought I to do? What kind of person should I be? How ought I to live my life?"

Any book for young readers that invites us to consider questions of these kinds is a philosophically provocative text, at least for those who have the eyes to discern what is being asked. Some books pose philosophical questions overtly and directly; others pose the same questions more obliquely, in a way that has to be teased out of the story. Some books are written in defense of a particular answer to the question posed; some present a choice between competing answers; others leave the question unanswered, inviting the reader to answer it for himself or herself. Teachers and parents can help children locate philosophical questions in a story and then evaluate the answers the story offers, or grope toward answers of their own.

In what follows, I survey various categories of children's literature to highlight the kinds of philosophical questions that they might raise, as well as identifying relevant titles in each category. Many of the books I cite are recognized classics; others are ones I came upon in recent reading (or that I wrote myself), where I can offer no guarantee that these books will endure. My point, however, is to call attention to the way that sensitive and open-minded readers, under the guidance of sensitive and open-minded teachers, can start to find and explore philosophical questions everywhere.

FANTASY/SCIENCE FICTION

Perhaps the most fertile category of children's literature for provoking philosophical questions is fantasy and science fiction. Authors who create other possible worlds that are both similar to our own and different in important ways have the luxury of being able to design those worlds to contain features chosen to invite reflection on central philosophical concepts like freedom, equality, and justice. These authors are then well placed to offer ethical evaluation of other ways of living: in what way is this alternative world superior or inferior to our own? Many of the fantasy worlds offered to young readers are dystopias rather than utopias, although dystopias motivated by (perhaps twisted) utopian aspirations. Such portraits encourage readers to speculate on the degree to which we might be collectively heading toward a problematic future of our own and whether certain elements of our current way of living invite parallel moral criticism.

In my view, the most philosophically interesting novels are ones that do not simply pit good against evil, light against dark, love against hate, freedom against servitude. It isn't philosophically interesting to demonstrate that good is superior to evil or that love is superior to hate! Even some highly acclaimed fantasy novels seem to involve a formulaic battle between the forces of good and the forces of evil: where "good" and "evil" become more like names of opposing athletic teams or armies than actually marking off different moral orientations. Years ago, when I first read Susan Cooper's admittedly evocative and beautifully written novel *The Dark Is Rising*, I had the sense that we couldn't tell apart those characters aligned with "good" from those characters aligned with "evil" by anything they actually *did*; seemingly good characters, who were doing all kinds of good things, could turn out to be allied with the forces of darkness, rooting for the "wrong" side in this cosmic competition. Of course, even as I criticize Cooper's novel on these grounds, this only means that readers can engage in philosophical argumentation on this very topic: what is it, exactly, that makes a "good" character *good*, or an "evil" character *evil*?

Celebrating the 50th anniversary of its publication this year, Madeleine L'Engle's Newbery-winning *A Wrinkle in Time* remains one of the most powerful children's books that portray alternative worlds for young readers to enter and ponder. Misfit Meg Murry travels by means of "tesseract" with her friend Calvin and younger brother Charles Wallace to rescue her scientist father from kidnappers who are holding him prisoner on the planet Camazotz. There the trio encounters a conformist society dominated by an evil disembodied brain called IT. In the climactic scene of the book, Meg rescues Charles Wallace, who has also succumbed to the dark power of IT.

Meg first reacts to IT with rage and hatred and then realizes that "Hate was nothing that IT didn't have. IT knew all about hate" (194). The only thing Meg has that IT doesn't have is love, and so she loves Charles Wallace hard enough to break IT's hold over him. L'Engle does not offer moral nuance in her presentation of Camazotz, or of IT; nonetheless, she implicitly invites readers to ask themselves exactly which features of Camazotz make it so morally disturbing. Is there something inherently problematic in trying to produce an orderly society in which "Nobody suffers" and "Nobody is ever unhappy"? (133). That is to say, is the goal of a society without any unhappiness itself problematic? Consider Meg's comment to her brother, "Maybe if you aren't unhappy sometimes you don't know how to be happy" (133). If a peaceful and orderly society is indeed a valuable goal, on the other hand, could such a society be achieved without having to sacrifice individuality in the process? Why or why not?

The Giver, by Lois Lowry, also creates an egalitarian society marked by social conformity, engineered to minimize socially problematic "difference" as well as to eradicate all experience of pain and other negative emotions: the "giver" of the title is the person who is charged with taking on the painful memories and experiences spared to the rest of the society. This is a world without colors, because with color comes difference, and with difference can come discrimination and inequality. Although one of my writer friends read *The Giver* and declared that she could tell that Jonah's world was "completely evil" from the get-go, I was impressed by the degree to which Lowry allows us to entertain the possibility that features of this society that prove ultimately disturbing do have arguments that can be offered on their behalf. For example, when little Lily comes home from school angry about some visiting child's disregard of playground rules, Lily's father asks her, "Do you think it's possible that he felt strange and stupid, being in a new place with rules that he didn't know about?" (6). It certainly seemed to me as if there could be advantages to redirecting painful and divisive emotions in the direction of compassion and understanding. Likewise, I found some appeal in the program of creating affectionate and caring families on a nongenetic basis according to gender-neutral principles. The novel thus provokes a host of probing philosophical questions. How far should we go as a society to eliminate pain and to monitor pleasure? Does "difference" compromise or violate an egalitarian vision of distributive justice? Can family ties be problematic? Is it a good thing to "release" elderly and infirm people into death before the quality of their lives declines too far?

The Giver invites comparison with Plato's construction of what he intends to be the model of a perfectly just, though perhaps unattainably ideal, society in his *Republic*. Plato designs his "beautiful city" by dismantling the traditional family and then breeding and educating individuals to occupy designated social roles, in either the crafts (working) class, the auxiliaries (military), or the ruling class of the guardians. Like the engineers of Lowry's dystopia, Plato seeks to develop social unity by eliminating biologically based familial attachments and to produce individuals with well-regulated souls where desire is effectively governed by reason, rather than allowed to become a destabilizing force on the individual or societal level. If we are disturbed, as Lowry evidently intends us to be, by the world she creates, does this mean that Plato is wrong about what a just society would look like? Is individual freedom more valuable than social unity and social equality?

It is impossible to write even a brief account of philosophically rich middle grade fantasy novels without mentioning the Harry Potter series. While J.K. Rowling certainly delivers the classic stark battle between good and evil, represented by Harry and Voldemort respectively, her characters are morally complex, especially the fascinating Snape: readers are left in doubt until book seven as to whether Snape is a "good guy" or "bad guy." The fantastic elements of the wizard world are marshaled effectively to raise moral and philosophical questions. Edmund M. Kern, in a book-length exploration of ethical questions raised in and by the series, analyzes *Harry Potter and the Sorcerer's Stone* as developing the theme of Harry's ability to make choices in the face of fate, in particular the universal fate of death itself, which the sorcerer's stone is crafted (unwisely) to cheat. According to Kern, the culminating moral moment in *Harry Potter and the Chamber of Secrets* is Dumbledore's pronouncement to Harry: "It is our choices, Harry, that show what we truly are, far more than our abilities" (qtd. in Kern, 62). *Harry Potter and the Prisoner of Azkaban*, on Kern's reading, is "a single, extended commentary upon the tensions between rules and the moral principles they are intended to sustain . . . The book's entire plot suggests that truth-telling, submission to authority, and following the rules are not always the moral things to do, particularly when the stakes are high" (72). That even Dumbledore breaks the Ministry's rules when enough is at stake motivates discussion over the role of rules in moral thinking. How are moral rules justified? When may they be justifiably broken? Each book in Rowlings's series is arguably built around a moral question played out in a complex and multilayered way.

To turn to a more recent and lesser-known title, *The Shadow Speaker*, by Nigerian American fantasy author Nnedi Okorafor-Mbachu, is set in Africa of 2070, a land that has been infused with magic ever since the nuclear fallout from the "Great Change." Fourteen-year-old Ejii is a "shadow speaker," who can communicate with the hovering shadows all around her, and through them, with the innermost being of those she encounters. But the world of the future is no less brutal and warlike than our own world of today, and Ejii is sent on a dangerous mission with the Red Queen of the Niger, who in the past beheaded Ejii's own savagely controlling father to put a bloody end to his tyranny. Ejii must learn whom she can and cannot trust, and how much she is willing to risk to save her endangered planet. Is deadly violence, even to oppose great evil, ever justified? This kind of philosophical question finds a home in debates over utilitarianism's evaluation of acts only in terms of their ultimate consequences.

Not all philosophically rich fantasy novels involve the creation of an entire alternative world; some introduce fantasy elements into our own ordinary world, clearly employed to raise philosophical questions. For example, Will Weaver's recent novel *Defect* has at its heart the question: What price should we be willing to pay for a rare, extraordinary gift? What if that gift is made possible only by the possession of a body regarded by others as disfigured, distorted, and defective? When is difference from others a curse, and when is it a blessing? Fifteen-year-old foster child David has a short face, bug eyes, a stooped back, painfully sensitive hearing—and wings. As the story develops, David is confronted with a choice: should he have reconstructive surgery that will give him a conventionally handsome appearance—but clip his wings forever? Like L'Engle and Lowry, Weaver's unusual and compelling novel raises questions of intense interest to any philosophical heir of John Stuart Mill or Friedrich Nietzsche who has pondered the price of conformity. And it is the fantasy element here that allows these questions to be raised in a fresh and striking way.

HISTORICAL FICTION

Just as fantasy and science fiction can transport readers to a morally problematic future, historical fiction can transport readers to a morally problematic past, giving readers the opportunity to inhabit alternative worlds that not only could exist, but did exist, as a matter of historical fact. Historical fiction can reveal to children how certain crucial concepts and values are understood differently at different times, inspiring critical interrogation of how we understand these values and concepts today. To realize that people once thought differently from how "we" now think is to realize that how "we" think is not the only way that people can conceptualize and evaluate their world.

In the same way that philosophically rich futuristic fiction avoids posing stark black-white moral alternatives, the most philosophically interesting historical fiction does not simply acquaint readers with the atrocities of the past: the horrors of the Holocaust, the unspeakable evils of chattel slavery. Of course, it is important that children be exposed to the darkest chapters of our collective past, and such exposure can have a lifelong effect of sensitizing children to injustice. I have one friend who grew up to be a philosopher devoting his career to analyzing philosophical questions about poverty and racism because when he was a little boy, his mother read him Mildred Taylor's *Roll of Thunder, Hear My Cry*, her powerful saga of the racism experienced by the Logan family in Depression-era Mississippi. Such a book can be a catalyst for forming moral character.

However, the most philosophically rich historical fiction for young readers resists the temptation to see how "we" think as clearly right and how "they" used to think as clearly wrong. It may do this either by letting us see that how we think today is not as different as we would like from how people once thought, or by showing us that in the past even people who were in some sense "good" people entertained views considered problematic today, raising the possibility that future readers of historical fiction set in 2012 will find how we now live as problematic as we find novels about slavery in the antebellum South or the rise of fascism in 1930s Germany.

Philosophically rich texts tend to be ones that give us not sharp moral contrasts, but, as in the title of Carolyn Reeder's award-winning novel about the Civil War, shades of gray. The 12-year-old protagonist of Reeder's *Shades of Gray* reevaluates his conceptualization of courage and honor when he is sent to live, in the immediate aftermath of the Civil War, with an uncle who refused to fight for the Confederacy. Ultimately Will comes to realize that "it took a lot of courage for [his uncle] not to go to war when all the other men did" (145). The novel allows readers to identify with a boy who himself identifies with what we (at least we Yankees!) now view as the "wrong" side of the War Between the States, already a morally destabilizing and philosophically interesting subject position for us to enter. The novel goes on to explore what it is to be courageous, a philosophical question discussed at least since the time of Aristotle. This can be a springboard for raising a series of philosophical questions about courage. Does courage involve the absence of fear, or having the appropriate amount of fear for the situation? Who is more brave: the person who has no fear or the person who acts heroically despite his fear? Can courage be displayed in ordinary life as well as on the battlefield?

Another critically acclaimed novel, *My Brother Sam Is Dead*, awarded a Newbery Honor in 1975, raises similarly thought-provoking questions about a war that has remained extremely popular in the American national consciousness: the American Revolution. Tim Meeker is torn between being a Loyalist like his father or a Patriot like his older brother, Sam. The darkest and most disturbing moment of the novel comes when Sam is executed by his own side for cattle thievery, despite his innocence: General Putnam needs to make an example of somebody to deter problematic troop behavior. The author's note at the end of the book poses this question to readers: "Could the United States have made its way without that agony and killing? That is probably a question that you will have to answer for yourself" (215). What if the answer were no? Would all that agony and killing have been worth it?

Loyalties during World War II are problematized in Betty Greene's *Summer of My German Soldier* and Mary Downing Hahn's *Stepping on the Cracks*. In the former, a part-Jewish girl helps hide an escaped German prisoner of war; in the latter, two girls help hide a U.S. army pacifist deserter, even as the one girl's brother is off fighting (and dying) in combat in Europe. In general, as I have argued elsewhere, stories that depict characters making difficult moral choices, as they are torn between conflicting values and competing loyalties, map philosophically rich terrain. Such stories refuse to offer facile, moralizing oppositions between the obvious right thing to do and the obvious wrong thing to do, as comically presented in the popular *Highlights Magazine* cartoon feature, Goofus and Gallant (Mills, "Beyond Goofus and Gallant"). Philosophically rich stories do not preach, but probe and ponder.

Even novels that depict a completely problematic past can raise fascinating philosophical questions about how people could have helped seeing how problematic this past was. Sheila Gordon's 1987 novel of apartheid, *Waiting for the Rain*, depicts a friendship between two boys: Frikkie, a white child of privilege; and Tengo, the black boy who works on Frikkie's farm before growing up to become a freedom fighter. When the two meet later in life, Frikkie tries to defend himself against Tengo's accusations: "It's not fair, Tengo. You can't blame *me* for everything that's wrong with this country." Tengo replies, "I'm not blaming you for that . . . I'm blaming you for not *knowing*. For not *wanting* to know" (195). Readers can ask themselves: *should* Frikki have known that apartheid was wrong? And to what contemporary practices might we currently be wrongfully blind?

CONTEMPORARY REALISTIC FICTION

Finally, philosophical and ethical questions confront us not only in the fantastic future or in the re-created past, but in the here and now. Once again, philosophically rich fiction for young readers will not be books that convey a simple moral message such as "Bullying is bad," or even somewhat more complex moral messages such as "It is wrong not only to be a bully but to be a bystander to bullying." Instead, the strongest titles, from a philosophical point of view, pose conceptual and normative questions without insisting on any single correct answer. Some of the concepts explored by realistic fiction are close to the concerns of a child's everyday life. What is a family? Who is a friend? What is it to be normal? These are joined by normative questions: How desirable is it to be normal? What should we do when different values point us in different directions? What is worth standing up for, and at what price?

Let me just give a very few examples here. Many children's novels show children in the process of forming or re-forming a family, or trying to find a family for themselves in some unconventional way. Katherine Paterson's National Book Award-winning *The Great Gilly Hopkins* shows foster child Gilly fixated on reuniting with the mother who has abandoned her and whom she continues to idealize. The reader can see what Gilly cannot: that her new foster family, headed by loving Maime Trotter, is in all important ways as perfect a family as anyone could hope to find. Similarly, in Peg Kehret's recent *Runaway Twin*, 13-year-old Sunny Skyland, orphaned at age 3 and separated from her twin sister, Starr, is now living in her 7th foster home with a kind and loving foster mother. But Sunny sets off on a journey to find her sister (which to her means finding her family), a journey that allows Sunny, and the reader, to explore the question of what it truly means to be a family. *Between Mom and Jo* by Julie Anne Peters takes as its starting point the loss its protagonist experiences when his two lesbian mothers separate, and he is in danger of losing his relationship with his nonbiological mom, Jo: what is it to be a mother? Carol Lynch Williams's hilarious and heart-wrenching novel, *If I Forget, You Remember*, focuses on the bond between its child protagonist and her increasingly senile grandmother: in what ways does loss of memory compromise one's ability to engage in a meaningful relationship with others? What role does memory play in sustaining family ties?

Beverly Cleary's delightful *Ramona and Her Father* explores not what it is to be a family, but what it is to be a happy family. Ramona's father has lost his job; he's unsuccessfully trying to stop smoking; tensions abound. At one point Ramona wails, "[W]hy can't we be a happy family?" (158). Her father delivers his reply: "I have news for you, Ramona . . . We *are* a happy family." He goes on to explain, "No family is perfect. Get that idea out of your head. And nobody is perfect either. All we can do is work at it. And we do" (158). Readers can debate how much imperfection is compatible with judging the life of a family to be overall a happy one: what is it to be a happy person, a happy family? What is a happy life?

Joey Pigsza Loses Control by Jack Gantos problematizes the concept of what it is to be normal, a question that grips Joey as he struggles with his out-of-control attention deficit disorder. In a wonderful scene, Joey is admiring a department store mannequin, with his perfect hair, nose, chin, skin, and feet: "I just kept staring at him. There he is, I thought, the perfect kid, and I bet he is perfectly *normal* too." Joey hops up next to the mannequin and tries to imitate his perfect normality, but soon this becomes boring, and he then tries to attract the attention of passersby by various antics:

> I leaned way forward and stuck out my tongue until my mouth started to ache. People just walked by as if it was nothing. I crossed my eyes and drooled so much it dripped off my chin. Nothing. I did fake hiccups. Nothing. Nobody seemed to notice, because no matter how weird I was, they were just as weird. People argued and picked their noses and swatted their kids and talked to themselves and pulled at their tight underwear and spit chewing gum out in the corners and wiped their dirty hands on the clothes and sang off key and did all kinds of strange things that I did too, which made me feel like I was normal like they were and not perfect like my mannequin buddy. (109–10)

What a perfect entrée into a discussion about the nature and value of what it is to be normal. (For a different treatment of the same question, see *Define Normal* by Julie Anne Peters.) Echoing John Stuart Mill's discussion of liberty and individuality in *On Liberty*, readers can debate why, and under which circumstances, we should or should not want to be "normal." What is the value for our collective life together of having regulative social norms? Might that value sometimes be best served by subverting or challenging norms?

Many children's books show young characters facing crucial choices about how they should act. As I suggested above, the more genuinely difficult the choice, the more philosophical the story that builds to it. The choice, for example, between whether to be true to yourself or to make yourself over to please the popular crowd is not going to make readers ask themselves, "Hmm. Now what *should* she do here?" Oliver Wendell Holmes famously said that hard cases make bad law, but hard choices make good philosophy. Often in children's fiction the choice will be whether to keep a friend's confidence or to seek adult help to save the friend from an intolerable living situation (*Daphne's Book* by Mary Downing Hahn) or whether to follow moral rules or break them to secure some important objective (*Shiloh* by Phyllis Reynolds Naylor). This kind of choice is an entrée into discussions about deontological (duty-based) imperatives such as "keep promises" and "tell the truth" as opposed to consequentialist concerns for happiness and the welfare of all those affected by the act in question (Mills 1999).

While questions drawn from ethics and social/philosophy dominate philosophically rich children's literature, other areas of philosophy occasionally are engaged as well. Andrew Clements's middle grade novel *Frindle* invites discussion of issues in the philosophy of language. Stalling for time in class, Nick asks where words in the dictionary come from; calling his bluff, his teacher assigns him to write a paper on how words get their meaning. Nick decides to create his own word, "frindle," an alternative word to refer to a pen. The word catches on around school, to the great displeasure of Nick's teacher, and then spreads in the wider world, until a generation later the word actually makes its way into the latest definitive edition of the dictionary. Here readers can consider what gives a word its meaning and how language is created and changed.

In addition to locating books that foreground philosophical reflection, I would also encourage teachers to be sensitive to philosophically and morally interesting questions that emerge "along the way" within a book: questions that may not be central to the story line as it unfolds, but that nonetheless present fodder for discussion. Consider this one priceless moment in Melissa Thomson's recent chapter book, *Keena Ford and the Secret Journal Mix-Up*, when "mean muffinhead" Tiffany explains to Keena that the parent-dictated sentences she is copying onto her homework paper don't count as plagiarism because "it's not copying when a mom writes it. My mother told me so!" What an ethical conversation opener that one line could be.

As a children's book author myself, reflecting on my own creative process, I have found that the theme of a book is generally a marker that points the way to a philosophical question, broadly understood. In writing my books, I find a philosophical question at the heart of many of them. *Losers, Inc.* features an average-achieving boy who feels inferior to his more successful older brother. Its central theme/question becomes this: should we define ourselves primarily in comparison to others? The seventh grade protagonist of *Standing Up to Mr. O.* refuses to dissect animals in her biology class: Is this practice as morally problematic as Maggie thinks it is? (Her lab partner, for one, certainly doesn't think so.) In *How Oliver Olson Changed the World*, an overprotected third grader strikes a blow for his own independence in the process of making a "protest" diorama of the solar system on behalf of poor excluded planet Pluto. In the course of the book, Oliver comes to reconsider his defense of Pluto, by considering the question: is the fact that something has always been done a certain way a good reason to continue doing it that way, and if not, why not? In my view, these are all philosophical questions—questions about identity, about animal rights, about autonomy and the value of tradition—lying not very far beneath the surface of a child's day-to-day life.

CONCLUSION

Marcel Proust is widely quoted as saying "The real voyage of discovery consists not in seeking new landscapes, but in having new eyes." Philosophically rich children's books provide a way of giving children new eyes, or perhaps more modestly, prescription eyeglasses that reveal unsettling questions that call for thoughtful consideration. Recognizing these questions means reading a book not only to find out what happens, but why it matters, what it meant, why some author thought this chunk of human experience was worth recording between the front and back cover of a book. It means focusing not only on what, but why, or by subjecting the "what" to critical moral scrutiny. When children begin to learn this, they are on their way to becoming philosophers, or at the least, to growing up to be more active citizens and more thoughtful human beings.

REFERENCES

Cleary, B. (1975) *Ramona and Her Father* New York: HarperCollins.
Clements, A. (1996) *Frindle* New York: Simon & Schuster.
Collier, J.L. and Collier, C. (1974) *My Brother Sam Is Dead* New York: Simon & Schuster.
Cooper, S. (1973) *The Dark Is Rising* New York: McElderry/Atheneum.
Gantos, J. (1998) *Joey Pigsza Loses Control* New York: Farrar, Straus & Giroux.
Gordon, S. (1987) *Waiting for the Rain* New York: Orchard Books.
Greene, B. (1973) *Summer of My German Soldier* New York: Penguin.
Hahn, M.D. (1991) *Stepping on the Cracks* New York: Clarion.
———. (1983) *Daphne's Book* New York: Clarion.
Kehret, P. (2009) *Runaway Twin* New York: Dutton.
Kern, E.M. (2003) *The Wisdom of Harry Potter: What Our Favorite Hero Teaches Us about Moral Choices* Amherst, NY: Prometheus Books.
L'Engle, M. (1962) *A Wrinkle in Time* New York: Farrar, Straus & Giroux..
Lowry, L.(1993) *The Giver* New York: Houghton Mifflin.
Mill, J. S. (1978, orig. 1859) *On Liberty* Indianapolis, IN: Hackett.
Mills, C. (2012) "Beyond Goofus and Gallant: Morally Charged Choices in Morally Complex Children's Literature" In *Philosophy and Education: Introducing*

Philosophy to Young People (eds. Mohr Lone, J and Israeloff, R.) Newcastle, UK: Cambridge Scholars Press.

———. (2009) *How Oliver Olson Changed the World* New York: Farrar, Straus & Giroux.

———. (1999) "The Structure of the Moral Dilemma in *Shiloh*" *Children's Literature* 27: 185–197.

———. (1998) *Standing Up to Mr. O* New York: Farrar, Straus & Giroux.

———. (1997) *Losers, Inc.* New York: Farrar, Straus & Giroux.

Naylor, P. R. (1991) *Shiloh* New York: Atheneum.

Okorafor-Mbachu, N. (2007) *The Shadow Speaker* New York: Jump at the Sun/Hyperion Books.

Paterson, K. (1978) *The Great Gilly Hopkins* New York: Crowell.

Peters, J. A. (2006) *Between Mom and Jo* Boston: Little, Brown.

———. (2000) *Define Normal* Boston: Little, Brown.

Plato (1991) *Republic* Translated by Bloom, A. New York: Basic Books.

Reeder, C. (1989) *Shades of Gray* New York: Simon & Schuster.

Rowling, J. K. (1999a) *Harry Potter and the Prisoner of Azkaban* New York: Scholastic/Arthur A. Levine.

———. (1999b) *Harry Potter and the Sorcerer's Stone* New York: Scholastic/Arthur A. Levine.

———. (1998) *Harry Potter and the Chamber of Secrets* New York: Scholastic/Arthur A. Levine.

Taylor, M. (1976) *Roll of Thunder, Hear My Cry* New York: Dial.

Thomson, M. (2010) *Keena Ford and the Secret Journal Mix-Up* New York: Dial.

Weaver, W. (2007) *Defect*. New York: Farrar, Straus & Giroux.

Williams, C. L. (1998) *If I Forget, You Remember* New York: Delacorte.

13 The Moral Impulse
Talking About Moral Philosophy and Genocide with Middle School Students

Jana Mohr Lone

Why do some people act to help others and other people become bystanders?

What keeps people silent in the face of moral wrongs?

Is indifference morally wrong?

Can inaction, or being a bystander, be a morally acceptable choice?

Do we have a moral obligation to help others?

What is a community? What shapes its identity?

How does knowledge of past wrongs affect our moral responsibilities?

Is it morally permissible to resist authority in certain situations? Is it ever morally obligatory to resist?

Who has the power to forgive oppressors? Is forgiveness always possible?

What is courage?

Middle school students often face difficult moral choices. What is the right thing to do when a peer is being treated badly by friends or acquaintances? Should you try to help a student being bullied, or should you go along with the crowd so as not to call attention to yourself and make yourself a possible victim? What obligation do you have to speak out when something is happening that you believe is wrong? To help middle school students approach these questions thoughtfully, we can turn toward philosophical inquiry, and invite students to consider such moral issues as the consequences of inaction and silence, and whether obedience to authority is always right.

Some years ago, I became aware that middle school students at our local school were reading *The Diary of Anne Frank*; and *Night*, by Elie Wiesel, but were not really engaged in examining the moral issues provoked by the Holocaust and other genocides. I approached the eighth grade English teacher about visiting her classroom to facilitate discussions about the moral questions raised by these novels. Eventually the eighth grade history teacher also became involved, as well as the art teacher. The unit developed into a series of sessions on moral philosophy and genocide; a literature and genocide unit; and a language arts/history project with a theme entitled "In Honor of the Human Spirit," in which the students create a thematic essay using video (a copy of the assignment is in Appendix I). As part of this unit, many of the students also read *Daniel's Story* by Carol Matas, a novel about a Jewish family in Nazi Germany. The art teacher engaged students in creating line drawings that illustrated their reactions to learning about the Holocaust.

The unit involves inquiry about some of the moral questions connected with the Holocaust and other genocides, and is taught primarily through the use of film. The entire eighth grade participates in the series of seven sessions, each 80 minutes long. The first two sessions involve an introduction to philosophy generally and to moral philosophy in particular. The remaining five sessions consist of viewing and discussing four different films (the resources for which include eight key questions for each film, as well as thought experiments and other discussion-generating prompts). Over the years, we have also involved parents in this unit, inviting them to attend and participate. Parents love being involved, as the opportunities for working in middle school classrooms are limited, and this creates opportunities for parents and their children to continue these discussions at home. In several years, we have invited Holocaust survivors to visit the school and speak to the students.

We designed the curriculum to help the students think for themselves about some of the difficult questions raised by the history of the Holocaust and other genocides. We consider the nature of indifference and the way that indifference and silence are central aspects of genocide—the behavior and choices of bystanders. Is indifference morally wrong? What is the difference between inaction and indifference? Our discussions touch on issues that are meaningful to the students, including peer pressure, bullying, and the rights of students.

The following is a detailed depiction of the unit, including a description of the content of each session and the key questions involved.

INTRODUCTION TO PHILOSOPHY: PLATO'S *CAVE* ALLEGORY

We start with a general philosophy unit, to give the students some background about the discipline of philosophy and an introduction into philosophical inquiry. The first class focuses on epistemology, or what can we know about the world? We read Plato's *Allegory of the Cave* and talk about how we can know things about the world, as well as related issues. Here is the adaptation of the story we use:

Plato imagines people living as prisoners in an underground cave that has a wide entrance open to the light. They have lived in the cave all of their lives, and so it is all they know. These people's bodies are chained at the legs and neck, so that they can only look straight ahead at the back wall of the cave. They cannot see one another. Behind the prisoners is a fire burning and in front of the fire is a high wall, which acts as a kind of puppet stage. Along this wall, people carry various artificial objects, such as the figures of men and animals.

The prisoners can see only the shadows of the objects, which are cast by the firelight onto the cave wall in front of them. The cave has an echo so that when the people in back of them speak, the prisoners believe the sounds come from the shadows on the cave wall. Since the cave dwellers have been in this position since birth, they believe that these shadows are all that exists.

Imagine, Plato suggests, that one of the prisoners manages to free himself from the chains. He turns around and is overwhelmed and distressed by the sharp light of the fire and the clarity of the figures, because until now he has seen only their shadows. Eventually, the prisoner climbs over the wall and gets past the fire to the world outside the cave. At first, he is even more distraught because of the strong light of the sun, which causes him to be unable to see. But over time he begins to make out the objects in the world more clearly, and struck by the world's beauty—its color, form and vibrancy—he understands that what he has all his life thought was reality was just shadows.

The former cave dweller could have stayed out in the world and enjoyed the beauty he found. But he feels sorry for his former fellow prisoners, and so he goes back down and tries to convince the others still imprisoned there that the shadows on the wall are just flickering reflections of "real" things. But they don't believe it, and they become enraged. They think he is mad.

After we read the allegory, the students break up into small groups and discuss the following questions:

1. Would you want to be released from the cave? Imagine that the cave was all you had ever known—how do you think it would feel to be outside it?
2. What is like the cave in our world? What are the things that we think are real but are only shadows?
3. How much of what we say we know, our ideas and beliefs, are shaped by other people? In what way does this take place? What about television, movies, and video games? The Internet? How do these things influence the way we see the world?
4. Are there things you know to be true? What are they, and how do you know them?

I've found that, in answer to the first question, most young people are inclined to respond quickly that they would want to be released from the cave. They express their curiosity about what else might be "out there," their desire for adventure, and their interest in knowing the truth; they imagine that they would regret it eventually if they didn't leave the cave. They envision the cave as a kind of prison, and it's hard for them to imagine not wanting to escape it.

Therefore, before they break up into groups, I ask the students to think about the first question by imagining that, instead of a cave, an alien from another galaxy appears and announces that everything they have experienced in their lives is an illusion. This alien, who radiates truth and kindness, will show them the true world. This will mean, however, leaving everyone they know and love, and the experience will likely change their lives and make it very challenging when they return, as only they will know the "truth." When I put it this way, the students are far more divided in their answers to the question about leaving the cave.

After they have had the chance to discuss the questions in their small groups, we come back together as a large group and debrief the groups' responses to the questions and have a class conversation about the issues raised by the allegory. We talk about what might be the basis for knowledge, and the differences between knowledge and belief. What is necessary for knowledge? On what do we base our beliefs and views?

MORAL PHILOSOPHY: PLATO'S "RING OF GYGES"

The second session in the unit is an introduction to moral philosophy. Because we will be exploring the moral questions raised by genocide, it's important that the students recognize when situations involve moral questions and begin to develop awareness of the moral dimension of human experience. In this session, students examine the following questions:

- What does "moral" mean?
- How do we know if a choice we are making involves a moral question?
- Why be moral at all?
- Are there moral standards that are common to all humanity?
- How do we know what the right thing to do is in particular situations?
- What does it mean to live a good life?

Moral questions are generally implicated in situations in which we are evaluating the effects of our actions on other people as well as ourselves. Whether to have vanilla or chocolate ice cream is not a moral question, for instance, but a question of taste or mood. However, if our choice about what ice cream to eat depends on the workplace conditions at the plant where the ice cream is produced, the decision might become a moral one.

We begin this session by reading Plato's story "The Ring of Gyges," from *The Republic*. Here is an adaptation of the story, from Gareth Matthews's *A Philosophy Startup Kit for Schoolkids* (Philosophyforkids.com)

Gyges was a shepherd in the service of the ruler of Lydia. One day there was a violent thunderstorm, and an earthquake broke open the ground and created a crater at the place where Gyges was tending his sheep. Seeing the big hole, Gyges was filled with amazement and went down into it. And there, in addition to many other wonders of which we are not told, he saw a hollow bronze horse. There were window-like openings in it, and peeping in, he saw a corpse, which seemed to be of more than human size, wearing nothing but a gold ring on its finger. He took the ring and came out of the crater.

Gyges wore the ring at the usual monthly meeting that reported to the king on the state of the flocks of sheep. As he was sitting among the others, he happened to turn the setting of the ring toward himself to the inside of his hand. When he did this, he became invisible to those sitting near him, and they went on talking as if he had gone. He wondered at this, and, fingering the ring, he turned the setting outward again and became visible. So he experimented with the ring to test whether it indeed has this power—and it did. If he turned the setting inward, he became invisible; if he turned it outward, he became visible again.

When Gyges realized that he had a ring that could make him invisible, he at once arranged to become one of the messengers sent to report to the king. And when he arrived there, he quickly became the queen's lover. With her help he attacked the king, killed him, and took over the kingdom.

The character Glaucon tells this story in a conversation with Socrates, and he asks Socrates to imagine two magic rings: one given to a morally good person and one to a person who is not morally good. Glaucon contends that there would be no difference in the way the two would behave. People only behave morally, he claims, because they are afraid of the consequences of getting caught if they behave badly.

After telling this story, I ask the students: what would you do if you had a ring that made you invisible? Students offer all kinds of possible behavior, including stealing from stores; winning at hide and seek; playing tricks on family members; getting on airplanes to travel; and, often, using the ring to help people. Every time I teach the unit, at least a couple of students declare that it would scare them to have the ring, that the power of it would change them in ways that make them uncomfortable, and that they would decline to utilize its power. The discussion usually leads to considering Glaucon's claim that we are good only because we are afraid of getting caught. Do people want to be good, or are they only good because they will get something out of it, like the approval of their parents or some other reward? What is a "morally good" person? What makes a choice the right thing to do?

We then discuss the various ways we might evaluate moral problems. It's helpful to give students some concrete problems to analyze. Two that I use frequently are now mentioned:

1. You have a friend, and you know this friend has been robbing houses and using the money for himself. You are worried about him, feel badly about the people from whom he has stolen, and you are trying to decide what to do. Should you tell someone?

2. You are spending the afternoon with a friend of yours who isn't very popular. You run into a group of your friends who invite you to go to a movie that you really want to see, and it is the last night the film is showing, but they say that your unpopular friend can't come. What is the right thing to do?

These situations inspire discussion about the ways in which we make moral choices: looking at the possible consequences, finding a moral rule that applies, paying attention to our intuitions or conscience, asking what's best for the community, etc. Middle school students often rely on a particular approach to morality—for example, relying on a rule (it's just wrong to lie!)—without having examined very deeply their own beliefs about what makes an action right or wrong. Thinking about moral problems from a wider range of viewpoints helps expand the moral universe for them, allowing them to see new options and reassess their own views.

IDENTITY AND COMMUNITY: *A CLASS DIVIDED*

After our two introductory sessions, we move into the first film of the "Moral Philosophy and Genocide" sessions. The film is titled *A Class Divided* and is a provocative work illuminating the ways in which people tend to divide into "us and them" groups.

When Martin Luther King, Jr. was assassinated in 1968, Jane Elliott, an Iowa third grade teacher, implemented an exercise in her classroom to help her students understand racism and discrimination. Elliott divided the class into two groups of students: those with brown eyes and those with blue eyes. With the class divided, she spent one day discriminating against the brown-eyed students and the next discriminating against the blue-eyed students, and encouraging the students to discriminate against each other. In 1970, the exercise was filmed by PBS. Fourteen years later, the students in the film reunited to watch the film and discuss the effect of the exercise on their lives.

During the exercise, the students labeled as the "superior" half of the third grade class for the day almost instantly take to discriminating against their peers, and even the students who were discriminated against the previous day waste no time settling into the mindset that they are now the superior group. In a very short time, Jane Elliott created an enormous gulf in her class. The exercise powerfully demonstrates the effect of the "us and them" mentality on a community. From this film come a few key questions that help facilitate moral and philosophical inquiry:

Questions

1. What happened to the children in the class?
2. How did Jane Elliott create division in the class in such a short time? What was effective about what she did?

3. What effect did the "us and them" mentality have on how the children felt about themselves and the other students in the class?
4. How do you think the classroom community changed after this activity?
5. Why do you think what Jane Elliott did affected the adults in the film years later?
6. What makes a group a community? How does a community determine who belongs to it?
7. Are communities necessarily exclusive?
8. Can I keep my individuality and still belong to a group?

The film is always compelling for students. After viewing it, we break up into small groups of four–five students each, spending about a half hour discussing the features of the film that surprised the students, whether it is natural for human beings to discriminate and when discrimination is acceptable and when it isn't, and the nature of community. Then the whole group comes back together, and we talk about the students' thoughts about the key questions.

The students generally are surprised by how quickly the third graders start to discriminate, even against children who had been their closest friends the previous hour. Reflecting about what constitutes discrimination and whether it is always wrong, whether communities are necessarily exclusive, and how easily people can accept a situation that puts them into a position of superiority over others, starts the students thinking about how an event like the Holocaust could happen. They reflect about the ways in which "us and them" groups have developed among their peers as well as in the larger community.

AUTHORITY AND CONFORMITY: *OBEDIENCE*

The "us and them" mentality, of course, is part of what shapes an environment that can lead to events like genocides. Also central to the conditions in which genocides occur are people's tendencies to conform to the situations in which they find themselves. Why do people obey authority even when they sense that what they're doing is wrong?

In this session, we watch a clip from the film *Obedience*, which documents the Milgram experiments. In the 1960s, Stanley Milgram, a professor at Yale University, decided to create an experiment to see how far people would go in situations in which they are ordered to inflict increasing pain on a protesting victim. Milgram wanted to see when a person would refuse to obey the experimenter.

The subjects of these experiments were told that the experiments were testing how learning is affected by punishment. Labeled the "teacher," the subject watched as the "learner" (who, unknown to the "teacher," was part of Milgram's team) was strapped into a chair with an electrode attached to each wrist. The "learner" was then told to memorize word pairs for a test and warned that wrong answers would result in electric shocks. Each teacher was taken to a separate room and seated before a shock generator with switches ranging from 15 volts labeled "slight shock" to 450 volts labeled "danger—severe shock." Each teacher was told to administer a shock for each wrong answer, with shocks increasing by 15 volts every time the learner responded incorrectly. The shocks were not real, but the teachers thought they were.

Before the experiment began, Milgram imagined that most volunteer subjects would refuse to give electric shocks of more than 150 volts, the point at which the learner starts to yell and complain of heart pain. A group of psychologists and psychiatrists predicted that slightly more than one-tenth of 1 percent of the volunteers (so 1 out of 1,000 people) would administer all 450 volts. However, more than 80 percent of people continued to administer shocks after reaching 150 volts, and more than 50 percent of the teachers gave the full 450 volts! The experiment and the results raise many disturbing questions about the capability of people to obey orders, even immoral ones, and even when they are in a position in which refusing to obey is as simple as saying "no" and walking away without repercussion.

The clip we watch involves one volunteer who gives the full 450 volts, even though it is clear that he is struggling with feelings of great uneasiness and discomfort about what he is doing. The clip is always somewhat shocking for many of the students. They are mystified at the way in which the subject continues to obey the person running the experiment, even when it seems apparent to him that the person receiving the shocks might be hurt or even killed by them. The students are surprised by the number of people who obey the experimenter, even when it is clear that the subjects are troubled by what they are doing. A few key questions from this film include the following:

Questions

1. The subject in the experiment is asked, "Why didn't you stop?" He answers, "He wouldn't let me." The person running the experiment said he would accept all responsibility for whatever happened. If the person hooked up to the machine had died or been seriously injured, whose responsibility would it have been?
2. Why did the subject laugh as he was giving the shocks?
3. Why do you think so many people "went all the way" in administering shocks? What encourages obedience? Is it fear of punishment? A desire to please? A need to conform to the group? A belief in authority?
4. Did the subject have a choice? What could he have done? Do you think most people usually obey the person or persons they think are the authority? Why or why not?
5. When we conform to what is expected of us (by parents, teachers, peers), are we obeying authority?

6. Is it ever right to defy authority? Why or why not? Is it ever wrong to obey authority?
7. Why do people choose to obey orders rather than resist authority, even when they sense or believe that what they are doing is morally wrong?
8. What forces influence people's moral choices?

In the small group conversations and then the larger class discussion, students tend to be interested in examining the question of responsibility and evaluating what responsibility the person inflicting the pain bears versus the responsibility of the person ordering the acts. They quickly make the connection to the Holocaust and all of the people who did not defy the edicts of the Hitler and the Nazis. We talk about the distinction between legal and moral obligation, and we analyze whether a person is ever morally obligated to defy authority and what it is about human beings that often results in widespread conformity. All of us have had experiences in which something was happening that we felt wasn't right, and yet we said and did nothing. What are the forces that lead us to silence and inaction?

RESISTANCE AND INDIFFERENCE: *HOTEL RWANDA*

It's important, in learning about genocide and the horrific acts people are capable of committing and allowing to happen, for students also to consider what it takes for people to resist such situations. What is resistance, and what leads some people to act instead of remaining silent and passive?

Hotel Rwanda tells the true story of one man's courage in the midst of genocide. When the film opens, Paul Rusesabagina, the manager of a Belgian-owned luxury hotel in Kigali, is doing his job pleasing the hotel's (mostly white) guests, the Rwandan army officers who frequent the hotel bar, and the local businessmen with whom he deals. Paul, a Hutu, is married to a Tutsi, and his children are considered mixed. When the genocide begins, Paul's Tutsi neighbors show up at his house, seeking refuge. Reluctantly, Paul takes them in and bribes a Rwandan army officer to allow him to bring them to the hotel. This is the beginning of Paul's acts to save people during the genocide. Through his connections and courage, he saved not only himself and his family, but also 1,268 innocent people. The questions this film inspires include the following:

Questions

1. At the beginning of the genocide, Paul is focused on protecting his family and doesn't want to get involved in protecting his neighbors. But over time his sense of obligation to his neighbors and others deepens. At one point, rather than abandon the people he is sheltering, he tries to send his family to safety while he stays behind. Is his decision

The Moral Impulse 161

the morally right one? Do we have greater moral obligations to our family members than to others?
2. Why didn't the international community intervene in Rwanda? Why did the foreign troops get all the foreign citizens out of Rwanda but not help the people who lived there? Should governments value the welfare of their own citizens more than that of people from other countries?
3. The UN colonel tells reporters that his troops are "peace-keepers," not "peace-makers." By UN mandate, UN troops were permitted to use their weapons only in self-defense. If the colonel had disobeyed orders and authorized his troops to fire on Interhamwe fighters, would he have done the right thing?
4. Was Paul a hero? What is a hero? What makes some people, regardless of risk, act to prevent moral wrongs, and others don't?
5. Many people who did not take part in murdering Tutsis did not help them either. Do you think they were all indifferent? What is indifference? Is indifference wrong?
6. What might be some other reasons that people did not act to help during the genocide? Is everyone who doesn't act indifferent?
7. What can we learn from the experiences of genocide survivors?
8. What small moral choices do people make in their everyday lives that can lead to them becoming either resisters or bystanders?

We watch this film in two sessions and then break up into small groups to discuss the key questions, after which we bring the class back together for a larger conversation that focuses on a few different questions. For example, Paul Rusesabagina risked his life to help his neighbors and other Rwandans. Was he morally obligated to do this? What forces led him to make the choices he did? Many people who hid Jews during the Holocaust say things like, "I didn't really think about it. I was asked to help and so I did." What is it that makes some people the kind of people who take risks to help others? Does this indicate a certain kind of character? In situations of great danger, is it wrong to protect your family and/or yourself rather than helping other people? At what point are we obligated to help others?

MAKING A DIFFERENCE: *NOT IN OUR TOWN*

When designing the unit, I decided that it should end by helping the students to envision ways they can become involved in their communities and the larger society and reflect about the kinds of people they want to become. I want them to develop an awareness of the power they have to impact the world around them.

This last session involves the film *Not in Our Town*, which describes a series of hate crimes and a town's reaction to these events. This episode of the PBS television program *We Do the Work* focuses on Billings, Montana, which came to national attention in 1993 when anti-Semitic hate crimes during Chanukah were met by solidarity from the primarily non-Jewish community, who placed menorahs in their windows to show support for the targeted Jewish population. The community pulled together a broad coalition to demonstrate to the neo-Nazi groups that hate would not be tolerated in their town. Key questions from this film are the following:

Questions

1. "The only thing necessary for the triumph of evil is for good men to do nothing." What do you think this quote by the philosopher Edmund Burke means? How does it relate to what the people in Billings did? What about Paul Rusesabagina?
2. Do you think people were scared to put up menorahs in their windows? Why or why not? If they were scared, why did they do it anyway?
3. The sheriff in the film comments that, "These hate groups have learned through experience that if a community doesn't respond, the community accepts. Silence is acceptance to them." Does the fact that hate groups see silence as acceptance mean that we are morally obligated to act when acts like the violence in Billings occur? Why or why not?
4. What keeps some people silent in the face of moral wrongs?
5. Can you think of a situation where you or someone you know accepted danger to help another person? If you refuse to help because there is danger, is that morally wrong? What about something less than danger? If I see someone being treated badly, like bullying at school, am I obligated to do something?
6. Are we morally obligated to make a positive difference in the world?
7. Is it always wrong to be a bystander? Sometimes wrong? Never wrong?
8. Can one person make a difference? Can you make a difference? How?

As part of our discussion, we ask the students to describe changes they'd like to see in school or in the larger community, and to think about how they might work to bring about such change, and to imagine the ways in which such involvement might change them. Young people often imagine that they have little power to effect change, and we talk about the dangers of adopting attitudes like "I can't do anything about this," "No one will listen to me," or "One person can't make any difference." We are committed to helping the students to recognize the power they do have and understand the importance of their voices being heard. The students often end up talking about the experience of adolescence, children's rights, and questions of justice and fairness.

At the end of the unit I ask the students to complete an evaluation form (a copy of which is included as Appendix II). They are often surprised by this, as asking middle school students to evaluate classes is unusual in public schools. Over the years, student comments and suggestions have helped enormously to improve the unit.

WHERE DO WE GO FROM HERE?

In 2008 the English and history teachers and I made a formal proposal to the local school board to adopt this curriculum in the district. As part of the proposal, we had to show that the unit helps students to meet certain state standards—for example, Washington State requires that a student "understands and applies reasoning skills to conduct research, deliberate, form, and evaluate positions through the processes of reading, writing and communicating"—and explain the academic benefits and the benefits to the school community. The unit was formally adopted in the district that year.

After six years of facilitating these sessions, this year I stepped away, and the two eighth grade teachers, Jane Orme and David Aspholm, are now teaching the unit. I think that this is a powerful model for a Philosophy in the Schools program. The unit was started as a kind of "add on" to an already-existing curriculum, and so was an easy fit with what was already going on in the classroom. As it developed, it became a more central part of the curriculum and thus was formally adopted by the school board. As the philosopher in residence, I was able to create the unit, introduce philosophy to the students, provide ongoing training for the teachers, and then relinquish the unit to them with absolute confidence.

Last year, in completing the evaluation form, one student stated: "I really liked listening to students begin to think for themselves and hearing people who I thought I knew say profound things." Being involved in moral inquiry with other students strengthens young people's awareness that they and their peers have meaningful, substantive ideas, and enhances their own ethical perspectives. This unit is not about getting students to do or believe what *we* think is right, but helping them to think *for themselves* about why certain things are right or wrong and what considerations matter when making moral decisions. The vast range of human behavior illustrated by these films leads students to better understand the complexity of such concepts as justice, obligation, right and wrong, forgiveness, and courage, and to reflect more deeply about the kind of people they want to be.

POSTSCRIPT BY JANE ORME, EIGHTH GRADE ENGLISH TEACHER, LIBERTY BELL JUNIOR/SENIOR HIGH SCHOOL, WINTHROP, WASHINGTON

The moral philosophy unit, introduced in my eighth grade English classroom six years ago, continues to flourish. This year, student teacher Elyse Fulcher, history teacher David Aspholm, and I planned the unit built on the elements described above. Our theme for this year was "Courage and Making Choices." This cross-curricular unit complements one of the main themes in the students' historically significant book choices—concern for individuals or families surviving and resisting in circumstances threatening to their well-being.

We focused on the following questions:

- Do we have a moral obligation to help others?
- Is forgiveness always possible?
- What is courage?

In history class, students investigated the choices that the colonists faced at the beginning of the American Revolution, and explored moral questions regarding choice, obligation, and courage. Near the end of the unit, we hosted a speaker from the Washington State Holocaust Education Resource Center who shared her experiences as a survivor. A key component of the unit remains the opportunity for students to engage in deep and often complex conversations. Students look forward to having serious discussions about the films, their readings, and the ethical choices that arise from historical events and their own lives. The unit enables students to think for themselves, to seek a fuller understanding of their own decision making, and to gain greater respect for one another through meaningful dialogue.

Appendix I

Video Quilt: Composing with Images Composition and Literature/U.S. History— 8th Grade

Rationale

The theme of this project is "In Honor of the Human Spirit." In this activity, you will create a thematic essay using the medium of video, focusing particularly on composing with images, text, and sound. After you select a topic, concept, or idea that relates to the theme stated above, you will create a 1½ to 2 minute movie of your chosen topic with visuals, graphics, text, audio, and visual transitions.

Procedure

Step 1: Choose a topic.
Step 2: Research your topic by taking notes from a variety of appropriate primary sources in the library and online.

Step 3: Write a one-page report focusing on the following: who the person is/ was, what the person did on behalf of others, and why the person is note- worthy. (The topic could be a group or event.) Your objective is to share what you know about this person, group, or event. Cite your sources.

Step 4: Meet with your group members and create a storyboard. Plan your story by referring to your edited one-pagers to consolidate and deter- mine the story you will tell about your topic. Use sticky notes or indi- vidual sheets of paper to move around your image ideas and text so that you can determine how you will tell the story with images and words. Transfer your ideas to the storyboard worksheets.

Step 5: Select images that relate to your topic. Use symbols and photos from the Internet as well as photos you have shot and uploaded. Make sure your photos are in focus and provide a reflection of the story you are telling. Save in your folder on the school server. Use a variety of images.

Step 6: Preplan the potential images with text by again using the storyboard,

Step 7: With your group members, open Movie Maker and review the pro- cess of creating a movie project. Make sure you understand how to make a movie and how to *save* your work. Use a flash drive to save folders of images and the work in progress.

Step 8: Select images, symbols, pictures and text and organize/tell your story using Movie Maker. Again, refer to your storyboard. While some of your text will be visible, remember that you will use audio to narrate and tell the story.

Step 9: Include your creative piece—poem, dialogue, photo images.

Step 10: Finalize images, text, and creative piece in linear order. Select ap- propriate special effects and transitions. Ask yourself if your project is a well-told story.

Step 11: Select and include appropriate music track.

Step 12: Provide an oral interpretation of text using a microphone. Make sure you have rehearsed your text so that the reading is smooth and flawless.

Step 13: Once you have closely revised and edited your movie, go to Movie Tasks and choose "finish movie." This is completely different than "sav- ing the project." Refer to "Using Movie Maker to Create Photomontage Movies," #15, for detailed instructions on how to save. Use your pro- vided flash drive.

Related Lessons

- Research: useful and appropriate websites; correct bibliography; note taking.
- Summary Writing: You are asked to respond to the question "What do you want people to know about this person, group, or event?"
- Image Search: organizing files/images; searching for images.
- Movie Maker instructions: manipulating images, using special effects and transitions, uploading audio files (music and voice), saving cor- rectly to home file and flash drives.

- Images and Text: selecting high impact words and phrases that tell the story, emphasis on "show not tell"; content includes responses to questions such as who, what, when, where, why. (You should imagine that this person or group has been selected for a humanity award, and your job is to tell their story with a minimum of words and images.)
- Tell the story by using description, statistics, quotations, examples, definitions, and repetition/restatement.
- Audio: Voice-clear, articulated phrasing appropriate to words and phrases being read; Music-background emphasis, appropriate for images and subject.

Expectations and Requirements

- Final draft one page summary of topic from each student—typed 12pt, 1½ lines spacing.
- All students in the group must participate in the creation of the movie—no loitering—divide the tasks so that all group members are full participants.
- Extensive "re-vision" and editing—make sure usage and spelling are correct.
- Creative piece should be an integral part of the movie.
- Last slide-photo of team and credits (cite resources correctly).
- After completing the project, all students will complete a self-assessment of their individual work on the assignment and are expected to explain their learning.

Appendix II

Philosophy/Moral Philosophy and Genocide Unit Evaluaton

1. Introduction to philosophy (Plato's *Allegory of the Cave*)
2. Introduction to moral philosophy (Plato's "Ring of Gyges")
3. Identity and Community (*A Class Divided*—blue eyes/ brown eyes exercise)
4. Authority and Conformity (*Obedience*—electric shock experiments)
5. Resistance and Indifference (*Hotel Rwanda*—two sessions)
6. Making a Difference (*Not in Our Town*—hate groups in Billings, Montana)

What do you think you will remember from this unit?

What did you like most about this unit?

What did you like least about this unit?

Do you have any suggestions for improving this unit?

THANK YOU!

14 Engaging Students—of Any Age—in Philosophical Inquiry

How Doing Philosophy for Children Changed the Way I Teach Philosophy to College Students

David A. Shapiro

Like most of my philosophy teacher colleagues, I didn't need much incentive, when I was a student, to be motivated to read and discuss philosophy. As a Philosophy major, I loved poring over classic and contemporary texts. Few things gave me more pleasure than talking about them with classmates, family members, friends, and even, when I got my nerve up, professors. I joyfully sat down with a pot of coffee and Descartes' *Meditations* for a marathon reading session; I happily underlined and annotated Mill's essay "Utilitarianism" for hours on end; I even wrote my own Cliff's notes version of Hume's "Dialogues on Natural Religion" so when it came time to write my paper on it, I'd be all set up and ready to go.

So, it's probably no surprise that when I first began teaching philosophy classes as a graduate student at the University of Washington, I was unprepared for how unexcited my own students were about the prospect of delving into philosophical texts and ideas. What was surprising—at least to me—was how much effort is required to engage many students in introductory philosophy classes in not just the ideas we are exploring, but the texts in which those ideas are often so beautifully presented.

I'm not ashamed to admit that when I first started teaching Introduction to Philosophy, I was clueless. I fully expected all I'd have to do was assign readings that I liked, and the next day, every student would come to class, having read the material, taken copious notes, prepared with lots of questions, and eager to discuss the esoteric points and troubling implications of arguments and conclusions of the material under investigation—just like I did when I was in their shoes.

These days, by contrast, I have in my teaching quiver a few arrows that can assist in slaying the beast of apathy that (often, but not always) afflicts students when they are presented with philosophical texts—even those that we, as philosophy teachers, have long loved.

Most of what I've learned about motivating college students has come to me from doing philosophy with precollege students. Concurrent with my first baby steps as a teacher of undergraduate philosophy, I was regularly working with middle school students in a philosophical community of inquiry. What I learned about doing philosophy with 11- and 12-year-olds didn't merely inform my classroom approach with 19- to 22-year-olds; it pretty much came to define it. I'm quite confident, in fact, that had I not been doing philosophy with young children as a neophyte instructor, I wouldn't have had the success (such as it is) in doing philosophy with young adults that has encouraged me to still be in the game today. Had I continued down that same instructional path I found myself on in those early days of teaching at the University of Washington, I probably would have despaired of the whole thing and never gone on to be teaching full time at Cascadia Community College.

And I attribute that, as I said, mainly to doing philosophy with kids.

So, in this chapter, I will discuss some of the transitions I went through as I learned from doing philosophy with precollege students about doing philosophy with college students. To do this, I will use, as an example, a philosophical text most teachers of Introduction to Philosophy courses are familiar with—Bertrand Russell's widely anthologized chapter from *Problems of Philosophy*, "The Value of Philosophy." The first time I assigned college students to read "The Value of Philosophy" was the first week of my first quarter teaching my own Introduction to Philosophy class. It was at the University of Washington, where with a newly minted master's degree in the graduate program in philosophy, I was eligible to teach my own stand-alone classes. I had arranged the course topically, and the first unit explored, as does Russell's essay, the purpose and value of studying philosophy. It was the third or fourth class of our five-day-a-week schedule, and I arrived in the classroom confident that students would have been as compelled by Russell's prose as I was and as ready and eager as me to talk about the ideas and arguments in his essay.

"So," I began, once students had settled into their seats. "What did you think of the essay?"

I was met with dead silence; in the film version, you'd hear the crickets-chirping soundtrack.

"What questions do people have? What made sense? What didn't?"

As my repeated attempts to solicit discussion about the piece repeatedly fell flat, I began to flail around even more. Eventually, it became obvious that most of the students hadn't done the reading, and most of those who had either didn't really get what Russell was saying or else found it, they seemed to indicate, so obvious that it wasn't worth talking about. I spent the rest of class doing my best to walk students through the essay, essentially giving a lecture, a mode of teaching that, for this material, I found only slightly less boring and lifeless than did my class. Basically, the day was a disaster. Fortunately for my psyche, I had a Philosophy for Children lesson to conduct that afternoon with a local fifth grade class I'd been working with for a few weeks, and thus began my first transition from a teacher who simply presented philosophical material to one who made a concerted effort to really engage student in philosophical inquiry.

In working with this fifth grade class, we were also wondering about the nature and value of philosophy. To motivate those discussions, though, I used a piece of writing that students took to immediately, without any prompting: Lewis Carroll's *Alice in Wonderland*, specifically the "Mad Hatter's Tea Party" chapter. We read it aloud together. The students generated questions they were interested in exploring, and we had a freewheeling discussion for nearly an hour about all sorts of topics, including the difference between saying what you mean and meaning with you say; the nature of time and time travel; and, of course, why a raven is like a writing desk.

It didn't occur to me at the time that I might import some of the techniques I was using in the Philosophy for Children class into my college class; instead, I came back to the undergraduates the next time with an outline that I figured would provide the proper "scaffolding" for students to successfully delve into Russell's prose. I handed out a paper to the class that looked something like this:

Outline of Bertrand Russell's *Value of Philosophy*, from Russell, Bertrand, *The Problems of Philosophy* (1912)

1. Russell asks why philosophy should be studied
   a. He points out many people consider it useless hair-splitting
      i. But this is because those people don't understand what philosophy is trying to do
   b. To understand the point of philosophy, we have to free our minds from the prejudices of "practical men."
2. Philosophy aims primarily at knowledge
   a. But it's the kind of knowledge that "gives unity and system to the body of the sciences"
   b. And it also explores questions that, by their very nature, are unanswerable
      i. Has the universe a purpose?
      ii. What is consciousness?
      iii. Do good and evil really exist?
3. The value of philosophy is to be sought in its very uncertainty
   a. ". . . while diminishing our feeling of certainty as to what things are, it greatly increases our knowledge as to what may be . . ."
4. Also, through the greatness of the objects which it contemplates, philosophy expands our minds
5. The study of philosophy encourages us to think about things other than ourselves
   a. ". . . true philosophic contemplation . . . finds its satisfaction in every enlargement of the not-self . . ."
   b. Thus, the study of philosophy makes us citizens of the universe.

6. Conclusion: "Philosophy is to be studied not for the sake of any definite answers to its questions . . . but rather for the sake of the questions themselves."

   a. And above all, because "through the greatness of the universe
   which philosophy contemplates, the mind is also rendered great."

My assumption was that by following this outline, students would be able
to easily grasp the main points of the essay, and that, as a result, great discussion would follow.

But pretty much the only question that came up after students looked
over the outline was, "Is this going to be on the test?" Again, I despaired
of much real philosophy occurring that day and went back to more or less
holding forth on Russell's views, an instructional strategy I thought I had
vowed to avoid.

It's not as if I had never had any success with outlines. The summer be-
fore, working with a group of fifth and sixth graders in the University of
Washington's Robinson Center for Gifted and Talented Youth's Summer
Challenge Program (a three-week long all-day philosophy "camp" experi-
ence entitled "The Meaning of Life: Philosophy and Its Application in the
Real World"), I'd had the kids generate their own outline of Descartes's
First Meditation.

We did so in two steps. First, I had the students "translate" Descartes's
prose into something that was more familiar to their ears. So, for instance,
one group turned this:

> Several years have now elapsed since I first became aware that I had
> accepted, even from my youth, many false opinions for true, and that
> consequently what I afterward based on such principles was highly
> doubtful; and from that time I was convinced of the necessity of under-
> taking once in my life to rid myself of all the opinions I had adopted,
> and of commencing anew the work of building from the foundation, if
> I desired to establish a firm and abiding superstructure in the sciences."
> (Descartes, 133)

into this:

> I used to believe a lot of lies. If I ever wanted to know anything, I had
> to start all over.

I next had the students trade their "translations" with each other. Each
student would then circle the sentence in the translation that he or she
thought expressed the key idea of the passage. I then gathered students
into groups of six to eight. Each student in the group read aloud the sentence that had been circled. The group's task, then, was to construct a
(more or less) coherent outline of what Descartes was saying by arranging

their sentences in a proper order. I can't say that every group's six to eight sentence essay was a perfectly faithful re-creation of Descartes's ideas, but it was certainly a lively, engaging, and philosophically intriguing exercise: a far cry from what happened in my college class where outlines were concerned.

Because of the success I'd had starting from questions when doing philosophy with precollege students, I figured what my Introduction students needed were some questions of their own. I provided them in the next class, with a handout that looked like this:

Inquiry Starters for Russell, "The Value of Philosophy"

1. How do the goods that philosophy seeks to achieve differ from those that the physical sciences seek to achieve?
2. What is a "practical" person? Why do practical persons find philosophy to be a waste of time? Who is your archetypical practical person?
3. What kind of knowledge does philosophy seek to acquire?
4. What are some philosophical questions for which philosophers have no answer?
5. How does philosophy free us from the "tyranny of custom?" Do you think it has its own tyrannies?
6. What does it mean to contemplate the "not-self?"
7. How does philosophical contemplation enlarge the self?
8. How does the act of philosophical contemplation carry over into everyday life? What do you think about this? A good or bad thing?
9. What does Russell think is the greatest benefit that comes from pursuing philosophy? What do you think?

"Let's answer these together!," I cheerfully announced at the outset of class. "Who wants to start?"

Since no one did, I jumped in with my response, pointing out the passage in the text where Russell makes the point. Students may not have been very impressed, but they were sufficiently savvy to realize that apparently, I already had in mind the answer I was looking for, so when we proceeded to the next question, they just waited me out until I offered the response they implicitly knew I wanted.

We dragged ourselves (or more to the point, I dragged them) through the remaining questions on the sheet, basically once more lecturing—albeit slightly more interactively (there were questions, at least!)—as I'd done earlier.

It was after that class that I realized—as I should have from my Philosophy for Kids experience—that the key to a good discussion had to be having it be motivated by the students' own questions, not mine. Here again marked another transition from passive presenter of material to active participant in classroom activities.

So, next time I came to class, I used the standard "community of inquiry" model that was familiar to me from my work in precollege classrooms: we would read together some text that had philosophical ideas embedded in it; students would write down questions inspired by the piece; and then, after putting those questions up on the blackboard, would select (usually by voting) which ones we wanted to explore together.

I handed out the following excerpt from Russell:

Excerpt from Bertrand Russell, *Problems of Philosophy, Chapter XV*

The value of philosophy is, in fact, to be sought largely in its very uncertainty. The man who has no tincture of philosophy goes through life imprisoned in the prejudices derived from common sense, from the habitual beliefs of his age or his nation, and from convictions which have grown up in his mind without the co-operation or consent of his deliberate reason. To such a man the world tends to become definite, finite, obvious; common objects rouse no questions, and unfamiliar possibilities are contemptuously rejected. As soon as we begin to philosophize, on the contrary, we find, as we saw in our opening chapters, that even the most everyday things lead to problems to which only very incomplete answers can be given. Philosophy, though unable to tell us with certainty what is the true answer to the doubts which it raises, is able to suggest many possibilities which enlarge our thoughts and free them from the tyranny of custom. Thus, while diminishing our feeling of certainty as to what things are, it greatly increases our knowledge as to what they may be; it removes the somewhat arrogant dogmatism of those who have never travelled into the region of liberating doubt, and it keeps alive our sense of wonder by showing familiar things in an unfamiliar aspect.

Apart from its utility in showing unsuspected possibilities, philosophy has a value—perhaps its chief value—through the greatness of the objects which it contemplates, and the freedom from narrow and personal aims resulting from this contemplation. The life of the instinctive man is shut up within the circle of his private interests: family and friends may be included, but the outer world is not regarded except as it may help or hinder what comes within the circle of instinctive wishes. In such a life there is something feverish and confined, in comparison with which the philosophic life is calm and free. The private world of instinctive interests is a small one, set in the midst of a great and powerful world which must, sooner or later, lay our private world in ruins. Unless we can so enlarge our interests as to include the whole outer world, we remain like a garrison in a beleaguered fortress, knowing that the enemy prevents escape and that ultimate surrender is inevitable. In such a life there is no peace, but a constant strife between the insistence of desire and the powerlessness of will. In one way or another, if our life is to be great and free, we must escape this prison and this strife. (Russell, 24)

We read it aloud together—in fact, we only read the first paragraph. Students came up with lots of questions without worrying whether they were sufficiently "philosophical." Some of them are included here:

- "What does it mean to be certain?"
- "What is knowledge?"
- "Why is Russell so sexist?"
- "Do things grow in our minds?"
- "Why do we obey custom?"
- "How can we keep our sense of wonder alive?"
- "What makes something valuable?"

We ending up talking about several of the above questions, but the one that students were most intrigued about was "What makes something valuable?" In discussion, without much prompting on my part, they come up with the distinction between intrinsically valuable and instrumentally valuable which, to my way of thinking, is one of the key points that Russell is making regarding the value of philosophy. Eventually, this brought us back to the essay and thankfully, for all involved, enabled us to put a cap on it and prepare for moving on to the next topic and reading, which was epistemology and, to begin with, Descartes's *First Meditation*.

Thinking about what had happened with the first topic and reading, and how my philosophy with kids experience informed what turned out, at last, to be reasonably successful, I resolved to start our unit on Descartes with the translation and outline exercise I used the previous summer with the Summer Challenge students. While I have to admit that it wasn't quite as successful as it had been with the fifth and sixth graders, it certainly got our exploration of Descartes off on the right foot and led, eventually, to a much higher level of student participation than I'd been experiencing in the class so far.

Plus, my learning also went the other way as well. Based on the "What makes something valuable?" exercise I did with the college students, I subsequently developed the following exercise for use in precollege classrooms:

LESSON PLAN: WHAT'S WORTH DOING?

Question/Topic: What is the meaning of life?
Age Group: 6th grade and up
Time: about 20 minutes
Materials: Students need a sheet of paper and something to write with

Description

This exercise is intended to get participants thinking about value, especially as it pertains to the value of the things that we do. In high school and college classes, I typically have students read a selection from Bertrand Russell's widely-anthologized piece, "The Value of Philosophy," but that isn't required. In the essay, Russell argues that the value of philosophy is not to be found in the answers it provides, but rather in the questions it encourages us to think about. In doing so, he opens up a distinction between intrinsic value (things that are valuable in and of themselves) and instrumental value (things that are valuable because they enable us to achieve some other value.) The hoped-for outcome from this activity is that students develop a better understanding of these concepts, and that they come to ponder together the degree to which philosophy, as a discipline and a practice, has either.

I begin the exercise by posing the question, "What's worth doing?" Students are then asked to write down ten things they consider worthwhile to do. I encourage them to be honest with themselves and really think about what they consider worthwhile. I emphasize that I'm not looking for a "right" answer, nor do I expect them to offer suggestions that would necessarily be approved by their parents and teachers; I really want to know what they really consider worth doing, no matter what that is.

When they've got their lists of ten, I ask them to partner up and share their lists with each other. Typically, they say things like, "travelling," "getting an education," "sleeping," "spending time with friends and family," and "updating my Facebook page." Based on what their partner says, students may then modify or append their own lists.

I then introduce the distinction between intrinsic and instrumental value. I ask students to look at their lists of what's worth doing and to ask themselves which sort of value they take the various activities they've listed to have. We typically engage, at this point, in a general discussion of the distinction; it's not uncommon for students to find the difference somewhat muddled. I think this is fine. It's not important that we come to agreement about whether a given activity is intrinsically or instrumentally valuable, or even that it's always possible to make the distinction. What I hope students get out of this is just an awareness of the distinction and an initial fluency in making it.

I then ask students to imagine that they've gone to their doctor, who has informed them that they only have five years to live. Looking at their lists, are there any activities they've listed that they would no longer consider worth doing? I ask for students to volunteer those activities with the larger group and we talk about it. Typically, there will be a few things that students mention at this point; usually, they are activities that have long-term instrumental value, like getting an education or starting a career.

I then ask students to imagine that their doctors have told them they only have a year to live. Are there any other activities they would then remove from their list? Again, I ask for students to volunteer their choices and we talk more about them.

I then proceed to continue shortening the time frame, to six months, then a month, then a week, until finally, I ask students to imagine that they only have 24 hours to live: which of the remaining activities would you still consider worth doing?

Typically, the kinds of things that remain are activities like spending time with family, giving praise to God, and occasionally, sleeping. We can make the point, though, that these are activities that students consider intrinsically valuable. Sometimes some students will want to argue that, if you only have a day to live, then nothing is worth doing. This can be an interesting discussion as well.

In any case, the typical upshot of the exercise is that students have developed a better vocabulary for discussing value and have thought a bit about what they consider valuable and why. This strikes me as a worthwhile outcome, one with both intrinsic and instrumental value.

By way of conclusion, I will reiterate that for me, the relationship between pre-college and college-level teaching of philosophy has turned out to be a two-way street. Consequently, I would go even further than merely suggesting that the two "inform" each other; I would assert that, for me at least, they have quite literally defined one another.

REFERENCES

Descartes, R. (2005) "Meditations on First Philosophy" reprinted in Abel, D., *Fifty Readings Plus: An Introduction to Philosohy*, NY: McGraw-Hill, pp.133–146.
Russell, B. (2005) "The Value of Philosophy," reprinted in Abel, D., *Fifty Readings Plus: An Introduction to Philosohy*, NY: McGraw-Hill, pp.21–27.

Part III

Ideas for Philosophy
at the High School Level

15 A Different Education
Philosophy and High School

Michael D. Burroughs

INTRODUCTION

The objective of this chapter is two-fold: first, I discuss the significance of introducing philosophy to young people, particularly at the high school academic level. Despite increases in precollege philosophy programs, philosophy classes for young people remain rare in the United States, especially in public schools. It is important, therefore, to offer justifications for the greater inclusion of philosophy in precollege curricula. Second, I discuss specific strategies and tactics for practicing philosophy with high school students through interventions into the high school classroom and curriculum. Taken in all, I aim to shed light on important elements of the process and great worth of practicing philosophical pedagogy with adolescents.

My discussion is informed by my own work in precollege philosophy spanning the past 10 years. During this time I have worked as a high school, middle school, and elementary school philosophy teacher, both nationally and internationally. Much of this work has occurred in Memphis, Tennessee (USA), through the "Philosophical Horizons" project, a community outreach program of the University of Memphis Department of Philosophy. Philosophical Horizons introduces the history and practice of philosophy to Memphis children (grade levels ranging from kindergarten to high school), particularly those who are socioeconomically disadvantaged, in schools that are the least likely to have the resources to implement philosophy into their curriculum. Philosophical Horizons initiatives are led by graduate and undergraduate philosophy students and take on a variety of forms: ranging from weekly philosophy discussion groups for elementary and middle school students to full-on philosophy courses for high school students. Working in Memphis public schools presents unique challenges, including some that will not be relevant for all practitioners of precollege philosophy. However, I regard much of my experience as generally applicable to those interested in implementing or continuing philosophy classes for high school students. I will focus here on these generally relevant experiences and insights gained in virtue of them.

180 *Michael D. Burroughs*

JUSTIFICATIONS FOR PRECOLLEGE PHILOSOPHY

The importance of offering justifications for precollege philosophy is initially highlighted by the fact that, in large part, the philosophical canon is not "child friendly." There is a need, then, for justifying philosophy for young people *within* the discipline of philosophy. Canonical philosophers continually overlook children as potential students of philosophy or, what is more, actively argue against children as proper subjects of philosophical pedagogy. For example, Plato regards the child as an illegitimate student of philosophy who—if engaged as a philosopher—"discredits" the discipline (Plato 2004a, 235), and Aristotle presents the child as possessing an appetitive nature, unsuited to the demands of philosophical engagement (Aristotle 1999, 157).

It is important to recognize this canonical challenge to the practice of philosophy for young people as it contributes to our conception of the proper subject of philosophical pedagogy. For Plato and Aristotle, the proper student of philosophy is not the child, but the rational adult (male). I will not respond to this challenge in full here. To do so adequately would require a work devoted solely to this task. For the purposes of this chapter, it is sufficient to note that the positions of these philosophers on philosophy for young people derive from their broader conceptions of adulthood, childhood, and education: many features of which the contemporary reader would certainly reject. To the extent we disagree with these philosophers and their primary characterization of children as appetitive and lacking in reason, we will also disagree with many of the conclusions derived from this characterization; namely, that the child *qua* child is devoid of philosophical ability and ineligible for participation in a philosophical education.

For the practitioner of philosophy for young people there is a more pressing area of need for the justification of precollege philosophy. The discipline of philosophy (in the United States) is generally not made available to students prior to the university classroom (if then) and, thus, most precollege students will never encounter a philosophy course in their curricula. In this case, the need for justification of philosophy for young people is *external* to the discipline of philosophy, originating instead within the ends of precollege education in the United States. Given that philosophy has largely been excluded from precollege classrooms, one must be capable of articulating sound reasons for its inclusion.

The justifications for precollege philosophy offered here are of two kinds: the first coinciding with the ends of precollege education as they presently stand, and the second arguing for the inclusion of a new dimension to these ends. First, the study of philosophy involves the development of analytic skills that are crucial for students regardless of their specific area of interest and future profession. Reading a philosophical text—such as Plato's *Republic*, Aristotle's *Politics*, or Rousseau's *Emile*—is not like reading a popular novel; students must learn to examine a text passage by passage, tracing the contours of an argument, and cultivating critical reading skills in the process. Writing a philosophical essay requires fully engaging a text. Students must move beyond a simple restatement of the "facts"; they must learn to develop an informed position, identifying essential passages and tailoring written arguments in response to the philosophical problem at hand. Finally, practicing philosophy with others requires that students learn to state positions logically and concisely and to ask productive questions that enrich a discussion.

Insofar as studying philosophy helps students to develop these skill sets, it also helps them to realize the aims of precollege education in the United States. When attempting to work with public schools (whether at the high school, middle school, or elementary school level), crowded curricula often provide administrators with little flexibility in the addition of new courses. Pressures to achieve increased averages on national and state standardized tests result in a focus on test preparation in most any extra space found in the curriculum. Given this educational context, practitioners of philosophy for young people do well to highlight features of their work that advance student writing and reading skills, logical argumentation, and abstract conceptualization. These skills aid students in standardized test taking and foster higher levels of academic achievement within the school while preparing them for greater success at the university level.

But (and this leads to the second point of justification) philosophy is certainly more than a means to the end of standardized testing. While it is true that demonstrating the practical use of philosophy can open the doors of particular schools, in order to gain a secure purchase in precollege education we must also present the *unique* contributions of philosophical pedagogy to a student's education. A high school education is not exhausted by the development of academic skill sets, nor is it exclusively constituted by high marks on standardized tests. Adolescents are reflective beings who possess both the intellectual ability and native interest to consider questions of fundamental import to the human condition. A unique attribute of philosophical pedagogy is its capacity for uniting an adolescent's academic maturation with the reflective developmental stage through which she encounters her world. The philosophical questions "what is justice?," or "what does it mean to live a good life?" do not find a place within the assessment strategies of standardized testing, but they *do* have a robust place in the lives of adolescents who are figuring out "who they are," whether as students, citizens, or friends. Philosophical pedagogy provides an intellectual space in the school day for formative engagement with these questions (and others like them) and in so doing helps students to critically encounter their social world and analyze and understand their location within it.

Further, if we think of education as involving, in part, the development of intellectual "tools"—such as analytic skills to do arithmetic or tools of composition to complete an essay—we can regard philosophical pedagogy as providing students with additional, no less essential tools for participation in a democratic society. Perhaps most important, philosophy students learn to take on a critical relationship with their values and beliefs. This is not to say that philosophical pedagogy calls for children to reject their beliefs and values offhand; rather, it requires students to identify sound reasons *both* in support of and in opposition to their own stated values and beliefs as well as an awareness of the social, cultural, and historical norms that inform them. A philosophy student learns that simply stating a position (say, "I believe that X is morally wrong") is not sufficient; she must also identify and relate sound reasons to others in support of such a position. In some cases this exercise will lead to a strengthened set of values and beliefs, in others it will lead to their revision or rejection. In any case, the formation of these tools— rational reflection, respectful discourse, and identifying reasons in support of and in opposition to one's own position—is essential for a student's own intellectual maturation and interaction with others in a democratic society.

The justifications for precollege philosophy offered here are not exhaustive. I present them in this form for two reasons. First, these justifications have served as useful guides for my own work as a practitioner of philosophy for young people. Advancing the academic skill sets and philosophical development of my students provides a framework for my work with each class. Second, I offer these justifications to demonstrate a useful exercise for others interested in beginning work in precollege philosophy. In the current climate of precollege education in the United States, it is essential that we reflect on *why* we want to work in precollege philosophy and *what* we can offer precollege students. Doing so can help one to find common ground with school administrators and teachers, as well as to articulate the unique value of adding (or continuing) philosophy in a high school.

STRATEGIES FOR PRACTICING PHILOSOPHY WITH HIGH SCHOOL STUDENTS

Having briefly considered justifications for precollege philosophy, I will now turn to a discussion of specific strategies and tactics for practicing philosophy with high school students. The challenge of providing a general account derives, in part, from the fact that every school and student is different. In some cases, a participating school will be interested in offering a weekly philosophy discussion group; in others, a semester long philosophy class. Many of the strategies discussed below come from my experience teaching philosophy courses to high school students in biweekly sessions. But whatever the format, one should expect to encounter students possessed of varying educational backgrounds and unique interests. Being an effective precollege philosophy teacher begins with an *awareness* of the diverse needs and interests of schools and students and continues by *responding* to them throughout a class and semester.

I respond to this diversity of needs and interests by instituting a high school philosophy curriculum that reflects *accessibility* and *openness*. A simple, yet effective exercise for introducing high school students to philosophy is to demonstrate that, in fact, philosophical questions as such are not foreign to them. Rather than diving into an opening lecture on the meaning of philosophy, I begin a first class by engaging students in the *practice* of philosophical discussion. To this end, I open with a philosophical question such as "what is justice?," or "what is wisdom?" Inevitably, students make claims in response to these questions, increasingly so as opposing claims are advanced by their peers. This opening activity (which can be modified and extended through several class or discussion group sessions) serves two purposes: first, it introduces students to the dynamic process of doing philosophy with others—collectively considering a philosophical concept, formulating and articulating positions, and responding to counterexamples. Rather than (or at least in addition to) lecturing on these skills, a philosophy teacher can draw attention to them as they arise organically in a discussion, thereby providing needed clarity on their purpose and pointing out the philosophical ability students *already* possess. Second, this activity allows students to recognize (with some prompting) that they have asked and considered philosophical questions in their own lives. The general relevance of this point—that philosophy is not foreign to their lives and concerns—contributes to students "buying in" to the philosophical process and can be strengthened throughout a semester by incorporating films, music, articles, or current events into class, thereby allowing students to use philosophy to critically engage significant elements of their world.

In addition, I often write and utilize philosophy dialogues (one example appears in the appendix) in early class or discussion group sessions. The use of these dialogues is advantageous for numerous reasons: First, philosophy dialogues concretize potentially abstract philosophical concepts and questions for students. Dialogues contain two or three main characters, each participating in a scripted discussion on a given philosophical concept (truth, justice, personal identity, etc.). These characters are generally of the same age as my students and voice their positions in common vernacular as opposed to philosophical jargon, providing for an open and accessible discussion for all involved. Second, students read the dialogue aloud, assuming the position of a given character in the dialogue. In doing so, they are engaged with the philosophical topic at the start of a session, giving voice to the contrasting positions that all class members will come to evaluate. Third, following the reading of the dialogue, students can focus on the philosophical positions represented in the dialogue as opposed to the positions of individual discussion group members. Students can begin to critique and explore philosophical positions without feeling that they are being intellectually aggressive toward their classmates (a common worry in students new to philosophical group discussion).

The dialogue activity introduces students to the practice of identifying and evaluating divergent philosophical positions. Much of this evaluation occurs between the group, with students referencing a stated position and explaining to others its merits or deficiencies. In order to foster this type of engagement in the class, it is best to conclude a dialogue with a lingering philosophical question as opposed to a defined answer. Whereas the former presents possibilities for further discussion, the latter closes off these avenues, leaving students with the task of finding the answer provided by the teacher as opposed to exploring a philosophical question or concept independently.

If successful, these opening activities provide an accessible starting point for students new to philosophy. As importantly, they set the ground for a transition into a significant feature of precollege philosophy at the high school level: student engagement with philosophical texts. Following early class discussions and/or dialogues, students have considered and formulated positions in response to philosophical questions. Students now have a "stake" in these questions—they are not indifferent to their resolution, but rather, have acquired a personal interest in considering and responding to them. From this position it is natural to ask: what do other philosophers offer us in their responses to these *same* questions? If class discussions have focused on the nature of justice and the good life, we can then turn to discussions of these concepts in Plato's *Republic*, Aristotle's *Nicomachean Ethics*, or Mill's *Utilitarianism*; if class discussions focused on the nature and purpose of education, we can turn to Rousseau's *Emile*, Dewey's *Democracy and Education*, or Paulo Freire's *Pedagogy of the Oppressed* (and so on).

Of course, philosophical texts are often convoluted and abstract; and for students new to the discipline, they can be particularly challenging. Although using these texts can enrich discussion and help students to develop philosophical and academic skill sets, none of this is possible if students are overwhelmed by a text from the start. It is important, then, to combine the use of these texts with a continuing commitment to accessibility. To this end, I use concise selections of a text (a paragraph to a few pages) that get at a major theme or philosophical question of import. For example, for the purposes of advancing a class discussion on the nature of justice I turn to Plato's "Ring of Gyges," Rawls's "The Veil of Ignorance," or a selection from Dr. Martin Luther King's "Letter from a Birmingham Jail" (as opposed to undertaking a large-scale reading of the *Republic* or *A Theory of Justice*). In introducing these brief selections, I provide ample time to read them as a class so as to elucidate unfamiliar terminology and encourage questions and discussion along the way. Presented in this fashion, a philosophical text is much less likely to intimidate a student already in the process of acclimating to new terminology and styles of argumentation. But none of this is to say that larger selections of philosophical texts should be off limits to high school students. I emphasize *beginning* with short selections rich in philosophical content as, in my experience, they serve as a manageable starting point for high school students. From this starting point it is common for students to develop an interest in a particular philosopher and to want to further explore his or her written work. Responding to students will then involve spending more time on a text or introducing others more relevant to their evolving interests.

The need to respond to the interests of students brings us to a second basic mode of approach for precollege philosophy at the high school level: as important as *accessibility* in a philosophy curriculum is *openness* on the part of the teacher. In many cases, high school students are accustomed to a *one-way* pedagogical approach—answers and relevant information come *from* the teacher *to* the student. In effect, students come to view themselves as recipients of a determined distribution of information rather than active participants in their own education. A crucial aspect (and opportunity) of doing precollege philosophy with high school students involves challenging this paradigm. Remaining open to the questions, insights, and interests of one's students constitutes an important part of this challenge. We can provide a different intellectual space for students to inhabit by approaching them as fellow philosophers with a significant role in determining the success of a class.

To illustrate more precisely what I mean by "openness," here it will be helpful to turn to a pedagogical distinction developed by Paulo Freire in *Pedagogy of the Oppressed* (Freire 2002, 72–86). Freire distinguishes between two fundamentally different approaches to education. First, the "banking concept of education" presents the educational process as akin to a bank transaction. The teacher approaches the student as a passive receptacle in which information can be "deposited." Describing this educational approach, Freire writes:

> Education thus becomes an act of depositing, in which the students are the depositories and the teacher is the depositor. Instead of communicating, the teacher issues communiqués and makes deposits which the students patiently receive, memorize, and repeat. This is the 'banking' concept of education, in which the scope of action allowed to the students extends only as far as receiving, filing, and storing the deposits. (Freire 2002, 72)

With this traditional approach to education, the student's primary tasks are to listen to the teacher, memorize necessary information, and demonstrate mastery of a predetermined lesson (the one-way pedagogical approach). If applied to precollege philosophy, for example, the banking concept of education would involve the student mastering those elements of a philosophical concept deemed significant by the teacher and, in turn, demonstration of this mastery for the teacher.

The "dialogical" or "problem-posing" method involves a radically different approach to education and the pedagogical relation between teacher and student, one of direct import for my pedagogical approach in this chapter. With this approach, the teacher engages students as fellow critical thinkers, as "critical co-investigators in dialogue with the teacher" (Freire 2002, 81). The student and teacher are viewed as equally responsible partners in the learning process:

> Through dialogue, the teacher-of-the-students and the students-of-the-teacher cease to exist and a new term emerges: teacher-student with

> students-teachers. The teacher is no longer merely the-one-who-teaches, but one who is himself taught in dialogue with the students, who in turn while being taught also teach. They become jointly responsible for a process in which all grow. (Freire 2002, 80)

The intended result is for the student, along with the teacher, to take ownership of the lesson; to question and apply the intellectual content of, say, a discussion of ethics to her daily life. Thus, in the study of philosophy the student's own questions, experiences, and insights are not tertiary to the lesson, but rather, are significant elements of the learning process itself.

As taken up in precollege philosophy, a dialogical or open pedagogical approach provides for a different educational experience with students, one that moves beyond one-way pedagogy insofar as it regards students as active members of a class or discussion group. Conducted in this fashion, philosophical pedagogy can have a *transformative* impact on students. To the extent a student takes ownership of an active role, she breaks from her common status as a merely passive recipient of information; she becomes more engaged in the philosophical work at hand and comes to see herself as a philosopher capable of making valuable contributions to a class.

We can manifest the open pedagogical approach in our work with students in a number of ways: first, after introducing a philosophical topic it is important to allow ample room for students to take ownership of a discussion. Given that many students are used to the one-way pedagogical approach, this will not happen automatically. Especially in early class sessions, students will focus on the teacher as the exclusive source of important information. Thus, the teacher's work begins with disrupting the pattern of one-way pedagogy; both the need to listen to others and the confidence to respond in turn—basic elements of philosophical discussion—must be encouraged in students. To this end, I keep lecture to a minimum, using this medium to clarify a discussion point from a past class or to introduce some particularly important elements of philosophical theory. In place of lecture, I often begin class with a philosophical contribution from a student, returning to a question or claim raised in a previous class. During subsequent discussion of this point, I ask students to listen and respond to each other as if they are contributing pieces for the construction of a "philosophical home": an opening philosophical question from a student acts as our foundation, and it is the responsibility of myself and other students to "build" on this substructure. We do so by contributing claims and questions that are both relevant to our foundation and capable of advancing the construction of our discussion. Most important, I point out to students that the teacher alone cannot achieve this task. My job is not to provide them with a ready-made philosophical worldview for them to appropriate as their own (a prefab house); rather, *our* task as class members is to contribute valuable components to a philosophical structure we all can inhabit.

Reenvisioning the role of students in a class (from passive to active participant) is aided by a corresponding alteration of their physical location in the classroom. In the traditional classroom structure, the teacher is positioned in front of the class with all students facing her. Both teacher and student take on roles akin to those we encounter while attending a play. The teacher is onstage as the sole focus of attention for an audience of students, eyes directed solely up front. Little is expected of audience members; they need only avoid being disruptive to others and attend to the show. Altering this classroom dynamic is essential for modeling a different pedagogical relationship between teacher, students, and the philosophical material at hand. In place of the traditional classroom structure, I have all class members (students and teacher) sit in a circle during sessions. This simple change to the structure of the class yields significant results. Seated in this way, students are in position to listen and respond to each other as equal contributors to class discussion. They can make eye contact and face each other in turn as various students raise questions and claims. Further, embedding the teacher within the class models our departure from the one-way pedagogical approach—students eventually learn that the front of the class (the traditional location of the teacher) is not the exclusive origin of important information. Through concrete changes in the classroom the questions, comments, and insights of class members are encountered as integral components of a philosophical education.

Like the structure of the classroom, the design of assignments can also help students to take an active role in a precollege philosophy class. In particular, it is important to include assignments that require students to perform self-directed philosophical work as opposed to a mere recapitulation of a lecture or philosophical argument. For example, I often begin class by asking students to complete a short writing assignment in which they respond to a philosophical prompt (a question raised by a class reading or class member). With their respective positions in hand, students are then asked to join in small groups with peers to discuss their written work, identifying both points of strength and those in need of revision. Following these dual activities, students have engaged with a topic independently and have presented their work to fellow class members. Students are then well prepared to take an active role in class discussion once we come back together as a group to discuss the same philosophical prompt.

As a culminating assignment on a major philosophical theme, I often have students participate in a class debate. Students are provided with a basic assignment framework (the debate topic, format, and team roles) and are asked to develop written position papers on the debate topic. In these papers students develop arguments in support of both "sides" of the debate, attempting to form sound arguments for each major position. Only after completing this exercise are students asked to choose the side they wish to defend in the class debate. Having formed arguments in support of either side, students better understand the contrasting positions of their peers as well as the merits and faults of their own. This assignment is not only successful in terms of student engagement (in my experience, debates are the *most* popular assignments with high school students), but also, it requires students to author a statement representative of their position as a philosopher. Although the teacher provides guidance and necessary instruction throughout the debate process, a primary focus is placed on the student synthesizing course material (relevant philosophical texts, notes from class discussions, etc.) and developing a sound argument to present in discourse with her peers.

CONCLUSION

In this brief chapter I have discussed important justifications and strategies for precollege philosophy, primarily at the high school academic level. There are, without doubt, numerous other justifications for this work, just as there are many tactics that I cannot cover here. Still, I have attempted to capture an essential element of precollege philosophical pedagogy: working in precollege philosophy is not simply a matter of bringing philosophy to young people; it is a process of *doing* philosophy *with* young people. This requires providing an introduction to philosophy for students (an introduction to certain philosophical questions, concepts, and skill sets). Just as importantly, however, it calls for the creation of ample "open space" for young philosophers to develop and articulate their own ideas. This is not possible if a teacher enters a class with a "closed" curriculum from the start, encountering students as mere "receptacles" for information as opposed to "critical coinvestigators." The essential point here, then, is to act as an educator who takes seriously the intellectual contributions of young students, thereby providing them with the intellectual space and necessary encouragement to be philosophers.

Appendix

A Dialogue on Justice

Derrick:	Hey Elicia, did you hear about the new rule just handed down from the school administration?
Elicia:	No, what is it?
Derrick:	Starting tomorrow all students have to wear ties and dress pants to school.
Elicia:	That is not fair, I mean, that is *unjust*.
Timothy:	What do you mean by *unjust*?
Elicia:	I mean that the students' voices weren't taken into account—that is *unjust*.
Derrick:	So it would have been *just* if students had a say in the new rule and supported it?

Elicia:	Yes.
Derrick:	No way. What is *just* is what is decided by the powerful. The powerful people (in this case, the school administration) say that we need to wear ties and dress pants. Therefore, it is *just* that we wear ties and dress pants.
Timothy:	I don't know about that. I have a different understanding of justice. *Justice* is whatever the majority of people in a community think it is. For example, the majority of people in this community (students at this high school) do not think that having to wear ties and dress pants is just. Therefore, wearing ties and dress pants is not just. What *is* just, then, is wearing what we want.
Derrick:	That seems like a dangerous understanding of justice.
Timothy:	Why dangerous?
Derrick:	Well, on your definition of justice, can't *anything* end up being just?
Timothy:	Sure, whatever the majority thinks is just *is* just.
Elicia:	What if the majority of folks in this city think the legal enforcement of racial segregation in schools is just? Does that mean legally enforced racial segregation is just?
Timothy:	Well . . . maybe not. But if you think my definition of justice and my argument supporting are no good, then what is yours?

REFERENCES

Aristotle. (1999) *Nicomachean Ethics*. Translated by Irwin, T. Indianapolis, IN: Hackett.
———. (1998) *Politics*. Translated by Reeve, C.D.C. Indianapolis, IN: Hackett.
Dewey, J. (1944) *Democracy and Education* New York: The Free Press.
Freire, P. (2002) *Pedagogy of the Oppressed* (30th Anniversary Edition). Translated by Ramos, M.B. New York: Continuum.
King, Jr., M.L. (1986) "Letter from a Birmingham Jail" In *A Testament of Hope. The Essential Writings and Speeches of Martin Luther King, Jr.* (ed. Washington, J. M.), 289–302, San Francisco: Harper Collins.
Mill, J.S. (2001) *Utilitarianism*, 2nd ed. (ed. Sher, G.) Indianapolis, IN: Hackett.
Philosophical Horizons. "Philosophical Horizons." Last modified September 1, 2011. www.memphis.edu/philosophy/philhorizons.php.
Plato. (2004a) *Republic*. Translated by Reeve, C.D.C. Indianapolis, IN: Hackett.
———. (2004b) "The Ring of Gyges" In *Republic*. Translated by Reeve, C.D.C., 38–40, Indianapolis, IN: Hackett.
Rawls, J. (1971) "The Veil of Ignorance" In *A Theory of Justice*, 136–142. Cambridge, MA: Harvard University Press.
Rousseau, J-J. (1979) *Emile or On Education* Translated by Bloom, A. New York: Basic Books.

16 Introducing Philosophy Courses in High School

Arik Ben-Avi

In 2009, I worked with another graduate student at Yale, Gaurav Vazirani, to start a philosophy outreach program. After connecting with a teacher at Hill Regional Career High School, a magnet school in New Haven known for its health sciences and business tracks, we arranged to teach a for-credit pilot course in the spring of 2010, through Career's independent study program. Based on the success of this pilot course, the philosophy course at Career has continued and is now being led by a different Yale graduate student.

I was personally involved in teaching two courses at Career: the pilot course in 2010, as well as another course in the spring of 2011. Not having taught at the high school level before, the curricular and pedagogical planning for these courses involved some guesswork, experimentation, and self-correction. Therefore, my plan for this chapter is straightforward: taking each of the two high school courses I taught, in turn, I will describe what we did in class and then offer my reflections on what worked and what didn't.

THE PILOT COURSE

Description

The pilot "Introduction to Philosophy" course—which I co-taught with Gaurav—was set up to meet in 90-minute sessions, once a week, for 15 weeks (although it ended up continuing for around 20 weeks) over the winter and spring marking periods of Career's academic year. Nine students were enrolled in the course for credit, with another four to six students (depending on the week) regularly showing up for classes despite not being officially enrolled in the course.

In designing this course, we agreed that our aim should not simply be to familiarize students with interesting and important philosophical questions and ideas, but also to make substantial progress in the development of students' critical reasoning skills. Our experience with undergraduates at Yale left us with the impression that, even at this level, many students lacked an adequate grasp of what makes for a good argument, what makes for good objections to an argument, and what makes for a good dialectical exchange in general. For example, when assessing a given argument in class discussion or in a paper, many undergraduates tended to focus on assessing the truth of the argument's premises, giving minimal attention to whether the conclusion of the argument could be false even if the premises were true—giving minimal attention, that is, to the *validity* of the argument in question. Our assumption was that high school students would be even less developed in the critical, dialectical reasoning skills of philosophical discourse, and therefore, that one of the more valuable things we could achieve with this course would be to help students make marked improvement with regard to these skills.

To give such skill development the attention we thought it deserved, we decided to begin our course with a five-week unit on critical reasoning. Using a mixture of short readings, didactic instruction, and exercises, we introduced students to the skills of identifying, charitably reconstructing, and pertinently challenging the soundness of a given argument, as well as to important concepts such as deduction, induction, validity, soundness, necessity, and sufficiency, and to a small set of common fallacies.

The readings we assigned to introduce critical thinking concepts and skills were mostly drawn from the first few chapters of a textbook called *Asking the Right Questions* (Browne & Keeley 2007). During several sessions of this unit we also worked with short pieces of philosophically interesting argumentative text to give students an opportunity to practice using the critical thinking concepts and skills covered in that day's session. These argumentative pieces included an excerpt from Martin Luther King Jr.'s "Letter from A Birmingham Jail" (King 1963), an excerpt from Plato's *Crito* (Jowett 1999), and an excerpt from James Rachels' chapter on Cultural Relativism in his book *The Elements of Moral Philosophy* (Rachels & Rachels 2006). After covering the critical thinking concepts and skills of the week and having students practice on the argumentative text in the first half of a class session, we then opened things up for a more engaging philosophical discussion of the text in the second half of class.

The questions we used to prompt the philosophical discussions were straightforwardly related to the texts at hand. For example, the discussion on the King excerpt focused on questions such as What distinguishes just from unjust laws? What types of civil disobedience are morally permissible? And what (if anything) grounds a moral duty to follow societal laws? Our discussion on the *Crito* excerpt mostly picked up on the latter question, regarding whether we have a moral duty to follow societal laws and, if so, what grounds this duty. And the piece by Rachels prompted discussion of questions like the following: Under what conditions might one person's moral duty be different—even opposed—to another person's moral duty? And is morality merely a set of established societal norms, or is it something more—and if so, what? Of course, we could not get very deeply into any of these questions in the half session devoted to philosophical discussion of each text, but these discussions did at least spark interest, as well as giving students an initial familiarity with the style of discussion to come in the topical units.

The remainder of the course consisted of short units on a variety of philosophical topics. Thinking that it mattered to us more that the students be interested in the topics covered than that the topics be ones we found particularly interesting or important, we gave students brief descriptions of some possible topics and had them vote on the topics to be covered. In this way, we still ended up with a fairly traditional mix of topics, including free will, arguments for/against the existence of God, aid to the poor, abortion, courage and cowardice, biomedical enhancement, and distributive justice.

Our pedagogical approach in this portion of the course was relatively loose in format—as we wanted to remain flexible to the developmental and engagement levels of the students—but we generally started off class either with a short lecture or by reading a section of assigned reading together as a class, and then transitioned to an intensive discussion on the topic at hand. Taking advantage of the fact that there were two of us teaching the class, sometimes we also broke the class into two discussion groups for a stretch of time, and then regrouped again for full-class discussion.

Class discussions usually began by asking students to reconstruct one or more of the central arguments put forth in the reading or lecture (although, when introducing a given topic or debate via lecture we often made sure to clearly construct relevant arguments, in which case it seemed unnecessary to have students do an argument reconstruction). Since we were wary of overly challenging the students' reading capacity, a number of the readings we assigned as homework were short topical overview chapters selected from a pop philosophy book we found, called *The Philosophy Gym* (Law 2003). For example, we used this text in introducing students to a few arguments for and against the existence of God, to the debate regarding free will and moral responsibility, and to a session on biomedical enhancement. Reconstructing the central arguments presented in these overview chapters was not too difficult for most students, particularly as they got more practice. We only assigned a few primary texts—Peter Singer's "Famine, Affluence, and Morality" (Singer 1972), Judith Thomson's "A Defense of Abortion" (Thomson 1971), and a debate between William Lane Craig and Walter Sinnott-Armstrong on the existence of God (Craig & Sinnott-Armstrong 2004)—and students generally needed more guidance in reconstructing arguments from passages of these texts.

Once a given argument was reconstructed, we asked students to offer their views on whether or not the argument was sound—and if not, where it seemed to them that there was a weakness in the argument. Based on student responses, we guided the discussion to focus on one of the premises that students found particularly questionable—soliciting students to further articulate their reasons for objecting to the premise, encouraging them to consider how the arguer might rebut their challenges or strengthen the targeted premise in light of the objections, and then asking them to reassess the argument in view of these objections and these considered responses. If this dialectical exchange left some notable holes or issues to explore further, we guided students to do so; otherwise, we moved on to examine some other questionable premise or weak point they found in the argument. Or sometimes we pressed students to more closely examine a reconstructed argument (or one of its premises) that they had all initially found quite convincing, by raising our own objections to this argument (or premise) and having students engage dialectically with these objections.

In some discussions there were certain premises or conclusions upon which there was pretty well-balanced disagreement among the students. In these cases our input was largely that of facilitators: making sure everyone participated, prompting students to clarify their comments as needed, and encouraging students to respond directly to each other's arguments—especially by pointing out connections and conflicts between the thoughts, claims, and questions of different students. Of course, at other times the discussion was heavily weighted toward one position—either because most students agreed on this point, or because those who disagreed were less vocal or skillful in challenging it or in defending their own opposing positions. In these cases we did intervene more substantively, perhaps challenging the favored position ourselves, or perhaps posing some scenario or pointing to some detail that supported the less-favored positions and giving the students holding these positions a chance to use our input to build stronger arguments or to discover and explore new, yet still amenable, alternative positions.

As an example of what a typical class discussion looked like, let me describe in some detail our discussion of Thomson's abortion paper. Before having students read the essay, we introduced the topic of abortion by asking students to state their positions on abortion and to articulate their reasons for holding these positions. As is happened, there were some students on either side of the debate (if not, we would have taken up the unrepresented stance ourselves), while a few were uncertain either way. We then read together the first few paragraphs of Thomson's essay—in which she introduces a standard line of argument against the permissibility of abortion—and guided students in the reconstruction of this argument. After giving students some time to freely discuss the soundness of this argument—a discussion which largely focused either on the premise about the personhood of the fetus or the premise regarding the mother's right to decide what happens with her body—we asked students to identify the premise Thomson herself plans to target. We then read together the paragraph in which Thomson presents her initial violinist thought experiment, and guided students in reconstructing how this thought experiment is used by Thomson to challenge her targeted premise. This class session then closed with a discussion of how the violinist case might or might not be sufficiently analogous to the standard abortion scenario to undermine the targeted premise.

By the next session, students had been assigned to read through the end of section 4 of Thomson's essay and to attempt to reconstruct a couple

more of its arguments; and the session was devoted to jointly reconstructing and then discussing these arguments. Since the paper seemed to us to
get somewhat more difficult in the fifth and sixth sections (when Thomson
talks about different uses of the term "rights" and distinguishes the Good
Samaritan from the "Minimally Decent Samaritan"), and would have required more time than we wanted to spend on this paper, we decided not to
cover beyond the fourth section.

The arguments we focused on during this second session regarded
whether or not the right to life entails a duty for others to provide you with
at least the minimum needed for survival (Thomson's Henry Fonda argument), whether or not it entails even simply a duty for others not to kill
you (the violinist case again), and what implications our answers to these
questions have for the permissibility of abortion. Here some attention was
also given to the purported moral distinction between killing and letting
die. We also focused on a crucial disanalogy between the initial violinist
case and the typical circumstances of abortion in the United States—namely,
that the woman seeking an abortion is usually at least partially responsible
for becoming pregnant with the fetus, while the victim in the violinist case
is clearly not—discussing whether or not Thomson's burglar and "people-
seeds" cases should be thought to successfully deflect the force of this line
of objection. Here some attention was also given to the question of when
people should be held responsible for the results of risky actions (given that
virtually all actions involve some uncertainty and possible downsides).

Although most class discussions, like the one for the Thomson paper,
were set up with either a reading or some didactic lecturing, the session we
did on courage and cowardice was one in which we instead used a series of
short narrative cases to prompt discussion. We came to class having written up around three or four scenarios in which someone acts in a way that
displays something in the vicinity of courage (but perhaps displays rashness
or simply exceptional training and practice, or perhaps aims at something
external, trivial, or evil), and another three or four scenarios in which someone acts in a way that displays something in the vicinity of cowardice (but
perhaps displays an exceptional lack of skill, or unusual—even selfish—
value priorities, or an overestimation of risk, etc).

Reading the first courage-related scenario together as a class, we then
asked students to assess whether or not they thought it was an instance of
courage, and to articulate their reasons for holding their views. After facilitating discussion of this case for a while and having students come up with
their own preliminary definitions of courage, we then introduced the other
cases depicting something in the vicinity of courage and facilitated a discussion in which students were prompted to test; debate; and, if warranted,
revise their own preliminary definitions of courage in light of their assessments of these further cases. We then followed a similar plan to get students
to formulate, test, debate, and revise their definitions of cowardice.

We decided to try out this approach after noticing that students often struggled in discussion to come up with examples of their own of whatever phenomenon was under examination. The examples they devised in illustrating or challenging a point inclined either toward the simplistic and cliché or toward the convoluted and confusing. And since working with an emaciated sense of the range of cases that might count as instances of a given phenomenon tends to limit the depth of insight one can have in formulating an understanding of this phenomenon, we figured it was worth seeing if we could helpfully circumvent this source of limitation when investigating courage and cowardice, by having a good number of potentially pertinent (and clearly described) cases on hand for the discussion.

Of course we had no control group for comparison in this experiment, but it seemed that this strategy did help a greater portion of the students than otherwise expected to quickly gain a wider perspective on the sorts of scenarios and criteria that might be in play when talking about courage and cowardice, and that this made the discussion more interesting and subtle than it otherwise would likely have been. On the other hand, one of the skills to develop in philosophical discussion is the ability to devise one's own cases that might be useful in testing out and revising one's articulated understanding of the phenomenon under examination; and while our strategy did serve to model the sort of imaginative case construction that is valuable in philosophical discussion, it probably would have been better to do a little less spoon-feeding here. For example, instead of thinking up the cases ourselves, we could have given a homework assignment or have set aside an adequate chunk of time in class for students to write up their own examples—say, one scenario depicting what they take to be an uncontroversial case of courage, and one or two scenarios in which they take it to be controversial whether or not the actions depicted display courage (and likewise for cowardice). The range of cases devised in this way may not have captured some of the nuances of our examples, but it probably would have been worth it to trade this nuance for the opportunity for students to develop their case construction skills (it also would have given us an even larger number of cases to work with in class). Probably the best alternative would have been to take a mixed approach: to have solicited student case contributions while supplementing these with our own cases, as needed.

Further Reflections

Overall, we think the course was a success. While some students seemed surprisingly resistant to doing their homework on a regular basis, students were generally enthusiastic about class itself—particularly about the discussion part of the class, which was invariably lively. The class was scheduled at the end of the school day, and not a week went by without four or five students staying around for another half hour or so after class ended to continue discussing either the topic of the day, a previously covered topic, or simply some miscellaneous philosophical question that had popped into their heads.

Students also seemed to make notable improvements in their critical reasoning skills during the course. Certain things, such as the concept of validity and the distinction between necessary and sufficient conditions, did not stick very well for most students during the opening, critical reasoning unit of the course. However, we continued throughout the rest of the course to draw students' attention to such critical thinking concepts and to help them build related skills; by the end of the course it seemed to us that students had come to understand and absorb at least some important pieces of what we were trying to convey in this skill area.

Although we didn't do any formal analyses to measure this progress, our sense that such progress was indeed made was based on our comparative evaluation of how students performed toward the beginning and toward the end of the course in terms of their homework assignments and their participation in class discussions.

For example, at the beginning of the course, we gave students a two-part assignment to initially assess their critical reading and thinking skills. In the first part of the assignment, we gave students a short argumentative passage to read and then asked them to identify the conclusion of the argument and the reasons given by the author in support of this conclusion, and then to indicate whether and why they found the argument convincing or not. In the second part of this assignment we posed an ethical question to the students, asked them to take a position on the issue and to indicate the reasons they had for holding this view, and then asked them to consider how someone might plausibly object to their argument and to respond to this objection. Then, at the end of the course, the students' final assignment was to write a short position paper, in which they were asked to offer an argument for which of two given distribution schemes for K–12 education they believed to be more just, to propose a plausible objection to their argument, and to attempt to rebut this objection.

What we found in comparing the students' responses in the second part of the opening assignment of the course with their performance on the final paper was that, by the time of the final paper, students were better at formulating non-question-begging arguments and at coming up with strong (rather than "straw-man") objections to their own arguments—that is, they were better at seeing an issue from multiple perspectives. And in comparing the students' responses in the first part of the opening assignment with their performance in reconstructing and evaluating argumentative passages toward the end of the course more generally, we found that students had improved in their ability to identify and restate the reasoning presented in such passages (even as these passages got more difficult), to raise good objections to these arguments, and to charitably imagine how the author of such a passage might respond to their objections. Particularly notable was that in the opening assignment, when asked to raise an objection to the given argument, many of the students were inclined to target the conclusion itself (rather than addressing the reasoning offered in its support) and to be less than charitable in imagining the author's rebuttal, while in later homework assignments and class discussions, students got more adept at offering objections that targeted an author's line of reasoning and at charitably taking the dialectical exchange a step or two further.

Our assessment of student progress was confirmed by the supervising high school teacher, who also said he saw marked gains in the focus and confidence of students in the way they analyzed arguments and engaged in class discussion. And, from a broader perspective, there was enough positive feedback about the pilot course from the students and the supervising teacher that we were welcomed by Career High School administration to continue offering the course for credit in the following year, with longer-term plans to have the course officially established within the school's curriculum.

On the other hand, this course was really our first foray into high school teaching, and we certainly took some missteps. Most significant, I think, was the way we handled the readings for the course. We were concerned enough about student reading ability to be rather cautious about assigning reading that might be too difficult, yet this concern apparently did not lead us to offer much in the way of substantive guidance to students in doing the reading we did assign. So, on the one hand, we assigned relatively few primary texts, and even these were mostly by contemporary authors whose writing seemed to us especially accessible. But, on the other hand, we did not, for example, create reading guides for students or do much intensive reading together in the classroom: we usually just assigned reading for homework, had students answer some questions about the reading (also for homework), and then reviewed in class—maybe even read together—a couple of central arguments from the reading, before turning to discussion.

This approach to the treatment of readings was not so much an oversight on our part, as a decision to focus the course on discussion of certain topics and questions, rather than on close textual reading and analysis. In reflecting on this experience afterward, though, it has seemed to me that there is great value in building a philosophy course around the careful reading in class of select primary texts—or at least in doing more to integrate close textual reading and analysis into such a course.

Especially convincing to me in coming to this conclusion has been my sense of the value of students learning how to move beyond their initial, more surface understanding of what a person is saying to reach a deeper and more charitable grasp of what the person means. Students are inclined to form quick, cursory interpretations of what someone says and then respond or move on. While this approach has its value in certain circumstances, we should also want students to learn the value of taking the time to pay closer attention to what someone is saying, to figure out what the person is really trying to communicate. What I came to realize more significantly is that working with a text provides a great opportunity for students to develop these skills, since what is being said by the author can easily be revisited and examined more carefully, to demonstrable reward. These skills are then more ready at hand when students set about interpreting each other in discussions, or even when students are trying to interpret their own thoughts and intuitions. I also came to see that primary texts are particularly valuable in this respect, since with these texts you are engaging with the actual views of the author and feel that you are getting a glimpse into the author's thought process, whereas with overview texts the writing is usually more critically detached from the positions presented and more "packaged."

Another pedagogical choice we confidently made, that afterward gave me some pause, was our decision to spend the first five or six weeks of the class covering a unit on critical reasoning. The first couple of sessions in this unit—the sessions in which we introduced students to the basic components of an argument, and then worked with students on identifying these components in the arguments found in passages of text (e.g., King's "Letter from a Birmingham Jail")—went rather well. Students were engaged and seemed to be picking up what we were trying to teach them, and we were able to smoothly transition from reconstructing arguments in the texts to philosophical discussion of these arguments.

Things went less well, however, when we got to the conceptually more difficult material, such as the concepts of validity and soundness, and the distinction between necessary and sufficient conditions. Because students struggled to grasp this material, we ended up spending a lot of time during these lessons explaining and illustrating these concepts, leaving us minimal time to move to more compelling philosophical discussion. The transition to philosophical discussion was also less natural, since we relied more on exercises than on provocative texts to illustrate and practice using these more difficult concepts. This meant that several lessons ended up being somewhat drier than we had intended; nor is it clear that they were sufficiently effective to have been worthy of such dedicated class time—especially so early in the course.

This is not to say that I left the class feeling we should not have spent time explicitly introducing students to the central framework and concepts of critical reasoning. I think of critical reasoning as essentially a self-aware and self-correcting form of thinking; and I firmly believe that such self-awareness and self-correction is significantly aided by familiarity with explicit concepts and criteria for describing and assessing one's own thinking. But I did leave the class feeling that we would have had more success had we found a way of better integrating the teaching of these tools with the more philosophically interesting material covered in the class: something more along the lines of what we were able to achieve with the first couple of critical reasoning lessons. It might even have helped to have just pushed the discussion of the more difficult concepts until a later point in the course, after the early critical reasoning lessons had been more thoroughly absorbed, and when questions about what makes an argument a good argument could have come up more naturally.

Aside from these more specific pedagogical points, however, I also left the class with a concern about its general tone, which inclined somewhat heavily toward the abstract and theoretical. Of course, this is far from unusual in a philosophy class. Indeed, I have no doubt that this tone is quite suitable for certain teachers and certain students of philosophy; nor would I deny that the tools and skills of abstract theoretical thinking are essential to any valuable sort of philosophical inquiry. However, I am also someone who thinks that philosophy is not just for highly analytical people, and that it is important to have concrete experiences and emotional perspectives brought into a philosophical inquiry. This view goes hand in hand with my conviction in the role philosophical reflection and discourse can play, not only in theorizing about the world and our lives, but in actually living those lives: for example, in dealing with conflicts among our values, in building bridges to people with whom we strongly disagree and resolving interpersonal disputes, in identifying and challenging injustices and other problems in our society, and generally in building authentically meaningful lives and relationships.

And yet (perhaps because of the focus we placed on the development of critical reasoning skills, or perhaps because of the years of training in academic environments geared toward an abstract theoretical approach toward philosophical inquiry), the way we ended up teaching the class seemed to make it more engaging and successful for students who were more analytically minded—or who were inclined toward precision and rational consistency over emotional complexity, or who were drawn to the intellectual challenge of argumentation and philosophical puzzles—than it was for students who, while bright and insightful, were less analytical and more emotion minded in their thinking.

Moreover, with a handful of notable exceptions, it wasn't obvious to me that we did much to impress upon students how the ideas and skills they were learning in the class might be translated into serious self-reflection or into fruitful discourse with others in their everyday lives. And, insofar as there were exceptions, all of them took place in discussions with individual students, or with small groups of students, *after* class sessions had ended.

One such discussion, for example, took place after a lesson on the problem of evil, when a group of three fairly observant—yet extremely thoughtful—Muslim students were trying to articulate and make sense of their views on free will and personal responsibility in light of their understanding of God, and invited me into their discussion. What followed was not just a fascinating lesson for me on various Islamic doctrines, but what I took to be a deeply sincere yet all-around respectful and open-minded discussion, in which we worked to examine and clarify the students' interpretation of Islamic doctrine, identifying where there were philosophical tensions to be either resolved, embraced, or simply recognized. It struck me that the students were using this conversation to genuinely reflect upon beliefs of significant importance to them: doing so in a way that was honest yet not emotionally detached, that was critical yet from a position of commitment—and, thus, that was truly constructive.

As wonderful and memorable as this conversation was for me—and although there were a few others like it that took place after class with these, or with one or two other, students—I don't recall any such discussions that took place during class itself, when we were officially teaching students how to engage in philosophical inquiry. Granted, it is more difficult to discuss personally important questions in the context of a larger group. However, this was a fairly small class anyway, and certainly by the middle of the course students seemed very comfortable with each other. More to the point, it really felt like a categorically different kind of discourse that was happening in these after-class discussions than the ones that were happening in the class itself—even when we broke out into two small groups, and I was able to lead a discussion among just six or seven students. And certainly one of my aims in teaching philosophy was (and is) to make personally meaningful discussion possible for students, even about interpersonally contentious issues, and even in the context of larger groups.

THE SECOND COURSE

Description

I was the sole instructor for the course I taught at Career High School in the following year—which (for better or worse) gave me full purview to adjust things in light of what I thought did and didn't work in the pilot course. In this 13-week course of weekly 90-minute sessions, I had 10 students, around three quarters of whom had taken our pilot course in the previous year, but all of whom were now officially enrolled for credit in the course. Some of these students had also taken the pilot course for credit; but since the content of the second course was different from that of the first one, there was no reason not to allow students to "repeat" the course for credit.

In designing this second course, it was important to me to continue focusing on explicit skills development, but this time to do so in a more integrated way and with an emphasis on skills of reading and discussion. Also important to me was to make class discussion less abstract and theoretical: to make it more engaging for a wider range of students and more pertinent to something deep and central in students' everyday lives.

In order to emphasize reading as a starting point for discussion, and as a main area of skills to improve, I decided to devote a significant portion of the course to a close reading of a single piece of text. The piece of text I chose to focus on was a 20-page excerpt from Erich Fromm's *Escape from*

Freedom (Fromm 1994), a section in which Fromm provocatively challenges the assumption that Western democracies regularly foster true individuality among their citizens.

This is not an easy text, but I chose it because it brings up questions like What is it to be one's own person, to have true individuality? What is it to be true to oneself? In what ways are these conditions desirable? To what degree are these conditions possible in our society? And to what degree does each student herself have true individuality and/or manage to remain true to herself? I figured that questions like these would be ones that adolescents would find compelling and so take seriously. I also figured that some of the more plausible answers to these questions would dovetail nicely with the sorts of values and skills that are at the heart of critical reasoning and philosophical reflection—so that in exploring these questions and answers, students would simultaneously gain substantive insight into the importance of the skills they have been learning in class.

My plan for the course was to begin by reading the Fromm text together in class over five or six sessions, including rereadings and reconstruction of important arguments. I supposed that by reading the entire text together in class, students would have the greatest opportunity to learn from me and from each other how to read this sort of text. On the assumption that students would have a solid grasp of the text after five or six sessions, I planned to then give students the freedom to decide which of the questions or positions presented in the text we would pursue more deeply—at which point I would look into any extra readings that might help.

As students made significant improvement in their reading skills, my plan was to begin focusing more on the explicit development of their discussion skills. Taking the central idea of the "Socratic Circles" movement (Copeland 2005) and adapting it, my plan for working on students' discussion skills was to structure several lessons so that the class time would be divided in half: in the first half of such a session, students would wrestle together with some philosophical issue (e.g., one raised by the Fromm text); and in the second half of the session, I would engage students in a meta-discussion about the discussion that took place in the first half. The meta-discussion of the second half would provide students with the opportunity to reflect together, and in a sustained way, upon what makes for a good philosophical discussion—thus giving them a more explicit grasp of how to improve, as individuals and as a class, in their approach to philosophical discourse.

Generally speaking, the course did follow this plan. Our close reading of the Fromm text was followed by a discussion, in the split-session format, of some of the text's central claims. Discussion especially centered on the balance of spontaneity and reflective thought in living a life in which one is true to oneself. Since many of the students placed heavy emphasis on reflective thought, the two other texts I ended up bringing into the discussion were an excerpt from Carl Rogers's *On Becoming a Person* (Rogers 1995), speaking to the importance of spontaneity and creativity; and an excerpt from Dostoyevsky's *Notes from the Underground* (Dostoyevsky 1864), illustrating some of the perils of overthinking.

This course was a significant learning experience for me in terms of teaching students how to read. It especially challenged me to try to balance, on the one hand, my urge to guide students in the charitable reconstruction of textual arguments and in seeing questions that struck me as important, with, on the other hand, my sense that students needed freedom to find things in the texts that moved them to further examination. It was a particular struggle for me to find this balance in the early sessions of the course, when I saw the difficulty students were having in understanding the text and wanted to give students as much concrete guidance as I could in how to read it. This led me to give them a couple of rather rigid, almost exercise-like homework assignments and lessons, that I shortly realized were not very helpful (at least not when and how I did them)—especially since they deprived students of a more natural and enjoyable engagement with the texts.

After correcting for this rigid guidance of student reading, I then ended up overcorrecting for this rigidity when working on students' discussion skills in the split-session format: by having students work out for themselves—with limited guidance from me—the criteria of a good class discussion. Wanting to avoid a scenario in which I would dogmatically list the criteria of a good class discussion and then have students mechanically apply these given criteria in assessing their own discussions, I instead asked students to start from scratch in thinking together about the criteria for a good class discussion.

These were certainly valuable sessions. It was very interesting to see how disoriented students became when I put to them the task of formulating their *own* evaluation criteria for assessing class discussions. Indeed, it took at least a full half session for students to get a handle on what I was asking them to do, and to start proposing some criteria.

In the following week's half session, students got into this task more seriously, and most of the criteria they proposed and debated had to do with student participation: did everyone get a chance to talk, were some people talking too much, should there be a minimum number of times each person participated, should each student's contribution be responded to by someone else before moving on to another point, and so forth. Students did also consider a few criteria regarding the quality of the content of the discussion: for example, that the discussions should be interesting and should leave students having learned something (although, what it might mean for students to "learn something" from the discussion was never adequately worked out).

In the third week of the split-session format, I prompted students to think more about the goal of *progress* in a philosophical discussion, and about what criteria would have to be met for the discussion to count as having made genuine progress. Here, students determined that learning more about one's own views, about the views of others, and simply about the topic under discussion would count as progress. Also mentioned was the epistemic aim of "getting closer to the truth"—although the nearest students came to articulating how to assess a given discussion in terms of this aim was to propose measuring this progress by the extent to which any students managed to eliminate contradictions within their own beliefs through the discussion (and several students balked at the adequacy of this criterion).

However, it was only in the fourth week of the split-session format that students could really start using criteria they had agreed upon to substantively evaluate the discussion that took place in the first half of the week's class session. This meant that almost a month went by with the first-order philosophical discussion of the course being constrained to just the first half of each session, yet without students getting the benefits of jointly reflecting upon these actual discussions. In other words, for several weeks of this split-session format, the second half of the session was spent on an inquiry (into the topic of what makes for good philosophical discourse) that was basically disjointed from the discussion in the first half—rather than being directly linked to the discussion of the first half, as a time for self-evaluative reflection upon that first-half discussion (which is what I had intended).

This is why I believe, in retrospect, that the second half of these split-session classes would have been more focused and productive had I begun by putting forth an initial set of criteria, which students could have immediately put to use in evaluating their first-half discussions. There is no reason I could not have started off the split-session classes in this way, while still giving students the opportunity to analyze and revise, or make amendments to, my initial set of criteria after they had gained some experience with this self-evaluative process. Nevertheless, it still strikes me as valuable to have used these split sessions; they gave, not just the students but me as well, a better understanding of the sorts of things to aim for in a philosophical discussion.

Further Reflections

Indeed, despite my frequent—and not always minor—stumbling, my general sense is that my teaching in this course improved upon my teaching in the pilot course in terms of the things that are especially important to me. Not only did the students' reading and discussion skills show improvement, but it really seemed to register with them that rereading a piece of text or revisiting a topic of discussion need not be tedious and repetitive, but can lead to new and deeper insights about the text or topic at hand. The central questions we tackled in this course did prove to be provocative for the students—especially when I allowed the discussion to roam a bit more. And while no discussion really approached my ideal of concretely engaged philosophical discourse, there were definitely moments in the class where students seemed to genuinely reflect on how the issues discussed applied in their own lives. So, I do believe that the various strategies I pursued in this course were quite successful in a number of ways—even if they could surely use to be further refined and more smoothly executed.

However, there still seemed to be an important gap between the more authentic and concretely engaged sort of philosophical discussion I was able to achieve while talking with a few students after class and the more abstract, detached sort of philosophical discussion that usually took place during class itself. This gap was notably reduced in the second course, but it still nagged at me. Since this course ended, therefore, I have been reflecting further on the question of how to make class discussions more concretely engaged.

While I've had several ideas that I find promising, I hesitate to discuss them before having tried them out in a classroom. There is, however, one pertinent line of thought about which I feel more solid—mostly because I think it accurately captures an important difference between what I did in the small, post-class discussions and what I did during official class time, that made the former more concretely engaged than the latter. In closing this paper, then, I'd like to briefly articulate the difference I have in mind.

Reflecting on what happened in class discussions, what I've noticed is that the context of these discussions was heavily focused on the back and forth of dialectical reasoning. I asked questions like "What is courage?"; and "When, if ever, is it morally permissible to kill a person?"; or "Is this argument for the incompatibility of free will and determinism a good one?" And when students answered these questions, I pressed them to support their answers with reasons, or I raised challenges to their answers, or I pushed them to explore the implications of their answers. Our focus in this process was on whether a given position is true, whether the reasoning offered in their support was good reasoning, whether the challenges pressed by me or others were good challenges, and so forth. Of course, I also asked students to clarify their comments or illustrate their points with examples, but my primary focus in these discussions was on the articulation and evaluation of dialectical reasoning. And since this was the model I was giving them for how to engage in philosophical discussion, this is generally what students themselves did when they engaged each other in these class discussions.

To an extent, this is surely how it should be in a philosophical discussion; and I certainly didn't abandon this dialectical questioning in the smaller, post-class discussions. But what reflecting on things has led me to realize is that, in the more informal discussions, I spent substantially more time than I did in class working to better understand the beliefs and values actually held by the students on the issue at hand and how these fit in with other things they actually believed and valued. When students asserted some position or critique in these post-class discussions, I was more inclined to respond by asking what they meant by some term or phrase that they used, or how they thought they had come to hold the stated belief or value. In other words, I was much better about helping students to *more fully and accurately articulate their vague thoughts and feelings.*

What this ensures is that, as we examined and evaluated these thoughts and feelings in the discussion, it was more likely that we were working with what the students *actually* believed and valued, rather than just with their quickly articulated impression of their beliefs and values, or with articulations that were perhaps defensively formulated in the context of demands for justification. Grounding the discussion as deeply as possible in what students actually believe and value, and in the reasons upon which these beliefs and values are actually based, is—it seems to me—crucial for making a philosophical discussion more concretely engaging for students, and for making students feel more like we are authentically working together in exploring the topic at hand.

In the more formal context of class, it seems I was somehow more inclined to take it for granted that when students expressed themselves, they were articulating their beliefs and values fully and accurately. I seem not to have appreciated as well as I did in the informal post-class context that being able to do this is a real *achievement* that requires much skill; and that for many (most?) students, developing these skills is greatly aided by an environment in which concerted efforts to better understand oneself and one's interlocutors are explicitly valued and fostered.

As I move forward, then, this is the sort of environment that I will aim to better create in my classrooms. Doing this, it seems to me, will require explicitly distinguishing for students between, on the one hand, a *descriptive* sort of inquiry—in which the purpose is simply to identify with as much accuracy and precision as possible what you (or someone else) believes on the issue in question and how this belief hangs together with other beliefs you (or the other) hold—and, on the other hand, a *critical/justification-seeking* sort of inquiry, in which the purpose is to assess the truth of these beliefs and the validity of the reasoning you (or the other) take as constituting the "hanging together" of the belief in question with the other beliefs.

But articulating this abstract distinction—while useful in naming, and thus preliminarily orienting students to these two different modes of inquiry—does not itself seem to me sufficient. Helping students put this distinction of modes of inquiry into practice requires giving students a more concrete understanding of what these two modes look like. Again, the critical mode of inquiry is more familiar in philosophy classes, so more immediate is the need to further flesh out a concrete picture of the descriptive, observational type of inquiry.

Since I don't have the space to do this here, a couple of quick thoughts will have to suffice for now. It is important that in the descriptive mode of inquiry, students as much as possible put out of their mind concerns about justifying and defending their own views, and of challenging views with which they disagree. Thus, when students state a position on some issue in discussion, before asking students "why," or "on the basis of what reasons," they hold this position, it seems to me that some time ought first be given to asking these students self-observational questions such as Can you give some examples of what you have in mind when you make this claim?

What other beliefs or feelings or images do you associate with this position? What do you mean by [some specific term used in stating this position]—can you restate this claim in other terms? And so forth. Since the purpose here is to help students become more accurate and precise in the way they articulate their beliefs to themselves and to others, it may also be useful—instead of simply asking students "what do you mean?" by some claim or term—to give a couple of interpretations of what I imagine they might mean with some claim or term, and then asking them if either of these interpretations captures what they mean, or if they mean something else entirely. Of course, I wouldn't want to put words in students' mouths or short-circuit their effort to carefully determine what it is they do mean, so it would be important for this technique to be used judiciously and skillfully.

Students should also have time to get practice using these techniques on themselves and on each other, which I don't think they have a sufficient opportunity to do in the context of regular (or even small group) class discussions, alone. Rather, I think it would be valuable to this end, to make use of "Think, Pair, Share" sorts of exercises, where students have time to reflect on their own and write down their thoughts on a posed issue in the class discussion, then pair up with another student to exchange their thoughts, and finally return to the full-class context to share their views with the wider group. When using this exercise for this purpose, students could be directed, in doing the "think" piece of this exercise, to ask themselves the descriptive/observational questions rather than any critical questions, and, in doing the "pair" piece of this exercise, to ask the other these descriptive questions. In particular, it would be valuable in the "pair" piece for each student to use the technique of articulating their interpretation of what the other student has said, and then asking the other to determine if this is what she really meant. Perhaps the "share" piece could then even be set up such that each student first shares her understanding of her partner's thoughts, and then the group (based on their understanding of this description) can query the partner further about whether this is quite what he had been thinking.

Again, these are just a couple of quick thoughts on how to create the context of descriptive, observational inquiry that I believe to be important in developing the skills of self-understanding and of charitably understanding others—skills that are essential to authentic, meaningful philosophical discussion. Ultimately, though, a skillful philosophical discussion is one that seamlessly moves back and forth between the search for a better descriptive understanding of a person's views and the effort to justify or challenge these views. Thus, in addition to further fleshing out and modeling the descriptive type of inquiry, it will also be important to figure out how to help students integrate this type of inquiry with the more critical one.

REFERENCES

Browne, M. N. & Keeley, S. M. (2007) *Asking the Right Questions, A Guide to Critical Thinking*, 8th ed. Upper Saddle River, NJ: Pearson Prentice Hall.

Copeland, M. (2005) *Socratic Circles: Fostering Critical and Creative Thinking in Middle and High Schools* Portland, ME: Stenhouse Publishers.

Craig, W. L. & Sinnott-Armstrong, W. (2004) *God?: A Debate between a Christian and an Atheist* Cary, NC: Oxford University Press.

Dostoevsky, F. (1864/1996) *Notes from the Underground* Project Gutenberg. http://www.gutenberg.org/files/600/600-h/600-h.htm.

Fromm, E. (1994) *Escape from Freedom* New York: Holt Paperbacks, Owl Books Edition.

King, Jr., M. L. (1963) "Letter from a Birmingham Jail" http://www.stanford.edu/group/King/frequentdocs/birmingham.pdf.

Law, S. (2003) *The Philosophy Gym: 25 Short Adventures in Thinking* New York: St. Martin's Press.

Plato. (1892/1999) *Crito*. Translated with an introduction by Jowett, B. 1892. Project Gutenberg. http://www.gutenberg.org/dirs/etext99/crito10.txt.

Rachels, J. and Rachels, S. (2006) "The Challenge of Cultural Relativism" In *The Elements of Moral Philosophy* (5th ed.) 15–29, New York: McGraw-Hill.

Rogers, C. (1995) " 'To Be That Self Which One Truly Is': A Therapist's View of Personal Goals" In *On Becoming A Person: A Therapist's View of Psychotherapy*, 163–182, New York: Houghton Mifflin Company.

Singer, P. (1972) "Famine, Affluence, and Morality" *Philosophy & Public Affairs* 1(3): 229–243.

Thomson, J. J. (1971) "A Defense of Abortion" *Philosophy & Public Affairs* 1(1): 47–66.

17 Finding Philosophy in High School Literature

A *Separate Peace* and *Beloved*

Sara Goering

INTRODUCTION

Philosophical themes and insights abound in great literature. Great authors don't simply tell stories, they explore the struggles that help define humanity. Their novels have staying power because they speak to enduring issues, questions that all of us contemplate at one time or another. They reflect our passions, insecurities, and existential struggles even as they invite us into worlds we have yet to experience ourselves. Although they are fictional, and as such, about characters that are made up, they resonate with truths that run deeper than any particular story. Indeed, they can teach us about the world and our places in it despite the fact the lessons come to us by way of stories about fictional beings.

Just as we struggle to figure out how to live, what to be, and who to befriend, we find in great novels other characters, striving like us to find answers, showing us a variety of ways of being in the world. Our philosophical thinking, then, is enriched by our attentive engagement with the lives of fictional characters. Philosopher Martha Nussbaum, reflecting on "the urgency of our engagements with works of literature, the intimacy of the relationships we form, the way in which we do, like David Copperfield, 'read as if for life,'" (Nussbaum 1990, 22) suggests that "moral philosophy . . . understood . . . as a pursuit of truth in all its forms, requiring a deep and sympathetic investigation of all major ethical alternatives and the comparison of each with our active sense of life . . . requires such literary texts and the experience of loving and attentive novel-reading" (Nussbaum 1990, 26–27, my emphasis).

Philosophy, then, not only resides in great literature, but perhaps cannot be fully understood without the aid of stories. Literary works provide us with vicarious life experiences and a wider range of perspectives on the world and the minds of others than we could ever fit into one short life, or than we could effectively relay in straightforward philosophical language. A telling quote from Nussbaum: "[T]here may be some views of the world and how one should live in it—views, especially, that emphasize the world's surprising variety, its complexity and mysteriousness, its flawed and imperfect beauty—that cannot be fully and adequately stated in the language of conventional philosophical prose, a style remarkably flat and lacking in wonder—but only in a language and in forms themselves more complex, more allusive, more attentive to particulars" (Nussbaum 1990, 3).

My aim in this chapter is to make explicit some of the compelling philosophical themes from two works of literature standardly assigned in high school courses, and to show how a teacher (or philosophy facilitator) might spark a philosophical discussion that would enrich the students' thinking in relation to the literature. Although excellent teachers may already broach these philosophical topics to some extent, my worry is that such topics often go un- or under-explored in the American system of schools. Students who read great literature are directed to concentrate on character development, plot structure, identification of key themes, and the use of symbolism more commonly than they are invited to explore and grapple with the philosophical questions at the heart of the stories. Those literary qualities are no doubt important to understand, and will lend insight into the value and meaning of a novel. Yet the philosophical themes deserve time and attention as well if we are to grasp fully the reasons we can be so moved by the story, and the compelling human struggles at the heart of it.

In what follows, I consider the philosophical dimensions of two standard high school novels: *A Separate Peace* (John Knowles) and *Beloved* (Toni Morrison). I recognize that not all schools will use these particular novels, though they appear on many high school reading lists. My hope is that by demonstrating even a small subsection of the wealth of philosophical material within each of these texts, I can show why it would be worth our while to enrich our current curriculum with philosophical explorations and discussions, and how to begin to do that. The rich philosophical themes these novels contain are but exemplars of the similarly robust philosophical entry points that can be found in most works of great literature.

A SEPARATE PEACE BY JOHN KNOWLES (1959)

In this coming of age novel, Knowles tells the story of a friendship between two boys at a New Hampshire boarding school at the start of World War II. The narrator, Gene, is academically gifted and relatively shy. He rooms with a charismatic athlete named Phineas. In a summer session prior to their senior year, the two friends support and challenge each other in ways that highlight their differing personalities and also their common bond. At one point, Gene begins to suspect a troubling rivalry between them, and when he discovers that he was wrong (i.e., that the competitiveness was really only coming from him), he feels not only embarrassed, but also morally inferior to his friend. He impulsively causes an accident that seriously harms his friend, ending his athletic future and taking him away from the school. As Gene struggles to come to terms with the meaning and consequences of his action and to find his own identity, Phineas returns to school. He encourages Gene to try to take on Phineas's own Olympic dreams. The two boys become ever closer, and in the face of World War II and the draft, they relish their protected and ideal circumstances, their "separate peace." Ultimately, however, Phineas dies from an unlikely complication from the accident. The story develops themes of friendship, identity and alienation, and moral evil (e.g., war, betrayal) and human responses to it.

Reading guides—such as online SparkNotes—designed to help students understand and appreciate the novel highlight themes such as "the threat of codependency to identity" and "the creation of inner enemies" and "the dark side of human nature." Yet the questions of identity and friendship at the heart of this novel are so much more robust than what is mentioned in these guides. From a philosophical perspective, these questions are related to a long tradition of contemplating the meaning, value, and practice of friendship, and its relationship to the formation of our identities.

Students reading the novel may find themselves both dismayed by Gene's action to shake the tree limb, causing Finny to fall, and also secretly and partially understanding of it, especially if they've experienced their own internal struggles of rivalry with a close friend. We think of friendship as a relationship of affection and love, where we are supposed to want what is best for our friends and to celebrate their successes. But we also tend to compare ourselves to our friends and to dislike coming up short. Faced with this apparent contradiction, we may question our friendship—our own commitment to it and honesty in it, or our friend's motives and allegiances. Gene suspects that Finny may not want him to be a top student (though Finny is clearly a top athlete) because that would make them even, and he begins to be suspicious that Finny may be deliberately trying to undermine his studying. When Gene realizes that Finny never felt the rivalry Gene had been experiencing, he is even more frustrated by his own apparent moral inferiority: "He had never been jealous of me for a second. Now I knew that there never was and never could have been any rivalry between us. I was not of the same quality as he. I couldn't stand this" (p. 51).

Students reading this section of the book could be invited to start their philosophical investigations by analyzing the definition of friendship. What kinds of friendship are there? Students in this Facebook era will likely have interesting things to say about who counts as a friend, what kinds of experiences are shared with friends, and who is restricted from access to more intimate details of one's life. Following such initial forays, students might be encouraged to consider their closest friendships, and then to analyze what makes a true friend, and whether there is any place for jealousy or competition in such friendships. The novel shows their close friendship in great detail, and as they reflect on their own friendships in light of this example, philosophical discussion can help them to generalize from their individual experiences and, through conversation with others, to recognize the features of their perspectives that are shared, as well as those that may limit their understanding.

Digging into these philosophical questions—exploring them carefully and critically—will give students a greater understanding of the novel than merely identifying "themes" and looking at plot structure. Innovative teachers may want to help their students delve even deeper into the novel's presentation of friendship. One of the best ways to do this is to pair philosophical writings with the book. Teachers might share sections of Aristotle's *Nicomachean Ethics* (Books VIII and IX) in which he describes three kinds of friendship: friends that are fun to be with, friends that are useful or advantageous, and friends that are virtuous. The first two kinds, while undoubtedly valuable in certain respects, are not steady—such friendships will end when the other's usefulness or capacity to amuse ends. True friends, for Aristotle, are virtuous, and like "other selves." We love them; are attracted to the other's virtuous character; and want what is good for the other, for his own sake. We care about them as we care about ourselves and share their joys and disappointments. Such friends are also typically pleasant and advantageous, to be sure, but we are not friends for those reasons. True friends, according to Aristotle, must be moral equals, who will challenge each other to reach their fullest potential by holding each other to high standards.

Given the benefit of such true friends, we might think that the more we have, the better. Yet Aristotle recognizes that it will be impossible to be truly close to more than a few people (his criterion is how many can "live together" because such individuals "spend their days together" and "share one another's enjoyments and distresses as their own") (Book IX, 11, 1171). Indeed, for the Facebook generation and for high school students facing worries about popularity, Aristotle's words may inspire careful reflection about the meaning of friendship. He warns, for instance, that "those who have many friends and treat everyone as close to them seem to be friends to no one" (Book IX, 11, 1171).

As students gain a sense of value of the historical philosophical work on friendship and its significance for understanding the book and their own friendships, teachers can invite students to widen their philosophical scope, exploring contemporary philosophical work that builds on but also partially critiques Aristotle's framework. For instance, teachers might also look to contemporary feminist philosopher Marilyn Friedman's work in *What Are Friends For?*, particularly chapters 7 (Friendship and Moral Growth) and 8 (Friendship, Choice and Change). This book explores the place of friends in moral theory and the tension between moral admonitions to treat everyone impartially and the requirements of partial affection and loyalty to close friends. Like Aristotle, she suggests that true friends will be equals, but she is careful to recognize that the friends might well have quite different sorts of strengths. Indeed, having different capacities can help spur friends to improve each other. Though her view has similarities to that of Aristotle, Friedman points out that true friends are alike, but still decidedly "other than oneself" and so are well placed to offer us opportunities for moral growth. "Through seeing what my friend counts as a harm done to her, for example, and seeing how she suffers from it and what she does in response, I can try on, as it were, her interpretive claim and its implications for moral practice" (Friedman 1993, p. 198). My closeness to my friend's experiences allows me to feel with her, to see her life played out in intimate detail, and this robust experience of another's world may reveal a moral perspective previously unrecognized by me.

Connected to this capacity for moral growth is the opportunity friendship presents to come to understand ourselves more fully. Friendship relies on trust so that with friends, we tend to let down our guard and share our deepest thoughts, feelings, and sensitivities. But in revealing these to another, we also gain insight into our own selves. Although we often presume that introspection is the most obvious and truest method to know our inner states, in many respects we are not fully transparent even to ourselves. We learn to listen to what our dearest friends tell us about ourselves, as a way of studying what might otherwise seem too close for clear observation. Who has not discovered something about herself in conversation with good friends?

Students reading *A Separate Peace* will find interesting connections to the philosophical themes raised by these philosophical works. For instance, when Gene sees Finny carried out of the hall after a second fall (the one that ultimately kills him), he notes "[H]e was by nature someone who carried others. I didn't think he knew how to act or even how to feel as the object of help. . . . My aid alone had never seemed to him in the category of help. . . . Phineas thought of me as an extension of himself" (171). As the quote suggests, we sometimes think of our friends as part of ourselves—not fully separate, but partially constituting us. In Finny's case, this meant that receiving help from Gene was significantly different from asking for help from others. How does our thinking about the nature of friendship change if we see friends as part of us, rather than even very close "other selves"? Are we fundamentally relational beings, creatures whose very existence is defined through our relationships? If so, how might that affect our thinking about what it is to be autonomous or self-determining? Students who are struggling to define themselves as different from their parents while feeling significant peer pressure not to be too different from their friends will have significant experience trying to navigate these troubled waters. Philosophical readings and discussions can give them uptake on their problems and the opportunity to puzzle through them together.

Friendship, like love, is a topic that cannot be ignored. Most of us interact daily with our friends; find reasons for delight, concern, or frustration; and have a difficult time not focusing on friends in need. Even high school students who have difficulty with reading, or whose motivation or time for working through long texts is lacking, will have a wealth of experience to call upon in philosophical discussions of friendship. Such topics, offered not as packets of information to be studied and remembered, but as challenges to be contemplated and carefully answered in their own way—in ways suitable to their vision of the world and their place in it—can reengage students who feel detached from their studies, and will enrich the studies of those who are already eager to learn.

BELOVED BY TONI MORRISON (1987)

This novel, based on a true story, takes place in the aftermath of the Civil War. It tells the story of Sethe, a slave woman who escapes from Kentucky with her children, and moves in with her mother-in-law in a free part of Ohio. It relays her struggles to protect her family, her abuse at the hands of previous slave owners, and the depth of her bond with her children. The story revolves around a nearly unimaginable event: Sethe, eventually pursued by a posse of her previous owners who are set on reclaiming their "property," impulsively determines that she must kill her children rather than allow them to be recaptured and tormented. She kills her oldest girl—a crawling child known as Beloved—before others realize what is happening and stop her. Her actions—her apparent craziness—scare away the posse, and her older sons eventually run off in fear. The novel relays the story of Sethe and her infant daughter, Denver, and the ways they are haunted by the ghost of Beloved, first in terms of a strange presence in the house, and then by an embodied adolescent girl, also known as Beloved, who turns up one day and seems to know parts of their past. (The story leaves open the possibility for other explanations for this latter Beloved's existence and appearance.)

This is a difficult book to read: the prose is dense; the subject matter is horrifying and heart breaking; and the characters are alienated from themselves in significant ways, making easy identification with them difficult. But the central themes of the book—the depth of mother/child bonds, the dehumanization and vicious treatment wrought by slavery, the long-lasting ramifications of such injustices on individual and community identities, the impossibility of moving on without speaking truth to historical injustice—are powerfully rendered and philosophically rich.

To initiate philosophical discussions on these themes, I would start students with the central question posed by the plot: can a way of life ever be so bad as to make dying preferable, or more precisely, can the sacrifice of one's own child ever be justified, given the grim possibilities that await? Students can begin to explore the reasons that Sethe might have acted as she did, and the arguments that might be offered in her defense. Although the book shows Sethe receiving a legal punishment—jail time—for her offense, Morrison does not clearly speak to the morality of her action, so the question remains open in the text. If they can imagine such actions being justified, how secure must the reasoning be? What likelihood of facing abuse and injustice would warrant this response? How grave must the future look? If they cannot imagine this action being justified, why not? What arguments could be given in favor of the value of life itself, regardless of its circumstances? Does it matter whether you make this choice for yourself or for your child? What about the mother/child bond might make seeing one's child be dehumanized worse than suffering that fate oneself?

To help students in discussing these issues, it might be useful to consider two passages from the book. The first is a passage in which Sethe talks with Paul D (also a former slave from her previous life). Confronting her about killing her child, he says, "Your love is too thick" to which she replies, "Too thick? Love is or it ain't. Thin love ain't love at all." He presses on, suggesting that her plan to keep her babies "safe" (away from slavery and abuse) didn't work. She claims it did work, because "They ain't at Sweet Home [the Kentucky farm]. Schoolteacher [the abusive owner] ain't got em." Paul D offers, "Maybe there's worse," and Sethe replies, "It ain't my job to know what's worse. It's my job to keep them away from what I know is terrible. I did that" (pp. 164–165). The second passage occurs later in the book. In it, another past slave—Ella—weighs in on the question of whether or not killing one's child to avoid an even greater harm for her could ever be justified. Having been treated miserably herself, by owners she calls "the lowest yet", it is said that she "understood Sethe's rage in the shed twenty years ago, but not her reaction to it, which Ella thought was prideful, misdirected, and Sethe herself too complicated" (p. 256). How could such an action be considered prideful? Is the point that others have suffered similarly, and endured, and so Sethe shouldn't have considered herself special, somehow powerful enough to take matters into her own hands, to resist in this manner? Or is it the pride for her own children, that they are too good, too precious, to ever face such degrading conditions? Perhaps Ella simply doesn't understand the depth of their familial bond, as Sethe experiences it. The narrator notes of Ella, for example, that "Nobody loved her and she wouldn't have liked it if they had, for she considered love a serious disability" (p. 256).

Asking students to focus on this last line could be quite philosophically productive. How might love be a disability? Or when is it a disability? How might Sethe's intense love for her children have contributed to her post-slavery despair? Can we choose not to love? Would it be worth avoiding this "disability" if we can? Of course, understanding how love can be a disability in general is a valuable question, but to understand how love might be a disability in Sethe and Ella's world, we have to know more about the history, more about the details of what they have suffered and endured.

Having considered how such "thick" love can be a burden, one that might even move a person to kill a loved one in order to protect her in a radically unjust world, students might then read a third passage, one that tries to show why Sethe acted in this way, killing what she saw as the best part of herself. The passage tries to explain why, horrible though the act of killing is, experiencing life in certain conditions might be worse. In so doing, it also identifies a tension between the importance of protecting oneself from unwanted takeover by others (loss of self) and the ways in which our nearest and dearest actually become part of ourselves (expansion of self). In the passage, the narrator describes how Sethe wants to explain to the girl she considers to be the embodied spirit of Beloved why she had to kill her, and the difficulty of doing so: "what it took to drag the teeth of that saw under the little chin; to feel the baby blood pump like oil in her hands; to hold her face so her head would stay on; to squeeze her so she could absorb, still, the death spasms that shot through that adored body, plump and sweet with life . . . worse than that [than dying would be] . . . that anybody white could take your whole self for anything that came to mind. Not just work, kill, or maim you, but dirty you. Dirty you so bad you couldn't like yourself anymore. Dirty you so bad you forgot who you were and couldn't think it up. And though she had lived through and got over it, she could never let it happen to her own. The best thing she was, was her children" (251).

Students who participate in philosophical discussions on these topics will gain a richer sense of the struggles at the heart of the book and deepen their thinking about themes raised by it. Rather than being swept up in story of the book, they will learn to pause to identify and reflect on the questions it raises, to participate in attempting to answer them, and to justify one's answers to others through dialogue. Teachers who want to expand their students' awareness of the philosophical issues related to *Beloved* could introduce a variety of contemporary philosophical readings to help students think through how we might approach such stark choices, how our identities can shift following significant trauma, and what it means to reclaim them and our place in the moral community.

On the first subject, students might consider the philosophical debate about acting so as to bring about a "lesser evil"—essentially it asks whether, faced with a moral dilemma (a situation in which whatever one does, a wrong will be done), one is justified in choosing the lesser evil. Thomas Hill Jr.'s essay "Moral Purity and the Lesser Evil" might be a place to start (Hill 1983), but there are also quite a few contemporary discussions that look at the topic of whether torture (or even "enhanced interrogation") could ever be justified in order to avoid even greater harms (e.g., major acts of terrorism). In such cases, commentators worry about whether the greater harm could really be avoided (i.e., will the information be accurate) as well as whether such infliction of harm could ever be justified in the name of preventing harm.

Of course, Sethe's situation is significantly different from scenarios of torture/enhanced interrogation done with the intent to save unknown others. Her deep and very personal love of her children is what motivates her action. She cannot bear the thought of her "best part" being spoiled and degraded. Part of what Morrison offers the reader is the opportunity to try to enter Sethe's world imaginatively, to grasp how one might feel in experiencing such a profound dilemma in relation to one's duties to loved ones. Here I think students would benefit from reading philosophical work on existential dilemmas. For instance, a moving depiction of an existential dilemma is contained in Sartre's "Existentialism as a Humanism," which describes Sartre's encounter with a young man, forced to choose between defending his brother's honor by going to war for his country, or remaining at home to care for his beloved and ailing mother. Whatever he does, he seems to fail in his moral duties. Yet, according to Sartre, there is no "right" choice for the young man to make: the choice is his alone. He decides what is right, and makes himself through his actions. As the existentialists proclaim, existence precedes essence. We define ourselves through our actions. By entering Sethe's world, the reader understands better just how desperate is her action, how seemingly necessary in the face of an unthinkable future for her children. Horrible as it is, we recognize in it a trace of our own commitments: we have to be able to live with our actions (and inactions).

Focusing on the philosophical difficulties related to re-forming a self after a traumatic event would also enhance discussion of *Beloved*. Philosopher Susan Brison's book *Aftermath* offers powerful reflections on the nature of identity and reclaiming identity after a rape. Brison's writing is accessible and moving. In Chapter 3—"Outliving Oneself"—she draws upon Holocaust narratives to discuss fractured identities, quoting one survivor who notes that "One can be alive after Sobibor without having survived Sobibor" (Brison 2002, 38). Someone lives on, but the former self is fragmented, if not obliterated. By thinking through her experiences and those of other survivors of trauma, Brison presents the reader with a picture of how such shattered identities can be re-formed, through acknowledgment of the past trauma and the capacity to integrate the trauma into one's ongoing story. "By constructing and telling a narrative of the trauma endured, and with the help of understanding listeners, the survivor begins not only to integrate the traumatic episode into a life with a before and an after, but also to gain control" (53–43). Even if we attempt to move forward by forgetting or repressing the past, we may fail to survive (with an intact self and identity) if we do not figure out a way to tell our story in a way that integrates the traumatic experience. Yet one cannot do this task alone. Sethe, isolated from the community after her murderous act, has no people to share her burden, to give uptake to her story, even if she could tell it. Until she meets Paul D and begins to acknowledge and tell her story, she is unable to reclaim herself. Having someone else bear witness to one's trauma story—hear it, give credence to it, bear it—is, in Brison's view, essential to the continuation of a self (Brison, 59). Brison's work will help students recognize why Sethe's identity continues to be broken until she learns to face her past, to tell it to others willing to hear. In so doing, she reclaims not only her identity through the period of trauma, but also her capacity to move forward. In addition to discussing questions related to Sethe's task of rebuilding her identity after trauma (after slavery, and then after killing her child), students would benefit from thinking through the value of bearing witness to the suffering of others. Indeed, although the story of Beloved is difficult to read, the reading of it is another sort of bearing witness to the wholesale suffering produced by slavery.

Finally, the story of *Beloved* calls out for examination of what some philosophers have termed "moral repair"—the work of addressing past wrongs and figuring out ways to reestablish moral relationships. Philosophical discussions on the value of truth and reconciliation commissions—like those instituted in post-apartheid South Africa or post-Pinochet Chile—offer stimulating fodder for our thinking about the value of setting the historical record straight, the difficulty of reestablishing moral relations, the meaning of reconciliation, and the possibility of forgiveness. Margaret Urban Walker's work on moral repair is excellent in this respect. In a paper available online, she not only writes accessibly on these central topics, but also considers them through the lens of another Morrison novel, *Jazz* (Urban Walker 2001).Urban Walker's piece points to the wide variety of ways we respond to wrongdoing—not just blame and punishment, but working out how we can go on together, how we set our relationships right and restore, at least in some ways, our trust in other humans and our hope for society as a whole. She points out that after some kinds of wrongdoing, morality itself may seem to need fixing. We face the question of how to restore "the reality of morality in our lives—its importance and its grip, its mattering to us rather than seeming like just somebody else's rules" (Urban Walker 2001, 113). For high school students, this piece will resonate with a challenging existential struggle of adolescence: how to grapple with the obvious injustices in the world while maintaining hope in humanity. How can we as agents, facing a troubled societal history of wrongdoing, figure out a way to move forward together, to reestablish meaningful moral community? Urban Walker examines the value of truth and reconciliation commissions, as well as some of their limitations, in thinking through the nature of social recovery from political injustice.

Readers of *Beloved* can use Urban Walker's philosophical examinations of moral repair to consider how our country might more directly grapple with the legacy of slavery. As Sethe explains to Denver, the past won't simply go away, even if the physical evidence of it is destroyed. "Where I was before I came here, that place was real. It's never going away. Even if the whole farm—every tree and grass blade of it dies away. The picture is still there and what's more, if you go there—you who never was there—if you go there and stand in the place where it was, it will happen again; it will be there for you, waiting for you. . . . [E]ven though it's all over—over and done with—it's going to always be there waiting for you. That's how come I had to get all my children out. No matter what." Denver replies, "If it's there, waiting, that must mean that nothing ever dies." Sethe agrees: "Nothing ever does" (36). Given that the past remains, our job is to figure out how to live with it, how to reconcile ourselves to it, how to move on together in way that rebuilds trust and hope. Sethe's journey through *Beloved* is story of coming to grips with that reality. Pairing *Beloved* with philosophical work on truth and reconciliation commissions will help students to see more fully how we might collectively deal with a past that cannot be escaped, with moral wrongs that have repercussions through generations.

CONCLUSION

I've offered two examples of high school novels that contain rich philosophical themes and started to show how philosophical writings on those themes will enrich discussions of the novels. My aim in doing so is twofold: to show teachers with a philosophical bent how they might enhance their class-room discussions by introducing these themes (and perhaps readings), and to show philosophy facilitators how they might link their efforts to readings already in the standard curriculum. Students who read great literature see, through the eyes of the characters in the stories, how people struggle to understand themselves, live well, and deal with adversity. All such stories contain within them richly textured instantiations of humans wrestling with the enduring issues at the heart of great philosophical questions. By inviting students to attend directly to these philosophical issues, and to grapple with them together—in light of the story as well as the students' own experiences—teachers can enrich and deepen students' understanding of the literature as well as the philosophical puzzles they explore. Students are already puzzling over such questions in their own lives, so addressing them in the context of classroom learning should be well received. As Katherine Simon found in her study of high school classrooms (reported in the book *Moral Questions in the Classroom*), "moral and existential questions abound but are barely discussed," and "when moral or existential questions are discussed in depth, students describe these as their best learning experiences" (Simon 2001, p. 12). Introducing philosophical discussion into the existing high school curriculum will help to foster these transformative experiences.

REFERENCES

Aristotle (1999) *Nicomachean Ethics*. Trans. by Irwin, T. Indianapolis: Hackett Publishing Company. Available online at http://classics.mit.edu/Aristotle/nicomachean.html.

Brison, S. (2003) *Aftermath* Princeton, NJ: Princeton University Press.

Friedman, M. (1993) *What Are Friends for?* Ithaca, NY: Cornell University Press.

Hill, Jr., T. (1983) "Moral Purity and the Lesser Evil" *Monist* 66: 213–232.

Knowles, J. (1959) *A Separate Peace* New York: MacMillan Company/Bantam Books.

Morrison, T. (1987) *Beloved* New York: Plume/Penguin.

Nussbaum, M. (1990) *Love's Knowledge: Essays on Philosophy and Literature* New York: Oxford University Press.

Sartre, J.P. (1946/2007) "Existentialism as a Humanism" Trans. Macomber, C. New Haven: Yale University Press. Available online at http://www.marxists.org/reference/archive/sartre/works/exist/sartre.htm.

Simon, K. (2001) *Moral Questions in the Classroom* New Haven: Yale University Press.

Urban Walker, M. (2001) "Moral Repair and Its Limits" In *Mapping the Ethical Turn: A Reader in Ethics, Culture, and Literary Theory* (eds. Davis, T.F. and Womack, K.), 110–127, Charlottesville: University of Virginia Press. Available online at http://epublications.marquette.edu/phil_fac/151/.

18 Philosophy in the High School Classroom
Film and Literature

Marina Vladova

Once when I was about eight years old sitting on my bedroom floor with my mother, probably putting toys away, I asked her if she ever thought about whether there were more animals than humans in the world. There probably were many more animals, she replied in a tone that lacked any evidence of the kind of superiority used to treat lightly or praise enthusiastically. We rarely have the foresight to determine when the brief exchanges or longer conversations we have with our children, our students, or each other will be epiphanic. But we can most readily imagine that to pay attention and not shrug off ideas that seem like self-indulgent musings, incontestable assertions, or pointed meditations can nurture the temperament of a future scholar or the will of an individual who will go on to live an examined life. My mother's slightly hesitant response granted credence to my question and encouraged me to ask, why, then, does it look like more humans populate the earth? This question had environmental, economic, and ethical implications. I would eventually go on to take college courses that focused on the origins of human exceptionalism and the environmental effects of industrial civilization. Throughout my life my best teachers, like my mother, did not necessarily introduce new ideas, but they served as guides who questioned, challenged, and encouraged my interests.

For the past five years, I have been teaching English courses at Andrews Osborne Academy (AOA), an international college preparatory day and boarding school just outside of Cleveland, Ohio. What I love most about teaching at AOA is the international perspective offered in any given classroom. Cooperative learning is truly interesting with critical responses from boys and girls representing a variety of cultures and ethnicities. My goal as an instructor is to expand and deepen my understanding of courses that I teach and to continue challenging the intellectual curiosity of my students. I believe that teenagers are cognitively sophisticated and are hungry to explore conceptual questions rather than passively receive instruction. Teenagers are deeply interested in basic complexities that are not typically addressed in core secondary school curriculum—questions that examine the gaps between the kinds of lives that we are encouraged to live as opposed to the kinds of lives that most of us live. These are questions ripe for philosophical investigation.

In this chapter, I relay how I incorporated philosophical readings and discussion into my courses on film and literature, and outline how my role as facilitator rather than expert has had far-reaching effects. My aim is to share some of the details of how I used a philosophical methodology to transform the content and outcomes of existing courses, and to report briefly on how my students responded.

BACKGROUND

Franklin Bobbitt, a founding father of U.S. curriculum theory and supported by behaviorists, viewed teaching as instruction of facts and skills to prepare the child for adult life. John Dewey, on the other hand, thought that education should be viewed as "a process of living and not a preparation for future living" (cited in Brooks and Brooks 1999, 9). Constructivist teachers (I hope to fall into this category) tend to agree with the latter view but also aim to prepare their students for a mature adult life by modeling inherent qualities of mind. Constructivists place greater value on classroom conditions and methodology than subject-matter expertise, and the reason for this has entirely to do with the locus of learning. In his essay, "The Creative Act," Marcel Duchamp (1973, 139) writes:

> The artist may shout from all the rooftops that he is a genius; he will have to wait for the verdict of the spectator in order that his declarations take on a social value [. . .] the creative act is not performed by the artist alone; the spectator brings the work in contact with the external world by deciphering and interpreting its inner qualification and thus adds his contribution to the creative act. This becomes even more obvious when posterity gives a final verdict.

Using the word "spectator" facetiously, Duchamp's view reflects the notion that learning is an active endeavor that constitutes the construction of new meaning rather than the ability to mimic conventions. When constructivist teachers have the interest and the courage to model themselves as learners and display willingness and ability to "alter both content and practice in the pursuit of meaning," they succeed in creating classroom conditions that support "students as self-initiating problem posers and solvers" (Brooks and Brooks 1999, 9).

During the fall of 2010, I began asking around about professional development courses that would help me to empower students to gain self-knowledge and effect social change rather than be mere spectators. Specifically, I was interested in incorporating more philosophical discussion in the classroom. Several History and English instructors enthusiastically suggested that I investigate the National Endowment for the Humanities (NEH) Summer Seminars and Institutes. NEH programs are designed to further the understanding of the humanities through reading, discussion, writing, and reflection.

In spring 2011, I was selected to be one of 15 participants in a summer seminar on Existentialism offered by the NEH. We stayed in a Mount Holyoke College dormitory and had full access to the library, gym, and seminar facilities. Mount Holyoke Professor of Philosophy Dr. Thomas E. Wartenberg directed our studies and hosted local outings throughout Western Massachusetts. Our seminar required at least four hours of reading each day. We read and discussed the works of Kierkegaard, Heidegger, Dostoevsky, Nietzsche, de Beauvoir, Camus, Sartre, and others. We considered how individuals engage in the world of things, history, and other individuals. We viewed films that illustrated existentialist ideas. What I loved most about that summer was the interaction with other passionate and dedicated teachers—from California, Massachusetts, New York, Connecticut, Illinois—who shared an enthusiasm and, to an extent, trepidation in relation to the subject matter. Our discussions helped us to connect seminar material to classroom applications. The relationships we built with each other have continued to grow since the NEH seminar ended and now serve as a resource for exchanging ideas about course development and teaching strategies.

A couple weeks into the seminar, I began thinking about how I could use these new resources—not just seminar material, but also Dr. Wartenberg's engaging teaching methodology—to redesign a basic film course that I had offered as an upper school elective at AOA. Until then, the course simply surveyed film techniques and genres and offered a brief examination of the tension between the art and commerce of filmmaking in the United States. After the seminar, however, I used NEH seminar material and referred to Dr. Wartenberg's book *Existentialism: A Beginner's Guide* (2008), Christopher Falzon's book *Philosophy Goes to the Movies* (2002), and Mary M. Litch's book *Philosophy through Film* (2002) to design a course called *Philosophy through Film*. I selected films and paired them with primary texts to introduce and discuss philosophical topics. Although the understanding of film techniques and the language of film was still part of the course, students were now asked to consider each film as a philosophical thought experiment, or as Dr. Wartenberg referred to film, as *philosophy screened*.

PHILOSOPHY AND FILM

The course focused on using film for philosophical reflection and argumentation. Becoming familiar with the language of film and with major philosophical works, students assessed the philosophical value of film. The aim was for students to become proficient readers of film who are also adept at writing analyses about the emotional, cultural, and philosophical dimensions of the viewing experience.

Although the film course had been a relatively popular elective, I needed to make sure that the 19 students who signed up for the course were aware that this was not going to be the kind of class where they could come in, get comfortable, watch films, and write researched responses. I wanted them to be prepared to get uncomfortable when they, perhaps for the first time, seriously considered some of the difficult existential questions that they have been asking for years. Questions like what's the point? What's it all for? Why do I need to know this or that? How do I know it is or I am real or that it or I matter? To give the students a clear idea of what they were in for on the first day of class, I used Falzon's as well as Litch's introductory discussions of philosophy and created a survey of *Big Questions*. This was the student handout:

> Your survey—the big questions are all basic questions. Each is among the first questions asked when building a framework for thinking about and acting in the world. The usual method employed by philosophers in examining any one of these questions is to consider the questions and then to argue for a particular answer (an answer that usually begets more questions). An argument is nothing more than a set of reasons to support a claim. For example, the skeptic argues for the view that we cannot know that an external world—a world outside of the mind—exists. He or she proceeds to support this argument by giving us reasons to believe that we cannot have knowledge that a world outside of the mind is real.

> 1. What is real? How do you know?
> 2. How do you know that a world outside your mind exists? In other words, can you know if an external mind-independent world exists?
> 3. What is Truth? Is Truth something that is discovered or something that is constructed?
> 4. Is your life meaningful? What makes it so?
> 5. Does the existence of God enhance or take away from your life's meaning?
> 6. Assuming God exists, is God's worship warranted?
> 7. Is your memory essential to your Identity? Conversely, would you still be you without your memory? If you had a different memory, would you then have a different Identity? If somebody had your memory, what would stop him or her from becoming you?
> 8. Is the rightness or wrongness of actions ever based on something other than consequences?

From students who came in expecting a film appreciation class and now facing a set of confusing questions, I saw visible signs of struggle in the classroom. Yet, I noticed a few subtle smiles from some students who seemed to be enjoying the unexpected twist to the class. Nonetheless, the class size on day two dropped off to 11 students. These were not necessarily overachievers or students who thought that the class would look good for college application purposes; 8 of the 11 were seniors who had already applied to college. The adolescent men and women who stayed simply seemed relatively more comfortable with ambiguity. For them, philosophical puzzlement was a form of excitement. These students were from vastly different cultural backgrounds—there were boarding students from China, Rwanda, California, Georgia, Texas, and day students from Ohio. Answers to the survey questions varied, but the prevalent idea among these students seemed to be that life is not inherently meaningful and that only an individual can place value on his or her life. These students were ready for philosophy.

On day two, I explained that film as a philosophical text functions like an argument: it presents a position in response to a big question. Unlike printed texts, films have the ability to address the big questions in ways that captivate our attention and show us a range of possibilities. I admitted that the survey questions were meant to be daunting and that some of them might even seem preposterous. I let them know that I understood why some of the students may have thought that some of the questions did not warrant time for serious thought. I explained that this initial reaction was normal and even expected, and I passed out a copy of Bertrand Russell's essay, "The Value of Philosophy" (Russell 1912). The assignment was to summarize in a single paragraph what, according to Russell, is the value or purpose or even utility of philosophy, and to respond to Russell's assertion. Students were intrigued by the following quote in the essay:

> [A]s soon as definite knowledge concerning any subject becomes possible, this subject ceases to be called philosophy, and becomes a separate science [. . .] those questions which are already capable of definite answers are placed in the sciences, while those only to which, at present, no definite answer can be given, remain to form the residue which is called philosophy.

Russell's delightful understatement in using the word *residue* suggests that the greatness of philosophy is its seeming uselessness. However, Russell is quick to clarify that pursuing philosophical studies is not fruitless self-indulgence. On the contrary, Russell argues that doubt and uncertainty is liberating and that skeptical contemplation frees the individual from his or her "narrow or personal aims" and material goals.

Next, I explained the role of film in the course and how it can be used to introduce and examine philosophical topics and paradoxes that on paper alone are often overlooked. For teenagers new to philosophy, Neo choosing the blue pill in *The Matrix*, for example, illustrates the empowering effect of doubt more vividly than Russell ever could in his entire oeuvre. I shared Litch's argument that a good film allows the viewer to identify with a character and therefore to suspend his or her own preconceived notions and "commonsense" views about how we think the world works (Litch 2002, 2).

Before we really began to develop our philosophical discussions or even to view and assess the philosophical value of any film, the class needed to learn how to talk about film and how to read film as text. So, at this point in the course, we worked on becoming familiar with the language of film. Students received a list of film terms to identify and wrote a few short analyses. Next we surveyed the history of film and the conventions that locate films in particular genres. After we got through these nuts and bolts—the mechanics of film—we entered the philosophical component of the course.

Our days were divided into Film Days, Prediscussion Days, and Discussion Days. On Film Days, students were expected to have read and annotated assigned literature and philosophical texts ahead of time (Descartes, Plato, Heidegger, Dostoyevsky, etc.). Each session, several students were assigned to introduce the film we were about to watch, and then we would watch a film together. The following is a guideline students used to introduce films:

1. Tell the class about when the film was made, who directed it, and which studio produced it.
2. What is the film's genre?
3. Discuss the critical and public reception of the film (what did the critics say and what was the word on the street?).
4. What, if any, awards did it win?
5. In a couple sentences and without giving anything away, say what it's about (not what happens).
6. Discuss anything special about the film, such as visual effects, or a famous line or scene.

A Prediscussion Day followed the film viewing days. Students worked in small groups to extract philosophical questions that they identified in viewing the film. This set up the framework for discussion the next day.

The Discussion Days were devoted entirely to incorporating the primary literature into the film. We started with sharing questions developed by the smaller groups in the previous session. The methodology, modeled by Dr. Wartenberg, was effective in that students learned by engaging with the material and with other students. A scribe from each of the small discussion groups wrote that group's questions on the board and the class proceeded to discuss the questions. Rarely did we manage to thoroughly explore every question. Regardless, the framework remained student centered.

Each student then had a couple days to write a 1½–2-page reaction paper in which he or she would evaluate the film's philosophical value. For this task, students considered the philosophical ideas from their reading assignments and class discussion and then decided to what extent the film they viewed—through various film techniques, specific dialogue, scenes, plot or character development, or symbolism—examined these ideas. Basically, students were asked to assess how effectively the film examined these philosophical ideas as well as the film's shortcomings, and they were free to make recommendations to bolster the film's philosophical value. The final project was to write a 2–3 page philosophical analysis of a film that the class had not watched. I provided a list of films from which to choose, or students were permitted to select a film with my approval. Alternatively, students were permitted to work in small groups to make their own short film and write a collaborative paper explaining that film's philosophical value.

FILMS WITH PHILOSOPHY TEXT PAIRINGS

1. *The Matrix* dir. Andy and Lana Wachowski 1999
   Selected excerpts from Christopher Falzon's *Philosophy Goes to the Movies*, excerpts from Plato's *Republic* on the myth of the cave, and excerpts from René Descartes's *Meditations on First Philosophy* on the evil demon and the illusory world; Kahlil Gibran's quote from "Handful of Beach Sand" in *Mirrors of the Soul*: "They tell me: if you see a slave sleeping, do not wake him lest he be dreaming of freedom. I tell them: if you see a slave sleeping, wake him and explain to him freedom" (Gibran 1965).
2. *Vanilla Sky* dir. Cameron Crowe 2001
   Excerpts from Martin Heidegger's *Being and Time* on throwness, temporality, authenticity, and death as the outermost horizon of being; excerpts from Jean-Paul Sartre's *Being and Nothingness* on bad faith as the human attempt to escape from freedom and responsibility.
3. *Run Lola Run* dir. Tom Tykwer 1998
   Readings and discussion about free will, Chronos (chronological/sequential time), and Kairos as the moment of vision; and Friedrich Kümmel's essay, "Time as Succession and the Problem of Duration" on the coexistence of the past, present, and future aspects of time; that is, time as a correlation and kinship of duration and succession of present moments and the individual's ability to "determine the order and content of his [or her] time" (Kummel, quoted in Fraser 1966). These ideas are interesting but also highly theoretical. To make them more accessible, students wrote and acted out a short skit where a character used sheer will—symbolized by Lola's scream in the film—to activate (or loosen) past, present, and future to reconfigure events. The three aspects of time were acted out by students and, when activated, they vibrated like little application icons on an iPhone screen right before the user can rearrange and manipulate them.

4. *Ikiru* dir. Akira Kurosawa 1952

   Readings included Abraham Maslow's hierarchy of needs and self-actualization and selections from the same readings from Heidegger and Sartre with particular focus on personal responsibility. David White's book *The Examined Life: Advanced Philosophy for Kids* provides key excerpts from Sartre's 1946 philosophical work *Existentialism Is a Humanism* (found in White 2005, 75–76).

5. *Eternal Sunshine of the Spotless Mind* dir. Michel Gondry 2004

   In this session, we focused on student-generated questions regarding memory and identity as well as the Heideggerian application of the idea that the imagined end of a relationship can function as the outermost horizon against which to project, value, and sustain the present relationship.

6. *Moon* dir. Duncan Jones 2009

   Again, we focused on student-generated questions associated with the future self and to what extent would corporations go for the sake of efficiency?

7. *Crimes and Misdemeanors* dir. Woody Allen 1989

   Two chapters—*Rebellion* and *The Grand Inquisitor*—from Fyodor Dostoyevsky's novel *Brothers Karamazov* and Ursula Le Guin's short story "The Ones Who Walk Away from Omelas"; the parable of the ring of Gyges from Plato's *Republic*; Lawrence Kohlberg's stages of moral development was introduced after viewing the film.

REFLECTIONS ON THE COURSE

I was astounded by the insight elicited from student discussion and reaction papers. For example, in response to *Run Lola Run*, students came up with questions such as In what ways does Lola transcend the order of time? Although in the film most of what we see is Lola running, who is truly passing? Lola or time? When are past, present, and future represented conjointly in the film? How does Lola transcend the order of time and actively mediate her present? What is time, according to the film? What does the song at the end of the film say about the relationship of beliefs and the power of human will?

Other films were equally philosophically productive. After viewing *Eternal Sunshine of the Spotless Mind*, student-generated questions considered the choices students would make had they the ability to see into the future: "If you met somebody with whom you were experiencing joy and wanted to have a relationship, but then were shown proof that it would end terribly, would you walk away or would you still pursue the relationship?" One student's response was, "Happiness isn't actively sought after; it is experienced. With some exception it's generally counterproductive to leave a relationship for the sole purpose of avoiding tragedy. You don't experience life trying to stay away from things and possibilities. Maybe it would cause some anxiety, but anxiety is the ambrosia of life!" Students also considered if memory is the essence of personality. Students discussed how the character, Patrick, is unsuccessful in seducing Clementine even though he duplicates her previous lover's words and gestures: "Even if someone has your memories, there's no guarantee that they'll make the same exact decisions as you. Too many variables cause constant formation of new experiences and decisions. Nobody can ever exactly be you." Two students were discussing personality formation and recalled a quote from *Total Recall*, a film that I had not seen: "You are what you do. A man is defined by his actions, not his memory."

Films like *Eternal Sunshine* and *Ikiru* help teenagers explore the role of personal agency in creating meaningful lives. This topic is pertinent for many high school students who find themselves oscillating between cynicism and idealism. A student wrote, "The film shows that Kanji Watanabe, a superfluous character living in a stagnant society, can start a revolution within his mind and affect the world by living creatively." Although I lacked the subject-matter proficiency to select appropriate literature to accompany the film *Moon*, the students organized themselves into groups and generated their own questions. Students considered how the film *Moon* raised moral and ethical questions associated with progress, focusing on a shocking quote from the film—"What is cheaper? Spending time and money training new personnel, or you just have a couple of spares [clones] here to do the job"— and arguing that expressions of "loneliness, anger, happiness, and despair inherited by a clone" should not be considered "forgeries."

Although ontological questions intrigued me personally, after completing the readings paired with *Crimes and Misdemeanors* and viewing the film, students seemed to be especially interested in questions about justice. Do we value ethical principles even when there are no repercussions to prevent us from using power to our own advantage? At this point I felt that the context was appropriate to introduce Kohlberg's theory of moral development. Sensing that the students wanted to continue discussing the nature of justice, I invited a philosopher of law and ethics from the University of Akron as a guest speaker who illustrated theories of justice with rich real and hypothetical anecdotes.

PHILOSOPHY IN LITERATURE COURSES

Including philosophy in the film course and in designing other courses has opened up creative avenues to engage students in the material. When I introduce a new literary period in American Literature, I ask students to consider the cultural impetus for change and to evaluate the new semblance of order put into place. Units center on essential questions such as What does it mean to be good? What is intuition, and is it reliable? How can a writer use language to transcend time and space? What is the difference between being self-reliant and selfish? How does ecstatic affection for people and place differ from nationalistic fervor? What is status? Does the Universe care? Toward the end of each unit, I schedule a Socratic Seminar based on one of our essential questions to allow students to demonstrate full familiarity with the ideas and specifics of the texts and to indicate how they tie into the essential question. It is important that the teacher remains an observer during the seminar. I limit my role to quickly looking up words online at the students' requests.

Socratic Seminars can also be used to examine narrative elements. For a character study after reading Arthur Miller's play *The Crucible*, students are asked to consider Is Abigail Williams [the teenaged orphan who accuses neighbors of witchcraft] pathetic or deplorable? Students begin by engaging in conceptual analysis of the two terms. Once they are satisfied with the meanings, boundaries, and distinctions they have come up with for the two terms, they proceed to discuss the kind of motivation that deserves contempt as opposed to pity. Some students suggest the need to examine Williams's actions in light of her backstory as well as late 17th-century social norms. Another student remarks that Williams becomes responsible and despicable for her actions as soon as she is placed in a position of power. Then the question is raised: how does one who engages in malevolent deeds maintain credibility in society? The list of student-generated questions and observations continues until the class ends. Students are then assigned to select one of the points made and develop it—supported by textual evidence—into a one–two-page reaction paper.

Another way I incorporate philosophy into my literature courses is by pairing philosophical texts with short stories or novels. I then ask students to compose "therapy sessions" or dialogues between the philosophers and selected fictional characters. For example, after reading "The Myth of Sisyphus," Albert Camus's philosophical essay about individual triumph in the face of meaninglessness, I have students assume the role of Camus to advise Nathaniel Hawthorne's bitter and disillusioned character, Goodman Brown, who is disappointed with his community and seems to be wallowing in despair and disenchantment. The results demonstrate the students' understanding of Camus's argument and the complexity of Hawthorne's character:

> Mr. Brown, if you are able to accept that life does not have meaning, and then to create a meaning of your own, you will be much better off. You may, once again, enjoy your wife and your neighbors and smile at your own reflection in a glass. Constructing meaning from nothing is much like painting upon a blank canvas. The paintbrush is in your hand, the acrylics by your side. Do with them what you will Mr. Brown, the choices are all your own.

and

I understand that you feel as if everyone has an evil nature and that you feel betrayed and deceived by the people that you live among, but they are not the cause of our problems. You are. Goodman Brown, you have the ability to create your own. You must define your own life, because it is yours and belongs to no one else. You defined yourself with your father, and generations before him. Now you define yourself with the flaws of everyone around you. Take my advice Sir—worry about yourself. I should clarify that when I say to worry, I do not mean to fret. I simply mean that you should be concerned with your actions and your motivations.

CONCLUSION

I am wildly passionate about the material that I teach and would never want to debase it through rote instruction. I much prefer to set up classroom conditions for students to explore, infer, and test their understanding. Existential or intellectual confusion does not worry me, particularly when I see how it can enliven the classroom. Selecting quotes from a complicated philosophical text for small groups to deconstruct and interpret usually yields favorable results. Allowing students to experience uncomfortable breaks with tidy notions or paradigm shifts and encouraging imagination can move students from living apathetically in the world as it is to creating a world they would like to have (Frye 1968, 23–24). This idea is exemplified in the following lines of Langston Hughes's poem *Let America Be America Again*: "O, let America be America again / The land that never has been yet / And yet must be" (Hughes 1999, 97). When a student like Sisyphus realizes that the locus of meaning in not in a particular novel or film or rock, but is in his or her interpretation of text, he or she then "negates the gods and raises rocks" by exercising responsibility for his or her own learning. This is enough to fill this teacher's heart.

REFERENCES

Brooks, J. G. and Brooks, M. G. (1999) *The Case for Constructivist Classrooms* Alexandria, VA: ASCD.
Dostoyevsky, F. (2002) *The Brothers Karamazov* New York: Farrar, Straus and Giroux.
Duchamp, M. (1973) *The Writings of Marcel Duchamp* New York: Oxford University Press.
Falzon, C. (2002) *Philosophy Goes to the Movies* New York: Routledge.
Fraser, J. T. (1966) *The Voices of Time* New York: George Braziller, Inc.
Frye, N. (1968) *The Educated Imagination* Bloomington: Indiana University Press.
Gibran, K. (1965/1999) "Handful of Beach Sand" In *Mirrors of Soul*. Trans. Sheban, J. Secaucas, NJ: Castle Books.
Heidegger, M. (1927/2010) *Being and Time*. Trans. Stambaugh, J. Albany, NY: State University of New York Press.

Hughes, L. (1999) *Hughes: Poems* New York: Everyman's Library/Alfred A. Knopf.

Le Guin, U.K. (2000) *The Wind's Twelve Quarters: Stories* London, England: Orion Books, Ltd.

Litch, M.M. (2002) *Philosophy through Film* New York: Routledge.

Russell, B. (1912) "The Value of Philosophy" In *The Problems of Philosophy* London: Williams and Norgate. Available online at http://www.skepdic.com/russell.html.

Sartre, J.P. (1956) *Being and Nothingness* New York: Random House.

Wartenberg, T. (2008) *Existentialism: A Beginner's Guide* Oxford, England: Oneworld.

White, D.A. (2005) *The Examined Life: Advanced Philosophy for Kids* Waco, TX: Prufrock Press Inc.

19 Project High-Phi

Mitchell Green

OVERVIEW AND AIMS

Project High-Phi was founded in 2009 with the support of the Teaching Resource Center and the College of Arts and Sciences at the University of Virginia (UVA). Its goal has been to facilitate philosophical inquiry in American high schools. Figure 19.1 shows its logo:

Why is such a goal worth pursuing? There are a number of reasons. First, unlike what is the case in Europe, formal instruction in philosophy in American high schools is the exception rather than the norm (Katz 2006). More often than not, students happen upon philosophical questions in the course of studying slavery as depicted by Mark Twain, human rights as appealed to by the American Founders, or freedom of will as contemplated by Hamlet. These and related issues are important topics for discussion in English, History, Government, and many other classes, yet it is my conviction that a large, untapped educational opportunity exists in secondary level philosophy instruction.

If you've wandered by the Philosophy section at a mainstream bookstore lately, you may have noticed, interspersed among the Plato, Sartre, and Kierkegaard, a number of titles having the form *X and Philosophy*, where X includes such pop culture topics as Star Wars, Buffy the Vampire Slayer, Hip Hop, The Simpsons, Mad Men, Stephen Colbert, Twilight, and Radiohead. Given the variety of topics paired with Philosophy, Open Court Publishing, which produces these volumes, evidently finds a market for them among teenagers. Similarly, over the last several years I have been invited to speak at both public and private high schools on various philosophical issues.

Figure 19.1 Project High-Phi logo.

In each case I was amazed at both the thirst for philosophical discussion I found among students in my audiences, and at these students' ability to engage constructively with the issues presented. Similarly, I have been a panelist since 2005 for the website, AskPhilosophers.org, to which anyone can submit questions about philosophy to be answered by an international panel of about 30 professional philosophers. My colleagues and I have answered questions from all walks of life, but it is clear that a large portion of such questions are from secondary level students who are exploring philosophy on their own but are having difficulty negotiating its complexities without guidance from their teachers. Here are a few examples:

> "Is it fair to force someone to learn even if it is for their own good?"
> "If you could recommend one novel for high school students about the subject of philosophy what would it be? I'm looking for a work that is readable, entertaining and raises important philosophical issues as they relate to the Theory of Knowledge. Many people online have recommended *Life of Pi* or *Tuesdays with Morrie*. Any other suggestions?"
> "I'm a high school student and the question I may be asking might seem dumb to others, but nevertheless. If matter cannot be created or destroyed then how could God create our world and everything surrounding it?"
> "My aunt once complained about how dumb the janitor of my high school was. He didn't seem very bright to me either. But, why do people think it's okay to put others down just because they are dumb? Am I warranted in having less respect for my aunt for being that way or is it hypocritical to be judgmental to people who are judgmental?"

These questions may not be highly polished, but they show curious minds engaging with important issues, and my fellow panelists and me on AskPhilosphers.org do our best to help those posing them to refine their thinking and, when possible, articulate a range of available answers.

There would seem, then, to be an unquenched thirst for philosophy at the secondary level. What is more, quenching that thirst could make a contribution to educational attainment, as well as to the level of public discourse in the United States. While all academic subjects involve some degree of criticism, analysis, and argumentation, philosophy is particularly well suited to the cultivation of critical reasoning skills. The thought processes central to this field, involving concepts like time, freedom, justice, and knowledge, depend crucially on precise verbal formulation, sometimes with explicit definitions and arguments elucidated in terms of premises and conclusions. Students of philosophy thus develop the skills of close textual analysis, as well as a sensitivity to fallacies in reasoning that often go unnoticed among educated adults.[1] What is more, even for secondary level students who do not continue to college, exposure to philosophy can have lasting benefits. Because this field encourages attention to clarity of thought and cogency of argument, high school graduates who have been exposed to philosophy may be better equipped to spot fallacious reasoning in the public sphere. As a result, they may well be prepared as adults to cast their votes based on reasoned argument rather than demagoguery, and to make choices as consumers reflectively and with a healthy skeptical attitude.

In addition, I have learned from many teachers with whom I've worked that philosophy properly taught has an uncanny ability to excite students who are capable but under motivated. Students who are otherwise apathetic are often the most vigorous contributors to class discussions touching on philosophical issues. As a result, philosophical education at the secondary level has the potential to inspire students who would otherwise plod through the rest of their education, however far it might carry them.

Finally, the cultivation of philosophical education in high school is a long-term investment in the humanities. All too often students taking a philosophy course in college treat it as one of so many items on a menu—to be sampled before, presumably, moving on to a main course of study that they expect to provide more sustenance for a dependable career. Such an approach makes it difficult for students to appreciate what philosophy as a classic humanistic discipline has to offer them even if they do end up with an ostensibly more practical major. By contrast, exposure to philosophy before college increases the likelihood of students coming to appreciate its lasting value. Regardless of the career path they later pursue, this early exposure can help our students come alive to the nuances and immediacy of life's most pressing questions, thereby engaging them actively rather than encouraging their uncritical acceptance of the pronouncements of political, religious, or other cultural authorities.

The foregoing observations and experiences inspired me to conceive Project High-Phi. Since its inception, we[2] have organized under its auspices a number of subprojects, including an Annual High-Phi Essay Contest (2011 and 2012); an NEH-funded Summer Institute for High School Teachers (July 2011); an undergraduate internship course at the University of Virginia (spring semesters 2011 and 2012); a public essay forum, known as the High-Phi Forum; and we are currently developing an interactive website, Socratic Method Online (http://jefferson.village.virginia.edu/), which will enable students and teachers to engage with philosophical problems in a digital environment. In the section that follows, I will describe each of these subprojects in fuller detail.

THE HIGH-PHI ESSAY CONTEST

For two consecutive years, we have sponsored a contest for the best essay by a high school student on a philosophical topic. For its first year, the contest was open only to residents of the state of Virginia. We restricted its scope simply to keep the logistics manageable, and to learn any lessons that needed bearing in mind before widening our scope to the national level. As of the time of the writing of this chapter, the contest is in its second year and is now open to students from any U.S. school, including public, private, religious, and home-school environments. In both inceptions, the essay contest has offered students a variety of topics to choose from as they prepared essays of up to 5,000 words in length. In its first year, the High-Phi Essay Contest was made possible by a generous grant from the Squire Family Foundation. In its second year, the contest has the good fortune of receiving support from both the Squire Foundation and the American Philosophical Association.

After the submission deadline, the contributed essays are judged by a panel of University of Virginia graduate students and faculty; and a winner, as well as runners-up, are chosen. In the first annual contest, we were able to sponsor an awards ceremony on the University of Virginia campus that was attended by the winner; runners-up; their families; and in some cases, even the students' teachers. For the 2011–2012 contest, participants were invited to write on any one of the following topics:

1. We often hear people talk about their rights and, by extension, about how others are obliged to respect those rights. What are rights and what is their source? How can we tell whether something is a right or is instead merely something that a person values highly? Are there any conditions under which society is justified in violating one or more of someone's rights, or is the expression "justified rights violation" an oxymoron? (Sources: John Locke, Thomas Paine, UN Declaration on Human Rights)

2. Some people feel that we have a moral obligation to help others who are suffering (from, for instance, famine) even if they live in distant countries. Others feel that our obligations only extend as far as our borders, so that we are at most obliged to come to the aid of our compatriots. Please take a stand on the question whether we are in any sense morally bound to aid fellow human beings irrespective of national boundaries, supporting your view as far as possible. (Sources: Singer, Pogge, O'Neill)

3. Many people worry that because we occupy a universe that is governed by the laws of physical causality, free will is a mere illusion. First, after elucidating what it is to have free will, please explain why one might hold that this freedom is challenged by the laws of physical causality. Next, take a stand on the question whether we have free will, defending your view against possible objections. (Sources: Green, Hume, Campbell)

4. Anthropologists point out that people's views of right and wrong vary dramatically from one culture to another as well as over time. Does this show that right and wrong are always relative to one's cultural milieu? Or, instead, is there such a thing as objective moral truth? Please explain and justify your answer. (Sources: Montaigne, WG Sumner, Green)

5. Can a machine think? (This is a question about what is *in principle* possible rather than what is technologically feasible either now or in the near future.) In your answer, please explain what you take "thinking" to mean. Also, and in light of your elucidation of thinking, please discuss how important it is to have a brain or a central nervous system to be a thinker. If you argue that it is not possible for a computer to think, please explain clearly what computers are missing. (Sources: Descartes, Turing, Dennett, Green)

The names listed at the end of each essay refer to readings that are posted on the High-Phi website for downloading by contestants. These readings are intended as supplemental only; students are not required either to refer to these essays or to presuppose them in their essays. Instead, they are intended to play a supporting role only.

Judging from the essays that have been submitted to the essay contest thus far, as well as conversations with some contestants, it appears that students find the task of writing them to be both challenging and rewarding. We have read many lovely essays that show students grappling with questions that are not normally addressed in their studies, but in a great many cases students rise to the occasion and write at a high level. Students would, however, benefit from greater guidance from their teachers, and this is one reason why I have also begun to work with high school teachers as well. It is to this topic that I now turn.

NEH SUMMER INSTITUTE

In communicating with teachers about philosophical pedagogy at the secondary level, I have learned that many who are interested in teaching more philosophy lack substantial training in the field. Further, because a philosophy class would be an elective, but not one that is supported with the prospect of an Advanced Placement exam, many high schools lack incentives to offer full-term courses on this subject. Instead, as I mentioned above, much philosophical discussion in high school happens by way of treating other subjects. Yet the educators I have polled are eager to deepen and broaden their teaching of philosophy in such contexts.

As a result of the foregoing observations, I sought and received funding from the National Endowment for the Humanities to offer a three-week Summer Institute in July 2011 entitled "Epic Questions: Mind, Meaning and Morality."

The Epic Questions Institute was quite different from other NEH Institutes of which I am aware. These tend to be focused on a specific topic—Jazz in America; Literature, Religion and Art of the Himalayas, and so on—whereas I aimed to provide brief but intensive exposure to a wide variety of areas within my discipline. My reason for doing so was that since many teachers whom I wished to serve have had little or no formal philosophical training, their first exposure to the field should provide some breadth of coverage. Such breadth is particularly important for philosophy because many of its subfields depend on one another intimately: discussions of justice and rights in Bioethics and Political Philosophy often depend on conceptions of personhood, a topic within Metaphysics; theories in the Philosophy of Science interact not just with the metaphysical issues of space and time, but also with Epistemology; current research in Ethics is even witnessing a quickened interest in Epistemology (DePaul and Zabzegski 2007). As a result, a civics teacher who aspires to bring Political Philosophy into her classroom does well to ground her thought in appropriate areas of Metaphysics; a science teacher wishing to explore with students what is involved in confirming or disconfirming a theory—a core topic in the Philosophy of Science—should be conversant with some main themes in Epistemology, and so on. Narrowing our approach would, I felt, hamper teachers' efforts. Yet, broadening our focus need not mandate superficial treatment. What's more, the Visiting Lecturers who contributed to the Institute were of such a caliber that even teachers who come to the Institute with, say, a primary interest in the Philosophy of Mind or Bioethics found, to their surprise, exciting opportunities for unexpected areas of philosophical pedagogy.

The main topics covered were as follows:

> *Logical Theory*: Argument construction, fallacies, method of counterexamples, conceptual analysis, conceivability and possibility
> *Metaphysics*: Free Will, Personal Identity
> *Philosophy of Language*: Meaning, Truth, Presupposition, Pragmatics
> *Epistemology* (Theory of Knowledge): Rationalism, Empiricism, Skepticism
> *Philosophy of Mind*: Consciousness, the Mind-Body Problem
> *Ethics*: Virtue Ethics, Utilitarianism, Deontology
> *Political Philosophy*: Justice, Theories of Rights, Political Obligation
> *Bioethics*: Research Ethics, Health Care Ethics

These topics were discussed by Visiting Lecturers (either current faculty at the University of Virginia or faculty at other Virginia institutions who received their doctorates in Philosophy from UVA) and/or me, in most cases over a two-day period of lecturing and question and answer. Summer scholars were given extensive reading from both historical and contemporary sources, and lecturers assigned such reading in part with an eye to what high school students would find accessible and useful. Lectures occupied the bulk of our time Mondays through Thursdays, while Fridays were set aside for "syllabus development," in which summer scholars would be invited to work either individually or in groups to develop lesson plans, units, or even new courses incorporating the material covered earlier in the week.

With the help of a website created for the Summer Institute, scholars have been able to remain in touch with one another since the completion of the program. Many have collaborated in development of courses and course units on topics of common interest, such as Environmental Ethics, Social Justice, Philosophy and Film, and Political Philosophy. We have also continued the dialogue begun in the summer of 2011 by organizing events around the United States in support of Philosophy in high school. For instance, one summer scholar, Steve Goldberg of Oak Park River Forest High School, has organized a session of the 2012 American Philosophical Association, Central Division meeting in which his students gave a "live" demonstration of their discussion of two philosophical issues: personal identity and genetic enhancement. Similarly, another American Philosophical Association meeting, this time at the Pacific Division, will be devoted to issues involved in developing a high school philosophy course.

Let me stress, however, that it is not to be assumed that the best way of introducing Philosophy into a high school is by developing a semester- or quarter-long course devoted to it. Great things can be done by incorporating Philosophy into other courses that are already established parts of the curricula. An English Literature class might be reading a dystopian novel such as *Brave New World*, and this would be an excellent route into discussion of the ethical question of what it means to lead a good life, and how such goodness relates to happiness. A Biology class might be studying the question how scientists find evidence in support of the theory of Evolution through Natural Selection; in such a study, discussion of the epistemological issues of confirming or disconfirming scientific theories could deeply enrich the class. The same can be said for the relevance of Political Philosophy to a course in Government. Similarly, any History course might find it useful to pause over one of the philosophers who lived in the period covered by that course: Ancient History could be enriched by reading and discussing the works of Plato or Aristotle, while a course that covers the history of Early Modern Europe could be enhanced by a study of Descartes or Hobbes. More generally, Philosophy is often at its best when studied alongside Literature, History, Science, or other fields, and one main aim of the Epic Questions Institute has been to equip teachers to draw these connections and thereby enhance their students' engagement with that they are learning.

UNDERGRADUATE INTERNSHIP COURSE

With support from an Academic Community Engagement Grant from the Office of the Provost of the University of Virginia, Project High-Phi has led internship courses for University of Virginia undergraduate students of Philosophy or related disciplines such as Political Philosophy or Bioethics. Students enrolled in the course are paired up with high school teachers at schools within a 30-mile radius of the university. These teachers are encouraged to share their aims in working with an intern, and then on this basis are paired up with students depending on common interests and backgrounds. Many of the students who enroll for this internship course are interested in exploring the possibility of a teaching career, and would like to get some classroom experience as they consider their options. Many who have enrolled in this internship course thus far have plans to enter Teach for America (teachforamerica.org), the City Year Program (cityyear.org), or aspire to careers in educational policy.

As with the Epic Questions Summer Institute, in designing the internship course we have gone to pains to meet teachers on their own terms rather than try to dictate what they do in their classrooms. For this reason, I insist that interns spend ample time early each semester just listening to the teachers with whom they are paired, and making sure they understand what will best serve the teacher's needs. Students also learn about Socratic method in teaching, and familiarize themselves with the notion of a Community of Philosophical Inquiry (see Mohr Lone 2012). Then, after consultation with their instructors (either myself or my colleague Jennifer Merritt of the UVA Women's Center), interns develop an outline of what they propose to contribute to the high school class. This might involve a discussion with students of some of the social and political philosophy that form the backdrop to a novel that the students are reading; or it might be an overview of some basic topics in logic to help students be better prepared to spot fallacies and rhetorical maneuvers in the media or politics. To take another example, Psychology has become a popular course in many high schools, and the field is allied with Philosophy in many ways. Students in our Philosophy Internship course are well placed to contribute to a Psychology course by, for instance, fleshing out the history of philosophical thinking about self-knowledge, introspection, and self-deception, all as ways of deepening students' appreciation of the role of the unconscious in contemporary psychological research.

All these cases and many more provide excellent opportunities for undergraduate students of philosophy and related disciplines to share what they have learned with high school students. I have long been committed to the view that you understand something only if you can explain it to an intelligent person who knows nothing about it—the so-called Intelligent Ignoramus Test. Students often find, as they try to explain what they have learned in college classrooms to younger students, that their grasp on that material is more tenuous than they had realized. This forces them to go back to that material and clear up misunderstandings, puzzles, or ambiguities. We try to minimize the likelihood of students being caught off guard by asking them to make practice presentations of philosophical ideas in front of other students in the Internship course. Their peers will do their best to behave like high school students whose interest in Philosophy cannot be presupposed, and we have great fun peppering these fledgling educators with questions and comments of varying degrees of relevance and respectfulness. Done in the spirit of camaraderie, this helps students relax a bit as they prepare for their first intervention in a high school classroom.

At the time of writing this chapter, we are mid-semester in a second Internship course. Based on student-submitted course evaluations from its first offering, as well as feedback from teachers with whom those students interned, it is clear that the course fills a need both for undergraduates who enroll and the teachers and students whom they serve. Aside from its support of philosophical inquiry in high schools, such a course dovetails with the worthy initiative many colleges and universities are undertaking in support of community engagement. As a result, we have reason to hope that other colleges and universities will develop similar courses in the future.[3]

HI-PHI FORUM

In 2011, Project High-Phi began to publish a series of occasional papers known as the *High-Phi Forum,* in which teachers at all levels are invited to share their reflections or innovative ideas on teaching a philosophical topic in the high school setting. In some cases, educators will reflect on what sorts of thought experiments work, and which do not, in stimulating discussion of consequentialist ethics in a high school classroom; in other cases we might find reflections and constructive suggestions as to how an art museum might be convinced to host an exhibit that raises philosophical issues for students and other visitors; another writer might discuss the potential value and challenges of community service projects in helping students to achieve a more intimate understanding of social justice; in yet a fourth instance, a teacher of literature might discuss which novels are particularly well suited to discussion of moral dilemmas, and how such discussions might best be initiated. Such essays might also include lesson plans and student evaluations in order to provide as many resources as possible to those wishing to adopt a new technique or strategy in their classroom.

All authors of articles in the High-Phi Forum are allowed to retain copyright of their work, and as result are welcome to subsequently publish their essays elsewhere if they choose to do so. In addition, the website on which the Forum articles are published has space for reader comments on all essays therein. As a result, we see the Forum as having a "working papers" format enabling authors to open their work to public view in the hope of benefiting from reader feedback, and in preparation for publication in other venues such as the journal *Teaching Philosophy.*

SOCRATIC METHOD ONLINE

During academic year 2011–2012, I have been working with the Institute for Advanced Technology in the Humanities (jefferson.village.virginia. edu/) to develop an online resource for students, teachers, and researchers of Philosophy. I have long believed that Philosophy is best taught not as a body of knowledge, but rather as a set of skills—of analysis, criticism, counterexample, definition, and articulation, all exemplified in the Socratic Method—used in the clarification and defense of controversial positions that are integral to our approach to the world.[4] For this reason, many uses of digital technology are not particularly well suited to supporting philosophical inquiry. For instance, while it is useful to have classical works of Philosophy online, particularly in searchable format (such as one finds in the Past Masters series), such applications do not exploit the full power of digital humanities. Instead, I aim to construct an online platform in which philosophical inquiry can be achieved with a system that *argues* with the user as an aid to her clarifying, refining, and articulating her position on a controversial question.

How might this be done? I take inspiration from a website entitled DebateGraph.org, which is ostensibly designed to support discussion of issues in European politics and economics. For each of a variety of issues, the reader sees a large bubble surrounded by a number of smaller ones, each labeled. The large bubble represents a thesis or idea concerning one or another social issue (such as "The G20 London Summit, 2009"), and the smaller bubbles surrounding it are problems or issues that challenge, develop, or otherwise complicate that idea ("What is the G20?," "The Global Financial Crisis," etc.). The user can also connect to larger bits of text that explain ideas in more detail. Further, in some cases when the user clicks on one of these smaller bubbles, she is taken to a new page on which that bubble is now the large one in the center and is surrounded by smaller ones that complicate, challenge, or otherwise develop *it*. In principle this process can go as many steps as the designers of the website wish, the only limit being the complexity of the issue.

DebateGraph is well suited to expose the depth and subtleties of debates on certain issues and helps users to see that many problems of concern to modern society are ones in which reasonable disagreement is possible. In addition, I would also venture that such a platform is well suited to enabling users to refine or clarify their views in light of various challenges. It thus helps users cultivate the skill, which is uncommon even among educated people, of asking skeptical questions even about one's own convictions.

Taking DebateGraph as a rough model, I aim to build a platform, Socratic Method Online (SMO), which supports philosophical inquiry specifically. On this platform, the user starts with any of a variety of core philosophical areas such as Ethics, Epistemology, Metaphysics, Philosophy of Science, Political Philosophy, and so on. She is then presented with a central question ("Is the will free?," "Do we have obligations to the State?," "Is the mind identical with the body or some part thereof?") and asked to take a stand by answering it. Choice of an answer then takes her to a new node in the SMO tree structure, in which her position is graphically surrounded by a variety of other nodes containing objections, nuances, possible clarifications, and so on. By clicking one of those bubbles, the user learns more about that objection, nuance, or possible refinement and is given a variety of options as to how to proceed from there: retract or refine her position, neutralize the objection, etc. SMO now updates her position in light of which option she chooses and then presents her with new challenges for the position thus revised. After a number of iterations, the user will, it is hoped, have reached a terminal node at which she has a refined and defensible position on a philosophical topic. That position will in all likelihood still be subject to various objections, but by now the user is at least aware of them; and by reaching her position by means of this process of elenchus, has "earned her right" to it. In addition, at this point, the user is invited to push back the frontiers of philosophical inquiry by adding new positions, responses to objections, and so on. These contributions would then be vetted by a webmaster for SMO, who may choose to include them in appropriate points of the website for future users.

The platform I am developing in collaboration with IATH is, accordingly, an aid to research in Philosophy as much as it is an aid to teaching and learning. I also hope it will provide an illustration of what is possible in the emerging field of Digital Humanities. If appropriately developed, SMO could harness the power of digital technology in ways that go beyond what a book or article can do, in order to bring out the dialectical structure integral to philosophical inquiry.[5] But it is also designed for a high school student to use on her own and at her own pace as she explores the subtleties and intricacies of philosophical reasoning.

Thus far I have given an overview of the main activities of Project High-Phi as of early 2012. In the coming years, I will be exploring with other organizations around the United States who share an interest in supporting Philosophy at the high school level, new opportunities to help reach that goal. Below I outline one exciting project on the horizon.

FUTURE DIRECTIONS: HIGH SCHOOL ETHICS BOWL

In recent years the Squire Family Foundation, the Parr Center for Ethics at the University of North Carolina, and other institutions have sponsored a number of ethics bowls for high school students. Their basic format is as follows. Approximately six weeks before the event, teams of five students at participating high schools are provided with real-world ethical scenarios and a number of associated questions. Under the guidance of a qualified coach, these teams then work in the following weeks to develop arguments in defense of answers to these questions. Their work culminates in the competition of the Ethics Bowl itself, in which all teams meet for an opportunity to explain and defend their answers. Judging depends not on style or theatrics, but on the logical rigor of the arguments provided in support of the position being defended. After one team has presented a defense of its own position, other teams are invited to challenge that defense. The presenting team is then permitted to respond to those challenges, and to answer any further questions that may be raised by the judges. These judges, who consist of college and university faculty and graduate students, school administrators, and local business leaders, then confer to score various aspects of the teams' performances and to decide on winners based on that scoring. Members of the press are always invited to these events in the hope that they will receive the widest possible publicity.

The ethical scenarios that form the basis of Ethics Bowl competition include issues of particular relevance to teenagers (including questions about cheating, plagiarism, peer pressure, bullying, abuse of social media, and privacy) as well as political and social issues such as free speech, gun control, environmental responsibility, and bioethical problems such as genetic enhancement and distribution of health care. Recent years have seen vigorous and exciting High School Ethics Bowls in the Research Triangle Area of North Carolina; on Long Island; at the University of Tennessee; the University of Baltimore; and in Pinellas County, Florida. Discussions are now underway to form a national-level competition in which those teams that qualify in their own regions advance to a national competition. As the Ethics Bowl movement grows, it will provide ever-greater opportunities for high school students to represent their schools in cordial and instructive competition while learning about Philosophy and the craft of argumentation.

I hope it is clear by now that a variety of intriguing opportunities are already available for the pursuit of Philosophy in high school, and more are on the horizon. In addition, whether you are a high school student, a parent of one, a high school teacher, or a faculty member at a college or university, there are exciting ways in which you can contribute to the growth of Philosophy at the secondary level. I hope you will avail yourself of the extraordinary resources represented in this volume to become part of the precollege Philosophy movement!

NOTES

1. According to an analysis of Nieswiadomy (2006), Philosophy majors are tied with economics majors as having the highest average LSAT scores of the largest disciplines (those with more than 1,900 students entering law school). Economics is tied for second (with philosophy/religion) behind physics/math in a set of 29 discipline groupings that the author created to yield groups of at least 450 students with similar majors.
2. I have had the good fortune to work with committed, enthusiastic, and talented program assistants Bryan Cwik, Deeva Shah, and Corin Fox. In addition, I've had the honor and pleasure of working with Professor Jennifer Merritt of University of Virginia's Women's Center on many High-Phi Projects including the NEH Institute and the Internship Course.
3. For an account of a service-learning philosophy course that does not involve teaching this subject to high school students, but which uses more traditional community service activities instead, see Giebel 2006.
4. For a fuller discussion, see Shah 2008 and Mullis 2009.
5. My work on SMO was recently discussed in a *Time* magazine article; see Paul 2011. A podcast of my discussion of SMO is available in Green 2012.

REFERENCES

DePaul, M., and Zabzegski, L. (2007) *Intellectual Virtue: Perspectives from Ethics and Epistemology* Oxford: Oxford University Press.

Giebel, H. (2006) "In Defense of Service Learning" *Teaching Philosophy* 29: 93–109.

Green, M. (2012) "Humanities in a Digital Age, Panel 2: Research and Teaching" *Digital Humanities Now*: http://digitalhumanitiesnow.org/2012/02/humanities-in-a-digital-age-symposium-podcast-2/.

———. (2006) *Engaging Philosophy: A Brief Introduction* Indianapolis, IN: Hackett Publishing Company.

Katz, S. (2006) "The Liberal Arts in School and College" *The Chronicle of Higher Education* 52: B46.

Mohr Lone, J. (2012) *The Philosophical Child* Lanham, MD: Rowman & Littlefield.

Mullis, E. (2009) "On Being a Socratic Philosophy Instructor" *Teaching Philosophy* 32: 345–359.

Nieswiadomy, M. (2010) "LSAT Scores of Economics Majors: The 2008–2009 Class Update" *Journal of Economic Education* 41: 331–333.

Paul, A. M. (2011) "Why Asking Questions Might Not Be the Best Way to Teach" *Time*, December 14, 2011, Ideas Section.

Shah, M. (2008) "The Socratic Teaching Method: A Therapeutic Approach to Learning" *Teaching Philosophy* 31: 267–275.

20 Philosophy Across the Ages
Some Observations on Content and Strategy

Kirsten Jacobson

BEGINNINGS

In the fall of 2009, I decided to create a philosophy outreach and service-learning program out of my sense that philosophy belongs to people, and should, therefore, not be confined within collegiate classrooms or in isolated conversations within journals or academic conferences. Instead, it is my view that philosophy ought to engage with everyday concerns and problems, and also that philosophy is a practice of thinking critically about values, choices, actions, and the nature of things—a practice from which all human beings could benefit. With this in mind, I developed "Philosophy Across the Ages" to connect University of Maine undergraduate students with high school students, and later with retirement community members, through seminar-style discussions of accessible and exciting philosophical texts. My hope was, and continues to be, for the program to bring this practice into the lives of people outside of the traditional collegiate atmosphere, and to do so through the activity of open, yet guided conversations.

My vision for each Philosophy Across the Ages session centers on four simple guiding tenets. First, I respect the intelligence and ability of participants to read, think, and discuss challenging ideas. Second, I trust in the great texts and ideas of philosophy as being relatable to the participants, and I work to find the pathway to connect "big" ideas to issues already present and alive in their lives. Third, I aim to craft a situation in which our discussion begins with a true question and from a place of true wonder. And, fourth, I entrust participants to play an essential role in shaping how the discussion develops: I strive to treat them, in other words, as true philosophical discussants, and I work at being open to being moved by them. Ultimately, this last principle includes these important demands: "Listen!" and "Respond!" It has also led me to ask students to lead off our sessions by asking our opening question, and by continuing to play a role in shaping the way the conversation develops.

The logistics for carrying out these tenets have been fairly simple. I began by finding a willing and intrigued pair of contacts—a guidance counselor and an English teacher—at a local public high school. With the support of these contacts, a half dozen undergraduates and I held two ice cream social/ informational sessions at the high school to introduce the program and entice students to consider participating. On the sides of both the high school students and the undergraduates participation would be entirely voluntary, and students would not be required to attend every session and also could arrange to leave early or arrive late if other after-school activities demanded. We were able to arrange to have the program count as a small piece of the high school's honors program, but any student choosing to take up this route would not gain "credit" for this program solely by attending our sessions. I wanted to ensure that people coming to the conversation were doing so entirely because they wanted to be there, not to serve an outside end.

We began the program with monthly discussions that were hosted at the high school directly after classes were over for the day. Our first sessions focused on Plato's *Apology* and Sophocles's *Antigone*—texts that helped to draw the students into some of the core practices of philosophical thinking, questioning, and discussing, and also to let them consider the significant and sometimes life-changing import of taking a stand on an idea. During the first year of the program, we moved our way through ancient to early modern (Descartes's *Meditations*) to contemporary texts (de Beauvoir's *Ethics of Ambiguity*).

We are now three years into the program, and owing to the project's popularity, sessions now occur every two weeks for at least two hours with the high school students. We have also responded to the high school students' desire to "check things out on campus" by moving the discussions to the philosophy department at the University of Maine. After our first year of sessions with undergraduate and high school students alone, we also expanded the program to include one additional monthly meeting with seniors at a local retirement home. This cross-generational meeting is typically one and a half hours in length, and we tend to select shorter readings that can be done "on the spot" rather than in advance. These sessions are coordinated through the retirement home's activities coordinator and take place in the facility's library.

While I have been principally in charge of choosing our texts, I regularly take into account themes of particular interest to the participants. Two different grants have enabled me to provide copies of the texts to all members of the discussions; while this is by no means a necessary part of the program's design, the high school students especially have expressed excitement at adding these significant philosophical texts to their personal libraries. I choose works from ancient philosophy all the way through to the contemporary; in addition to the texts mentioned above, some of the most successful texts for our discussions have included Plato's *Republic*, R. G. Collingwood's *Principles of Art*, Marshall McLuhan's *The Medium is the Message*, Iris Marion Young's essay "Throwing Like a Girl," and Alva Noë's *Out of Our Heads*.

My main focus in selecting a text is to find a work that can connect to issues relevant to the participants. This does not necessarily need to be an obvious connection; indeed, it is often most exciting and significant when a text that may seem "out of date" or obtuse can be shown to have remarkable relevance to us. For example, participants who initially may find Socrates's position on art in Plato's *Republic* to "reek of censorship" have been surprised to discover just how much resonance Socrates's ideas have with their own views of what is appropriate for children and their education.

The most important logistical element of these sessions involves preparing the undergraduate students who are volunteering their time to help me lead the day's discussion. Prior to each session with the high school students, I gather with my undergraduate students for 30 minutes to discuss the themes they saw as most salient and intriguing in our text for the day. During this pre-planning time, each undergraduate proposes an opening question that he or she thinks could launch the session. We discuss and refine these questions, and I select one student as the session's opening questioner, and I encourage other students to keep their questions ready in case the discussion lends itself to being positively shaped by their addition. (When we meet in the cross-generational meetings, I have included regular participants from among the high school students in these preparatory discussions and in select cases have chosen one of them to be our discussion leader.)

Involving the students in leading our discussions offers them the opportunity to experience what it takes to direct a class. It also pushes my students to think differently about the material we are studying: the undergraduates involved in the program have regularly told me that helping to lead these discussions has made them better thinkers and class participants by pushing them to feel more responsible for what they are saying and also to think more holistically about what a conversation as a whole needs to be successful. Above all, the undergraduate express that being involved in this project has helped them to feel the civic significance of doing philosophy.

To continue developing this very sense of the "civic" nature of our endeavors, I ask participants to introduce or reintroduce themselves before each session begins, and I remind them that our goal is to have a discussion with each other and to work our way into some of the core ideas that this text can open up for us. I participate in the conversation as a member, working especially hard to model listening and responding carefully to others, synthesizing the ideas that have been "on the table," connecting our ideas to the text and connecting the text to life experiences, and encouraging people to elaborate on their ideas and the reasons behind what they have said. Overall, however, I find I do not need to do much "work" to keep the discussion on track; it seems that the structure of the program itself helps to guide the participants into energetic, smooth flowing, and responsive conversations.

A GLIMPSE INSIDE

To give a fuller picture of the work we do in Philosophy Across the Ages, I will describe portions of a number of sessions that were particularly engaging for participants. I will discuss approaches we took to the texts, which others could replicate in their own outreach programs, and I will also begin to describe the immediate results of some of these discussions. In section 3, I will then speak further about the long-term outcomes of the program.

The very first text I read with any new group of participants is Plato's *Apology*. In this dialogue, we encounter Socrates articulating his view of philosophical practice as well as his sense of the significance of philosophical thinking for both the health of his own life as well as of his city. We gather from this dialogue that philosophy pushes us to consider our ideas and practices with a critical eye, and never to let ourselves settle into accepting things simply because they are given to us or because they come with the stamp of authority. We must, Socrates argues directly and in his actions, take up and consider for ourselves what matters and what we will stand by. So, this dialogue stands as an excellent starting ground for encouraging a group of thinkers to think for themselves.

Beginning questions that my students have raised for discussing this dialogue have included the following: What is philosophical about Socrates's way of approaching knowledge and truth?; How is—if it is—Socrates's practice of thinking different from that of politicians, artisans, and poets?; Why do you think Socrates is willing to die to stand behind his way of thinking and living? What is it that he is willing to die for?; What does Socrates mean when he describes himself as a "gadfly" necessary for the health of the city?; and, finally, is philosophical practice necessary for a healthy human life?

An interesting pattern has emerged regardless of which of these questions has begun our session: participants new to the dialogue have often felt quite critical of Socrates, and then through discussion they have tended to reverse their view. For instance, many participants often first described Socrates as stubborn and as shortsighted; they regularly expressed an initial wish that Socrates had appeased his jurors, and, in doing so, secured his acquittal. My undergraduate students, who have been reading Plato for some time, will often move carefully in to question this view. One student might ask, "Is there anything for which you would be willing to die?" Another might push the question further, "What message would it send to Athens if Socrates gave up on his path of questioning?" Slowly, a conversation has developed, allowing us to examine the power of keeping open a questioning attitude with respect to authority—even if this requires us to take great personal risks. Without fail, these discussions have retained some of the initial resistance participants brought into the conversation: they do not want to throw out *all* respect for the patterns of tradition or the power of authority.

The question often becomes, "How do we both question and respect authority?" This is a particularly rich discussion for a group of high school students to have, since they are beginning to be able and eventually will be required to define for themselves what they value and how they will and ought to live their lives. In this way, speaking about Plato's *Apology* becomes a performative act, and, thus, draws greater attention to many of the issues that Socrates himself is discussing in the dialogue. I have also found that even after this initial discussion of the *Apology* that young students express appreciation of being respected as people who have a voice. Allowing them to exercise this voice helps them to develop their sense of self. Exercising their voice in conversation with others also allows them to realize that with having a voice comes responsibility: one must speak and behave coherently, and one must answer to others.

We have worked our way further into such themes by reading the second and third parts of Simone de Beauvoir's *The Ethics of Ambiguity*. (I omit the first part because it is less concrete and the more abstract ideas are not necessary for setting up the rich and engaging conversations made possible by the latter parts.) In this text, de Beauvoir argues that while human beings are by nature free, we are not by nature prepared to take up this freedom adequately. Instead, she argues, we must undergo an "apprenticeship of freedom." De Beauvoir further maintains that the character of our childhood experience makes it challenging for us to enter fully into our freedom, for, in childhood, the world and its meanings tend to be given to us and experienced by us as fixed, as beyond our control. As we enter adolescence, we come to see that the way things count for us and our families is in fact a matter of accumulated choices and habits, and, as we grow older, it will be incumbent upon us to *decide* how *we* will value things.

Once again, this text is one that is particularly exciting to read and discuss with high school students, who are themselves often in the midst of some of their first "battles" with parents, teachers, and peers over differences in how they see and react to things and situations in their world. Undergraduate students in the program are also still thickly involved in this process of figuring their lives out for themselves and, perhaps more keenly than the high school students, are sometimes wishing that life's path were as "easy" as it was in childhood. To begin discussions of this text, we focus on the first three or four pages of the second part. Students have led us off by asking questions such as How are the worlds of children and of adults different?; What exactly is the "crisis of adolescence" that de Beauvoir argues we face and that is a necessary step in taking up our freedom adequately?; and, What is it about childhood life that makes it difficult for us to enter into our freedom? This last question has led participants to consider whether there is any other way for parents and teachers to raise children such that it would be easier for them, as they mature, to take up their nature as free beings. While some participants have suggested that adults should offer more room for children to exercise making choices for themselves, other participants have countered that children are not yet ready for this activity. The latter have further argued that the difference in existential structure that de Beauvoir notices between the worlds of children and of adults is indeed part of what enables humans to experience their freedom: without this point of contrast and the related shock of realizing that what seemed fixed is not indeed fixed, humans would not notice and feel the responsibility of their creative role in shaping meaning.

Continuing on to the later portions of part 2 and the beginning of part 3 of *The Ethics of Ambiguity* offers participants the chance to work through different ways in which people commonly fail to exercise their freedom adequately and fully. De Beauvoir presents these "failures" as well as steps toward successfully expressing one's freedom in the form of certain character types—for example, the subman, the serious man, the adventurer, and the passionate man. Participants can work quite deeply into the various problems and successes found in these forms of living. In these discussions, comparisons have often been made both to well-known film and television characters and even to participants' own ways of dealing or failing to deal with their responsibility for shaping their lives. This text was one of the earliest texts we used in the program, and students who partook in those discussions two years ago continue to refer to this text. One high school student even arranged, on account of his interest in this text, to enroll in my undergraduate course "Existentialism and Literature." Overall, the conversations surrounding this text served, the participants reported, as a "sort of wake-up call" and also as a "welcome to adulthood, its joys and its pains."

Two additional texts I chose for the program arose from specific interests expressed by the program's high school students. One group of students wanted to consider the role of technology in our lives, so we read portions of Marshall McLuhan's *The Medium Is the Massage*. This text gave us a chance to talk both about the way in which things become incorporated into our way of being and into our experience of our bodies, and also about the way that technology can subsequently change our way of experiencing and responding to the world and our ways of thinking. Undergraduates opened our conversation of this text by asking, To what extent are various pieces of technology (including clothing, glasses, pens, computers, cars, etc.) essential to what you do and how you think every day? Some participants were quite amazed to discover that simple things like reading or making a point became less easy for them if they were not allowed to hold a pencil in their hand; others came to realize how much a certain hat or a pair of glasses had become so much a part of their bodies that they felt "naked" without it; and one student observed that his entire sense of the world and his future changed from the day that he got his license and a car.

We continued conversations about this intertwinement of our bodies and tools as we read Alva Noë's *Out of Our Heads: Why You Are Not Your Brain, and Other Lessons from the Biology of Consciousness*—a text chosen to respond to a student's interest in the intersections between philosophy and contemporary science. *Out of Our Heads* allowed us the chance to think about what we typically take mind to be and what we typically take body to be. Echoing Descartes's observations in his *Meditations*, participants' first impressions of mind and body placed these at opposite extremes: mind is intangible, indivisible, and free; body is made of matter, can be dissected, and is bound by the laws of physics. Yet, after getting participants to make these very understandable distinctions, an undergraduate student challenged us to think about just where and how thinking happens. We talked at length about how we know how to type or play an instrument, for instance. One student noted that without her fingers on her guitar, she could not remember certain songs. Similarly, when students were asked to recall the order of the letters on a keyboard, they typically could not do so from mere memory; they began to be successful at the task when they moved their fingers in the air as if touching a keyboard. Both of these observations began to blur any distinct line one could make between mind and body. Noë's book pushed us further into these considerations through his studies of sensory substitution, habituation, the role of the environment in our perceptual capacities, and more. Students were particularly impressed by the book's argument that philosophy has an essential role in the scientific arena: indeed, Noë argues that phenomenological philosophy offers an important corrective to many of the contemporary approaches to understanding the mind offered by cognitive neuroscience.

At this point in the Philosophy Across the Ages program, most students already felt as though philosophy was an essential part of living well, but our discussions here pushed them to see that even (and perhaps especially) today philosophy can and should play the role that Socrates proposed it should thousands of years ago—namely, that of pushing people to question the assumptions on which they act and through which they shape our understanding of reality.

This point brings me to a final set of paired readings that have been particularly successful in the program—namely, the opening 30 pages of Rainer Maria Rilke's *The Notebooks of Malte Laurids Brigge* and his poem "The Archaic Torso Apollo." We used these readings toward the end of a series of sessions dedicated to considering the nature of art and its role in our lives. The particular session on which I will focus here involved high school students, undergraduate students, and retirement community members.

In this session, a high school student opened our conversation by asking, "What has art done for your life?" This seemingly simple question led us deeply into discussions of the life-changing value that making and witnessing art had for each participant in this group composed of people ranging from 16 to 90 years old. Participants spoke of art as sometimes leading them to see things in an entirely new light—something that they argued science had rarely accomplished for them on a personal level. Some people spoke about the activity of making art as allowing them to work through something, and others saw it as a means for capturing and letting someone else gain insight into their sense of something. As the discussion worked its way into Rilke's novel, participants saw, along with Rilke, the danger of living life and attempting to do art according to a prefabricated, third-person view of what life should be. Art, they argued, needs to move beyond the habitual ways of understanding things, and must instead arise from a person's own and authentic "hands on" struggle to express something anew about the topic. Art, they again thought with Rilke, is an undertaking—whether one is creating it or engaging with it—that demands "You must change your life!" The seniors in the group encouraged the younger participants to take seriously this charge, telling us stories of how pivotal their own creative experiences had been to giving lasting meaning to their own lives. The conversation ended by our noting that our discussion and Rilke's writings placed the power of art very close to that of the power of philosophy.

Both art and philosophy challenge us to continue to question and create meaning. Both challenge us to see every "end product" as a necessary point for beginning again. Both make the seemingly simple, but ultimately quite difficult, charge that we become involved in the making of our lives, and remind us that we are capable of and responsible for doing this until the day that we die.

OUTCOMES

The single most notable outcome of this project has been the growing enthusiasm for philosophical discussion expressed by all members—including myself. The conversations typically need to be forced to come to a close, and members generally leave quite "high" and refreshed by the experience. For me, I find that at the close of one session, I am already looking forward to the next. Two factors are regularly mentioned by participants as the reason that these discussions are so energizing and moving for them. First, these conversations do not arise from any requirement; participants are there because they want to be present and they are not "graded" on their performance in any way. Second, the cross-generational aspect of these conversations leads to surprisingly different perspectives and approaches to discussion.

The program allows its participants the chance to think for themselves and to do so in the encouraging and challenging environment of other engaged and respectful thinkers. For this reason, the English teacher who is my contact at Orono High School sees Philosophy Across the Ages as an unparalleled resource for his students. He writes:

> Dr. Jacobson has since provided our students a rare opportunity to do the very thing which, I believe, young people thirst for: the chance to consider in depth and with passion the great ideas of life. Philosophy Across the Ages takes place after school. The typical weariness of the student mind at such an hour evidently vanishes in these meetings. . . . The comment that best reinforces what this group has done for our students came from a high schooler who told me that she did not even realize she had those parts of her mind which Dr. Jacobson's discussions led her to.

Indeed, both high school and undergraduate students regularly report that the ideas we discussed have woven their way into their written and spoken contributions in their official classes and have often kept them up late at night in conversation with their friends. They are often amazed at how much philosophy can and has "changed their lives." One high school student found herself surprised by the program and by philosophy itself:

> I admit that I had some reservations about getting involved with the group. Philosophy seemed an aggravatingly idle and abstract pastime, the type of thing wealthy men had invented to fill their days. However, I have found it to be a delightful exercise. I'm getting to know my own

mind better, and I feel like parts of my brain [are] expanding and connecting to one another. It is really fun, and I always come home from sessions invigorated. This sort of thing is sadly lacking in public education.

A second high school student in the program was impressed by the power of philosophy and the program to help him think anew about his own life and his future intellectual and personal endeavors:

PAA could not have introduced itself to me at a better time. I was fifteen, in the most critical point in my struggle to identify myself. . . . For me, and I think for most people, this middle-of-high-school time was a sort of liquefied gap between the determinate identity my parents made me and the determined identity I would later decide for myself. In this weird zone I was busy making and breaking friendships, picking new sports, new social groups, and new defining activities (some people became "that fast swimmer," or "the rich kid"), and [through the texts and our discussions] I was given a tool [other high school students did not have]. My pursuit of philosophy reorganized my world, peeled off layers, and gave me the skills to see them [for myself].

When he first started Philosophy Across the Ages, this student was convinced that he would major in one of the sciences when he attended college. Though he continues to ponder this as a possibility, he is now firmly convinced that any field he pursues must be complemented by philosophy as a major. He writes:

When I first started going to PAA, I had eyes only for math and science, and was absolutely sure that that was what I wanted to do for the rest of my life. Two years later, I've slowly come to the realization that I will never be able to divorce myself from the practice or study of philosophy. . . . My world and my experience have undergone a radical change, and I'm sure now that whatever I do with my life, philosophy will be wound tightly to the core.

An undergraduate came to a similar conclusion through his involvement in Philosophy Across the Ages:

At its most basic, philosophy is about questioning your environment. It is this one thing that leads to just about everything people have. This is also of particular interest to be because I want to be a scientist. Without a philosophical way of thinking, a scientist is nothing more than a walking textbook, only able to repeat facts about the world given a specific query. It takes a philosophical way of thinking to truly understand and be able to figure new things out in science. And that's the kind of scientist I want to be.

In each of these cases, what strikes me is the ability of philosophy to push students to think critically about their choices in life as well as about their engagements in other arenas of thought. They, like Socrates, recognize philosophy to be like a midwife for their thoughts—that is, as a reflective support allowing them to give birth to strong and healthy ideas.

There are additional positive results that pertain to the specific "level" of the participant. The program connects local high school students with a university experience—both through contact with undergraduate students as well as through exposure to what is arguably the oldest academic discipline. For undergraduate students, the program gives them the exciting opportunity to experience what it is like to lead a class discussion, and also helps them to consider whether they aspire to teach philosophy in their future. Many of my students report developing a newfound respect for the skill involved in leading a discussion, and report themselves as having become notably stronger participants in their undergraduate classes due to their participation in the program. Finally, Philosophy Across the Ages connects retirement community members to lively, engaging, and relevant discussions with younger members of their community. The retirees have noted how exciting it is to hear the ideas of young people and to have been heard by them; they are impressed that the students want to spend their free time engaging in these discussions, and they have reported being specifically interested in the way in which the students "try on" different ideas so supplely. The students, in their turn, report how "blown away" they are by the retirees' comfort with "being themselves" and also by the richness and depth of their views; through the program, the students become more meaningfully aware of this portion of our society that is often concealed. For me, the program is one of the most rewarding things I have ever done as a professional and as a person.

REFERENCES

De Beauvoir, S. (1948) *The Ethics of Ambiguity*. Trans. Frechtman, B. New York: Citadel Press.

Descartes, R. (1999) *Discourse on Method and Meditations on First Philosophy*, 4th ed. Trans. Cress, D. Indianapolis, IN: Hackett Publishing Co.

McLuhan, M. and Fiore, Q. (2006) *The Medium Is the Message: An Inventory of Effects* Berkeley, CA: Gingko Press.

Noë, A. (2010) *Out of Our Heads: Why You Are Not Your Brain, and Other Lessons from the Biology of Consciousness* New York: Hill and Wang.

Plato (1961) "Apology" In *The Collected Dialogues of Plato*, eds. Hamilton, E. and Cairns, H. New York: Bollingen.

———. (1968) *The Republic of Plato*. 2nd ed. Trans. Bloom, A. New York: Basic Books.

Rilke, R. M. (2005) "Archaic Torso of Apollo" In *The Essential Rilke* Rev. ed. Trans. Kinnell, G. and Liebmann, H. Hopewell, NJ: Ecco Press.

———. (2009) *The Notebooks of Malte Laurids Brigge* Trans. Hulse, M. London: Penguin Classics.

Part IV

Strategies for Assessment

21 Can Philosophy Find a Place in the K–12 Curriculum?

Deanna Kuhn, Nicole Zillmer,
and Valerie Khait

INTRODUCTION

The writers, and likely the majority of readers, of this volume need little persuasion of the value to precollege students of engaging with philosophy. It certainly won't hurt them and there's such potential, it would seem, for intellectual gain. Alas, however, beyond this still small circle of writers and readers, it is not an easy case to make. We live increasingly in a culture of accountability, and this has become especially the case in education. Parents, teachers, and the administrators charged with making curriculum decisions will ask "How do you know this is the best use of our children's time, compared to the myriad of alternatives that compete with it?" "What is your evidence?" These are questions we must have answers to, and the constituencies expecting these answers want to see them identified in terms of tangible, measurable outcomes. Principals and superintendents—increasingly resource strapped and under pressure to demonstrate improved learning outcomes—will need to be convinced that squeezing philosophy into already jam-packed middle and high school curricula will yield benefits that outweigh the costs, both financial and in the instructional time that must be subtracted from other pursuits.

This accountability derives in part from the increasing attention accorded to standards. American school systems are now expected to precisely identify and measure expected learning outcomes by subject and grade level and to be held accountable for them. These anticipated outcomes are expected to align with the most recent and explicit rendering of these standards—the Common Core State Standards adopted by all but a few U.S. states (National Governors Association 2010). Curriculum maps and materials must make it clear how they lead to proficiency as defined by these standards. While standards-driven instruction may not be universally embraced, it is well on its way to becoming a reality.

We thus portray what appears a pessimistic picture regarding the prospects of philosophy finding its way into the K–12 curriculum to any extent beyond the present isolated pockets of such practice. In fact, however, there is a bright note. The developments in K–12 education just noted, in particular the remarkable attention being accorded the new Common Core Standards, will likely serve to make the environment for philosophy in the K–12 curriculum more hospitable than it has ever been. This is so for two reasons. First, the Standards highlight, in a way not seen before, intellectual proficiencies strikingly similar to the ones we see as the likely products of engaging young people in philosophical inquiry. Second, all the existing evidence indicates that precollege students demonstrate, at best, limited mastery of these intellectual skills.

INTELLECTUAL SKILLS FOR THE 21ST CENTURY

Today's students must be prepared for adult lives in the 21st century. We are not certain what they will need to know and hence can't be sure that we will teach it to them. At best, and most ambitiously, we can support their development of the intellectual skills that will equip them to survive and even prosper in this new world, learning what they need to know as they go along. One such skill we know they will need is working collaboratively, relying on reasoned argument to deliberate with others to determine the best solutions to difficult problems. It's thus encouraging that the new Common Core Standards (2010) accord more emphasis to higher-order thinking skills than have past standards. Moreover, this attention goes beyond endorsements of the loosely defined construct of "critical thinking" as an educational objective, to begin to identify more precisely the nature of such skills. Common Core writing proficiency standards specify that by the end of the middle school years, students must be able to: ". . . write arguments to support claims with clear reasons and relevant evidence;" to ". . . introduce claim(s), acknowledge and distinguish the claim(s) from alternate or opposing claims, and organize the reasons and evidence logically;" and to ". . . support claim(s) with logical reasons and relevant evidence, using accurate, credible sources and demonstrating an understanding of the topic or text." (National Governors Association 2010, 42). By high school graduation, they should to be able to "Develop claim(s) and counterclaims fairly and thoroughly, supplying the most relevant evidence for each while pointing out the strengths and limitations of both in a manner which anticipates the audience's knowledge level, concerns, values, and possible biases" (National Governors Association 2010, 45). Writing standards for middle and high school students have been formulated to align with those specified by the National Assessment of Educational Progress Writing Framework.

In the sizable body of published text defining curriculum standards that has accumulated over many decades and now culminates in the 2010 Common Core Standards, the appearance of this kind of explicit and specific language to identify particular intellectual skills is something new. We will return to the less positive fact that the new standards leave educators with little to go on with respect to *how* such objectives should be achieved. But first we should note a striking similarity between the intellectual skills the new standards specify and what Jana Mohr Lone (2012), in introducing an edited volume similar in purpose to the present volume, characterizes as the benefits of engaging with philosophy. "The hard thinking that philosophical inquiry demands," she claims, "provides students with some of the analytic skills they need to engage in thoughtful decision-making throughout their lives." More specifically, " . .[e]ngaging in philosophical inquiry trains young people to evaluate claims based on reason and analysis" (8). Perhaps, then, it will be possible to demonstrate that engagement with philosophy is an effective vehicle for fulfilling the objectives the new standards specify.

Before turning to the critical question of what it might take to achieve such demonstration, we should note that the current failure of the American education system to achieve such standards is not in question. According to the most recent results of the National Assessment of Educational Progress (NAEP), upon whose writing framework the Common Core Standards are based, just 26 percent of American high school seniors graduating in 2007 achieved proficiency in persuasive writing (Salahu-Din, Persky, & Miller 2008). The news is no better with regard to scientific thinking, which requires students leaving middle school to be able to "use evidence from investigations in arguments that accept, revise, or reject scientific models." Here, just 30 percent of 8th graders and 21 percent of 12th graders met critical benchmarks in 2009 (National Center for Education Statistics 2011a).

(HOW) DOES PHILOSOPHICAL THINKING DEVELOP?

Can empirical evidence of its benefits be brought to bear by those who seek the more widespread inclusion of philosophical inquiry in the K–12 curriculum? We have suggested that such evidence has not just a desirable but an essential role to play in this regard. This evidence, however, is less of the form of whether students' skills are weak or strong, but, rather, of exactly what they are. Put simply, to make the case for young students' engagement with philosophy requires that we draw on what is known about intellectual development during the first decades of life as an essential foundation for our argument. In seeking to bring the discipline of philosophy to young students, philosophers must ask, "What do young students bring to their engagement with philosophy?" The answers are multifaceted and extend across competencies, skills, and dispositions. Cognitive, developmental, and educational psychologists by now have accrued a body of knowledge across this wide range, although as always there is much more to learn, and what is known stands to support the cause of those who would bring philosophical inquiry into the K–12 classroom.

Philosophers have been known to claim that the proper domain of philosophy is only that set of questions that cannot be answered by empirical investigation. But that is not to say that there are not domains of empirical inquiry that can inform philosophical investigation—a demonstration that Piaget (1970) long ago sought to provide in his studies of children's developing understandings of time, space, and other concepts in what he coined genetic epistemology—a field of study founded on the view that insight is gained into the nature of complex concepts by studying their evolution in the intellect of the developing child. Moreover, Piaget taught us that the reasoning skills that are the hoped-for product of engaging children in philosophy are a moving target. Children's reasoning skills develop in extended and often complex trajectories that require careful analysis. In addition to identifying these trajectories, as educators we must take on the challenging questions of mechanism. When and how, developmentally, do we optimally "catch" most children as they proceed through the precollege grades?

The most directly relevant trajectories that we know something about are those in epistemological understanding and in argumentive reasoning. The origins of epistemological understanding lie in early childhood. Three-year-olds are unwilling to attribute to another a belief they know to be false (Perner 1991). The incomprehensibility of false belief reflects an epistemology in which beliefs come directly from the external world, rather than being constructed by the knower. Hence, there are no inaccurate renderings of events. Even after false beliefs are acknowledged, the products of knowing remain at least for a time more firmly attached to the known object than to the knower. At this *absolutist* level of epistemological understanding, knowledge is thus understood as an accumulating set of certain facts.

By adolescence there is typically some progress toward a *multiplist*, or relativist, level of epistemological understanding. The discovery that reasonable people, and even experts, disagree may serve as a source of recognizing the subjective and uncertain dimension of knowing. This recognition may assume such proportions, however, that it eclipses recognition of any objective standard that could serve as a basis for evaluating conflicting claims. Knowledge consists of opinions, freely chosen by their holders as personal possessions. Knowledge is now seen as emanating from the knower rather than the known, but at the significant cost of any discriminability among competing claims.

This developmental progression has been documented as typical and has been characterized as an extended task of coordinating the subjective and objective elements of knowing (Kuhn, Cheney, & Weinstock 2000). Far from universal, however, is progression to the next, *evaluativist* level in which some opinions can be more right than others. Rather than facts or opinions, knowing entails judgments, which require support in a framework of alternatives, evidence, and argument. Research by King and Kitchener (1994) and others (Hofer & Pintrich 1997) indicates that even college students may barely attain a "quasi-reflective" stage. Still, even elementary school children, in the supportive contexts of interest to readers of this volume, show the capacity for the more nuanced thinking of an evaluativist. Indeed, our interest is in how to nurture and develop it in these early years.

Recognizing the role of human interpretation and judgment poses somewhat different challenges in scientific and social domains (Iordanou 2010).

In science, entry of human interpretation into what was previously regarded in absolutist terms is to be understood in positive terms: Science comes to be appreciated as a human construction and interpretation as an essential resource for knowing. The "filter" that human minds represent empowers the scientific endeavor. In the social domain, in contrast, when human subjectivity first impinges on the absolutist realm of objective fact, it is typically regarded in negative terms as the intrusion of human "bias." The danger is one of a permanent stall in the multiplist's radical relativism. In the social domain, then, the major developmental challenge is to conquer the view that human interpretation plays an unmanageable, overpowering role. In the science domain, the challenge is to recognize that human interpretation plays any role at all.

If reflective judgment, founded in consideration of alternatives and evidence, is the developmental goal, examining the effects of practice in argumentive discourse seems an apt avenue of investigation. Such practice may be seen as the dynamic enactment of reflective judgment. Our studies of developmental trajectories in argumentive reasoning have shown that young students can devise cogent arguments to support a claim if it is something important to them—why they should have some privilege, for example—although their typically poor performance in expository essay writing has been widely noted. Where we have found middle school students to be most notably deficient is in dialogic argument—in particular, in listening and responding to an opponent's arguments. The tendency instead is to reiterate one's own arguments with more force and elaboration, with the sense that they will eventually prevail with persistence, and the opponent's claims merely fade away in the face of their power.

If one subscribes to a Vygotskyan (1978) model of development, where development of individual thought is a process of internalizing interpersonal dialogue, encouraging good thinking lies not in some intervention unrelated to everyday experience, but instead in strengthening the nascent argumentive discourse skills evident in normal human interaction. Intensive, sustained argumentive practice offers a natural corrective to the immature thinker's egocentrism by providing what Graff (2005) terms the "missing interlocutor" in students' written work—a dialogic partner that gives the activity its point and in the process holds a mirror to the thinker's assumptions for both to examine, thereby facilitating individual thinking skill. The fact that argumentive practice provides an externalization of internal thought processes is of particular importance to the educator or researcher who wishes to better understand its nature and how best to support it.

SUPPORTING THE DEVELOPMENT OF ARGUMENTIVE DISCOURSE SKILLS

Dense and extended engagement in dialogic argumentation with peers about meaningful issues, we have found, is a sufficient remedy for young students'

262   Deanna Kuhn, Nicole Zillmer, and Valerie Khait

initial weaknesses. Students begin to attend to and engage their peers' ideas, contributed to by the fact that student dialogues in our research are conducted electronically—what an opposing peer has expressed thus sits on the screen to be responded to and is not so easily ignored. In the case of verbal discourse, in contrast, statements disappear as soon as they are spoken and thus become more difficult to serve as objects of reference.

We have done this work with middle school students in the context of what is presented to them as a class in philosophy, although, like the majority of authors in this volume, our aim is to engage them in doing philosophy, more than to teach them about philosophy. The topics they address are contemporary social issues—whether parents should have the right to home school their child or whether organ sales should be allowed—but they inevitably invoke deep and enduring philosophical topics.

Students engage a topic for an extended period of 13 twice-weekly class sessions, with minimal intervention by adult "coaches." They begin work in same-side small groups devoted to generating reasons why the position the group favors is the better one and assembling a set of "reason cards" to represent supporting reasons. A second session focuses on evaluation and ranking of reason cards with respect to their strength as support for the position. Later in the year, after the class has completed work on several topics, coaches in these early sessions introduce a set of "evidence claims" as possibly of use in developing their arguments. This evidence at first doesn't provoke great interest, but gradually it becomes an increasing focus as students come to recognize its relevance and power, and by the second year of their engagement they begin to generate their own questions ("Are there any questions that having answers to would help in making your arguments?") and are assisted in obtaining answers to them. Other activities during the initial sessions on a topic focus on (a) anticipating what the other-side's reasons might be, (b) how they might be criticized and weakened ("counters"), (c) anticipating how the other team will counter our reasons, and (d) conceiving of ways to rebut these counters ("comebacks").

During the middle sessions of the sequence, each student is paired with a same-side teammate (but one they did not work with in the preceding small-group sessions), and together the pair argues against a series of opposing-side pairs, one each session. During this electronically conducted discourse, pairs are reminded to collaborate with their partners in deciding what to say to the opposing pair. While waiting for the opposing pair to respond, the pair works on a reflection sheet, referring to the ongoing dialogue transcript that appears on the screen before them. These are of two forms (alternated across sessions)—one asking the pair to identify and reflect on one of their own arguments and the other on one of the opponents' arguments.

During the final phase of the sequence, students return to same-side small groups to prepare for a final whole-class debate. They review the other-side arguments encountered in the dialogues and their counterarguments against them, as well as reviewing their own arguments, expected counterarguments, and rebuttals. In a debrief session following the debate, students are guided through an argument map—a diagram that the class coaches prepare of the debate with points awarded for effective argumentive moves (notably counterarguments and rebuttals and use of evidence) and points subtracted for ineffective moves, such as unwarranted assumptions and unconnected responses. Points are summed and a winner declared. Finally, students are assigned to write individual final essays justifying their positions on the topic, due at the next session, when a new topic cycle begins.

We have conducted various kinds of assessments at the onset, during, and following participation in this curriculum, and our evidence indicates that the experience develops intellectual values (Michaels, O'Conor, & Resnick 2008) as well as intellectual skills, with both being empirically measurable kinds of gains. With respect to values, they are more likely to judge serious discourse with peers as worth the effort it requires (Kuhn & Park 2005; Kuhn, Wang, & Li 2011). With respect to skills, after two years of participation, middle school students, in assessments involving new topics not part of the curriculum, show not only greater attention to the opponent's arguments but increased use of direct counterarguments aimed at weakening them—one of the two goals of argumentation proposed by Walton (1989). These gains, moreover, extend to individual written expository arguments, a noteworthy outcome in light of educators' continuing concern regarding students' weak expository writing skills. Students also show increased awareness of the role of evidence in argumentation (reflected in their requests for it) and make use of it more often in their arguments. All of these observed gains are relative to comparison groups who participated in an equivalent number of class sessions devoted to more traditional, whole-class discussion of similar topics led by a teacher (Kuhn & Crowell 2011).

These gains, moreover, encompass not only production of argumentive discourse but extend to measures of meta-level understanding of argumentation, as well as the valuing of it noted earlier. Analyses of students' electronic discourse showed advances in frequency of statements *about* the discourse (distinguished from the statements that conduct the discourse), for example, "How do you know that?," or "You have a point." This "meta-talk," we have found, increases in both quantity and sophistication, becoming more regulatory in nature. Meta-level regulatory discussion affords arguers the opportunity to glean feedback from the opponent (remember the "missing interlocutor") regarding their own meta-strategic skill and understanding. We also have observed meta-talk to become more reciprocal in nature— whereas initially students tend to ignore opponents' rare meta-level utterances, later on meta-statements are likely to initiate extended discussions.

These indications of students' growing epistemological understandings of the nature and purposes of argumentive discourse are further supported by assessments in which we asked them to evaluate short transcripts of argumentive discourse, a task at which they outperform nonparticipant comparison groups. They similarly excel in an assessment in which they are asked to construct an argument between two interlocutors, based on some background information regarding their positions. We correctly predicted that they would show greater meta-level understanding of argumentation, relative to a comparison group, in depicting the dialogue as one in which the participants were engaged in addressing and countering one another's points, drawing on and integrating available evidence, rather than simply "taking turns" asserting their own positions (Kuhn & Zillmer 2011).

CONCLUSIONS

We have stressed the issue of measurable gains because we believe it to be so critical. The first essential step is to more precisely identify these intellectual skills, and the next is to develop accurate, robust ways of measuring them. Einstein may have been right that we don't know how to measure all that is important, but we must pursue the effort. Especially because these skills, as we have noted, are a moving target, those who would bring philosophical inquiry into young students' classrooms must know what these children and adolescents bring to the pursuit in the way of intellectual resources and how these competencies and dispositions change over time.

A third step is then to devise the kinds of classroom experiences devoted to philosophical inquiry that will align with these intellectual resources and engage their use and further development. This is a demanding agenda, but we believe there is no simpler way to advance the objectives shared by the contributors to this volume.

REFERENCES

Crowell, A. (2011) *Assessment of a three-year argument skill development curriculum* Unpublished doctoral dissertation, Teachers College, Columbia University.

Felton, M., & Kuhn, D. (2001) "The development of argumentive discourse skills" *Discourse Processes* 32: 135–153.

Graff, G. (2003) *Clueless in academe: How schooling obscures the life of the mind* New Haven, CT: Yale University Press.

Hofer, B. and Pintrich, P. (1997) "The development of epistemological theories: Beliefs about knowledge and knowing and their relation to learning" *Review of Educational Research* 67(1): 88–140.

Iordanou, K. (2010) "Developing argument skills across scientific and social domains" *Journal of Cognition and Development* 11(3): 293–327.

Kuhn, D. (1991) *The skills of argument* Cambridge: Cambridge University Press.

Kuhn, D. (2001) "How do people know?" *Psychological Science* 12(1): 1–8.

Kuhn, D. (2005) *Education for thinking* Cambridge, MA: Harvard University Press.

Kuhn, D. (2010) "Teaching and learning science as argument" *Science Education* (Published online: Mar26 2010 DOI: 10.1002/sce.2039).

Kuhn, D., Cheney, R., and Weinstock, M. (2000) "The development of epistemological understanding" *Cognitive Development* 15: 309–328.

Kuhn, D. and Crowell, A. (2011) "Dialogic argumentation as a vehicle for developing young adolescents' thinking" *Psychological Science* 22: 545–552.

Kuhn, D. and Park, S. H. (2005) "Epistemological understanding and the development of intellectual values" *International Journal of Educational Research 43:* 111–124.

Kuhn, D. and Udell, W. (2003) "The development of argument skills" *Child Development 74*(5): 1245–1260.

Kuhn, D., Wang, Y., and Li, H. (2011) "Why argue: Developing understanding of the purposes and value of argumentive discourse" *Discourse Processes 48:* 26–49.

Kuhn, D. and Zillmer, N. (2011) "Developing norms of discourse" Paper presented at the conference *Socializing Intelligence through Academic Talk and Dialogue.* Learning Research and Development Center, University of Pittsburgh, September 2011.

Michaels, S., O'Connor, C., and Resnick, L. (2008) "Deliberative discourse idealized and realized: Accountable talk in the classroom and in civic life" *Studies in Philosophy and Education 27:* 283–297.

Mohr Lone, J. (2012) "Philosophy and Education: A Gateway to Inquiry" In *Philosophy and education: Introducing philosophy to young people* (eds. Mohr Lone, J. and Israeloff, R.) 7–9, Newcastle Upon Tyne: Cambridge Scholars Publishing.

National Center for Education Statistics (2011a) *The nation's report card: Science 2009* Institute of Education Sciences, U.S. Department of Education, Washington, DC.

National Center for Education Statistics (2011b) *The nation's report card: Civics 2010* Institute of Education Sciences, U.S. Department of Education, Washington, DC.

National Governors Association Center for Best Practices, Council of Chief State School Officers (2010) *Common core state standards* National Governors Association Center for Best Practices, Council of Chief State School Officers, Washington, DC.

Piaget, J. (1970) *Genetic epistemology* New York: Columbia University Press.

Salahu-Din, D., Persky, H., and Miller, J. (2008) *The nation's report card: Writing 2007* (NCES 2008–468). National Center for Education Statistics, Institute of Education Sciences, U.S. Department of Education, Washington, DC.

Vygotsky, L. S. (1978) *Mind in society: The development of higher psychological processes* Cambridge, MA: Harvard University Press.

Walton, D. (1989) "Dialogue theory for critical thinking" *Argumentation 3:* 169–184.

22 A Whole School Approach to Philosophy in Schools
Outcomes and Observations

Lynne Hinton and Sarah Davey Chesters

All which the school can or need do for pupils, so far as their minds are concerned . . . is to develop their ability to think.

Dewey, 1916

INTRODUCTION

Increasingly in education, learning is being measured through standardized testing that assesses the same skills in different children. While it is questionable if this particular process is a true reflection of the learning that is occurring, given what we know about different learning styles and multiple intelligences, the fact that education *requires* such outcomes is integral to informing practice (Gardner 1999). Education, derived from the Latin *educare*, means literally to "lead out" and at its very core is concerned with bringing about some kind of change however we like to measure it. This chapter will discuss the outcomes, both measurable and beyond measure, of a transformation of one school, from the perspective of a school principal.

In 1997, a small inner-city Australian school in Brisbane, Queensland, embarked on an approach to teaching and learning based on philosophy. The intention of the transformation of the school curriculum to embrace philosophy was to teach children to think, with the expectation that this would lead to better learning. While most educators would argue that teaching children to think is the core business of schooling, the measures through which teaching and learning are recorded reflect the primacy of literacy and numeracy in education. However, John Dewey argues that "[i]f education is life, all life has, from the outset, a scientific aspect, an aspect of art and culture, and an aspect of communication. It cannot, therefore, be true that proper studies for one grade are mere reading and writing . . ." (Dewey 1897, 77–80). Taking heed from Dewey, educating for life in the instance of this particular school was teaching children to think, as an outcome in and of itself.

Educational philosopher Philip Cam (2006) argues that we are concerned about children leaving school illiterate or innumerate, hence the move toward providing junctures throughout school to measure the progress in these areas, but as yet there is not the concern that children will leave school "insocratic." According to Cam, being *socratic* has just as much importance as being literate or numerate. Cam believes that being socratic is a disposition with its own inherent value. Being socratic involves thinking "about the issues and problems that we face in our lives," and being able "to explore life's possibilities, to appreciate alternative points of view, to critically evaluate what we read and hear, to make appropriate distinctions and needful connections, and generally to make reasonable judgements" (1).

These same attributes are identified by Australian proponents of educational philosophy, Knight and Collins (2010) as key "graduate attributes." They illuminate the fact that critical judgment, among other qualities, is widely recognized as a key graduate attribute by both secondary schools and tertiary institutions, and yet, as they lament, there is still little systematic focus on philosophy as a vehicle to develop such qualities in students. While critical judgment, critical thinking, and reflection are highlighted as desirable outcomes, there is no specific way to suggest that teachers may achieve these outcomes. Hence, until there is widespread recognition of both the academic and social value of philosophy in education, we must instead highlight the outcomes consistent with those in the current education vernacular.

CHAPTER OVERVIEW

While there are studies attesting to the contribution that philosophy in schools makes in relation to IQ and social and emotional development, among other qualities (see Millet and Tapper 2011; Tricky and Topping 2004; UNESCO 2007) this chapter, by contrast, is a case study of the development of one school. It is presented as a reflection and draws from personal experience over a period of 14 years. It includes two main elements: outcomes that were observed by school principal Lynne Hinton from 1996 until 2009, and also a description of the outcomes that were measurable by both state and national standardized tests.[1]

First, the chapter foregrounds the community demographic to help to elucidate the culture of the school. While there is sometimes skepticism that the school already draws in "the best children," it is important to have a full understanding of the children who attended the school during this period. If we view them only as those who come to the school with assumed capabilities, then we negate the potential for a philosophical approach to pedagogy, but more importantly, we have not understood the genealogy of the school that started as a federally funded "disadvantaged school" to what it is today. The Australian "Disadvantaged Schools Program" used national census data to identify schools in low socioeconomic areas. Through the program, these schools received extra funding. Second, we address the ideas behind the school reform and the reasons for placing thinking at the forefront. As Dewey (1897) suggests, schools are in every essence a reflection of life, and teaching children to think is at the very core of teaching children how to live "the good life."

The chapter then gives an overview of the literacy and numeracy outcomes from the school during the period 1996 to 2009. More importantly, however, the chapter describes student outcomes not measured by standardized tests; those which could be considered reflective of "educating for life" such as changed attitudes toward learning and marked, positive changes in behavior. Other positive changes are also described, including staff attitudes toward their roles in the schools and toward the students, as well as community attitudes toward the school.

What occurred at Buranda State School went far beyond simply improvements in academic performance, although that is acknowledged as being significant. What gently unfolded was a strong and unifying sense of purpose, an excitement about teaching and learning, a willingness to seek and offer help, an ability to work productively with others (including being able to explore disagreements respectfully), and a sense of a job being done well—on the part of both children and adults. It was unexpected, gratifying, and way beyond anything the school community could have imagined.

REFLECTIONS OF A SCHOOL PRINCIPAL IN THE BEGINNING . . .

I was appointed to Buranda State School, an inner-city school in Brisbane, Australia, in 1996. At that time, the area around the school was identified by the Australian Bureau of Statistics (ABS) national census data as serving families who were considered to be of low socioeconomic status. These families were also likely to be migrants. The school was part of the federally funded "Disadvantaged Schools Scheme" (later known as the "Special Programs School Scheme") and had a reputation for being rough. Enrolments had plummeted and were expected to continue to do so. The school population was very diverse. Academically, students ranged from those with serious learning needs to those with high academic achievement (in later years, some seriously gifted children were brought to the school because of specific programs offered). Culturally, about 10 percent of the student population had English as their second language. At that time, these were mainly refugees from areas such as Afghanistan and the Middle East. Today, refugee students at the school come mainly from Africa.

Socioeconomically, there was a very small number of children who came from privileged homes, as well as children who lived in quite difficult circumstances—homes where substance abuse was an issue or where a parent was in jail. These days there are proportionately fewer of the latter group. Some children at the school displayed very challenging behaviors, although the environment that was eventually developed ameliorated these to the extent that it became possible to admit some students each year who had been suspended or excluded from other schools. Interestingly, the school had, and continued to have, a ratio of four boys to three girls.

The biggest problem to my mind was that the children didn't really like being at school. There was no joy for them in learning. Not surprisingly, their academic outcomes were very poor. I wanted these children to enjoy their learning. I wanted their learning to be fun, surprising, challenging, interesting, and joyful. I wanted to build on the curiosity and wonder that children come to school with, and for them to question, talk, imagine and think—for there to be an excitement about learning. I firmly believed that we needed to develop across the school a culture of thinking, in all its forms: creative, critical, reflective, and caring.

PHILOSOPHY AS THE FOUNDATION FOR THINKING: THE IMPETUS FOR SCHOOL REFORM

Over the years, I have done a lot of wondering about the reason schools exist. And I'm clear it is because we need our children to be as successful as they can be—every single one of them—in everything they do. That's the core business of schools; it's why they exist. As Sizer (1992) suggests, "[t]he school's central focus must be on the intellect, on helping each young citizen learn to use his or her mind resourcefully and well" (142). Ideally, schools help children learn to operate in the world as competent, confident, thoughtful, ethical, and reasonable people, and able to make good judgments about all aspects of their lives in order that they can live satisfying and productive lives. If they can do this when they're children, there's a good chance they will do it as adults. Imagine that.

I am also clear that the prerequisite for developing these competencies is the ability to think. Children need to operate in the world as thinkers. They need to think about how to be a good friend, how to do 2-digit subtraction with regrouping, how to address global warming. Aristotle argued that what sets people apart from other living things is their capacity to think and acquire wisdom. He says we are the most human when we think, and we are best when we think well, and attain wisdom. This, then, has to be the core business of schools: teaching children to think. I believe we need to develop in our schools a culture of thinking. I believe also, that if we teach children to think, it is reasonable to expect it will lead to better learning.

A WHOLE SCHOOL APPROACH

To develop this culture of thinking, it was clear that thinking needed to be both the aim and the means of education. Philosophy seemed to fit the bill. The children would learn about thinking by doing it. Our intention was to turn our children into thinkers and learners by engaging them in philosophy.

We would do whatever it took to achieve this. Matthew Lipman (1994) suggests that the purpose of doing philosophy with children is not to turn them into philosophers but to teach them to be more reflective, more considerate human beings.

This is where the notion of leadership underpinned what was happening in the school. The implementation of philosophy teaching was lengthy and collaborative. Initial agreement was sought from teachers and the parent body, which proved to be easier than expected, as we all shared the common goal of helping the children learn better. Once we had agreed to do this, it became integral that as principal I would expect teachers to commit to philosophy in their classroom, and also that it would be done as proficiently as possible—which, in turn, required time and money. To some extent it was a leap of faith: first, that we could learn how to do this well; and second, that our students would benefit as a result. One teacher commented that it worked in our school because of "vision, leadership, faith and trust," with a group of researchers once describing the leadership style in the school as "a warm demandingness." A real sense of "we've decided to do this, now let's do it well" developed, with an almost palpable sense of energy, enthusiasm, and commitment. People began working as a team with the same goal—the evolution of our perception of the ideal school—a school where children can and do think. Philosophy became a core subject at the school: English, Mathematics, Science, and Philosophy. It was taught for at least an hour a week, timetabled in the mornings, in all classes, by all teachers. I took the view that every child would do it; therefore every teacher would need to teach it.

The results were stunning. The school won a number of awards for leadership, school improvement, and curriculum, the funding from which contributed to ongoing teacher development. We had a number of visitors from Australia and around the globe who came to see what was happening. As a school, we had a responsibility to show people what we are doing, provided it did not impact negatively on our teachers or children. We found that provided it is managed carefully, visitors to the school bring and leave behind as much as they take away. Similarly, the school was noted in several publications, including those by Stephen Law (2006), Bob Lingard et al. (2003), and the Australian Department of Science, Education and Training (2003). All of these factors attested to the fact that what was happening was unique and had tapped into the interests of a number of educationalists.

ACADEMIC CHANGES—MEASURABLE OUTCOMES

My first year as principal at Buranda coincided with the first systemic testing of academic performance in government schools across the state of Queensland. Reading and writing would be tested in the sixth year of primary school. Speaking generally, and as has been shown in systemic testing since, Queensland achievement is often quite poor when compared with other states of Australia (the possible reasons for this are many and varied and are beyond the scope of this paper). Nevertheless, at that time, Buranda State School students scored below state mean in both areas. Philosophy teaching at Buranda State School began (in hindsight, very poorly) in late 1997. By 1999 we were noticing that the students' results were beginning to improve.

Not long afterwards, the systemic state tests became more comprehensive, with more areas of literacy and numeracy being tested. All students in years three, five, and seven were to be included. By 2002, Buranda students were above the state mean in everything tested; in some cases, "statistically significantly" above. We had been teaching philosophy for less than five years. This state testing continued until 2007, during which time the school's results remained above or significantly above in all areas tested, except for the occasional, explainable anomaly. The school remained part of the Disadvantaged Schools Scheme (Special Programs School Scheme) for most of this time, which shows that the demographics of the school had not changed significantly during that time. Buranda State School students scored more highly than the state means for the life of these tests. As would be expected, some year level groups were more successful than others, but even so, results remained above the state means and were sustained.

As would be expected, the release of these data led to comments like, "It's easy for you—you get all the good kids." The state of Queensland also checks all children in early year two in order to identify those needing early intervention. The number of children at Buranda State School identified as needing intervention in year two was comparable to the norm across the state. Clearly we didn't get all the "good kids." Yet by year three, they were achieving well.

In 2008 the state tests were replaced by national tests: the National Assessment Program for Literacy and Numeracy (NAPLAN). This provided us with an opportunity to see how we compared to the whole country. Since this time, reading and viewing, writing, spelling, grammar and punctuation, and numeracy have been tested in years three, five, and seven. It is mandatory for all schools to participate, so this includes all public, private, church, and selective schools.

In that first year, Buranda State School was above the state and national means in all 15 areas tested. In more than half of the 15 areas, our average was higher than that of the highest scoring state. This was the same result in the following year, which was also my last year at the school. By this time the demographic of the school had changed to the point where it was no longer part of the Disadvantaged Schools Scheme (Special Programs School Scheme).

REFLECTIONS FROM THE CHILDREN—OBSERVABLE CHANGES

From the outset, the children took to philosophy like the proverbial fish to water. They understood and enjoyed: the collaborative nature of the activity ("using all your brains together at once"), the deep issues discussed ("a study of the way life works," "a place where you are able to reflect on life"), and the intellectual challenges invoked ("using the thinking part of your brain"), yet at their own level of development, ("discussing mysteries like, is it better to be smart or pretty?"). Children would bounce into my office saying things such as "I have a great question for philosophy! 'What is it that makes me, me?,'" and "I have thought of something really interesting . . . for every right answer there is an infinite number of wrong ones!" and even, "I'm wondering . . . can a negative number have a square root?"—the last of which indicates that the curiosity and wonderment encouraged in philosophical discussions really does find its way into other areas of the curriculum.

CHANGES IN THE PLAYGROUND: SOCIAL OUTCOMES

When we began this, our focus was to improve academic outcomes by teaching the children to think. What we didn't foresee, but perhaps should have, was that children who learn to think well, through doing philosophy, think about a lot more than just the academic side of their lives. We also didn't foresee how the respect that is generated in the community of inquiry spills out everywhere. The children learned to listen to one another, explore disagreements respectfully, see things from other points of view, and have the courage of their well thought-out convictions.

When discussing the social benefits of doing philosophy, the children talk about respect for self and others, putting oneself in other people's shoes, considering ideas different from one's own, and learning to think before doing things in the playground. One child even commented, "Without philosophy, this school would have bullies."

I remember an occasion when an older boy was reported to me for bullying behavior toward a younger student at after-school care. I brought the boy to the office and began by asking him why he thought so many people traveled past other schools to bring their children to our school. "It's because of philosophy," he said confidently, ". . . and also because there's no bullying." At this point he looked dismayed and burst into tears as he realized . . . "and I'VE BEEN BULLYING AND I SHOULDN'T BE! Buranda kids don't bully!" He left the room hurriedly, saying he had to go and "fix it up," which he did.

I also remember overhearing a couple of boys, one of whom was often in need of guidance for his behavior. The other boy was saying to him kindly, "You know, you really need to think carefully before you speak in situations like that."

An almost palpable settling occurred across the whole school seven years after we began teaching philosophy—even more profound than the not-insignificant settling that had occurred to that point. It was the beginning of the school year, and we had begun as if we had been away for only a long weekend, rather than for the long summer holiday. Children and teachers were happy to be there, serious work was underway on only the second day of the year, and there was a lovely sense of calm. Wondering why that particular year was more effortless than any previous years led me to the realization that the children who had first encountered philosophy in their first year of schooling were now in their final year at the school. Thus, for every child in the school, philosophy was something they had always done at school. It was normal. It showed. At Buranda State School, academic and social outcomes improved following the implementation of philosophy across the whole school, regardless of whether this was a causal or contributory link.

SCHOOL CULTURE: STAFF OUTCOMES

It was clear from the outset that success would be achieved only if a serious, consistent, ongoing, long-term commitment was made to teacher development. We knew nothing about how to teach philosophy. We improved our own practice through trial and error. We undertook extensive professional development activities, ongoing reflection alone and together, presented papers at conferences, and willingly shared our expertise with one another and with other schools. The result was a group of teachers with expert knowledge of and passion for teaching children how to think. We knew about philosophical thinking, and we knew how to teach children to inquire and think. We became good at helping children to learn to think for themselves. As for the teachers, there can be little as satisfying as knowing that the job you are doing is succeeding, particularly in such a spectacular manner. This satisfaction was reflected in all their dealings: with the children, with their colleagues, with the wider school community, and with all aspects of their work. This attitude was reflected in Scholl, Nichols, and Burgh's 2008 study of teachers who adopted philosophical inquiry in their classrooms. They noted that

> [p]hilosophical communities of inquiry have been shown to have wonderful benefits for student thinking . . . it can in turn have a very positive effect on pedagogy and teacher thinking, in a time and resource efficient manner. In classrooms where teachers philosophise with students, these interactions cause teachers to reap the benefits themselves of critical, creative and caring thinking, within the community of inquiry, and more broadly in their lives. They become thoughtful people and reflective practitioners. (2008, 6)

We began to help other schools with training. With support we wrote an online course which was offered through the Queensland Department of Education for seven years and is now licensed to the Institute for the Advancement of Philosophy for Children at Montclair University. We also wrote a book because we wanted more material for teachers to use with younger children (see Cam et al. 2007). These activities further contributed to the well-deserved feelings of efficacy for the staff, leading to high levels of staff morale and satisfaction.

COMMUNITY ENGAGEMENT: PARENT OUTCOMES

At all stages in the process, we kept the parents involved and informed. The school developed a long waiting list for enrollment. It is understood that sometimes people even moved into the catchment area in order to be eligible for enrollment, a fact that has led to questions about the results of the school. It is important to understand that this was not always the case. However, what it shows is the interest that a school adopting philosophy can draw for parents.

ASSESSMENT OF PROGRAM OUTCOMES

The emphasis in this story is on the outcome of *thinking as an end in and of itself*. Regardless of the benefit of fine-tuning children's ability for reasoning, judgment, and the generation of ideas, the ability to think effectively has an inherent value. This fact may not always be understood when the focus is on the technical aspects of learning. When Knight and Collins (2010) engaged in teacher training for philosophy in schools, they found that the biggest hurdle was in changing the views of teachers who could not see the inherent value in teaching philosophically in a climate of standardized tests, mentioning that "[a]longside citing concerns about workload and the overcrowded curriculum, many teachers express their frustration at losing precious teaching and learning time to discussing abstract ideas that are seemingly irrelevant to the concerns of the mainstream curriculum" (2010, 2). Knight and Collins believe that it is the teacher's own beliefs about knowledge or what they term their "epistemic beliefs," due to the increasing pressure in Australia (as with many Western countries) to display results in literacy and numeracy, which contribute negatively to the attitude toward philosophy. The task then, for practitioners who work with teachers seeking to engage their students in philosophy, is to show how discussing ideas can have a positive impact on learning—through an emphasis on thinking.

The outcome of encouraging children to think was recognized on a global scale by UNESCO in 2008. The UNESCO study into the outcomes of adopting philosophy in schools reported the overwhelming benefits of philosophy for its contributions to society. However, until there is a systematic recognition by governing bodies that philosophy is an educational imperative, practitioners must continue to show outcomes that are consistent with recognizable quantifiers. As Dewey (1916) and Lipman (2004) both suggest, teaching children to think is the core business of education, so the onus is on those involved in teaching children to think to show the overall outcome of such a venture. The results reflected upon herein elucidate how children exposed to philosophy for one hour a week experienced increased outcomes in literacy and numeracy. While there were a number of demographic changes over time, the changes in results from children in their early school years, where many presented as struggling in literacy and numeracy, to later primary where outcomes were above the state and national means, attest to the benefit of adopting philosophy across a whole school. These observations point to the contribution of philosophy to measured improvements in student learning, and certainly from the point of view of the school principal, there is an undeniable link between philosophy and improvements in literacy and numeracy

In addition to the outcomes demonstrated though the literacy and numeracy testing, other wider-reaching outcomes are also notable. Teachers reported staff satisfaction above the average recorded across the state. While this may be evidence of a number of different factors that underpin the school culture, teachers identified involvement in philosophy across the school as one of the main reasons for increased motivation.

CONCLUSION

While acknowledging it is difficult to prove that adopting philosophy in the classroom has a direct causal link to an increase in literacy and numeracy outcomes, this chapter shows that at the very best, philosophy has contributed to the enhancement of literacy and numeracy; and at the very least, has had no negative impact on such outcomes.

Knight and Collins (2010) reported that one of the greatest reluctances of teachers to adopt philosophy was their concern that time devoted to "the curriculum" would be usurped by discussions about abstract ideas. However, through timetabled philosophy sessions, teachers in this case study didn't lose time but rather gained it, by developing in students the dispositions necessary to achieve in other, more measurable areas. Similarly, teachers gained a greater commitment to teaching and learning through increased satisfaction. The links here cannot be quantitatively substantiated, but through reflecting on these results we can see that the children clearly benefited from the inclusion of philosophy in both measureable and observable ways.

In 1997, a small school set out to change its approach to teaching and learning. By adopting a whole school approach to philosophy in the classroom, the principal, together with the teachers and school community, transformed their school curriculum and, in turn, experienced an increase in literacy and numeracy outcomes, staff morale, and parent satisfaction. These results present an opportunity for practitioners to communicate the benefits of adopting philosophy in the classroom and teaching children to think by speaking through the language of standardized testing. It is an attempt to make what is not currently counted count in mainstream education.

NOTE

1. The data collected by the school during the 14 years was unable to be released for publication. This chapter, hence, speaks to the reflections of the school principal who has firsthand knowledge of the trends in this data.

REFERENCES

Cam, P. (2006) *Twenty Thinking Tools* Camberwell, Victoria: ACER Press.

Cam, P., et al. (2007) *Philosophy with Young Children: A Classroom Handbook* Canberra: Australian Curriculum Studies Association.

Department of Education, Science and Training (2003) *Australia's Teachers: Australia's Future. Main Report* Canberra: Commonwealth of Australia.

Dewey, J. (1897) "My pedagogical creed" *School Journal, 54*, 77–80.

Dewey, J. (1916) *Democracy and Education: An Introduction to the Philosophy of Education* (1966 ed.) New York: Free Press.

Gardner, H. (1999) *Intelligence Reframed* New York: Basic Books.

Knight, S. and Collins, C. (2010) "What must teacher education programmes do to open teachers' minds to philosophy?" *Philosophy of Education Society of Australasia Conference*, December, Western Australia.

Law, S. (2006) *The War for Children's Minds* Abingdon, UK: Routledge.

Lingard, B., Hayes, D., Mills, M. and Christie, P. (2003) *Leading Learning. Making Hope Practical in Schools* Maidenhead, UK: Open University Press.

Lipman, M. (2004) *Thinking in Education* Cambridge: Cambridge University Press.

Millett, S. and Tapper, A. (2012) "Benefits of collaborative philosophical inquiry in schools" *Educational Philosophy and Theory 44*(5), 546–567.

Ritchhart, R. (2002) *Intellectual Character What It Is, Why It Matters, and How to Get It* San Francisco: Jossey-Bass.

Scholl, R. et al. (2008) "Interactions within a philosophical community of inquiry: Can they transform pedagogy and what do teachers learn in the process?" AARE Conference, Brisbane.

Sizer, T. R. (1992) *Horace's School. Redesigning the American High School* New York: Houghton Mifflin Company.

Trickey, S. and Topping, K. J. (2004) "Philosophy for children: A systematic review" *Research Papers in Education 19*(3), 365–380.

Trickey, S. and Topping, K. J. (2007) "Collaborative philosophical enquiry for school children: Cognitive effects at 10–12 years" *British Journal of Educational Psychology 77*(2), 271–288.

UNESCO (2008) *Philosophy: A School of Freedom, Teaching Philosophy and Learning to Philosophise: Status and Prospects* Paris: UNESCO Publishing.

23 Examining the Effects of Philosophy Classes on the Early Development of Argumentation Skills

Caren M. Walker, Thomas E. Wartenberg, and Ellen Winner

INTRODUCTION

Theories of learning have long emphasized the essential role of social factors in the development of early reasoning abilities (Vygotsky 1962). More recently, it has been proposed that the presentation of conflicting perspectives may facilitate children's understanding of knowledge claims as potentially subjective—one of many possible representations of the world (e.g., Cook & Schulz 2008; Felton 2004). Understanding the inherent subjectivity of knowledge claims is an important determinant of intellectual performance and is central to the development of reasoning abilities that are critical for academic success (Kuhn & Udell 2007). Despite these claims, there has been a surprising lack of empirical research that explores the effects of exposure to conflicting perspectives in the classroom on the development of children's early ideas about subjectivity and the subsequent development of argumentation skills. This chapter describes the methods and results of a research program that was designed to explore whether the dialogue-based pedagogical model that lies at the heart of the Philosophy for Children programs influences early epistemology and the development of argumentation skills in early childhood.

Understanding Subjectivity and the Development of Argumentation Skills

Coming to understand that the mind actively influences the representation of knowledge and contributes to the formation of beliefs is a major cognitive milestone in early childhood (e.g., Astington, Harris, & Olson 1988; Perner 1991). By age seven, children begin to show explicit understanding that reality itself may be open to a variety of interpretations—that a given knowledge claim is not a direct reflection of reality, but rather a representation of the world that is generated by human minds in a social context (Kuhn, Cheney, & Weinstock 2000). For example, children discover that knowledgeable people—even experts—often disagree, and that people's varying exposure to different experiences may lead to differences in their knowledge or the unique perspectives about the same scenario. Children therefore develop an appreciation that it is possible for people to hold conflicting beliefs about the same event (Taylor, Cartright, & Bowden 1991) and that knowledge claims are open to interpretation and evaluation.

One cognitive skill that appears to be highly correlated with this developing understanding of the nature of knowledge is the ability to understand and produce sound argumentation (Kuhn 1991; Mason & Boscolo 2004; Weinstock & Cronin 2003). Because good argumentation skills require that one be able to engage with the view that one intends to argue against, successful argumentation hinges upon the ability to consider the possibility of multiple perspectives. In other words, claims must be understood to be open to evaluation in order to be candidates for productive argumentation.

In support of this proposal, Felton and Kuhn (2001) demonstrated that when social and verbal production demands are factored out, the failure to consider the opposing view remains the critical weakness in students' performance in argument tasks. According to Graff (2003), students who simulate an imaginary opponent when producing written arguments produce more authentic and meaningful content and structure in their work. Further, previous research on the development of argumentation abilities has suggested that unskilled arguers tend to focus too heavily on providing sufficient support for their own claims, and therefore repeatedly ignore the claims of their opponent (Kuhn & Udell 2007). This is characterized by the novice's failure to consider the dual objectives in argumentation: (1) to evaluate incoming information from an interlocutor, and (2) to formulate a response that effectively clarifies the merits of one's own position. This process of coordinating opposing perspectives involves embracing the potential subjectivity of knowledge claims—a skill that develops over the course of early childhood.

The Benefits of Dialogue

One type of experience that may be essential to coordinating objective and subjective elements of knowing is the opportunity to engage in dialogue in both formal classroom settings and in everyday social contexts with peers. Dialogue exposes the learner to the presence of conflicting views about a particular topic, and thereby encourages evaluation of the relative merits of each of these views. Dialogue-based pedagogy has therefore been proposed to encourage the development of students' knowledge about *how* to think critically, as well as *what* to think critically about (Reznitskaya et al. 2009).

In a review of 19 studies on dialogic interaction in adolescents, Webb (1989) reports a strong correlation between student achievement and group interaction when students were asked to produce explanations or elaborations during class discussion. In reviewing the literature on the educational importance of these types of interactions, Glachan and Light (1982) concluded that cognitive benefits are most pronounced when students offer support for their own opinion and offer counterarguments against a conflicting claim through dialogue, and that differences in student perspectives that promote socio-cognitive conflict lead to greater learning. More recently, a variety of studies examining adolescents and adults have shown that participation in dialogue in the classroom leads to measurable improvements in written argumentation skills (e.g., Kuhn, Shaw, & Felton, 1997; Kuhn & Crowell 2011). For example, Kuhn et al. (1997) traced the appearance of argument elements in a writing task to the presence of those same elements during informal exchanges that had taken place among study participants prior to the task.

Despite this growing body of research that supports the benefits of engaging in dialogical interaction, few studies have examined how this may be successfully incorporated in the classroom (Kuhn & Crowell 2011; Nussbaum 2008). A recent multiyear study conducted by Kuhn and Crowell (2011) examined the effect of a novel educational method that explored the role of dialogic interaction on developing the maturity of written arguments in middle school students. Students who were encouraged to engage deeply with the discussion topics over the course of multiple semesters and produce relevant evidence for both sides of each topic showed significant improvements in their subsequent use of evidence in written essays. While this educational program demonstrated that argumentative reasoning skills can be successfully assessed and developed in the classroom, this method requires a large time investment in "non-curriculum-embedded" material and is specifically designed to be applicable to older students.

The study reported here assessed the effects of a short-term, dialogue-based pedagogical program that is accessible to much younger students (aged seven–eight), and easily embedded within a typical elementary school curriculum without special teaching materials or training. Unlike in previous work, the current program does not directly teach argumentation skills or expose students to novel content in the classroom. Instead, the goal of this educational program was to explore the potential effects of early, informal exposure to the presence of multiple, potentially conflicting perspectives in a familiar, naturalistic context.

Pedagogical Method: Philosophy for Children

The educational method investigated was based upon the Philosophy for Children (P4C) program developed by Matthew Lipman in the 1970s that introduces dialogic inquiry in elementary school classrooms (Lipman 1981). There is now a growing body of research examining the educational benefits of this program. Lipman's method is based on reading and discussing philosophical novels in elementary school classrooms, and is typically introduced to children at about the age of six. During each P4C session, children listen to a chapter from one of the novels, and then engage in collaborative dialogue about the philosophical content and themes. Using this method, P4C creates a "community of inquiry" in the classroom, in which the teacher facilitates student discussion in a supportive environment. The stated goal of the program is to "improve children's reasoning abilities and judgment by having them thinking about thinking as they discuss concepts of importance to them" (Lipman 1981, p.37).

While there is a large literature reporting the various benefits of the P4C program, there are a limited number of controlled experimental designs investigating its effects (Trickey & Topping 2004). In one longitudinal study examining the short- and long-term benefits of P4C on elementary school students, Topping & Trickey (2007a) demonstrated significant improvement on student performance on verbal and nonverbal aspects of the Cognitive Abilities Test (CAT3) following 16 months of weekly instruction. This benefit was maintained over the subsequent 2 years, even after students had transferred to secondary school with no further philosophical training. Using longitudinal data from this same study, the authors investigated the quantity and quality of teacher-student and student-student dialogue in the classroom to assess the impact of P4C on promoting participation in dialogic inquiry (Topping & Trickey 2007b). Results demonstrated increases in teacher use of open-ended questioning, proportion of student engagement in dialogue, number of student's reasoned responses to another's view, and amount of support provided for the student's own views.

THE CURRENT STUDY

Across the diverse set of research paradigms exploring the benefits of P4C and related philosophy programs, the strength of this pedagogical model has been largely attributed to its use of the dialogic process. Here, we report the procedures and results from a recent study exploring the benefits of this model on the development of argumentation skills in young children (Walker, Wartenberg, & Winner 2012). The particular philosophy program that we assessed is a method called "Teaching Children Philosophy" (Wartenberg 2009), which largely shares the theoretical orientation and educational goals of the original P4C program from which it evolved. Unlike P4C however, Wartenberg's (2009) curriculum does not require special training or materials, and is based upon well-known works of children's literature that are broadly accessible. The stated goal of the program is to assist children to engage in productive dialogue with one another and help them to "discover, express, and support their own answers to questions that concern them" (Wartenberg 2009, 17). Previous research in educational psychology has shown that collaborative discourse is fostered when teachers solicit explanations of students (with some prompting for elaborative thinking), rather than provide explanations of material (Webb et al. 2008). This type of student-focused model is the central pedagogical technique utilized by the Teaching Children Philosophy program. At the beginning of each philosophy class session, children are introduced to six rules for discussion: (1) state your position, (2) figure out if you agree or disagree, (3) present a real example of the abstract issue being discussed, (4) present a counterexample to a claim that has been proposed, (5) offer a revised version of the claim, and (6) support your position. This program therefore creates a supportive environment that explicitly introduces the concept of the subjectivity of ideas through collaborative discourse in a naturalistic setting.

Experimental Design and Procedure

The experiment assessed the effects of a 12-week semester of philosophy classes on the development of argumentation skills in seven-year-old second grade students. This study sought to confirm claims regarding the impact of dialogic interaction on argumentation across a variety of knowledge domains, and to extend this work to assess much younger children. It was hypothesized that participation in philosophy classes would lead to general improvement in even very young students' ability to both support their own perspective and consider the opposing perspective when confronted with conflicting claims.

Twenty-three second grade students participated in the study. Children were recruited from a single second grade class at an international public charter school in Massachusetts, and most children were bilingual in English and Chinese. None of the children had been exposed to a philosophy program prior to enrolling in the study. Research was conducted over the course of one academic year. Children were randomly assigned to either the philosophy or control program (art history) for the first semester, and received the alternate program in the second semester. Eleven children received the philosophy class in the first semester; 12 children received the philosophy class in the second semester.

Each philosophy session occurred once a week for a 12-week semester and was taught by a trained undergraduate instructor who read a preselected picture book aloud to the children. Books were chosen based on their philosophical content, and all of the standard fields of philosophy, from epistemology and metaphysics to ethics and aesthetics, were covered by the various picture books. This read-aloud activity served to initiate a child-centered discussion about the issues raised by the book, during which children were encouraged to engage in dialogue with one another, with the instructor acting as facilitator. The instructor asked open-ended questions to initiate the discussion in order to get the children to reflect on the philosophical issues in the books. The children were asked to respond, to support their ideas with explanations, and to say whether and why they agreed or disagreed with one another (for a detailed description of the method, see Wartenberg 2009).

An art history program served as the control for the philosophy program. Because we were particularly interested in assessing the role of dialogue, the art history class was designed to be as similar as possible to the philosophy class, but without any dialogical interaction. Both groups read a picture book each week, with the philosophy group reading a book with philosophical content, and the art history group reading a book about a well-known artist (e.g., Leonardo da Vinci, Henri Matisse). Those in the philosophy group engaged in group dialogue after the reading, while those in the art group created an art project inspired by the artist of the week. The same teacher taught both the philosophy and the art history classes for each group, and art history and philosophy classes were identical in length and frequency.

Three individual assessments of argumentation skills were administered over three time points and served as pre- and post-program measures for both semesters: a pretest one week prior to the first semester (time 1); posttest 1 one week after the first semester (time 2); and posttest 2 one week after the second semester (time 3). Testing took place in 20-minute, one-on-one sessions with the experimenter, and all testing sessions were audio recorded for later analysis.

The argumentation skills task was adapted from an assessment originally designed by Valle, Tighe, and Hale (2009). The task presents children with a four-page illustrated book depicting conflicting claims chosen to be relevant to children. Each page represented a conflicting claim from one of four domains of knowledge: (1) aesthetic (e.g., rock music is better/classical music is better), (2) value (e.g., children should/should not be allowed to have candy in school), (3) social (e.g., children learn more from family/friends), and (4) physical (e.g., there is/is not life on other planets). On each page, children were presented with both sides of the conflicting claim. The following is an example from the value domain: "*Some school lunchrooms offer soda and candy to students. Some people say that soda and candy should be sold in the lunchroom at school. They think that kids should decide what they eat and drink. Other people say that soda and candy should not be sold in the lunchroom at school. They think that parents should decide what kids eat and drink.*"

Children were asked to report which side they agreed with. Children were then asked the following four questions: (1) "Why do you agree with that side?" (*own argument*), (2) "Can you be sure that you are right?" (*certainty*), (3) "Is it possible you could learn something new that would make you change your mind?" (*falsifiability*), and (4) "What would someone from the other side say if he/she were trying to convince you that he/she was right?" (*opposing argument*). The order of presentation of the four kinds of claims was randomized, and three versions of each book were created, one with each order. One third of the children received each version at each time point to avoid practice effects. Pilot testing determined that the three versions of the task were highly correlated and yielded no difference in performance.

Responses were scored for each conflicting claim, based upon the maturity of participant answers. Questions assessing *own* and *opposing arguments* were scored from zero to four. Zero points were awarded in cases where no answer was provided (e.g., "I don't know."). One point was awarded for simply choosing a side or repeating the claim provided in the book (e.g., "Children should not have candy in school because parents should decide what they eat."). Two points were awarded for citing the word "evidence" or "proof," or for recognizing the need for evidence by some form of irrelevant supporting information (e.g., "Children should not have candy in school because there is proof that parents should decide what they eat," or "Children should not have candy in school because school is for learning math."). Three points were awarded for providing relevant but anecdotal evidence from personal experience (e.g., "Children should not have candy in school because once I got a tummy ache from too much candy."). The full four points were provided for supporting their chosen side with relevant, non-anecdotal evidence (e.g., "Children should not be allowed to have candy in school because parents know what is good for their kids, and they know that sugar will make kids crazy and they won't be able to sit still in class."). Because there were a total of four claims, participants could receive up to 16 points for the *own argument* questions and 16 points for the *opposing argument* questions, yielding a total of 32 possible points. Two trained raters who were blind to the child's assigned group independently scored responses. Inter-rater reliability was high with a mean of 95 percent agreement.

Questions assessing children's *certainty* and their beliefs about *falsifiability* were scored from zero to two. One point was awarded when responses indicated lack of absolute certainty, and one point was awarded when children endorsed the potential falsifiability of their chosen claim. Participants could therefore receive up to two points for each of the four knowledge claims, yielding a total of eight possible points for these items.

Results

Results of the questions assessing children's *own* and *opposing arguments* appear in Figure 23.1 below (reprinted from Walker et al. 2012). Time 1 was the pretest for both groups; time 2 was the a posttest for the first semester philosophy group and the pretest for the philosophy 2nd semester group; time 3 was the long-term posttest for the first semester philosophy group and the posttest for the second semester philosophy group.

There was no difference in argumentation skills between the philosophy and control group at time 1 (pretest). At time 2 (posttest for the first semester program), the philosophy group significantly outperformed the control group. Additional analyses of children's scores at times 1 and 2 revealed that the scores of the philosophy group increased from pretest to posttest, while the scores of the control group remained stable. At time 3 (long-term posttest for the first semester philosophy group and posttest for the second semester philosophy group), there was no difference between groups.

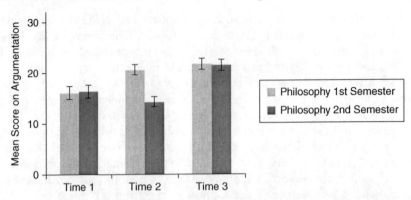

Figure 23.1. Mean score (out of a possible 32) for first and second semester philosophy students on the argumentation skills assessment. Mean score includes the combined score for *own argument* and *opposing argument* questions for each of the four domains. Time 1 served as a pretest for both groups, time 2 served as a posttest for the first semester philosophy group and a pretest for the philosophy second semester group, and time 3 served as a long-term posttest for the first semester philosophy group and a posttest for the second semester philosophy group. (Reprinted with permission from Walker et al., 2012)

Results from time 3 therefore replicate results from time 2 with the second semester philosophy group, who demonstrated improvement equal to that of the first semester philosophy group. These results also demonstrate that the first semester philosophy group improvements in argumentation skills did not decline following a subsequent semester without further philosophy training (See Figure 23.1).

We next analyzed children's responses to each of the questions individually. Because the *own argument* and *opposing argument* questions assess performance on distinct argumentative skills—producing arguments that support one's own views and producing arguments that support alternative perspectives to one's own views (see Mercier 2011)—we were particularly interested in assessing whether the philosophy program targeted one skill over the other. Responses to both types of questions paralleled the overall pattern of performance on the task. While scores on responses supporting the child's own argument were generally higher than scores on responses supporting the opposing argument at both pre- and posttests, performance on both types of responses showed similar patterns of improvement following the program: there was an effect of the philosophy program on children's arguments that were consistent with their own view and those consistent for the opposing view. However, there was no effect of the philosophy intervention on children's *certainty* or beliefs about the *falsifiability* of their views.

This study demonstrates that when young children are asked to consider conflicting claims, their argumentation skills improve. This program led to improvements in generating an argument, and this improvement was maintained following a subsequent semester without further philosophy training.

These results provide support for the impact of exposure to dialogic interaction in a pedagogical context on argumentation skills in very young children.

CONCLUSION

There are few pedagogical models that have been shown to support the development of critical thinking skills in very young children. The experiment presented here shows that children as young as seven years old improve their argumentation skills when they are encouraged to ask questions, justify their own reasoning, and evaluate the reasoning of other individuals in the classroom. Children who received the philosophy program demonstrated greater skill in their capacity to attend to the subjective element in generating a novel argument. These findings contribute to our understanding of how dialogic inquiry and naturalistic exposure to conflicting beliefs fosters the development of argumentation skills and awareness of subjectivity (Duschl & Osborne 2002; Lehrer, Schauble, & Lucas 2008). This style of inquiry has been shown to support learning and promote maturation of metacognition in the development of scientific thinking (e.g., Kelly & Crawford 1997; Polman & Pea 2001; Wertsch 1991), and the current studies extend the potential benefits of these cognitive gains to very young children's beliefs about the subjectivity of knowledge in other domains as well. More generally, these findings support claims regarding the role of social factors in learning and reasoning, and show that exposure to contrastive beliefs in the context of collaborative discourse has important effects on the development of early reasoning.

This research has implications for classroom practices, in which teacher-fronted, monological, and traditional methods have remained the dominant pedagogical strategies for elementary education (Alexander 2003). Educators' resistance to embracing dialogic interaction in the classroom is most commonly attributed to the complexity and potential inconsistency associated with its implementation (Reznitskaya et al. 2009). Introducing a Philosophy for Children program in elementary school classrooms may help teachers to use effective dialogical processes. Additional longitudinal research examining the benefits of introducing dialogic inquiry to elementary education is necessary to explore the potential long-term benefits for critical thinking skills and academic achievement.

ACKNOWLEDGMENTS

Thanks to the parents and children of the Pioneer Valley Chinese Immersion Charter School in Hadley, MA, who participated in the study: to Kathleen Wang, Leigh Doherty, and the second grade teachers for their support and aid recruiting participants; and to Ariel Sykes and Nicole Giambalvo from

Mt. Holyoke Philosophy Department for their contribution teaching the philosophy and art history classes. Finally, I thank Angelina Hawley and Erin O'Connor for their help in conducting all aspects of the research, and the Psychology Department at Boston College for funding.

REFERENCES

Alexander, R.J. (2003) *Talk for learning: The first year* Northallerton, UK: North Yorkshire County Council.

Astington, J.W., Harris, P.L., & Olson, D.R. (1988) *Developing theories of mind* Cambridge: Cambridge University Press.

Cook, C., & Schulz, L. (2009) *Bob thinks this but Emily thinks that: Contrastive beliefs improve kindergartners' scientific reasoning* 31st Annual Proceedings of the Cognitive Science Society Conference in Amsterdam, Netherlands.

Duschl, R., & Osborne, J. (2002) "Supporting and promoting argumentation discourse in science education" *Studies in Science Education 38*: 39–72.

Felton, M.K. (2004) "The development of discourse strategies in adolescent argumentation" *Cognitive Development 19*: 35–52.

Felton, M.K., & Kuhn, D. (2001) "The development of discourse strategies in adolescent argumentation" *Cognitive Development 19*, 35–52.

Glachan, M., & Light, P. (1982) "Peer interaction and learning: Can two wrongs make a right?" In *Social cognition: Studies of the development of understanding* (eds. Butterworth, G. and Light, P.) 238–262, Chicago, IL: University of Chicago Press.

Graff, G. (2003) *Clueless in academe: How schooling obscures the life of the mind* New Haven, CT: Yale University Press.

Kelly, G.J. andCrawford, T. (1997) "An ethnographic investigation of the discourse processes of school science" *Science Education 81*(5): 533–560.

Kuhn, D. (1991) *The skills of argument* Cambridge: Cambridge University Press.

Kuhn, D., Cheney, R., and Weinstock, M. (2000) "The development of epistemological understanding" *Cognitive Development 15*: 309–328.

Kuhn, D. and Crowell, A. (2011) "Dialogic argumentation as a vehicle for developing young adolescents' thinking" *Psychological Science 22*(4): 545–552.

Kuhn, D., Shaw, V., and Felton, M. (1997) "Effects of dyadic interaction on argumentative reasoning" *Cognition and Instruction 15*: 287–315.

Kuhn, D. and Udell, W. (2007) "Coordinating own and other perspectives in argument" *Thinking and Reasoning 13*: 90–104.

Lehrer, R., Schauble, L., and Lucas, D. (2008) "Supporting development of the epistemology of inquiry" *Cognitive Development 23*(4): 512–529.

Lipman, M. (1981) "Philosophy for Children" In *Developing minds: Programs for teaching thinking* (ed. Costa, A.L.) 35–38, Alexandria, VA: Association for Supervision and Curricular Development.

Mason, L. and Boscolo, P. (2004) "Role of epistemological understanding and interest in interpreting a controversy and in topic-specific belief change" *Contemporary Educational Psychology 29*: 103–128.

Mercier, H. (2011) "Reasoning serves argumentation in children" *Cognitive Development 26*(3): 177–191.

Nussbaum, E.M. (2008) "Collaborative discourse, argumentation, and learning: Preface and literature review" *Contemporary Educational Psychology 33*(3): 345–359.

Perner, J. (1991) *Understanding the representational mind* Cambridge, MA: MIT Press.

Polman, J., and Pea, R. (2001) "Transformative communication as a cultural tool for guiding inquiry science" *Science Education* 85(3): 223–238.

Reznitskaya, A., Kuo, L., Clark, A., Miller, B., Jadallah, M., Anderson, R. C., and Nguyen-Jahiel, K. (2009) "Collaborative reasoning: a dialogic approach to group discussions" *Cambridge Journal of Education* 39(1): 29–48.

Taylor, M., Cartwright, B., and Bowden, T. (1991) "Perspective taking and theory of mind: Do children predict interpretive diversity as a function of differences in observers' knowledge?" *Child Development* 62: 1334–1351.

Topping, K. J. and Trickey, S. (2007a) "Collaborative philosophical inquiry for schoolchildren: Cognitive gains at 2-year follow-up" *British Journal of Educational Psychology* 77: 787–796.

Topping, K. J. and Trickey, S. (2007b) "Impact of philosophical enquiry on school students' interactive behavior" *Thinking Skills and Creativity* 2: 73–84.

Trickey, S. and Topping, K. J. (2004) "Philosophy for children: A systematic review" *Research Papers in Education* 19(3): 365–380.

Valle, A., Tighe, E., and Hale, J. (2009) "Domain-related patterns in epistemological understanding: Evidence from questionnaire and parent-child conversation data" Poster presented at *Society for Research in Child Development*.

Vygotsky, L.S. (1962) *Thought and language* Cambridge, MA: MIT Press.

Walker, C.M., Wartenberg, T., and Winner, E. (2012) "Engagement in philosophical dialogue facilitates children's reasoning about subjectivity" *Developmental Psychology* appeared in online first publication, September 3, 2012. doi: 10.1037/a0029870

Wartenberg, T. (2009) *Big ideas for little kids: Teaching philosophy through children's literature* Lanham, MD: Rowman & Littlefield Education

Webb, N.M. (1989) "Peer interaction and learning in small groups" *International Journal of Educational Research* 13: 21–40.

Webb, N.M., Franke, M.L., Ing, M., Chan, A., De, T., Freund, D., and Battey, D. (2008) "The role of teacher instructional practices in student collaboration" *Contemporary Educational Psychology* 33(4): 360–381

Weinstock, M. and Cronin, M.A. (2003) "The everyday production of knowledge: Individual differences in epistemological understanding and juror-reasoning skill" *Applied Cognitive Psychology* 17: 161–181.

Wertsch, J. (1991) *Voices of the mind* New York: Harvester.

24 Assessing the Outcomes of Philosophical Thinking with Children

Steven Trickey and Keith Topping

It has been suggested that children derive a range of benefits from their participation in philosophical inquiry. For example, Fisher (1998) noted gains in achievement scores, democratic values, self-esteem, and creative thinking. More recently, Gaut and Gaut (2012) stated that "by doing philosophy," children develop a range of skills including critical thinking, creative thinking, concentration, listening, communication, and social skills. This chapter considers how some of these developments might be assessed. It is based on methods used in a study of the evaluation of the Thinking through Philosophy program (Cleghorn 2002) in Clackmannanshire in Scotland. This chapter focuses on an overview of the methods used for evaluating the outcomes of the project.

Detailed discussion of the results of the Clackmannanshire study can be found elsewhere (e.g., Topping and Trickey 2007a, 2007b, 2007c; Trickey and Topping 2006, 2007). However, it would be appropriate in this discussion of assessment approaches to also identify the main findings arising from this evaluation of philosophical inquiry in the classroom. These findings included evidence that one hour of philosophical inquiry each week in elementary schools classrooms can be cost-effective in promoting developments in cognitive ability, increase participation in classroom discussion, and help children develop socially.

The methods described here are provided as examples of potential ways of assessing the outcomes of Philosophical Inquiry. The authors recognize that different evaluation methods have different strengths and weaknesses, and therefore investigators will need to take into account the purpose of their assessment when deciding what assessment instrument they wish to use. Indeed, cautious investigators will choose to use at least two diverse methods of evaluation and triangulate them. Mercer (2010) discussed the advantages and disadvantages of quantitative, qualitative, and mixed methods for analyzing classroom talk. This could be applied to the analysis of discussion in philosophical inquiry. Fisher (1998) also focused on the analysis of transcripts of classroom discussion when he suggested various ways in which teachers could assess progress in philosophical discussion including the following:

- tracking a whole discussion using a checklist of discourse skills,
- tracking the contributions of every individual participant,
- tracking a particular discourse or cognitive feature (e.g., counting examples of reasoning, measuring the extent of utterances), and
- analyzing the student teacher ratio of contributions to discussion.

The last two of the above approaches were incorporated into the video analysis evaluation method used in the Clackmannanshire study. This evaluated the outcomes of the Thinking through Philosophy program in eight elementary schools (and controls). The study used three evaluation methods each of which had their strengths and weaknesses. While these methods were diverse in nature, their focus frequently overlapped, allowing a triangulated approach from different perspectives. Strong consistencies in results from diverse methods provided evidence of the reliability of conclusions drawn from the evaluation of the project.

The Thinking through Philosophy project was an adaptation of Lipman's 'Philosophy for Children program (see Lipman, Sharp, and Oscanyon 1980, for a description of this program). The Philosophy for Children program emphasizes the development of critical reasoning skills through questioning and dialogue between student, teacher, and peers. The Scottish evaluation of the Thinking through Philosophy project investigated the outcomes of one hour of weekly collaborative inquiry—particularly with regard to developments in cognitive ability, developments in critical reasoning skills, the quality of classroom discussion, and social developments. Previous evidence was available supporting these outcomes. In the early stages, the authors (Trickey and Topping 2004) critically reviewed previous research literature relating to the evaluation of Philosophy for Children. This review indicated a consistent educationally significant effect size across the studies selected for inclusion in the review.

The authors used a traditional two-by-two pre-post experimental design for the larger part of the research. This involved collecting a range of data from two comparable populations of children before the initiative started. One population of children participated in one lesson each week using the Thinking through Philosophy program, while a matched group pursued their curriculum as before. Both populations were then retested at a later stage under the same conditions. The experimental group, that is, the children who have been involved in Thinking through Philosophy, were also involved in an additional qualitative evaluation. The overall evaluation thus aimed to provide a triangulated approach to assessing the outcomes of the Thinking through Philosophy program through a combination of the following:

- standardized tests to provide (pre-post) *quantitative* measures of the outcomes,
- video analysis of classroom discussions to provide (pre-post) *qualitative and quantitative* measures of the outcomes, and

- systematic analysis of questionnaires (post-test only) to provide a further *qualitative* indicator of outcomes.

METHOD 1: USE OF STANDARDIZED TESTS

The standardized tests used were the Cognitive Ability Test (CAT) (Smith, Fernandes, and Strand 2001) and Myself as a Learner (MALS) (Burden 2000). Although Burden and Nicholls (2000) have argued that the above design may not the best means of evaluating this type of intervention, the design had the advantage of allowing the relationship between the groups to be precisely defined and in ways that could be subject to external scrutiny and replication.

The evaluation tasks in this study were randomly shared across classes to minimize disruption to each class's activities and demands on their teachers while they were in process of developing new skills and a new pedagogy. For example, video recordings were made of discussions taking place in six Primary 6 classes (the children were 10 years of age), whereas a different group of Primary 6 classes had their cognitive abilities assessed. The control schools were comparable to the experimental schools in terms of pupil ability, size of school, and social disadvantage factors. For example, the pre-test mean standardized cognitive ability score was 100 for the experimental pupils (standard deviation 12.1) and 101 for the control pupils (standard deviation 11.1). Both of these measures were normally distributed.

The Cognitive Ability Test was used in the Clackmannanshire study to investigate whether there was any change in cognitive abilities following regular participation in philosophical inquiry. The cognitive abilities of the children who were going to participate in philosophical inquiry and the control children were assessed using the updated version (Smith, Fernandes, and Strand 2001) of the Cognitive Abilities Test (Lohman, Thorndike, and Hagen 1986). The Cognitive Abilities Test provides reliable and valid standardized scores of verbal ability, nonverbal ability, and quantitative ability for each pupil, using a series of multiple-choice questions. Each of these three ability measures had three subtests. This assessment thus provided raw scores for a total of nine subtests for each pupil.

A brief description of each of the nine Cognitive Ability Test subtests follows:

Verbal Classification Test requires the selection of a word from five choices that goes with three other words, such as "green, blue, red."

Sentence Completion Test requires selecting a word from five to complete a sentence that has a word missing.

Verbal Analogies Test provides two words that go together (e.g., "new" and "old" and a third word that similarly goes with one of five choices.

Number Analogies Test provides two sets of numbers that are linked in some way (e.g., "2/3" and "6/7,"' and another number on its own.

A number has to be selected from a choice of five that belongs with the number on its own.

Number Series Test provides a series of numbers that are linked by a rule that needs to be worked out. The correct number must then be selected from a choice of five to follow on from that series.

Equation Building Test provides three numbers and signs that can be combined to make different answers. Only one correct answer is provided in the choices.

Figure Classification Test provides three figures that are similar in some way. The similarity has to be worked out and the correct choice selected that belongs with the first three figures.

Figure Analogies Test provides two figures that are related in some way (e.g., two squares). A third figure is provided. The correct choice must be selected from five that belongs with that third figure.

Figure Analysis Test shows an example of how a square of dark paper is folded and where holes are punched into it. The choice must be selected that will show how the paper will look when it is unfolded.

"Pre-project" standardized scores were obtained in the three overall abilities (i.e., verbal, nonverbal, and quantitative reasoning) and raw scores in the nine subtests for 177 experimental and control children aged 10 years. Post-intervention testing took place 16 months later. This length of time had two potential advantages. First, it took into account the probability that any gains in cognitive development were likely to be gradual, and second, it reduced potential "practice effects" arising from rapid repetition of the same test procedure.

The main finding arising from the use of Cognitive Abilities Test was that there was an average gain in cognitive abilities scores of 6.0 standardized points for children who participated in regular philosophical inquiry. This finding was highly statistically significant (i.e., the probability of the result occurring by chance was less than 0.001; less than one in a thousand). There were also highly significant gains for the philosophical inquiry children in the three component abilities (verbal, quantitative, and nonverbal). There were no gains in the cognitive ability scores of the matched control group. Further statistical analysis took place by gender, school, and subtest. For full results, see Topping and Trickey (2007a).

There was a further follow-up assessment of both "treatment" and "control" children two years after the initial intervention study had been completed, again using the Cognitive Abilities Test. At the time of follow-up assessment, the students were aged approximately 14 years. Despite the lack of any further philosophical inquiry following transfer from elementary to secondary school, the experimental students had retained their cognitive ability gains nearly two years into their secondary school education. (See Topping and Trickey 2007b, for a full description of the follow-up study).

The second standardized measure used in this study was Burden's (2000) "Myself as a Learner Scale" (MALS). MALS was constructed to have a deliberate focus upon "academic self-concept" and provided a suitable measure to investigate changes in self-perception. Burden's emphasis on "academic self-esteem" contrasts with a more all-embracing notion of general "self-concept" and more specific academic-related scales (e.g., reading or mathematics self-concept). MALS provides a measure of "students' perceptions of themselves as learners and active problem solvers within educational settings." The scale comprises 20 statements, for example, "I need lots of help with my work." The students rate themselves on each statement on a five-point scale.

MALS presented as a reliable and valid measure. Burden indicated that academic self-concept was closely related to measures of cognitive ability and academic achievement and cited a correlation between the Cognitive Abilities Test (CAT) and MALS of around 0.7. The Clackmannanshire study aimed to consider the effect of the Thinking through Philosophy program on both cognitive ability and self-esteem in learning environments. MALS thus appeared an attractive measure to use in view of the correlation with CAT scores and academic self-esteem, together with its ease of administration.

The children who had regularly participated in the philosophy program improved their self-esteem scores on MALS. The difference between the pre- and post-test total MALS scores for the experimental pupils was statistically significant. There was no significant difference between the pre- and post-test results of the control pupils. See Trickey and Topping (2006) for a full account of the use of "Myself as a Learner Scale" in assessing the effects of philosophical inquiry.

METHOD 2: VIDEO ANALYSIS OF CLASSROOM DISCUSSIONS

The second method used in this study may be more practical for teachers to use in assessing the effects of philosophical inquiry in the classroom than the use of standardized tests. However, analyzing and scoring video sequences can be time consuming. In the Clackmannanshire study, pre-project video recordings were made of classroom discussion of the somewhat ambiguous Greek fable "Mercury and the Axe" (Aesop). The teacher first read out the story and then explored its meaning through discussion with the class. The following "prompt questions" (from Fisher 1999) were provided to each teacher to help structure a discussion of "What is truth?"

1. Do you think this is a true story? Why?
2. What do we mean when we say something is true?
3. What do we call something that is not true? What does "false" mean?
4. What is a lie?
5. What do we call a story that is not true? What is fiction / a fable / a fairy tale?
6. Which man in the story was honest? What does "honest" mean?
7. Which man in the story was a liar? What does "liar" mean?

   8. Is it better to tell the truth or to tell lies? Why?
   9. Have you ever told a lie? Can you say when or why?
   10. Is it every right to tell a lie? Is it ever wrong to tell the truth?

Both the philosophy classes and the control classes repeated the same task with the same instructions six months later, and the discussions were again video recorded. The first 10 minutes of each video recorded classroom discussion was scored using a structured observation schedule. This process aimed to determine the incidence of the following specific behaviors during that period of discussion:

- Occurrence of pupil supporting his view/opinion with a reason
- Occurrence of pupil agreeing or disagreeing with a view expressed by another pupil *and* providing a reason for this
- Occurrence of teacher asking an open-ended question (including follow-up questions)
- Number of discrete pupil utterances
- Ratio of the amount of time pupils were talking to the amount of time their teacher was talking

The first four of these measures was gained through counting the number of occasions that these behaviors were observed during the 10-minute observation period. The final measure was obtained by fixed-interval observations taken every 30 seconds, to determine whether the teacher was talking or whether a pupil was talking at that precise moment. Twenty observations were therefore made over a 10-minute period for each recorded discussion. A percentage was then calculated for the amount of time the pupils were talking, as against the amount of time their teacher was talking.

Specific behaviors that were selected for the observation schedule were chosen on the grounds that they were readily observable and measurable (countable). A measure of inter-observer agreement was gained to ensure the observation schedule (and the observers) was sufficiently reliable. Two observers received brief training to enable them to use the schedule accurately. The observers independently scored a random sample of video recordings, and these scores were compared. With practice, the observation schedule was found to be reliable and, with its focus on readily measurable behaviors, proved relatively straightforward to use. Other observation measures were also originally to be included in the scoring. However these were discounted on account of reliability concerns, that is, they lacked sufficient inter-observer reliability in the early pilot phase of testing out the schedule.

The first two measures (i.e., "occurrence of pupil supporting their view/opinion with a reason" and the "occurrence of pupil agreeing or disagreeing with a view expressed by another pupil and providing a reason for this") were seen as providing an indicator of critical reasoning skills (in terms of the student's ability to justify a viewpoint with evidence or reasons). The third measure provided an indicator of changes in teacher behavior during the project.

The fourth measure scored the number of discrete utterances made by pupils during the first 10 minutes of the discussion. This score in isolation is not particularly significant. However, dividing the fixed interval scores from the fourth measure by the number of utterances provides an indication of the length (elaboration) of individual verbal contributions made by the pupils.

The last measure provided an indication of the level of pupil participation in the discussion relative to the verbal contributions made by the teacher. The level of pupil participation was thought important, as it provided a "quantity" measure of "pupil talk." Mercer (2000) has cautioned against the use of quantity of talk as an indicator of dialogue. However, a measure of quantity together with a quality critical thinking indicator (incidence of reasoning) was considered to provide an indication of the extent to which developments in classroom dialogue took place in this study.

The analysis of the video recordings of the classroom discussions provided evidence that the children's regular involvement in the Thinking through Philosophy program had resulted in the following:

- increased participation in classroom discussion,
- increased occurrence of children supporting their views/opinions with reasons,
- more elaborated responses from the children,
- an increase in the use of open-ended, follow-up questions by the teachers.

See Topping and Trickey (2007c) for a full discussion of the quantitative results of the video analysis.

In addition, transcripts were made of the recordings to provide examples of actual dialogue taking place. Such examples provided an indication of the nature of the thinking that was developing in children as the philosophical inquiries proceeded. One transcript example is provided below:

Stuart (discussing happiness):	Happiness is inside you. It is sort of chained to you so it can never leave you.
Teacher:	Do we use happiness up? If I am happy too much might I run out of it when I'm older?
Holly:	No, it's like a car going to the petrol station to get more petrol. When something makes you happy it sort of tops it up again.
Teacher:	But where is happiness?
Holly:	Happiness is not to be found without—it can only be found within.
Hannah:	Things are not real happiness—they are just like a comfort blanket over you that make you think you are

	happy. It's the same *you* underneath. Money won't make you happy.
Teacher:	Can you say more about that?
Hannah:	Happiness is better thought of as a contentment inside.
Sam:	Happiness is like a spark in a fire—it's always there but it needs something extra to make it come to life.

METHOD 3: ANALYSIS OF STUDENT QUESTIONNAIRES

Questionnaires were also used to assess the outcomes of philosophical inquiry following seven months involvement with the Thinking through Philosophy program. In addition, feedback from teachers involved in the Philosophy for Children lessons came from verbal comments recorded during group feedback meetings arranged to support the teachers. Teachers also provided written comments in observation diaries that they had been asked to maintain. Head teachers were asked to record their impressions as the Philosophy for Children initiative progressed.

While the teacher observations provided anecdotal evidence of inquiry outcomes, the student questionnaires were subject to more detailed analysis. A sample of students completed a questionnaire that had been designed to elicit their views and experiences of Philosophy for Children. These questionnaires were then subjected to systematic analysis. The initial pupil questionnaire was piloted on a group of 12 pupils. Feedback from both teacher and pupils indicated that only minor amendments were necessary. A random sample of 77 pupils was then asked to complete the questionnaire anonymously.

The questions consisted of one closed (multiple-choice) question (that determined the extent to which the children had enjoyed the inquiries) and nine open-ended questions. The open ended questions were typically preceded by a yes/no choice before the open-ended question was put to the children. The nine open questions used in the student questionnaire were as follows:

1. What do you like best about the philosophy lessons?
2. What do you do not like about the philosophy lessons? Why is that?
3. Can you think of any changes that you have noticed in how you and others do things in the philosophy lessons as the year has progressed? If so, what changes have you noticed?
4. Do you think that the philosophy lessons helped you in any way? If so, how have they helped you?
5. Can you think of any changes in what happened in any *other* lessons as a result of what is done in the philosophy lessons? If you have noticed any changes, what changes have you noticed?
6. Can you think of anything you have learned during the philosophy lessons? (This can be about yourself or other things.) If so, what is it that you have learned?

7. Have the philosophy discussions changed your views on anything? (for example, your views on fairness, beauty, or anything else you have discussed). In what way has your thinking changed?
8. Can you write one thing that makes philosophy different to any other subject you do in school?
9. What does the word "thinking" mean to you? Please complete this sentence. Thinking is _____.

The responses of each child for each open-ended question were assigned to categories that were then judged to reflect themes in the students' responses. Student responses that did not readily fall into a specific category were placed in a category termed "Other." Although 77 pupils participated in this exercise, the total number of responses varied for each question because occasionally pupils would record more than one response or occasionally a pupil would omit to record any response for a particular question.

The reliability of this approach was gauged by obtaining inter-rater comparisons. Two raters allocated a sample of the overall pupil responses to existing categories. This procedure was carried out blind (i.e., the raters had no knowledge of the decisions of the other). These ratings of the two raters were then compared. The number of agreed ratings was divided into the total number of pupil responses and multiplied by 100 to calculate the percentage of occasions that the two raters were in agreement. This calculation provided an inter-rater comparability of 85 percent. Variability was noted between the reliability in the 10 questions. The lowest reliability was recorded in Question 10 (What is thinking?). The inter-rater comparison for all the other questions indicated the process to be sufficiently reliable for the purpose of this study. Any tendency for the children to provide responses they thought their teachers wanted should have been minimized through clear instructions to the teachers to seek unbiased, honest, anonymous feedback from the pupils.

The analysis of the children's questionnaire responses indicated that they perceived their participation in classroom discussion to have increased as the inquiries progressed. This result was consistent with that of the video analysis. The questionnaire study also provided evidence that the children perceived improvements in their communication skills, confidence, and concentration. It also indicated that the children perceived that their experience of regular inquiry helped them to learn to manage their feelings and impulsivity more appropriately. See Trickey and Topping (2007) for a full discussion of the analysis of the questionnaire results.

CONCLUSION

This chapter has considered the methods used in one study to assess the outcomes of philosophical inquiry programs in the classroom. While these were used in a wider evaluation of a specific program being used in elementary schools in Scotland, the authors see scope for adapting these methods so that teachers can structure assessment of programs used in their own classrooms.

The study described in this chapter used diverse methods to investigate the impact of the program on participating children. The emergence of a consistent pattern of outcomes from such diverse methods added to the reliability of findings from this study. For example, evidence of gains in reasoning abilities were found in the results of both standardized tests and video analysis. Similarly, evidence of gains in student participation in inquiries was found in the analysis of student questionnaires and the analysis of the videoed discussions. The authors also looked for consistency within the same measure, such as consistency in the overlapping responses to different questions in the student questionnaire. The use of more than one method would therefore seem to confer advantages in assessing possible outcomes.

However, teachers should keep in mind the purposes of their assessments of philosophical inquiries. Audio recording classroom inquiries and the analysis of transcripts of classroom discussion may provide a more practical way of assessing progress in philosophical discussion through facilitating the tracking of progress in specific discourse skills. Similarly. regular metacognitive reflection following each inquiry could provide a simple and practical way of assessing students' views of how the inquiry went. For example, the teacher might ask young children questions following an inquiry such as "Did we ask good questions?" "Did we listen to each other well?" "Did we give good reasons for our answers?" "Did anyone change his mind?" See Fisher (1998) for further examples of such questions.

Teachers and philosophers need to assess the outcomes of using philosophical inquiry with children in the classroom for a variety of different reasons. Teachers investing time and energy into such inquiries will wish to know whether such activities are having beneficial effect on the children's development and what aspects of the inquiry process need attention if the children are to experience maximum benefit. In times of curricular pressure, the need to evaluate the outcomes of philosophical inquiry in the classroom may be particularly pressing. Lipman, Sharp, and Oscanyon (1980) refuted the argument that the use of philosophy does not need to be justified by empirical evidence and argued that such a position is unlikely to be persuasive to those responsible for administering our school systems. They further argued that if the use of philosophy is to gain wider acceptance in schools, "it will succeed in doing so only if it can demonstrate to those who run the schools that it can make a significant difference to the child's overall performance." The various methods discussed in this chapter will provide ideas to facilitators to help them assess the social and cognitive outcomes of their inquiries with children rather than relying on their intuitions of possible benefits that may or may not have been experienced by the participating children.

REFERENCES

Burden, R. (2000) *Myself as a learner scale* Windsor, UK: NFER-Nelson.

Burden, R. and Nichols L. (2000) "Evaluating the process of introducing a thinking skills programme into the secondary school curriculum" *Research Papers in Education* 15(3): 293–306.

Cleghorn, P. (2002) *Thinking through philosophy* Blackburn, UK: Educational Printing Services.

Fisher, R. (1998) *Teaching thinking: Philosophical inquiry in the classroom* London: Cassell.

Fisher, R. (1999) *First stories for thinking* Oxford: Nash Pollock.

Gaut, B. andante M. (2012) *Philosophy for young children* Abingdon: Routledge.

Lipman, M, Sharp, A. M., and Oscanyon, F. (1980) *Philosophy in the classroom* Philadelphia: Temple University Press.

Lohman, D. F., Thorndike, R. L., and Hagen E. P. (1986) *Cognitive abilities test* Windsor, UK: National Foundation of Educational Research.

Mercer, N. (2000) *Word and minds: How we use language to think together* London: Routledge.

Mercer, N. (2010) "The analysis of classroom talk: Methods and methodologies" *British Journal of Educational Psychology* 80(1): 1–14.

Smith, P., Fernandes, C., and Strand, S. (2001) *Cognitive Abilities Test 3 pupil book* (Levels B and C) Windsor, UK: NFER-Nelson.

Topping K. J. and Trickey, S. (2007a) "Collaborative philosophical enquiry for school children: Cognitive effects at 10–12 years" *British Journal of Educational Psychology* 77: 2271–2288.

Topping, K. J. and Trickey, S. (2007b) "Collaborative philosophical enquiry for school children: Cognitive gains at two-year follow-up" *British Journal of Educational Psychology* 77: 781–796.

Topping K. J. and Trickey, S. (2007c) "Impact of philosophical enquiry on school students' interactive behaviour" *International Journal of Thinking Skills and Creativity* 2: 73–84.

Trickey, S. and Topping, K. J. (2004) "Philosophy for children: A systematic review" *Research Papers in Education* 19(3): 363–378.

Trickey, S. and Topping, K. J. (2006) "Collaborative philosophical enquiry for school children: Socio-emotional effects at 11–12 years" *School Psychology International* 27(5): 599–614.

Trickey, S. and Topping, K. J. (2007) "Collaborative philosophical enquiry for school children: Participant evaluation at 11 years" *Thinking: The Journal of Philosophy for Children* 18(3): 23–34.

25 Unexpected Philosophers
The Advantages of Teaching Philosophy to Disadvantaged Children

Lena Harwood Pacheco

Desks sit empty and abandoned. Textbooks and reading anthologies remain on the cart at the front of the room. Worksheets are in stacks to be graded, or stuffed into desks and folders to take home to share with families.

The students of room 204 are crowded onto the rug at the back of the classroom, leaning in, completely engaged. They hang on the teacher's every word, as she reads from Neil Gaiman's *The Wolves in the Walls*. Students laugh and smile. They call out in excitement, pointing at the illustrations. They sit as tall as they can, practically falling forward onto their knees, hoping to get an even better view of the telling of the story. When the book comes to an end, students applaud uproariously. "Can we read it again?," they ask.

Then, students move into small groups, one group seated on the rug with the teacher, two additional groups at small round tables. Facilitators take out prewritten question sets, prepared to guide a discussion on the nature of bravery and the nature of reality. Students gather around in a circle, so that every member of the group can see every other. They settle in, and await the first question so that their discussion might begin. In this third grade class, it is *time for philosophy*.

It comes as a surprise to most of my colleagues that I spend Thursday afternoons engaged in philosophy lessons with my students. For one, I teach third grade. This means that my students are typically eight and nine years old. Most of us don't imagine eight- and nine-year-olds as philosophers. My students still play with Beyblades and Pokemon Cards. They enjoy video games and are upset when I ask that they read at home every night.

Though my students' ages may make it hard for my colleagues to imagine my students participating in philosophy, the greatest obstacle in most people's minds is location. My students are from Hartford, Connecticut. They attend a more traditional, neighborhood school, in a portfolio district increasingly populated by specialized charter and magnet schools. The school spans from pre-kindergarten to eighth grade, with a significant cohort of students who attend the school for the entirety of their elementary and middle school years.

The student population of my school is diverse in the best sense of the word. The greatest percent of our student population is of Spanish decent.

Students' families hail from Puerto Rico, Mexico, Chile, Peru, Colombia, and the Dominican Republic. Additionally, we have a strong African and African American community. Families that recently immigrated from Bosnia, Albania, Romania, and Turkey also have a strong presence in our school community. This creates an interesting school culture, in which no one identifies purely with a race—I have never heard anyone describe themselves as white, black, or Latino—instead, they identify strongly with their families' specific culture or ethnicity. Students cooperate well and form friendship groups that incorporate classmates from every race and culture in the class. In my third grade classroom, culture is something to be celebrated rather than scorned.

Though their cultures are celebrated, my students are not immune to institutionalized racism and classism. My students face many challenges, particularly based on class. All of my students receive free breakfast and lunch at school. It is not uncommon—or unreasonable—for me to worry that some of my students may not have eaten since I've last seen them. In class, students are forced to read texts that do not reflect their own cultural experiences. Students take high-stakes assessments that are far above their reading levels. Students experience the lowered expectations of others, and begin to question if education is really for them. Over time, these expectations become reality. Students enter my classroom significantly below grade level in every subject.

Given these facts, it may sound even more surprising that I take time out of my week to do philosophy lessons with my students. Certainly, it is true that I need to devote as much time as possible to improving my students' fundamental skills. Reading growth, for example, is among the top priorities on my list. However, I initially became involved in teaching philosophy to children based on the following two convictions:

My students, perhaps more than others, need to develop strong critical thinking and communication skills. Regardless of academic ability, my students will face many obstacles based solely on their race and class backgrounds. After successfully improving my students' fundamental skill sets last year, I began teaching this year with many questions in mind: What will my students do when they get into college and their peers suggest they were accepted due to affirmative action? What will my students do if treated disrespectfully during the admissions process, during class, or when they apply for jobs? Will they know how to advocate for themselves? Will they know how to thoughtfully and compellingly identify injustice, and respectfully face antagonists head on, in order to gain the respect and the rights they deserve? Will they be able to identify the history of how they and their families came to have so little, when others have so much? My students need to be able to reason and frame an argument effectively if they want to navigate these issues as they move through life. Philosophy lessons provide students with an opportunity to develop these skills over time, through strategic teacher guidance and support.

My students, just as much those in affluent districts, deserve the opportunity to engage in rich, interesting, rigorous content. Schools often track students from low-income areas into classes that have low levels of academic rigor. Students in low-income communities are more likely, statistically, to engage in tasks at school that involve coloring and rote memorization than students attending schools in more affluent communities. Moreover, students from my school—and schools like it—are taught to think about their academics in a purely vocational way. If they do go to college, they are encouraged to go into a major field of study that has a very clear vocational trajectory for its graduates. Liberal arts and the humanities take a backseat to fields that are perceived as more practical. This in and of itself is an injustice. Philosophy should not be a luxury afforded only to the few. My students deserve the opportunity to participate in philosophy and other liberal arts programming just as much as upper-middle class suburban kids do.

With these convictions in mind, I began this academic year determined to fit philosophy into my teaching schedule, regardless of the barriers that I may face along the way. Though I felt strongly that philosophy would benefit my students, I could not have anticipated the results that I have now experienced firsthand. The changes that teaching philosophy has had on my classroom—both in terms of a direct impact on my students and my own practice as an educator—have been more than worth the time sacrificed.

Integrating a philosophy program into my classroom couldn't have been much easier. I began by implementing the Teaching Children Philosophy program, as developed by Tom Wartenberg as part of his course at Mount Holyoke College. In this program, elementary students are read a thought-provoking picture book. Following the reading, students sit in a circle and engage in a Socratic-Method style dialogue about the philosophical content embedded in the story. As they discuss the story, students take on most of the control over the discussion. They respond directly to their peers, using language such as "I agree with you because. . . ." As the teacher, I take on the role of facilitator, simply guiding the discussion by reframing students' responses and calling attention to the most critical parts of their answers. This allows the discussion to remain productive, focused on the questions at hand. To get the conversation initially started, I use question sets that have already been generated on the program's website—planning for my lessons was as simple as printing the predetermined question sets and highlighting the questions I hope to focus in on.

Planning on the unit level has been equally simple. The Teaching Children Philosophy website lists three thematically cohesive units of study, each of which can be taught over the course of eight weeks. This year, I have implemented all three of these units, with few modifications. We began with an Introductory Unit, which provided students with a brief introduction to Ethics, Social and Political Philosophy, Metaphysics, Epistemology, Philosophy of Language, and Aesthetics. The books in this unit are the easiest for students to respond to, as the philosophical content is relatively straightforward. This provides students with an opportunity to get comfortable with the rules of philosophical discussion and to gain confidence in their own philosophical skills in a relatively safe and simple way. Additionally, because the unit covers a wide variety of philosophical ideas, it provides students with a breadth of topics with which they can become engaged in. Students who may gravitate to one topic or another do not have to wait long to discover that they do in fact enjoy philosophy.

After completing the Introduction to Philosophy Unit, I moved on to two subsequent units—one focused on ethics, and one focused on epistemology and metaphysics. These units become progressively more challenging for students in terms of the ideas and discussions that they generate. Our study on ethics provided students a unique opportunity to hone their philosophical prowess while still tackling simple issues of right and wrong that they likely had thought about before in some capacity. Unlike many ethics programs for kids, the unit is not teacher-dictated morality instruction. Rather, students are engaged in the process of looking at an ethical dilemma and then attempting to generalize rules about what sorts of behaviors are and are not ethical and why. For example, students engaged in an incredibly sophisticated discussion of rights after reading *Hey, Little Ant* by Philip and Hannah Hoose. The story is framed as a dialogue between an ant and a little boy who wants to squish the ant. Readers are asked to consider—should the boy squish the ant? In the course of the discussion, students tackle more complicated philosophical considerations, such as the role of respect in making ethical decisions, whether or not animals have rights, whether animal rights exist uniformly for all living creatures or are contingent on other factors, whether power should influence ethical determinations, and how societal pressure does/should impact ethical dilemmas. Students immediately started drawing parallels from the book to more complicated ideas about power related to dictatorships, bullies, and more. Thus, the ethics unit, while it addresses topics students are familiar with in many ways, still provided our class with incredibly rich discussion.

Our study of epistemology and metaphysics then allowed students who immensely enjoyed philosophy to dig a little deeper into the field and ask and answer questions that they may have never considered before. While still responding to picture books, students get the opportunity to think about incredibly complex issues. For example, when reading *Little Blue and Little Yellow* by Leo Lionni, students have the opportunity to discuss metaphysics and epistemology as it relates to personal identity. In this apparently simple story, Little Blue decides to play with Little Yellow, and in so doing, they appear to become Little Green. Chaos ensues as Papa and Mama Blue do not recognize Little Blue. Students are forced to consider How do you know what you know? Can you trust the appearance of things—and if not, what else could qualify as sufficient evidence for knowledge? How do you draw the line between changing from one state to another and changing from one being into another? Does Little Blue just look like Little Green or has he truly changed into something new, which could be called Little Green? In my class, students were particularly interested in the idea that perhaps what you see—or think you see—isn't sufficient evidence for knowledge. They provided many personal examples of when things appeared to be one way, but ended up being different than expected. Personal examples like these, along with continually referencing the text, helped ground students' discussion in the concrete, which proved helpful as sometimes third graders struggle to consider generalities and abstract reasoning.

The format of these philosophical discussions changed over time in my classroom. When the year began, I taught the Introduction to Philosophy Unit to the whole class together. My entire class sat on the rug in the back of the classroom to hear the story, after which we formed an immense circle on the floor so that everyone could be included in the discussion. This format was adopted for purely practical reasons. I am the only adult teaching in my classroom. As such, there was no way—at the time—to break the class up into smaller groups for concurrent discussions. I considered holding multiple philosophy sessions at different times in the day, but this seemed as though it would only create further problems—what would the other students do while I was holding a discussion group? Would they be engaged in a writing prompt or follow-up activity still related to the book? Would the assignment still be philosophical in nature, or would they do something completely different? Could I trust my students to work quietly and independently enough that I could truly have a fruitful discussion with my group at the same time? I worried that the answer was no; my students were not independent enough as learners at the time to enable me to hold multiple discussion sessions, which meant that I had to make do with whole class philosophy sessions.

Over time, these whole class philosophy sessions seemed less and less effective. It was challenging to get every student to participate in a significant way when we only had about 30 minutes for our discussion, and 25 students were there waiting to speak. Quiet and apathetic students found it easy to disengage from the discussion and not participate at all. Moreover, students struggled to really hear and respond to one another. They tended to repeat the same discussion points over and over, without moving the discussion forward. Perhaps most frustrating were the logistical concerns. Our circle of students did not fit on the class rug. It did not even fit around the class rug. Students found their backs butted up against other tables, desks, and chairs. Not every student could see every other clearly. It became evident pretty quickly that something had to change.

Now, I have established a structure that allows every student to participate in philosophy in a meaningful way. High achieving middle school students, who often find themselves bored in class and in need of enrichment, were selected to come to my classroom once a week to assist in facilitating philosophy sessions. Specifically, two eighth grade girls come to my class every Thursday for about one hour. All of my students, and the two eighth graders, sit on the rug while I read aloud the picture book for the day. Then, I hand each of the middle school students a copy of the question set that corresponds with the book read aloud. They each facilitate a discussion for a group of my students, meaning that students can now work in 3 groups of about 8 students, rather than one group of 25. All students have ample opportunity to participate and to receive feedback on their argument from the instructor. Since having made this change to the structure of our philosophy lessons, sessions have been much more successful.

Success within the area of philosophy has translated into many benefits for my students. First and foremost, my students have developed the ability to follow, and even develop, their own arguments. Take, for instance, our classroom discussion about the nature of bravery as it played out after reading *The Wolves in the Walls*. Students demonstrated that they had developed the ability to agree and disagree effectively, as students proposed various explanations for the correlation between danger and bravery. Some students felt strongly that to be brave, you must do something dangerous. The character Lucy is brave, they argue, because she goes back into the house even though there are wolves in the house, and it could be dangerous. Other students disagree, and do so using appropriate language. "I disagree because. . . ." starts each rebuttal. Students then suggest a myriad of possibilities. Lucy is not brave because she did something dangerous—she is brave because she did something important. She is brave because she did what she thought was right. Or perhaps she isn't even brave at all—she spends most of her time hiding in the walls! In sharing these ideas, students learn how to have a debate without becoming uncivil.

In developing their own arguments, students also come to recognize that creating a valid and sound argument is perhaps more challenging than it first appears. Many students initially fall into the trap of framing arguments that are inconsistent. At first, they suggest that Lucy is brave because she does something dangerous. However, when I ask whether or not it can simply be foolish to do dangerous things, they share a resounding yes, and are quick to give real-life examples: every child seems to have a cousin who jumps out of trees or inexplicably touches the stove. The kids agree that these actions are just foolish, but do not initially recognize that this flies in the face of their previous argument that danger yields bravery. While this initially presents a challenge, over time students learn to recognize that things aren't as simple as they may have thought. They learn to rethink their initial argument and respond with a more nuanced answer when they are challenged by me or their peers. Ultimately, they come to learn that a less popular opinion may sometimes be the most valid. The one student who initially suggested that bravery is not just determined by the danger a person experiences comes to sound a lot more reasonable once students see the flaws in their own arguments. Though at this point my students do not recognize on their own whether or not their arguments are consistent, they are developing strong habits for times when it is brought to their attention that they have formed an inconsistent argument. Rather than giving up, students try to determine how their two, seemingly inconsistent beliefs may in fact work together. If they cannot find an answer, they realize that they may have to rethink their initial assertion. Perhaps Lucy isn't brave after all . . . or if she is, it's not just because what she did was dangerous.

In addition to providing students with the opportunity to develop their argumentation abilities, philosophy engages students in critical thinking that forces them to subscribe to truth claims about our world more cautiously and thoughtfully. Particularly during the ethics unit, students are forced to develop their own ethical frameworks that they use to evaluate actions, rather than simply relying on whatever dogmatic set of morals they have inherited from their parents. While students begin the year saying that Max, in *Where the Wild Things Are* by Maurice Sendak, should not have a bad attitude because his mother will punish him, eventually they come to articulate more compelling justifications for their ethical evaluations. Perhaps Max should not have a bad attitude because it will impact those around him. Maybe Max should not have a bad attitude because it is disrespectful to others to speak so rudely. Regardless, they come to see that fear of punishment should not be the most significant factor in making ethical determinations. I often invite students to "kick their parents out of the room" metaphorically so that they start to ask themselves why the rules exist as they do in the first place. . . . if it's just because mom says so, then maybe mom is wrong.

Philosophy lessons allow students to challenge more than just conventional morality; additionally, students come to have a clearer understanding of the difference between beliefs and knowledge. After reading *Owl at Home* by Arnold Lobel, in which Owl is sure that the moon is following him home because they're friends, students begin to ask "Is the moon really following Owl? Does believing that the moon is following you make it true? Is a belief the same as knowledge?" Immediately, students brought up religion as an example of a set of beliefs. We then had a passionate discussion about whether or not you could "know" that there is a god. Some students felt that all religious beliefs were just beliefs—more akin to an opinion than to a fact—and others felt that they "knew" God existed, because they had evidence, even if it was unconventional evidence. This opened up another great discussion about what qualifies as sufficient evidence for knowledge. Throughout this discussion, students were challenged to think for themselves, rather than simply repeat what they've been taught. I find this an incredibly compelling reason to study philosophy: not out of any desire to dissuade religious believers, but because the practice of thinking for yourself and deciding what to believe on your own terms is a practice that can be incredibly useful throughout life. I have seen students in my class transfer this skill from philosophy to other situations. For example, students in my class did particularly well on literacy lessons on the difference between fact and opinion. Students even rephrased my definition of an opinion by saying,

"It's like philosophy. You could agree or disagree." My kids are beginning to use what they learn during philosophy time to strengthen their ability levels in other content areas.

One of the greatest impacts philosophy has had on my students is that it has strengthened their oral communication skills. This is particularly noticeable in shy students and English Language Learners. Davonte, my shyest student, used to visibly tremble whenever he was asked to speak in class. It appeared that nothing scared him more than to talk in front of our large group. However, during our small-group philosophy sessions, Davonte has gained the confidence he needs to feel more comfortable speaking in class. In a safe, eight-person setting, he has the opportunity to regularly share his ideas. This has had a major impact on Davonte. Now, he is much more vocal during regular class. Sometimes, he even raises his hand to respond of his own volition! Unified Arts teachers have also noticed the difference in him. Many have stated that they recently heard him speak for the first time in their class. Perhaps most surprisingly, on a recent survey that I administered in class, Davonte self-assessed himself at a 3 on a 1–5 scale for the statement "I feel comfortable speaking in front of a group." As he has become more comfortable speaking in class, his oral reading has improved. His confidence has made it easier for him to read aloud fluently. This is a major change—one that could provide Davonte with lifelong benefits.

More noticeable still was the change in my student Juan. Juan began the year as a new arrival from the Dominican Republic. He had moved to Hartford about halfway through the previous school year, but over the summer he had little opportunity to practice his English. He arrived at room 204 this year unable to speak more than one English word at a time. Juan appeared anxious about his ability to speak properly; as such, even when he knew the correct words to convey a message, it was rare for him to speak during class. Another Spanish-speaking student was assigned to be his buddy so that if at any point he didn't understand the directions in class, he could get a rough translation from a peer. Even in writing this reflection, it is hard to even visualize what class was like for Juan at that time, as he has come such a long way. I first recognized how far he had come during a philosophy lesson on *The Lorax* by Dr. Seuss. Most students in my group agreed that it is wrong to kill all of the trees, as happened in the story, because we need trees to survive. However, they were caught in a disagreement about the ethics pertaining to killing just one tree. Some students said that we have practical reasons to kill trees, such as needed paper, and that those needs make it okay to kill trees so long as we plant new ones in their place. Juan watched this conversation with fascination. Finally, very passionately, he said, "I disagree. Because . . . the tree is the home of the monkey!" In that moment, Juan was able to find English words to convey a complex idea. He was able to engage in a philosophical dialogue with his peers. He was able to genuinely take our discussion to a new place. This is not to say that his quick acquisition of the English language is entirely due to philosophy;

however, having the regular opportunity to practice oral language skills in a small-group discussion certainly had an impact on his development as an English speaker.

The final, perhaps most significant impact that philosophy has had on my students' development is that it helped them develop the mindset that learning is not about rushing toward a predetermined answer. Learning is about thinking. It is a process. My students see the struggle—during philosophy lessons, they regularly get frustrated when I challenge them to articulate clearer reasons for their answers, or when I carefully suggest that their argument is inconsistent or invalid. My students often wish to have the "right" answer more quickly. However, in muddling through, they develop the intellectual stamina that will be needed to think through more complex problems. In math, my students are more likely to work through a complex application problem using trial and error than they were at the start of the year. Before, if they didn't get the right answer immediately, they just moved on. Now my students know that solving a problem can be a process.

This is not to say that teaching philosophy hasn't presented any challenges in my classroom. I have struggled immensely to help students understand what counts as a "reason" for their answers. Often, they do what they think they have been taught to do during literacy lessons—cite the story. However, they typically just restate an event from the story without explaining how that event proves that their assertion is valid—in part because often, the event they choose does not actually prove anything. For example, when reading *The True Story of the Three Little Pigs* by Jon Scieszka, many students stated that they believed the wolf's side of the story. When pushed to explain why, they said that they believed the wolf because he didn't mean to hurt the pigs, he was just looking for some sugar. I tried to explain to the students that this isn't a reason for their belief, as the wolf could be lying, and that what I wanted to know was not what his story was, but why they believed his story. At this point, students just repeated that the wolf wanted to get the sugar. I became exasperated and eventually decided that we would have to continue the lesson another day.

This challenge to my teaching has allowed me, however, to improve my own practice. I have come to realize how confusing it is to a third grader—particularly those who do not regularly engage in these sorts of discussions at home—to give a reason for their answer. As teachers, we always ask students for reasons, but we never explicitly teach students what counts as a reason. I strongly believe that this is not a shortcoming of teaching children philosophy, but an opportunity to use this program to even greater benefit. My intention is to create my own unit on Logic for kids so that they come to understand very clearly what does and does not count as a reason for an argument.

Perhaps the most significant change to my teaching, however, has been that I have been able to successfully create a climate and culture in my classroom that encourages students to think more critically about the world around them. It is not significant to me whether or not students truly grasp metaphysics, or whether they go on to be philosophy majors. It is important to me that I develop a group of strong, young thinkers who challenge convention and ask the big questions. In my classroom, students are comfortable grappling with big questions and forming their own opinions about them. It is not uncommon for us to discuss social justice issues at length, especially with regards to the books that we read during my literacy block. For example, once my students asked me why there is war. Almost spontaneously, our class entered into a debate about the nature of war, and whether or not there are circumstances in which war is justifiable. When I reminded students that this is an issue we won't all come to an agreement on, they themselves drew the parallel—"It's like doing philosophy; you can agree or disagree." I then was able to make the connection more explicit and remind them that in philosophy, we give reasons for our answers, so we have to think carefully about *why* war is or is not justifiable.

At the start of the year, my students were hesitant to participate in philosophy. They were quiet, in general, and they struggled to come up with their own opinions. Now, my students are confident communicators, who give reasons for their answers—to the best of their ability—and do their best to tackle complicated questions, even if an answer isn't immediately apparent. There is perhaps no better testimony to the importance of philosophy in my classroom than this. Recently, I conducted a survey in my classroom that asked students what they liked and disliked about doing philosophy. Three students actually responded that what they disliked about philosophy was that it ends too soon. Kids truly do appreciate real learning.

REFERENCES

Gaiman, N. (2003) *The Wolves in the Walls* New York: HarperCollins.
Lionni, L. (1995) *Little Blue and Little Yellow* New York: HarperCollins.
Lobel, A. (1982) *Owl at Home* New York: HarperCollins.
Hoose, P. and Hoose, H. (1998) *Hey, Little Ant* Berkeley: Tricycle Press.
Scieszka, J. (1996) *The True Story of the Three Little Pigs* New York: Puffin
Sendak, M. (1988) *Where the Wild Things Are* 25th anniversary edition, New York: HarperCollins.
Seuss, Dr. (1971) *The Lorax* New York: Random House Books.

Index